Teaching Statistics and Quantitative Methods in the 21st Century

This work, which provides a guide for revising and expanding statistical and quantitative methods pedagogy, is useful for novice and seasoned instructors at both undergraduate and graduate levels, inspiring them to use transformative approaches to train students as future researchers.

Is it time for a radical revision in our pedagogical orientation? How are we currently teaching introductory statistics and quantitative methods, and how should we teach them? What innovations are used, what is in development? This ground-breaking edited volume addresses these questions and more, providing cutting-edge guidance from highly accomplished teachers. Many current textbooks and syllabi differ in only superficial ways from those used 50 years ago, yet the field of quantitative methods—and its relationship to the research enterprise—has expanded in many important ways. A philosophical axiom underlying this book is that introductory teaching should prepare students to potentially enter more advanced quantitative methods training and ultimately to become accomplished researchers.

The reader is introduced to classroom innovation and to both pragmatic and philosophical challenges to the status quo, motivating a broad revolution in how introductory statistics and quantitative methods are taught. Designed to update and renovate statistical pedagogy, this material will stimulate students, new instructors, and experienced teachers.

Joseph Lee Rodgers earned his PhD in quantitative psychology, with a minor in biostatistics, from the University of North Carolina at Chapel Hill in 1981. He worked at the University of Oklahoma from 1981–2012, where he is George Lynn Cross Research Professor Emeritus. He joined the Quantitative Methods program at Vanderbilt in 2012. He has published two co-authored books, two edited books, and more than 150 journal articles/book chapters in the professional literature. He has also had a career commitment to classroom teaching and has written many articles in the statistics and quantitative methods literature that are didactic teaching-oriented articles.

Multivariate Applications Series

Sponsored by the Society of Multivariate Experimental Psychology, the goal of this series is to apply statistical methods to significant social or behavioral issues in such a way so as to be accessible to a nontechnical-oriented readership (e.g., nonmethodological researchers, teachers, students, government personnel, practitioners, and other professionals). Applications from a variety of disciplines such as psychology, public health, sociology, education, and business are welcome. Books can be single- or multiple-authored or edited volumes that (1) demonstrate the application of a variety of multivariate methods to a single, major area of research; (2) describe a multivariate procedure or framework that could be applied to a number of research areas; or (3) present a variety of perspectives on a topic of interest to applied multivariate researchers.

Anyone wishing to submit a book proposal should send the following: (1) author/title; (2) timeline including completion date; (3) brief overview of the book's focus, including table of contents and, ideally, a sample chapter (or chapters); (4) a brief description of competing publications; and (5) targeted audiences.

For more information, please contact the series editor, Lisa L. Harlow, (University of Rhode Island) at e-mail LHarlow@uri.edu.

- *The Essence of Multivariate Thinking: Basic Themes and Methods, Second Edition* written by Lisa L. Harlow (2014)
- *Longitudinal Analysis: Modeling Within-Person Fluctuation and Change* written by Lesa Hoffman (2015)
- *Handbook of Item Response Theory Modeling: Applications to Typical Performance Assessment* co-edited by Steven P. Reise & Dennis Revicki (2015)
- *Longitudinal Structural Equation Modeling: A Comprehensive Introduction* written by Jason T. Newsom (2015)
- *Higher-order Growth Curves and Mixture Modeling with Mplus: A Practical Guide* by Kandauda A. S. Wickrama, Tae Kyoung Lee, Catherine Walker O'Neal, & Frederick O. Lorenz (2016)
- *What If There Were No Significance Tests?: Classic Edition* by Lisa L. Harlow, Stanley A. Mulaik, James H. Steiger (2016)

A full list of titles in this series is available at: https://www.routledge.com/Multivariate-Applications-Series/book-series/LEAMAS

Teaching Statistics and Quantitative Methods in the 21st Century

Edited by
Joseph Lee Rodgers

Routledge
Taylor & Francis Group

NEW YORK AND LONDON

First published 2020
by Routledge
52 Vanderbilt Avenue, New York, NY 10017

and by Routledge
2 Park Square, Milton Park, Abingdon, Oxon, OX14 4RN

Routledge is an imprint of the Taylor & Francis Group, an informa business

Library of Congress Cataloging-in-Publication Data
A catalog record for this book has been requested

ISBN: 978-1-138-33685-8 (hbk)
ISBN: 978-1-138-33686-5 (pbk)
ISBN: 978-0-429-44281-0 (ebk)

Typeset in Perpetua
by Apex CoVantage, LLC

Contents

List of Contributors   viii

Preface — Camilla P. Benbow   xi

Foreword — Robert C. MacCallum   xiii

1   Teaching Statistics and Research Methods in the 21st Century:
    An Introduction to 17 Chapters on Statistical Pedagogy, Curriculum,
    Philosophy, and Administration   1
    JOSEPH LEE RODGERS

SECTION I
Meta-Issues Related to Teaching: Curriculum, Content,
Philosophy, and Supply-Demand Issues   11

2   The Role of Philosophy of Science When Teaching Statistics to Social Scientists:
    Two Constructivists Walk Into a Bar (or Do They?)   13
    MICHAEL C. EDWARDS

3   Optimizing Student Learning and Inclusion in Quantitative Courses   30
    A. T. PANTER, VIJI SATHY, AND KELLY A. HOGAN

4   Not the What of Quantitative Training but the Who   55
    LEONA S. AIKEN

5   Is Methodological Research Moving Into Practice? The Critical Role of Formal
    Methodological Training   70
    JESSICA K. FLAKE, IAN J. DAVIDSON, AND JOLYNN PEK

6   Singletons: Reevaluating Course Objectives When an Introductory Statistics
    Course Is a Student's Only Statistics Course   87
    MATTHEW S. FRITZ

7   When Statistical Assumptions Are Interesting Outcomes Instead of
    Nuisances—Looking Beyond the Mean   102
    RACHEL T. FOULADI

8   Teaching Introductory Statistics to Applied Researchers in the 21st Century:
    A Dialectic Examination   123
    JOSEPH LEE RODGERS

SECTION II
Modern Classroom Innovations in Teaching Statistics
and Quantitative Methods   135

9   Teaching Quantitative Skills Across the Psychology Curriculum   137
    CHARLES S. REICHARDT

10 The Eyes Have It: Emphasizing Data Visualization When Teaching Students
    Meeting a Quantitative Literacy Requirement   153
    ROBERT TERRY AND VINCENT T. YBARRA

11 Low- and Medium-Tech Complements to High-Tech Tools for Teaching
    Statistics: The Case for Using Appropriate Technology to Implement
    Cognitive Principles for Teaching   170
    DAVID RINDSKOPF

12 Hands-on Experience in the Classroom—Why, How, and Outcomes   182
    PASCAL R. DEBOECK

13 Who Benefits From the Flipped Classroom? Quasi-Experimental Findings
    on Student Learning, Engagement, Course Perceptions, and Interest in
    Statistics   197
    VIJI SATHY AND QUINN MOORE

14 Teaching Research Methods Using Simulation   217
    WILLIAM REVELLE

15   Teaching Statistics With a BYOD (Bring Your Own Device) Student Response
     System   238
     R. SHANE HUTTON AND DEREK BRUFF

16   Personally Relevant Project-Based Learning in Graduate Statistics Curriculum
     in Psychology   249
     RACHEL T. FOULADI

17   Using Projects to Teach Statistics in Social Sciences   266
     JENNIFER D. TIMMER AND CAROLYN J. ANDERSON

18   Teaching Statistical Concepts Through a Scale Development Project   281
     KEVIN J. GRIMM AND JONATHAN L. HELM

     Index   290

Contributors

Leona S. Aiken is Professor Emerita of the Department of Psychology at Arizona State University. Until her retirement in May 2018, she regularly taught advanced undergraduate statistics, as well as two graduate courses, regression analysis, and multivariate analysis.

Carolyn J. Anderson is Professor of Educational Psychology with affiliations with the Departments of Psychology and Statistics at the University of Illinois, Urbana-Champaign. She regularly teaches graduate statistics courses including multilevel modeling, categorical data analysis, Bayesian statistics and modeling, and multivariate data analysis. She has also taught introductory undergraduate and graduate statistics and tests and measurement in psychology.

Derek Bruff is director of the Vanderbilt University Center for Teaching and a principal senior lecturer in the Vanderbilt Department of Mathematics, where he teaches courses on statistics, linear algebra, and cryptography.

Ian J. Davidson is a PhD candidate in the Historical, Theoretical and Critical Studies Program in the Psychology Department at York University (Toronto, Canada). He has published research on the history of personality psychology and the theory of methodology. He began assisting and tutoring statistics and research methods courses while completing his undergraduate degree, and, over the past few years, has been teaching psychology students how to use R and RStudio in the lab sessions of Intermediate Statistics.

Pascal R. Deboeck is an Associate Professor in the Developmental Psychology program at the University of Utah. He is also a member and statistical consultant for the University of Utah's Consortium for Families and Health Research. He primarily teaches graduate courses in quantitative methods for social, behavioral, and medical data. His most recent courses have included a course on approaches to modeling temporal data, and the second graduate course in psychology which covers the Generalized Linear Model, Mixed Models, and Exploratory Factor analysis.

Michael C. Edwards is Associate Professor of Psychology at Arizona State University. He has taught undergraduate and graduate introductory statistics courses along with graduate-level courses in psychometrics, factor analysis, item response theory, and multivariate statistics.

Jessica K. Flake is an assistant professor in the Department of Psychology at McGill University in the Quantitative Psychology and Modelling area. She teaches undergraduate and graduate courses in introductory statistics, multilevel modeling, and research design. She also gives workshops on open science practices such as transparency in measurement, writing preregistrations and registered reports, and navigating researcher degrees of freedom.

Rachel T. Fouladi is Associate Professor in the Department of Psychology at Simon Fraser University. She is a quantitative psychologist in the Department's History, Quantitative, and Theoretical Psychology area. Over the past 25+ years, she has regularly taught introductory undergraduate and graduate statistics courses, including topics of experimental design, correlation and regression, and other multivariate methods. Most recently, she has started teaching courses on questionnaire design/evaluation and use, with specific applications in studies of well-being.

Matthew S. Fritz is an assistant professor of quantitative, qualitative, and psychometric methods in the Department of Educational Psychology at the University of Nebraska–Lincoln. He regularly teaches graduate statistics courses in Introductory Statistics, Analysis of Variance, Multivariate Data Analysis, and Longitudinal Data Analysis, for which he won a College of Education and Human Sciences Outstanding Teaching Award in 2018.

Kevin J. Grimm is Professor of Psychology in The College of Liberal Arts & Sciences at Arizona State University. He teaches graduate courses in the analysis of variance, growth modeling, machine learning, and structural equation modeling.

Jonathan L. Helm is Assistant Professor of Psychology in the College of Sciences at San Diego State University. He teaches introductory courses in ANOVA and regression analysis to both undergraduate and graduate students, as well as an advanced course in multilevel modeling to graduate students.

Kelly A. Hogan is a biologist and the Associate Dean of Instructional Innovation at the University of North Carolina at Chapel Hill. She oversees curricular and pedagogical innovations across the university, researches how course design decisions affect student learning, and has won multiple awards for her teaching of large gateway biology courses.

R. Shane Hutton is a senior lecturer in the Quantitative Methods program at Vanderbilt's Peabody College. He regularly teaches an undergraduate introductory statistics course and graduate courses on statistical inference, applied statistics, regression, and survival analysis.

Quinn Moore is a Senior Researcher at Mathematica Policy Research. He applies quantitative methods and program evaluation techniques to studies of public policy.

A. T. Panter is a quantitative psychologist and the Senior Associate Dean of Undergraduate Education at University of North Carolina at Chapel Hill. She is an award-winning teacher of quantitative methods, conducts research on curricular design and student support, and oversees the academic mission related to 19,000+ undergraduate students at her university.

Jolynn Pek is an assistant professor in the Department of Psychology at The Ohio State University. She teaches introductory undergraduate and graduate statistics courses. She also teaches courses in multilevel modeling, factor analysis, and structural equation modeling.

Charles S. Reichardt is Professor of Psychology at the University of Denver. He teaches a graduate level course in multiple regression and two undergraduate courses (a first-year seminar and a capstone advanced seminar) in which he regularly uses the data and statistical interface described in Chapter 9.

William Revelle is a professor of psychology at Northwestern University, where he teaches courses on research methods and personality research to undergraduates and psychometric theory and latent variable modeling to graduate students. He is the author of a psych package in R, which is a useful tool for psychological research.

David Rindskopf is Distinguished Professor of Educational Psychology and Psychology at the City University of New York Graduate Center. He has taught courses in categorical data, structural equation models, Bayesian statistics, missing data, evaluation research, R, multilevel models, item response theory, and statistical consulting.

Joseph Lee Rodgers is the Lois Autrey Betts Chair of Psychology and Human Development at Vanderbilt University and George Lynn Cross Research Professor Emeritus at the University of Oklahoma. He regularly teaches undergraduate and graduate statistics courses, as well as courses in exploratory and graphical data analysis, scaling and measurement, psychological testing, and behavior genetic methods.

Viji Sathy is a teaching professor in the Department of Psychology and Neuroscience and Special Projects Assistant to the Senior Associate Dean of Undergraduate Education. She is an award-winning professor who teaches large undergraduate quantitative courses: statistics and research methods, as well as smaller courses in advanced methodology and a first-year seminar in quantitative psychology using makerspaces.

Robert Terry is Professor of Psychology at the University of Oklahoma. He regularly teaches introductory undergraduate and graduate statistic courses, as well as courses in measurement, skeptical thinking for the social sciences, and the history of psychology.

Jennifer D. Timmer is a postdoctoral research fellow in the Department of Leadership, Policy, and Organizations at Peabody College, Vanderbilt University. She has taught online introductory statistics courses for undergraduate and graduate students, and she also served as a teaching assistant for a graduate-level course in quasi-experimental design.

Vincent T. Ybarra is a graduate student in the Department of Psychology at the University of Oklahoma. He regularly teaches introductory undergraduate statistics courses and studies the role of graphical literacy in decision-making.

Preface

You hold in your hands not only a scholarly work, admirably edited by Vanderbilt University's Joseph Lee Rodgers, but a call for reform in the way we teach certain quantitative skills that are critical for success in the 21st century. If the pedagogical practices described in this volume were to be widely adopted, the results could yield more knowledgeable students, professionals, and leaders as well as better-informed citizens and a more effective democracy.

For me, this volume represents a happy outcome. My first encounter with work presented here was when I gave a brief welcome to a number of the authors represented at a mini-conference Joseph Lee Rodgers organized at Vanderbilt University in 2017. As dean of Vanderbilt's Peabody College of education and human development, I was happy to greet the attendees, who constituted cutting-edge scholars in quantitative methods from the educational and psychological sciences. They had come to Vanderbilt for a day-long discussion about statistical pedagogy. One of Vanderbilt's strengths is its own highly regarded cohort of quantitative methodologists, which draws on a long history at Peabody College (including my graduate advisor and mentor, Julian C. Stanley), and a long history of excellence in psychological research. Peabody has been fortunate over the years to have a number of scholars well versed in experimental design, psychological measurement, and statistical modeling.

The mini-conference this volume grew out of was intended to explore a particular problem. While quantitative methods have evolved quite rapidly in recent decades, the teaching of these methods has not kept pace. This problem is epitomized in the textbooks that introduce statistics to college students. The pedagogical challenge is particularly acute in the social and behavior sciences, where students often have their first encounter with the subject matter. Building upon the presentations and discussions that took place two years ago, the contributors in this volume now put forth a work intended to "motivate a broad revolution." Not only is this revolution overdue, it is imperative. Indeed, the American Statistical Association has been calling for reform since at least 2005, with updated *Guidelines for Assessment and Instruction in Statistics Education* published again in 2016.

Schools of education have an important role to play here in two regards. The first is in continuing to develop the knowledge base and methodological tools to further the research that advances the psychological and learning sciences. Context-sensitive research methods, statistical modeling, and techniques for psychological measurement are crucial to experimental design and the iterative cycles of intervention design, implementation, evaluation, and refinement. At Peabody, we have methodologists involved at every stage of research, from conceptualization of grant proposals through publication of findings. Their input strengthens substantive research on learning disabilities, autism spectrum disorders, intellectual precocity, educational neuroscience, reading disorders, mathematics learning, or how children cope with adversity, to name just a few.

The second role for education schools is in the teaching of statistics and quantitative methods. It is here where this new volume shines. This volume articulates a philosophical framework that justifies the need to radically revise introductory texts and coursework, using approaches derived from several decades of innovation about what constitutes best practice. I am pleased to see another Peabody faculty member, R. Shane Hutton, contributing a chapter here on the classroom use of personal devices. Although it hardly needs rehearsing here, the importance of statistical literacy cannot be overstated. To cite just a few examples from our collective lives, one could point to politicians who routinely use statistics to mislead rather than inform or to uncritical journalists who pass on context-free study findings about the dangers of eating certain foods or the correlations between specific behaviors and cancer risk. We all share in the dangers of failing to properly understand the data and communicate intelligently about climate change.

Statistical literacy is an important component of scientific literacy. Increasingly, statistical literacy is necessary for participation in democratic life. Yet too many of our fellow citizens lack basic skills for analyzing data, looking for patterns, forming hypotheses, and drawing quantitatively informed conclusions. Fewer still can communicate information using data to inform discussions about public policy. Ultimately, we cannot hope to have either a just or a prosperous society unless we also have a populace capable of gathering, analyzing, and interpreting data. The principles and practices discussed in this book can help to move us in the right direction. The authors set the stage for a dialogue with the readers of this work. Even better, they facilitate the development of a community around its topic, with members interacting and discussing one another's ideas. Ultimately, these ideas should be shared widely in dynamic and ongoing conversations.

Looking forward, it is important for the continued growth of the field to seize the opportunities afforded by advances in data science, technology, and student interest. The authors who contribute here are great methodologists as well as expert teachers. They can, and in this book they do, point the way forward.

Camilla P. Benbow
Patricia and Rodes Hart Dean of Education and Human Development
Vanderbilt University's Peabody College

Foreword

About five years ago, I was having dinner with my old friend Joe Rodgers when Joe brought up the topic of how we in the field of quantitative psychology go about teaching introductory statistics. He asked if I had any general thoughts about it, and I had an immediate response. I said that I thought it was the thing we do worst. That I thought we did a lot of things well in terms of development and study of quantitative methods, and implementation of those methods in applied research, as well as teaching of advanced methodology. But that we did a relatively poor job of teaching introductory statistics. My concern primarily involved course content in the sense that these courses do little to introduce students to quantitative methods as they are used in applied research and also do little to prepare students for study of these methods. For example, few introductory statistics courses in our field provide even a hint regarding topics such as model specification and testing, an approach which dominates much of our research and methodology literature. There seems to be a disconnect between the content of these courses and the content of our research literature. I made a comment at that dinner with Joe that I had made before—that it always surprised me when a student just completing an introductory statistics course expressed an interest in taking a second course.

Joe, of course, had already been thinking long and hard about various aspects of the general issue. We were in full agreement about the matter of course content, and Joe went further, expressing concerns about inherent aspects such as the long-stagnant content and market for textbooks as well difficulty in staffing courses. Joe had been thinking about organizing a conference on the topic of teaching introductory statistics in our field, potentially yielding a book of chapters by conference participants addressing various aspects of the current state of affairs along with proposals for making things better. I was enthusiastically supportive and am delighted to see that his efforts produced a highly successful conference and, in turn, this outstanding volume.

Contributors to the conference and this book are all well-trained and well-known methodologists as well as experienced teachers with deep concern about course content and quality of instruction. Topics cover not only the critical aspects of course content but also the matter of who should best teach these courses, as well as creative and innovative approaches to teaching such content. The volume provides an outstanding set of contributions, each one being insightful, thought provoking, and of real value for anyone who seeks to improve on instruction of introductory statistics in our field.

So, what do we do now? My own hope is that this book can serve as an impetus for further action that could start to counteract the inertia that plagues our teaching of introductory statistics. There are substantial obstacles to such change, of course, clearly presented in Joe Rodgers's introductory first chapter. But perhaps the reader will tolerate my taking this opportunity to suggest a next step. I believe we could find two or three prominent methodologists who are recognized as extraordinary teachers who would be willing to jointly head a task force on reforming the teaching of introductory statistics in our field. These leaders would need to accept their roles as involving a significant commitment over a period of several years. The leaders would recruit other members for the task force, including additional distinguished methodologists and teachers, with some of these people in positions at large universities with large student enrollments in the relevant courses. The task force should also include representatives from one or two prominent publishing companies. The mission of the task force would, ideally, involve developing a draft outline for two semesters of introductory statistics, as well as a corresponding textbook outline. The task force would also attempt to secure commitments of several kinds: (a) one or more accomplished authors or co-authors to write a new text; (b) a publisher to publish it; and (c) multiple universities that would commit to offering this new course to large enrollment classes in introductory statistics, thus guaranteeing an initial market for the publisher and author(s). To get all this work done, the task force would need some funding. I believe such support could be secured from multiple sources, including professional societies, publishers, quantitative psychology programs, grants, and probably concerned individuals in our field. Like me. If some version of this idea gets started and fundraising is underway, I offer to match up to a combined $5,000 in contributions to the task force provided by the two quantitative psychology programs where I spent my career—Ohio State University and University of North Carolina.

I recognize that it is easy to identify weaknesses and uncertainties in this task force proposal. The proposal is rough and loose, but so are most initial proposals. I believe it could be refined and made workable with sufficient commitment and cooperation—the kind of commitment and cooperation that ultimately produced the book that you hold in your hands. More important than the specific approach is the general principle that we need to do something to break the inertia and to dramatically change the culture of how our field teaches introductory statistics. Further, it should happen soon. The status quo does a serious disservice to our students and our field. Change toward creating an introductory foundation that connects content of these courses to the content of our literature would yield widespread benefits. The current book provides some foundation and impetus for such change. *For the first time, I believe there is some hope for real change to begin.*

Robert C. MacCallum
University of North Carolina at Chapel Hill

## Chapter 1

Teaching Statistics and Research Methods in the 21st Century

An Introduction to 17 Chapters on Statistical Pedagogy, Curriculum, Philosophy, and Administration

Joseph Lee Rodgers

This edited book is about teaching statistics, in particular within social and behavioral science programs. Most of the chapter authors work in psychology departments or in quantitative methods programs in colleges of education. The 18 chapters in this book address the philosophical challenges of teaching statistics (and related quantitative methods) and propose innovations that can help improve our teaching of statistics. Ultimately, the whole book coheres to produce a call for reform. In this introductory chapter, I'll first organize a community effort to share in the "improve our teaching" initiative. Following, I'll present a summary and then define past efforts to stimulate teaching reform. Next, I'll summarize the 17 substantive chapters. Finally, I'll present 10 pieces of teaching advice, styled for teachers in the arena of statistics and quantitative methods.

The Rodgers Challenge

I begin this introductory chapter with a challenge. I'll present the challenge and the reward—and then elaborate. The challenge is addressed to anyone reading this particular sentence, which is just one sentence out of a rather longer book. But to be transparent, the challenge is most applicable to those who teach statistics at the introductory level, and especially in behavioral or social science settings.

The challenge: Read the introduction of *every single chapter* in this edited book—17 chapters, not including the introductory chapter. Then choose *at least three of the chapters* and read them, carefully and completely. Once completed, send me an e-mail addressed to joseph.l.rodgers@vanderbilt. edu or to jrodgers@ou.edu, and let me know that you've completed the "Rodgers Challenge" (and please be sure to put "Rodgers Challenge" in your subject line). In your e-mail, let me know which chapters you read. Also, include any comments you may have about your reaction to the chapters: Did you like them? Did you disagree with certain features? Do you believe the chapters will inspire statistics teaching? Did they inspire you? Do you believe that statistics teaching in the behavioral and social sciences needs to be redefined and reformed? Does this book have the seeds to stimulate that reform? How will we know when such a reform has begun and when it will be completed? In your e-mail, feel free to ignore these questions, or address every one—it's up to you.

The reward: To those who accept the Rodgers Challenge and contact me by e-mail, I'll send you back a summary of what you and others have said about teaching statistics and the chapters in this book. I'll include your e-mail in the summary, along with those of all others who respond. I'll make a short statement to encourage interaction and discussion. In fact, I'll expect and hope to be one of the discussion leaders. If your immediate response to this challenge is, "For reading three chapters and responding, all I get is a crummy e-mail summary," then please feel free to opt out of the challenge. If what you say is, rather, "I think my own teaching will be enhanced and stimulated by interacting with others and with others' opinions, and maybe I'll really enjoy reading these three chapters," then the Rodgers Challenge was designed, specifically, exactly, for you!

To belabor the point: Why is this challenge worth doing? If you engage in this exercise, you will be voting and connecting. You will be voting with your feet, indicating that teaching statistics is important and is worth doing well. You will be connecting with others who agree. That connection, alone, will be worth the small effort to join the Rodgers Challenge. (And also, let's be clear—many of the chapters in this book are awesome and amazing—get ready to be impressed!)

I have one other quick comment about the Rodgers Challenge, and then I'll move onto a more traditional introductory chapter. I'm not sure exactly when I'll circulate the summary. Once the book is published, it'll take some time for the potential audience of statistics teachers to find out about it, consider it, purchase it, and then eventually put "eyes on the introduction." And then it'll take some time to read those three chapters. But obviously, this is a dynamic process, one that ultimately has no end date. I expect to circulate summaries not just once but on a regular basis—maybe once every six months, for several years. And each will be as updated as you, the audience of responders to the Rodgers Challenge, provide material to support that process. So here's the take-home message: Don't worry that it's too late. It isn't. Whenever you read this introduction, all chapter introductions, and then at least three chapters, you're on!!! If it's been six weeks since you read about the challenge and you've now completed it, then great, send me an e-mail. It's been six years since you first read about the challenge but you've only now completed it, no problem, send me an e-mail! And once on, unless you opt out, you're a part of the circulation list in perpetuity. I look forward to hearing from you with great pleasure and anticipation!

Overall Summary

The book you hold in your hand (or that you see on the screen in front of you) is an effort by around two dozen practicing quantitative methodologists to improve our teaching craft as it applies to introductory statistics (and related quantitative methods). At least that's the starting point to motivate this book. There's more, though. I list three goals, explicitly:

Goal # 1: We present several philosophical/administrative/organizational chapters that can help orient, improve, and motivate better teaching of introductory statistics and quantitative methods within the social and behavioral sciences. That's the first major section.

Goal #2: We present a number of chapters that carefully describe innovations, new methods, revised old methods, and general approaches to teaching statistics and quantitative methods to introductory students. That's the second major section.

Goal #3: The overall set of 18 chapters is designed to motivate a broad revolution in how statistics and quantitative methods are taught at the introductory level. That's the broad purpose of the whole book.

Thus, if you're a teacher and you have a teaching philosophy (or want to develop or improve one), study the papers in the first major section. If you're a teacher and you are interested in "best practices," new approaches, and how to teach well, study the papers in the second major section. If you feel that teaching statistics has become fairly rote and rather stagnant and needs to be revitalized, then this is the book for you. Please, in that case, study the whole book.

Teaching Reform

Several times in this book, you will see the assertion that the tables of contents of most introductory statistics textbooks have hardly changed in the past 50+ years. Similarly, syllabi for introductory statistics courses have been relatively fixed over the past several decades. Although the textbook TOCs and the syllabi have remained stable, the whole discipline of statistics and quantitative methods has exploded, with exciting developments and intellectual fireworks. When I began my teaching career in 1980, structural equation modeling was just being proposed. Multilevel modeling barely existed, with little formal development or coherence. Categorical data analysis, hazards modeling, mixture modeling, latent growth curve modeling, and modern Bayesian methods including Bayes factors were still in development or, in some cases, only on the horizon. One would assume that with the explosion of new methods, the foundation upon which those methods have been built would somehow reflect the overall growth of the field. But that assumption would be, mostly, incorrect.

A few efforts at statistical reform can be identified during the past half century. In the field of statistics, whole issues of core journals have been devoted to statistical pedagogy (e.g., see Horton and Hardin (2015), who introduce a special issue of *The American Statistician* devoted to "Statistics and the Undergraduate Curriculum"). The American Statistical Association has twice published standards for teaching statistics, in 2005 and 2016. The GAISE guidelines refer to the *Guidelines for Assessment and Instruction in Statistics Education College Report*. In commenting on the 2016 revised GAISE guidelines, Wood, Mocko, Everson, Horton, and Velleman (2018, pp. 53–54) noted the following changes since the 2005 report: First, "More students study statistics"; second, "The growth in available data has made the field of statistics more salient and provided rich opportunities to address important statistical questions"; third, "The discipline of 'data science' has emerged as a field that encompasses elements of statistics, computer science, and domain-specific knowledge"; fourth, "More powerful and affordable technology options have become widely available"; fifth, "alternative learning environments have become more common"; sixth, "Innovative ways to teach the logic of statistical inference have received increasing attention."

I'm a quantitative psychologist, as are most of the contributing authors; many of us are also members of the American Statistical Association and participate in both quantitative psychology and statistics conferences and publish in both types of journals. The sense of reform that emerges from careful study of the preceding paragraph is not so evident in the statistics classes taught in the social and behavioral sciences. There are several causes and consequences. First, many of the teachers of social and behavioral science introductory statistics courses are not well trained in sophisticated quantitative methods. Many are, rather, substantive psychologists (or sociologists or economists, etc.) who step into the statistics course as a service to the department or as a way to enhance their own methodological skills. Unlike the authors of the chapters in this book, those teachers are unlikely to encounter the GAISE guidelines. Second, publishers and book authors have cornered the market on a long-term financial bonanza. Virtually all behavioral and social science departments require an introductory statistics course, creating demand for hundreds of thousands of textbook purchases each semester. The intellectual and financial momentum that emerges from that simple statement is both profound and nearly impossible to confront. Many introductory statistics textbook authors—like many of the introductory statistics teachers themselves—are not trained methodologists. (Most trained and practicing methodologists have been busy developing and evaluating the methods that I listed earlier in this chapter rather than writing textbooks.) The textbook authors are often teachers at small colleges and universities, ones that do not support an overall quantitative methods program, writing textbooks to respond to the large demand for such textbooks. It is not surprising that those textbooks tend to follow a relatively standard formula—one that has changed only slightly during the past 50+ years. Third, there do exist examples of "reform-oriented textbooks," and without exception, those are written by highly trained methodologist and statisticians. A few examples include Judd, McClelland, and Ryan (2017), Abelson (1995), Maxwell, Delaney, and Kelley (2017), Cohen, Cohen, West, and Aiken (2003), and Freedman, Pisani, and Purves (2007). Notably, most of these texts were published a long time ago, and the dates given are for second, third, or even fourth editions. Also notably, none of those textbooks have been widely adopted for teaching introductory statistics courses. Nor were they intended for introductory teaching; most of those were written for more advanced courses.

In comparison, very few, if any, undergraduate statistics textbooks have been written to emphasize innovation or modern statistical methods. Perhaps of greatest concern, statistics textbooks in 2019 (when this introduction is being written) have no component that appears to link to more sophisticated quantitative methods. The assumption is that how statistics was taught in 1970 is just fine for how statistics should be taught in 2020. Garfield et al. (2011) further support the principle that the field needs much more than just minor adjustments in how we teach introductory statistics.

This edited book is, in a fundamental and very real sense, a corrective effort. Whether the goal of teaching reform emerges from efforts around 2020 or sometime in the distant future, the preceding paragraph should make clear that there are substantial challenges standing in front of the goal of improving and modernizing the enterprise of teaching statistics. But this edited book represents such an effort. The chapter authors have, without exception, two remarkable traits. First, they are outstanding methodologists. Second, they are committed and excellent teachers. They are exactly who should signal the directions toward which statistical pedagogy is heading. I turn now to a summary of the chapters in this book.

Chapter Summaries

Section One

Chapters 2 through 8 define the first major section, titled "Meta-Issues Related to Teaching: Curriculum, Content, Philosophy, and Supply–Demand Issues." This section treats the discipline of teaching statistics. It may be surprising to some (though not to introductory statistics teachers) that statistics is a whole discipline and not just a set of procedures. Further, statistics does overlap into philosophy in fascinating ways.

Michael C. Edwards, in Chapter 2 ("The Role of Philosophy of Science When Teaching Statistics to Social Scientists: Two Constructivists Walk into a Bar (or Do They?)") brings philosophy-of-science issues to bear on teaching statistics and quantitative methods. He not only discusses how to do so, he has been "walking the walk" in his own teaching. Read his lively account of the challenges he has encountered in bringing formal philosophy of science concepts into statistical pedagogy.

A. T. Panter and colleagues, in Chapter 3 ("Optimizing Student Learning in Quantitative Courses") treat a broader level than introductory statistics, as they embed statistics within STEM (science, technology, engineering, and mathematics) teaching. These authors have worked within their home institution to implement learning communities directed toward positive student outcomes. Further, the implementation was carefully evaluated in relation to those outcomes in the context of a randomized trial.

Leona S. Aiken, in Chapter 4 ("Not the What of Quantitative Training But the Who"), treats a critical issue for those interested in reform and innovation in statistical pedagogy: Who will deliver that reform and innovation? Drawing on several decades of careful data collection and analysis, she argues that modern hiring practices mitigate against progressive and sophisticated pedagogy, as much (even most) introductory statistics teaching is done by those who are relatively untrained in formal quantitative methods.

Jessica K. Flake and colleagues, in Chapter 5 ("Is Methods Research Moving Into Practice? The Critical Role of Quantitative Training"), treat the issue of how sophisticated quantitative methods are taught and then subsequently enter into routine use in applied settings. Using two subtopics (psychometrics and mediation analysis), they study the path from training to the production of "defensible psychological knowledge." They document often ineffective applications, traceable to ineffective training.

Matthew S. Fritz, in Chapter 6 ("Singletons: Reevaluating Course Objectives When an Introductory Statistics Course Is a Student's Only Statistics Course"), treats a relatively common though seldom considered problem. Many students only take a single statistics course; how does that inform our teaching? He argues that objectives and assessments should be adjusted in relation to this realization (and teachers should naturally encourage students to take more than just one statistics course).

Rachel T. Fouladi, in Chapter 7 ("When Statistics Assumptions Are Interesting Outcomes Instead of Nuisances—Looking Beyond the Mean"), treats a relatively sophisticated teaching issue, the assumptions underlying the conduct of statistics analysis. She quite correctly notes that assumptions are not just procedural details to be evaluated following statistical analysis but rather may be valuable to inform the statistical process. This realization necessarily must inform our teaching, and she offers both orientation and examples to support better teaching.

Joeseph Lee Rodgers, in Chapter 8 ("Teaching Introductory Statistics to Applied Researchers in the 21st Century: A Dialectic Examination"), expands on a topic introduced earlier—that there is a disconnect between static introductory statistics teaching and the dynamic quantitative methods field that the teaching is supposed to be targeting. Using an old philosophical mechanism, the dialectic, he presents arguments from a number of different positions for several critical pedagogical questions and attempts to resolve those arguments.

Section Two

Chapters 9 through 18 comprise the second major section, which is devoted to "Modern Classroom Innovations in Teaching Statistics and Quantitative Methods." This section is oriented toward classroom teaching and presents a number of exciting and novel ways to approach the teaching of statistics. Without exception, the innovations presented in these chapters have been developed, refined, and used by the authors themselves in their successful presentation of statistics material.

Charles S. Reichardt, in Chapter 9 ("Teaching Quantitative Skills Across the Psychology Curriculum"), demonstrates how to use large archival datasets (and their associated statistical software interfaces) to simultaneously teach statistics and important content areas within the field of psychology. In fact, his approaches can be used to inform statistics teaching with substantive import and also to teach substantive courses that are sophisticated methodologically. The particular database on which he focuses is the General Social Survey.

Robert Terry and Vincent T. Ybarra, in Chapter 10 ("The Eyes Have It: Emphasizing Data Visualization When Teaching Students Meeting a Quantitative Literacy Requirement"), focus on using modern and sophisticated graphical methods in the classroom to display quantitative information. Their graphical applications are designed to stimulate interest in students and are drawn from a wide variety of content areas. Many of their applications use software that easily can be extracted from the web. Their goal is to present graphs that "hit you right between the eyes."

David Rindskopf, in Chapter 11 ("Medium- and Low-Tech Complements to High-Tech Tools for Teaching Statistics: The Case for Using Appropriate Technology to Implement Cognitive Principles for Teaching"), argues the value of high-speed computing and other high-tech support, but he also suggests that older "low-tech" tools that have fallen in disuse are actually quite valuable for teaching and learning. What are those tools? He presents a charming set of examples, and illustrates how to apply them in statistics teaching.

Pascal R. Deboeck, in Chapter 12 ("Hands-On Experience in the Classroom—Why, How, and Outcomes"), uses a "reverse classroom" to teach categorical data analysis. In this classroom, the lecture is moved outside of the classroom, as students watch video lectures before class. Then class time is spent on more active learning approaches, including a great deal of interaction between the instructor (and the TA) and the students, using a small-group and workshop orientation.

Viji Sathy and Quinn Moore, in Chapter 13 ("Who Benefits From the Flipped Classroom? Quasi-Experimental Findings on Student Learning, Engagement, Course Perceptions and Interest in Statistics"), also use the reverse or flipped classroom to improve student learning and to build better student engagement. They present results of a formal evaluation exercise using outside lectures and focusing on active learning during class time. Their results provide evidence-based support for the value of the flipped-classroom approach.

William Revelle, in Chapter 14 ("Teaching Research Methods Using Simulation"), directly confronts the challenge of modern methods by taking them straight into the classroom. Using a web-based simulation system, and R as the software system for statistical analysis, he builds realistic (though simulated) real-world data examples. Of great advantage, the instructor thus knows the model that generated the data and can take advantage of that knowledge in teaching and evaluating the course.

R. Shane Hutton and Derek Bruff, in Chapter 15 ("Teaching Statistics With a BYOD (Bring Your Own Device) Student Response System"), take advantage of the use of personal electronic devices (e.g., laptops, cell phones) for in-class student assessment and interactive exercises. The methods support active learning during class. They show general advantages, specific advantages that apply in particular to teaching statistics, and illustrate a number of exercises that can take advantages of the BYOD format.

Rachel T. Fouladi, in Chapter 16 ("Personally Relevant Project Based Learning in Graduate Statistics Curriculum in Psychology"), like other authors, documents a method to support active learning within (and outside) the classroom. Her approach involves assigning student-developed projects, which are of the breadth and magnitude of academic research projects. Students develop each phase of a research project—design, data collection, analysis, and write-up—and are evaluated on each phase.

Jennifer D. Timmer and Carolyn J. Anderson, in Chapter 17 ("Using Projects to Teach Statistics in Social Sciences"), also develop a project-based pedagogical system to support active learning. Their focus is on the undergraduate level and on matching projects to the individual interests of each undergraduate statistics student. The challenges of evaluating each student are addressed, and they emphasize the value of project-based teaching for instructors, who can better understand student successes.

Kevin J. Grimm and Jonathan L. Helm, in Chapter 18 ("Learning Statistics Through a Scale Development Project"), use a psychometric arena to motivate learning statistics. Students define a construct of interest, build a scale to measure the construct, and then collect data (from one another) using the scale. The method, like many others, emphasizes active learning within the classroom.

Conclusion: Top 10 Pieces of Advice for Teaching Statistics

One of the best professional compliments I've ever received was when a colleague said that he realized a long time ago that I had a "heart for teaching." I've always hoped that my commitment and enthusiasm for teaching shows through, and I was pleased that he recognized that. This volume is filled with a whole teaching community of academics, each of whom has a serious case of the same academic affliction, a "heart for teaching."

Working in a university, in an academic department, has many outstanding features. One is that there are feedbacks at many different time intervals, ones that complement one another. When we begin a research project, we're aware that it may be several years before we see the reward of having the results eventually published (if we're lucky). When we begin to serve on a student's master's committee, it will be at least a year before the reward of seeing a student successfully defend the thesis occurs. When we begin a semester, it will be several months before we assign final grades and both provide and receive feedback on how successful our teaching has been at a broad level. One of the shortest-term, and in many ways the most important, types of feedback for academics—one that keeps us going on a short-term and daily basis—is the interaction with students within the classroom. Anyone can build their "heart for teaching," and it pays us back on a day-to-day, even moment-to-moment basis, in a profession where many of the rewards are extremely long term.

Over a teaching career that will soon move into its fifth decade, I've developed many methods, stories, approaches, and tricks of the trade. To conclude this introduction to a book titled *Teaching Statistics and Quantitative Methods in the 21st Century*, I'm listing here my top ten pieces of advice for those who are in the "teaching statistics" profession. Some of these bits of advice are generally applicable to almost any college teaching setting; most are specific to teaching statistics in particular. They are not quite in any particular order, though I'll use the David Letterman countdown method to build suspense and intrigue.

Teaching Tip #10: Take ownership of your class. You're empowered to do that by your university and by your department. You're empowered to do that by virtue of the teacher–student relationships that you'll be developing. There should never be a doubt who the instructor is, in terms of pedagogy, class management, and accountability. Taking ownership does not mean being heavy-handed. It means being carefully organized, always prepared, exceedingly pleasant, energetic, and always in charge.

Teaching Tip #9: Students are naturally interested in you, and you are (hopefully) naturally interested in them. But the relationship is asymmetric. You don't have time to get to know 20 or 100 or 350 students (I've taught introductory undergraduate statistics classes to all of those sizes) as well as they'll get to know you. And they are getting to know you. Remember that everything you do in class is building a relationship with the students. Some of the success of those efforts is invisible to you but nevertheless of great ultimate importance.

Teaching Tip #8: The more you let your love of statistics show through, the better you'll teach. The more you let your love of statistics show through, the more students will learn. The more you let your love of statistics show through, the more likely students will become enthusiastic about the subject.

Teaching Tip #7: Try to avoid solving subtle and specific classroom problems on your feet in front of the class. For example, early in my career, I used to answer grading questions after a quiz in front of the class; I quickly learned not to do that. The nuances of individual grading decisions are better made during an interaction with a student. (E.g., Question: "I used the word 'ordinate' instead of 'ordinal'; will that be full credit?" Answer: "Let me please address specific grading questions with you individually after we return the quizzes.")

Teaching Tip #6: Testing is evaluation, and all students are entitled to know how they are being evaluated. When I was in college, I was once told by an instructor, "You got a B because I'm an expert in this area, and I judged your paper to be worth a B. That's all I can say." That was infuriating and arbitrary—and impeded my learning. Students are entitled to know what the grading rules are, how they were followed, who did the grading (e.g., instructor versus TA), and even how the question fits into the course material. Students may not agree with grading standards, but they should know what they are. I often use the example of a double-clutch heavily covered layup in a basketball game, which logically should be worth more points than a simple wide-open layup. But the rules say it's not, and basketball players know the rules for baskets worth one point, two points, and three points. Students deserve to know grading rules.

Teaching Tip #5: Testing is not only evaluation, it is also pedagogy. Good teachers can use testing to teach. Students learn as they're taking tests as well as in preparing to take tests. Students can learn a great deal from well-constructed tests. I give mini-quizzes, almost every day, that help students prepare for quizzes. I give quizzes, most weeks, that help students prepare for the midterm and final. When students learn how to take tests by actually taking tests, they are engaging in a form of active learning. (Garfield et al., 2011, further developed the principle that assessment feeds back into student learning and vice versa.)

Teaching Tip #4: Many students have substantial anxiety about taking a statistics course. Combining some kindness, fairness, and honesty about the course can go a long way toward relieving anxiety. (Statistical cartoons help, too!) There are no magic "anti-anxiety" pellets, but your own enthusiasm for the material and good pedagogical practices will help most (not all) students a great deal.

Teaching Tip #3: Many students expect statistics to be boring. But statistics is, in fact, fascinating. Most of us who are teaching statistics know that it's not boring (at least not to us). Make it your goal—and state that to the class—to deliver statistics for what it is: a way to talk about the real world in a language designed to portray that world honestly, objectively, and fairly. If the world is interesting—if education, sports, health, television, and interpersonal interactions are interesting—then so is statistical analysis, as it is designed to allow us to better understand those areas.

Teaching Tip #2: The ability to tell stories using graphs is one of the best tools that students can take out of an introductory statistics course. In 20 years, it's unlikely that most students will have ever used the robustness properties of the t-test in their daily life (with a few exceptions, of course). In 20 years, by far the majority of your students will have produced graphs for some useful purpose.

Teaching Tip #1: The more students do statistics, the more they'll learn statistics. One of the several threads that runs through the chapters in this book is the value of active learning. That applies to computation, to using software, and to learning concepts. When students stand up and create a "living histogram," they'll likely understand, appreciate, even like histograms more than if they see you sketch one on the board. There is no substitute for doing statistics and drawing conclusions from that process about the world in which students live.

References

Abelson, R. P. (1995). *Statistics as principled argument*. Hillsdale, NJ: LEA.

Cobb, G. W. (2015). Mere renovation is too little too late: We need to rethink our undergraduate curriculum from the ground up. *The American Statistician*, 69, 266–282.

Cohen, J., Cohen, P., West, S. G., & Aiken, L. S. (2003). *Applied multiple regression/correlation analysis for the behavioral sciences*. Mahwah, NJ: LEA.

Freedman, D., Pisani, R., & Purves, R. (2007). *Statistics* (4th ed.). New York: W. W. Norton & Co.

Garfield, J., Zieffler, A., Kaplan, D., Cobb, G. W., Chance, B. L., & Holcomb, J. R. (2011). Rethinking assessment of student learning in statistics courses. *The American Statistician*, 65, 1–10.

Horton, N. J., & Hardin, J. S. (2015). Teaching the next generation of statistics students to "think with data": Special issue on statistics and the undergraduate curriculum. *The American Statistician*, 69, 259–265.

Judd, C. M., McClelland, G. H., & Ryan, C. S. (2017). *Data analysis: A model comparison approach to regression, ANOVA, and beyond* (3rd ed.). New York: Routledge.

Maxwell, S. E., Delaney, H. D., & Kelley, K. (2017). *Designing experiments and analyzing data: A model comparison perspective* (3rd ed.). New York: Routledge.

Wood, B. L., Mocko, M., Everson, M., Horton, N. J., & Velleman, P. (2018). Updated guidelines, updated curriculum: The GAISE college report and introductory statistics for the modern students. *Chance*, 31, 53–59.

Section I

Meta-Issues Related to Teaching: Curriculum, Content, Philosophy, and Supply-Demand Issues

The Role of Philosophy of Science When Teaching Statistics to Social Scientists

Two Constructivists Walk Into a Bar (or Do They?)

Michael C. Edwards

Once upon a time, I was a graduate student. During my graduate training, I took a required course called something like History and Systems, which provided an overview of intellectual trends informing psychology as well as more specific information on the trajectory of the discipline itself. At least, that's what I think happened. I can't find the syllabus. I have some vague memories along those lines, but that's about it. This was the extent of my formal (read: required) training in philosophy during graduate school. *Informally*, I was fortunate to have folks around me who were interested in philosophy of science, and so I was exposed to more than I might have been otherwise. It wasn't just a matter of exposure, it was a matter of timing and integration (more on this later in the chapter). At the time, I was just beginning to learn basic statistics at a deeper level and had just been exposed to more complex models (e.g., structural equation modeling). I noticed occasional snippets of conversation—or the odd paragraph in a paper—that seemed to think about philosophy of science and statistics. Until quite recently, that was the extent to which I had really thought about philosophy of science and how it might relate to understanding/teaching statistics.

Fast-forward a bunch of years, and I now teach an introduction to psychometrics course on a roughly annual basis. This includes a discussion of validity theory[1] and how we go about building a coherent argument that we are measuring what we think we are measuring. It also includes latent variables, factor analysis, and the role these statistical concepts and models play in the psychometric enterprise. Once I had taught the course a few times, I slipped into that comfortable zone teachers will recognize in which the material is familiar and doesn't require too much energy to deliver reasonably well. This allows one to pay more attention to the students and to "read the audience" a bit more—noticing when faces go from "Uh huh, I follow you" to "Wait . . . what?" I noticed times where a flash of confusion would pass over faces and then dispel as I moved on. Over time, I started to note what I was saying that might have prompted this confusion. One semester, with the cooperation of some very tolerant students, I did some exploration to see if I could unpack what was going on. There turned out to be a few issues at play, but a major one was this: (Most of) my students were realists when it came to thinking about constructs, but I was (mostly) a constructivist.[2]

This realization led me down a very enjoyable rabbit hole of philosophy of science readings. In the rest of this chapter, I hope to do three things. First, I'll provide a very brief overview of philosophy of science—giving a basic sketch of important developments and pointing interested readers to excellent and accessible resources to learn more. Second, I'll make the beginnings of a case for why we may want to consider integrating some discussion of philosophy of science into statistics courses. Lastly, I'll float an idea that is likely to get me into trouble but that has emanated from some of my thinking about philosophy of science and the teaching of statistics.

Philosophy of Science 50.5

Until the aforementioned foray into philosophy of science, the entirety of what I knew about it could be summarized as follows:

1. Something must be falsifiable to be a useful scientific theory (from Karl Popper) and
2. Science mostly proceeds in slow and steady increments, but occasionally the paradigm shifts and there is a "revolution" (Thomas S. Kuhn)

If someone knows two things about philosophy of science, the smart money bets that it is these two things. The problem is that modern philosophers of science have identified serious problems with both ideas. On the plus side, they have had a lot of other interesting ideas since the time the major works of those two great philosophers were published.[3] My goal in this part of the chapter is to sketch an overview of major milestones in philosophy of science and mention some of the more recent ideas that I have found particularly interesting. An important caveat before we move forward: I am not a philosopher. I am, on a good day with a strong tailwind, capable of reading what they write and understanding some of it. I do my best to represent the ideas I have encountered accurately, but know that none of them are mine, and I'm just summarizing things other folks have (probably) said (better).

To that end, before moving on, I'll give credit where credit is due. Four books were instrumental in helping me understand the grand narrative of philosophy of science as well as more recent trends:

1. *Philosophy of Science: A Very Short Introduction* (Okasha, 2016)
2. *What Is This Thing Called Science?* (Chalmers, 2013)
3. *Theory and Reality: An Introduction to the Philosophy of Science* (Godfrey-Smith, 2003)
4. *Philosophy of Science: The Central Issues* (Curd, Cover, & Pincock, 2013)

I enthusiastically recommend each. The order they are listed in is the order in which I would recommend reading them. The *Very Short Introduction* is, indeed, very short. The author writes in an accessible manner, and it covers an astonishing array of information with great clarity. Chalmers and Godfrey-Smith cover the same topics but in more detail. Although there is considerable overlap between their treatments, there are enough differences that I enjoyed reading them both. Their voices are distinct, and their philosophical orientations differ, both of which come through in their work. The last book is an edited volume, with content spanning a wide array of philosophical issues. My recommendation would be to keep a running tally of ideas that are particularly interesting to you while you read Okasha, Chalmers, and Godfrey-Smith and then pursue more advanced specific readings on those topics in Curd, Cover, and Pincock. That's what I've been doing, and it has been an immensely satisfying intellectual experience.

Some Quick Definitions

Philosophy is the study of general and fundamental problems concerning matters such as knowledge, values, reason, mind, and language. (I took this from Wikipedia, but you'll find a similar definition in many places.) Epistemology is the branch of philosophy concerned with knowledge, evidence, and rationality (Godfrey-Smith, 2003). Metaphysics is the branch of philosophy concerned with more general questions about the nature of reality (Godfrey-Smith, 2003). Philosophy of science is the branch of philosophy concerned with (mostly epistemological) questions about science.

What Is Science?

That leaves us with one last term to define before moving on. What is science? Before reading on, please pause for a second and really think about a definition. Write it down if you're feeling adventurous. Go ahead. I promise I won't go anywhere while you're thinking about it.

Done Yet?

It's hard, isn't it? You're not alone if you found it difficult to succinctly define science. Indeed, the title of Chalmers's book (#2 in the list) suggests that it's probably not a quick-to-answer question. The authors we have already met offer a variety of answers, including:

1. The attempt to understand, explain, and predict the world we live in (Okasha)
2. A falsifiable theory (Popper)
3. Derived from facts (Chalmers)
4. Produced through the use of the scientific method (several authors)
5. Something we know when we see (Godfrey-Smith)

Numbers 1 and 3 are only offered by their respective authors as too-simple definitions that are then disproven (to some degree). Number 2 receives points for concision (conciseness? Both sound odd to me) but is perhaps overly simple. Number 4 is interesting, but then we must define the scientific method, which also turns out to be harder than one might anticipate. Number 5 isn't a direct quote from Godfrey-Smith but rather my crude distillation of some of his clever observations (e.g., "The work done by physicists and molecular biologists when they test hypotheses is science. And playing a game of basketball, no matter how well one plays, is not doing science"). Godfrey-Smith goes on to provide a more elaborate answer to the question that explains science through an interaction of empiricism (the ultimate source of real knowledge about the world is experience), mathematics, and social structure.

I love the fact that science turns out to be hard to define. It's a great teachable moment when you're teaching things to would-be scientists. Feel free to steal the idea the next time you have a collection of such folks in your classroom. Ask them to define science and see what you get. I bet lots of fictional created-to-make-my-point money that you'll see some confused/bemused facial expressions. Setting all that aside, I don't want us to get too bogged down in defining science. Whether or not individual scientists have a ready definition for science—and whether their individual definition is particularly defensible—we still seem to be doing a lot of what we call science. Most philosophers of science deal with the complexity of defining science in one of two ways: (1) They give a reasonable approximation to a definition and move on or (2) They say that to some extent, defining science is part of the goal of a philosophy of science and move on. Moving on . . .

Logical Positivism and Logical Empiricism

I'm not going to say too much about logical positivism and logical empiricism. That is mostly because they are no longer viewed as acceptable mainstream ways to grapple with philosophy of science. It is also because they can get super tedious and confusing. Logical positivism was a linguistically oriented view of knowledge that focused on things like the analytic-synthetic distinction and the verifiability theory of meaning to understand knowledge and hence science. It was viewed as very reductionist, and after sustained criticism from philosophers (see, e.g., Quine, 1953), it evolved into logical empiricism, which tried to expand its view to something more holistic (in the sense that meaning was dependent on something's place in a larger whole) while still maintaining the empiricist belief that we only learn about the world through experience.

Deduction and Induction

Deduction is a kind of logic by which, given the truth of certain statements, we can derive (or deduce) additional true statements. For example, if I tell you that all cats have four legs and that I have a cat named Miss Marple, you could deduce that Miss Marple has four legs. That's a potentially powerful way of learning about the world, and there are instances in which we use it to great effect. As a way to organize scientific knowledge, though, it suffers from one fatal flaw: You can't use deduction to establish the truth of the items used to deduce new things. Here's what I mean: If I tell you that all cats have *five* legs and that I have a cat named Miss Marple, you would logically deduce that Miss Marple has five legs. That's a valid deduction, but unfortunately, it is incorrect, because one of the facts used to produce the deduction is wrong. No matter how far back in the deductive reasoning chain you go, at some point you must accept something as true to get the ball rolling.

Induction is another kind of logic that is often mentioned in concert with deduction. Chalmers (2013, p. 42) tells us that "a characteristic of inductive arguments that distinguishes them from deductive ones is that, by proceeding as they do from statements about *some* to statements about *all* events of a particular kind, they go beyond what is contained in the premises." An example of induction is: I have woken up every day this month and tomorrow is another day of this month, so I will wake up. While this may not seem earth-shatteringly different from deduction, it is. While the claim is *probably* true, it isn't guaranteed to be. By using a limited sample of information to generalize/predict beyond it, we open ourselves up to the possibility of making errors. The sad (for me at least) fact is that, one of these days, I am not going to wake up.[4] It probably won't be tomorrow—at least based on my actuarial tables. But it could be, which makes induction problematic as a way to think about building knowledge. If induction seems kind of familiar to you, it should. Inferential statistics are inductive in nature. We make an inference about a population from a sample, but when doing so, we know there is a chance that we are wrong.[5]

Chalmers has a nice description of how induction and deduction can be paired up to provide a way to think about science. Through observation, we use induction to come up with laws/theories, and we then use these deductively to predict/explain things. That process works well if our observations lead us to accurate laws/theories. While some have seen this as a weakness, other thinkers have based their philosophy of science around the possibility of making predictions and then seeing if they are wrong.

Falsifiability

Karl Popper, one of the more famous philosophers of science, stated that "I *wished to distinguish between science and pseudo-science*; knowing very well that science often errs, and that pseudo-science may happen to stumble upon the truth" (Popper, 2013, p. 3, emphasis in original). Basically, he was trying to define science. His thinking along these lines led him to several conclusions. First, it's easy to see things that confirm a theory if we go looking for things to confirm a theory. Because of that, confirmations don't count for much in Popper's view. He also comes to believe that "every 'good' scientific theory is a prohibition: it forbids certain things to happen. The more a theory forbids, the better it is" (Popper, 2013, p. 7). We next get to what most of us know as the crux of what Popper believed, that the only way to really test a theory is to try and falsify it. Viewed in this light, you can see why he was focused on prohibitions in theories. If a theory says Thing A can't possibly happen, then you can look to see if Thing A happens, and if it does, you know the theory is wrong. The more things the theory says can't happen, the easier it is to show that it is in error. Popper goes on to say that, in cases where a theory *cannot* be falsified, it is not a proper scientific theory (i.e., it is pseudo-science). While Popper focuses primarily on falsification, he does allow for what he calls corroborating evidence if it is the result of a serious effort to falsify a theory.[6]

I'll mention two areas where I see Popper's ideas most clearly reflected in our statistical practice. First, any time I think about falsification, my first thought is null hypothesis significance testing (NHST). We state a hypothesis and then try to reject (aka, falsify) it. It's a very Popperian thing to do. It's also very Popperian that we never *accept* a null hypothesis. They exist in two states: Rejected or Not Yet Rejected. Acceptance isn't part of the system. Statistically, that's an accurate statement. Practically, most students seem to struggle with this a bit. Me too. If an NHST is the result of a prediction made by a theory, then rejecting it kills the theory.[7] Failure to kill the theory doesn't mean it is right—it just means we haven't killed it yet. And the good scientist goes on trying to kill the theory until she succeeds. Then we start over. It's like *Groundhog Day*, but with more killing, albeit of the theoretical kind. A more elaborate extension of this notion can be found in the ideas of model comparison and selection. As our theories get more complex, testing them can outstrip the capacities of tools like the NHST. Rodgers (2010) discusses this point in detail in a very good paper about transition from NSHT to more holistic modeling approaches in psychology. Life in the "postmodeling revolution" world can look quite different than what we see when we are focused on NHST, but still we feel Popper's influence. One of the primary ways we evaluate a model is to use *competing* models and reject the one that does a poorer job by whatever criterion we are using (typically some combination of the ability to fit the data and parsimony). While we see this in practice, we also see a lot of wrong-headed attempts to replicate NHST. For example, in structural equation modeling, we have a bunch[8] of measures of approximate fit. There is no defensible justification for treating these like p-values or drawing sharp lines allowing us to "accept" or "reject" a model. It can make sense to prefer models that fit better than competitors, but even that is only a tendency and not a rule. Saying something like "all models with an RMSEA > 0.1 are unacceptable" is indefensible. So why do people try to do NHST-like things even when they aren't appropriate? I suspect in part because NHST is often *simpler* than more elaborate model-building exercises, but I *also* suspect that some subset of scientists know about Popper (at least the famous bit about falsification) and think that's the only way science works.

Here's the problem with thinking that falsification is the only way science works: It isn't. In the time since Popper's ideas were widely disseminated, there have been many philosophers thinking about them. In interacting with his ideas, they have found some pretty substantial problems. First, when our observations do not match what our theory predicts, how can we be sure it is the theory that is wrong and not the observations? Science is rife with examples where our power of observation was not capable of seeing the data that would have supported a theory. In several famous cases, it was scientists' stubborn persistence despite disconfirming evidence that eventually led to a breakthrough. Second, most theories have a host of supporting assumptions on which they need to rely. If a theory is disproven, how do we know that we have not simply disproven one of these supporting assumptions? It isn't always easy/possible to make a clear distinction (this is known as the Duhem-Quine problem). Third, what if we reject the only theory we have? Do we just stop? Are we permitted to still use it for some purposes? How do we regard a theory that is in the "yet-to-be-rejected" state? Lastly, in practice, a world where something *never* happens and one where something happens *incredibly rarely* are hard to tell apart. If our theory says Thing A can never happen and we never see it, it could be that our theory is right. Or it could be that we just haven't seen Thing A *yet*. This is a problem with inductive reasoning and the use of observational/experimental evidence to support a claim.

There are more modern spins on Popper's ideas that attempt to salvage some of the core bits and deal with some of the functional and philosophical challenges. One development comes from a philosopher named Deborah Mayo. She developed an idea she calls "severe testing" that provides a more elaborate framework for understanding how and when experimental results support or refute a theory. The interested reader is directed to Mayo (1996) to hear from the scholar herself.

Descriptive or Normative: A Brief Aside

Something I mentioned in the last section warrants a slightly longer comment. When I was reading a lot of philosophy of science, I repeatedly found myself muttering (to myself), "Clearly this philosopher doesn't know any *actual* scientists." Having seen science at arm's length on occasion (and, indeed, having done some of it myself) the descriptions I read often seemed very much at odds with my experience. It's worse than that, because famous scientific discoveries in the last hundred or so years sometimes come with very good documentation and, by and large, they don't look like what the philosophies of science describe. This leads to an important question: Is the goal of philosophy of science to describe what scientists *actually* do (descriptive) or to describe what they *should* do (normative)? The answer, which proves to me that statisticians and philosophers have more in common than I would have guessed, is that it depends. Some theories are meant to be descriptive. Some are meant to be mostly descriptive with some normative pieces. Some are meant to be entirely descriptive but end up having normative pieces anyhow. If you do get into reading more philosophy of science, just realize this is a good question to have running through your head as you engage with a philosopher or idea.

Paradigms

Thomas Kuhn introduced the idea of paradigms to explain the nature of the changing face of science over time. Kuhn described science as moving on two levels. On the "higher level" were paradigms. Kuhn thought of a paradigm as "a package of claims about the world, methods for gathering and analyzing data, and habits of scientific thought and action" (Godfrey-Smith, 2003, p. 76). Chalmers defines a paradigm as "made up of the general theoretical assumptions and laws and the techniques for their application that the members of a particular scientific community adopt" (2013, p. 100). Okasha adds, "When scientists share a paradigm they do not just agree on certain scientific propositions, they agree also on how future research in their field should proceed, on what the appropriate methods for solving those problems are, and on what an acceptable solution of the problems would look like. In short, a paradigm is an entire scientific outlook" (2016, p. 75).

On the "lower level" was what Kuhn termed "normal science." Normal science consisted of all the work done within a given paradigm. Interestingly, although Kuhn allowed for a kind of progress within a paradigm—i.e., we could learn more and solve problems using the accepted tools/methods/theories—he *did not* think one could talk about progress between paradigms. This is an element of Kuhn's thinking about paradigm shifts of which I was completely unaware. In Kuhn's mind, paradigm shifts were the scientific equivalent of popularity contests. Here's how Kuhn described the paradigm shift. First, we have scientists beavering away within their current paradigm. For any of us who do research, this is what we recognize as our jobs: Creating theories, designing studies, collecting data, doing analyses. Over time, says Kuhn, we encounter oddities that are difficult to reconcile with our current understanding of how the world works. One or two of these isn't a huge deal—humans are incredibly skilled at ignoring things they don't want to think about[9]—but then there are four, eight, a dozen, and the field experiences a crisis. At this point of crisis, there will be one or more new paradigms offered up as alternatives. Critically, though, these paradigms are *incommensurable*, meaning it isn't possible to compare them and say Paradigm A is better than Paradigm B. The metrics of success are different when you change paradigms, which is one of the things driving incommensurability. How, then, do scientists choose a new paradigm? The cool kids win. Basically, since there was no rational or scientific reason to prefer any one new paradigm over any other, human behavior played a very large part in determining which new paradigm was adopted. While many practicing scientists feel that something like paradigms and paradigm shifts are reasonable (indeed, there are even historical examples that roughly match aspects of Kuhn's description), these same scientists would probably balk at the idea that progress is only made locally within a paradigm and that we are not progressing toward some global maximum.

This "relativist" way in which paradigms shifted troubled many philosophers. Two of the more famous "fixes" came from Imre Lakatos and Larry Laudan. Lakatos admired both Popper and Kuhn, who are usually seen as adversarial and proposing competing theories of how science works. In addition to his work expanding the idea of falsification, Lakatos offered some interesting modifications to Kuhn's work. He preferred the term "research program" instead of paradigm and did not believe that only one program would be operating at a time. To him, it seemed likely there would be multiple competing research programs in operation at any given time. He believed there was a "hard core" of ideas that defined a research program. These were essential ideas without which the research program couldn't function. There was also a "protective belt" of ideas that allowed the research program to interact with the world. These ideas *could* be discarded and replaced without triggering the kind of crisis Kuhn saw precipitating paradigm shifts. Lakatos's ideas also softened the notion of incommensurability somewhat. Laudan had similar ideas (he called the macro changes "research traditions" instead of paradigms or programs) but pushed a great deal of flexibility into what made a research tradition as well as whether one could compare different traditions in a rational way. Another interesting idea we get from Laudan is the distinction between acceptance and pursuit. Laudan wanted to explain decision-making in science (by scientists) in some rational way. He agreed with Lakatos that more than one research tradition/research program/paradigm could be in operation at any given time. Further, he believed an individual scientist could dabble in multiple research traditions. The difficulty was this: If a researcher accepted a popular research tradition, how did it make sense for them to do research that wasn't aligned with this worldview? That's where pursuit comes in. The notion of pursuit is novel in this context and implies that one does not have to accept an idea to think it is worth exploring. This allowed Laudan to investigate the rationality of scientists choosing what to do when confronted with multiple traditions/programs/paradigms as well as theories within those levels. A scientist could accept one popular research tradition but still rationally invest time pursuing ideas from a less popular (perhaps even antithetical) research tradition that were potentially useful.

Realism, Antirealism, and Scientific Realism

Whether they know it or not, many scientists hold beliefs that roughly mirror a philosophical position called naïve realism. Naïve realists believe that the world exists independent of them and their senses provide an accurate representation of the way the world really is. More relevant to our topic is the concept of *scientific* realism. As defined by van Fraassen, a scientific realist believes that "Science aims to give us, in its theories, a literally true story of what the world is like; and acceptance of a theory involves the belief that it is true" (van Fraassen, 2013, p. 1062). In contrast, we have what are varyingly called antirealists, instrumentalists, constructivists, or constructive empiricists.[10] There are differences when you get into the details, but van Fraassen again does a nice job defining constructive empiricism as the belief that "Science aims to give us theories which are empirically adequate; and acceptance of a theory involves as belief only that it is empirically adequate" (van Fraassen, 2013, p. 1065). Discussions about realism in the domain of science seem to happen in two layers. First, there is some discussion about the extent to which there is what I call "Capital T" Truth. Truth, as I am using it here, boils down to whether there is a unique and correct answer to any question we ask about the universe. Realists think yes, and constructivists are divided. Next, there is some discussion about the point of science. Realists think the point of science is to discover True things. Constructivists believe: (1) There is Truth but science can't know it, (2) There isn't Truth and hence science can't know it, or (3) I don't care if there is Truth because that's not science's job.

Debates about specific *kinds* of realism and constructivism are probably best left to philosophers. What I'll focus on here is realism and constructivism more generally, and as they are understood in the context of science. One of the big differences is in how each camp thinks about the goals of science and about the roles of theories and models. Realists think that theories are attempts to describe the world as it is. Constructivists just want the theory to work. By "work," they tend to mean that it helps us predict what's going on around us and leads to new ideas. The first thing I thought of when I ran into this was latent variables. They are statistical artifacts—a means to partition variance in a way that we find useful. Many users of these models, however, believe that this arrangement of variance gets at something that lives outside the model. In a realist sense, the goal (or at least *a* goal) of creating a statistical model is to try and reflect what is going on in the real world. That's not how I think about latent variables or psychometric constructs. They are vastly oversimplified representations of a hopelessly more complex reality. I'm fine with that. I think the reality that is out there is so complex it is functionally unknowable. I'm fine with that too. I want my theories to help me know what to do in the world. It seems to me that they don't have to be True to do that—but they do have to be empirically adequate.

I suspect though, for people who tend towards the realist position, it is easy to be realist about statistical models. I think that can be dangerous—or at the very least misleading. Even if you are a realist, the statistical models we use are only ever approximations. It's a tautological part of their nature. I suspect this has some implications for how we might best explain models as approximations. I don't have any data on this, but I wonder if more quantitatively focused researchers (i.e., quantitative psychologists) tend toward more constructivist views. If that was true, then it's another potential difference between us and many of our students (i.e., we are constructivists and they are realists) that probably warrants some consideration.

Realism and Constructivism in the Classroom

I mentioned way back in the introduction that I had bumped into some issues in my psychometrics course related to realist and constructivist views of the world. My default when talking about latent variables is to assume that the statistical entities in the models don't need to have a real analog out in the universe to be useful (i.e., it turns out I'm mostly a constructivist). But many students in my course—students who spend their lives focused on whatever the latent variable/construct/factor was—felt differently. They believed (more often than not) that the construct(s) existed in the universe in much the same way that they and their colleagues understood it (i.e., they were realists, at least of a kind), and the job of the model was to capture/reflect that. I think psychometric models can support both constructivists and realists in their endeavors. What I found when teaching the class is that there are instances where what you think about the world impacts how you think about a psychometric topic.

I'll highlight one example that I think demonstrates this relationship. It is a bit of a complicated issue, but I'll skip many of the details and focus on aspects that are relevant for our purposes. There is a phenomenon in factor analysis (structural equation modeling more generally, really, but let the ignoring begin) called equivalent models. Equivalent models are, by the statistical measures we use, completely exchangeable. Put another way, they are exactly as good as each other using any statistical criteria we have. What's interesting about these models is that while they are equivalent on *statistical* criteria, they are often not equivalent on *substantive* criteria. To a constructivist, the fact that you can use statistical models to partition variance in two or more statistically equivalent ways is maybe interesting and potentially useful. To a realist, this can precipitate a crisis of confidence in all statistical models.[11] If the statistical model is indifferent to two wildly different substantive models, then what's the point? And we don't even have to go into the weird world of equivalent models to engage with these issues. There are many cases where substantively different models have very similar statistical performance—equivalent models are just the extreme case where the models are exactly the same in terms of statistical performance.

Lest you leave this section thinking life is a barrel of kittens for constructivists and nothing but pain and suffering for realists, let me assure you that this is not the case. If you believe there is a right answer (Truth), then it is easy to see models as approximations to that Truth. If you *don't* believe there is a right answer, then what exactly are the models approximations of?

In addition to adding lectures that explicitly discuss philosophy of science, I try to raise issues like this throughout class. What my students see when they look at a latent variable, at least at the end of the class I hope, is a statistical representation of a researcher's conceptual representation of a construct. I think that works whether you are a constructivist or a realist.

Other Cool Topics

As much as I'm just touching on the topics we've covered to this point, there are many more that I have been completely ignoring. Some of them are intriguing, but I only have so much space, so they are relegated to this section. My goal here is to say a bit about each and provide you with some references if it piques your interest.

Bayesianism

Bayesianism takes Bayes' theorem and tries to make a philosophy of science out of it. Bayes' theorem says that the probability of some hypothesis being correct given evidence is equal to the probability of some hypothesis being correct without any evidence multiplied by the ratio of the probability of the evidence existing if the hypothesis were correct to the probability of the evidence happening at all. Using Chalmers's notation, this can be written as:

$$P(h/e) = P(h) * \frac{P(e/h)}{P(e)}$$

In the context of philosophy of science, Bayesianism is the notion that this formula can be used to help understand the progress and function of science. Chalmers[12] notes that there are "subjective" and "objective" Bayesians. Objective Bayesians think we can figure out the probability of a hypothesis being correct using objective means. Subjective Bayesians believe that the probability of a hypothesis being correct (called the prior in Bayesian statistics) instead reflects an individual subjective degree of belief. For some writings in favor of Bayesianism as a model of science, see Howson and Urbach (2005) and Salmon (2013). For criticisms, see Mayo (2013). Also, a clever line from Chalmers (2013, p. 229), "Indeed, the most useful applications of Bayesianism are in gambling rather than science," nicely captures some of the skepticism in the community at large regarding Bayesianism.

Prediction Versus Explanation

I had believed for a long time that there was something like a symmetric relationship between prediction and explanation. It turns out this isn't true. The classic example of this is the shadow cast by a flagpole. If I know the height of the flagpole and the angle of the sun, I can both predict and explain the length of the shadow. If I know the length of the shadow and the angle of the sun, I can predict the height of the flagpole, but I cannot explain why it is that height. It's a simple example, but once I knew about it, I started to see asymmetries in prediction and explanation everywhere. For those of us who are quantitative researchers, I believe the relationship between prediction and explanation will be a tremendously important topic in the next decade as we begin to wrestle with/integrate machine learning approaches. Achinstein (2013) is a good place to start learning more about this issue.

Laws and Facticity

Nancy Cartwright has a book called *How the Laws of Physics Lie* (1983). It blew my mind. She has a shorter chapter in Curd et al. (2013) called "Do the Laws of Physics State the Facts?" It hits all the high notes from the book but in fewer pages. What she does in this chapter (and her book) is explain that "the fundamental laws of physics do not describe true facts about reality." This is not merely a constructivist tautology but rather an observation of under what circumstances the laws should be expected to function. She starts with the law of universal gravitation, pointing out that this well-established law doesn't actually describe how any two bodies will behave in relation to each other *because there will always be other forces at work in the real world*. Laws are derived in a vacuum—asymptotic main effects in a world rampant with error and interaction. These "true" statements about the universe are not true anywhere in it. To make them true requires framing them so that they do not describe anything real. There are clear and obvious parallels to statistical models. I'm just beginning to get my head around what Cartwright is saying and what it might mean for users of statistical models, but I have found my mind drifting to this topic often.

Epistemological Anarchism

Into the midst of all this work on structure and systems of knowledge came the work of Paul Feyerabend. His approach, which he labelled epistemological anarchism, does not think there should be any special approach to science. Scientists should do whatever works for them and not worry so much about the various ideals and systems the philosophers were trying to impose on their work. Godfrey-Smith (2003) nicely describes two main points in Feyerabend's best-known work, *Against Method* (2010). First, Feyerabend notes that an honest history of scientific discovery seems to fly in the face of the ideals of philosophers like Popper or Kuhn. Second, he notes that science is viewed a little too reverently in society, and its highly structured practice was antithetical to human freedom. His work is very different from much of what we have talked about up to this point but provocative and worth a read.

Should We Teach Philosophy of Science in Our Statistics Courses?

When I teach graduate courses, I ask students if they have had a philosophy of science class (or something like it) in their graduate training. Of the roughly 200 doctoral students I have asked, fewer than 10 have indicated having taken such a class. That's about 5%. Now, I don't pretend that my sample is random—I teach courses like Psychometrics, Factor Analysis, and Item Response Theory—but that doesn't mean the observation isn't informative. I will also note that, living in Psychology departments as I have the entirety of my career, I was surprised that only one or two of the roughly ten students who had some philosophy of science coursework were from my home department. My expectations were thus: (1) Students likely hadn't had a philosophy of science course, and (2) If they had it wasn't part of their coursework in psychology. It would be very interesting to do a little more data collection[13] and see what role, if any, philosophy of science has in psychology graduate training generally.

Now, you may be objecting to the way I framed the question, which is fair. I was interested in course-length treatments, but that doesn't mean they didn't have *any* contact with basic philosophy or some philosophy of science. So now I shift to an even smaller sample size: The roughly 70 doctoral students who have taken my graduate psychometrics course since I added a philosophy of science lecture. Based on the reactions I get during class and the questions I get after, this is the first time many of these students have been exposed to most of these ideas.[14] Even if it isn't the first time, it's the first time someone has talked about the concepts in philosophy of science as they relate to statistics, the models we use, and the inferences we make.

I am, at heart, a pragmatic guy. So it breaks my aforementioned pragmatic heart to know that I am not likely to convince my department to add a course on philosophy of science to the required graduate sequence. That required graduate sequence, by the way, has been very small at both institutions I have worked at, consisting largely of an introductory statistics sequence.[15] This is perhaps unsurprising, as psychology departments often leave the specifics of training up to an area-based structure. It does mean that, to the extent students receiving a PhD in psychology have any common coursework, it is one or two statistics courses. If that's where the audience is, *then maybe the solution is to take philosophy of science to where they are*.

I don't think we would have to completely overhaul introductory graduate statistics courses to inject some relevant philosophy of science into them. Some topics that seem to fit in easily include: (1) statistics and epistemology, (2) explanation versus prediction, (3) causal reasoning, and (4) realism versus constructivist positions. I could imagine thinking about NHST or frequentist methods as a paradigm (or research program/tradition as your personal tastes go) and how that might make for an interesting conversation when you're considering more general models or Bayesian statistics. A more basic way to start would be to think about *what we want to learn from using statistics* and comparing that to *what we can reasonably expect to infer from our results*. In my experience, this is something that can get short shrift in favor of more esoteric content. This basic theme runs through all models/procedures we use, so it could be something of a unifying structure throughout a statistics curriculum. As we move into more complex models (e.g., structural equation modeling), we can use the existence of latent variables to motivate a realist/constructivist conversation. We can also review other examples in science where unobservable constructs have been used. In my experience, that provides a useful and broad background when trying to get your head around what latent variables are/do.

What's Wrong With Cookbooks, Exactly?

Remember way back at the beginning of the chapter when I said that I'd float an idea that would likely get me into trouble? Here we are. I don't want to blame anyone else for this idea, but it is completely Chuck Klosterman's fault. He wrote this great book called *But What If We're Wrong?* (2016). I had read an earlier book of his (also great, called *I Wear the Black Hat*, 2014), and when I stumbled across this one, I decided to read it. I'm glad I did. It singlehandedly reignited my interest in philosophy and got me to read all the philosophy of science books and chapters I've been telling you about. Oversimplifying a lot, the basic premise of the book is this: At least some of what we know is true today is not. For scientists, you either believe that today is a unique epoch in the history of science where we are right about everything we know, or you believe that today is probably like all the days before it, and some of the things we know to be true are, in fact, not true. If you are like me, then you believe today probably isn't special and conclude that some of what we know is true is not. Klosterman's book has a subtitle: *Thinking About the Present as if It Were the Past*. That's an idea he has about ways we can try to figure out which things we know to be true may turn out not to be. I liked the idea and it started me thinking more critically about basic things I had just assumed to be true. What follows is a work-in-progress based on some of that questioning.

Quantitative psychologists love statistics. It's a topic we are excited about and for most of us plumbing the depths of some corner of the statistical world is how we justify our continued employment. That and teaching students about various corners of the statistical world. One trend I have noticed among quant folks[16] is a fetish-level love of R. R is a free, syntax-based piece of statistical software. There is some basic core functionality, but everything else comes as a package that is written by someone with varying degrees of skill and clarity. You can also just use R like a basic programming language. It is an incredibly flexible program. That's great if you need that flexibility. What if you don't need it? What if, like many of the students who take our courses, you just need to run an ANOVA? Syntax-based programs are, it seems to me, harder to use than point-and-click programs (SPSS comes to mind as one exemplar). Quant people hate SPSS. We teach it in our courses sometimes, but you will not generally see it gracing the pages of *our* journals. Now, don't get me wrong, SPSS has some issues. For example, if you try to do an exploratory factor analysis in SPSS, it defaults to a principle components analysis, despite the fact that these are two different analyses (see, e.g., Widaman, 2007). But SPSS does make it easier for researchers to do analyses, and I think that's probably something we should think about a bit more.

I used to think SPSS was too easy to use, and that led to people doing analyses they didn't understand. I still think that happens, but now my primary complaint with SPSS is that *it has too many options*. Do most users want to know enough about statistics to be able to make informed choices about when to use all those options?[17] I don't think so. I think we need to create a new software package that has a button you push when you want to do an ANOVA. All the options are fixed. They default to reasonable things. We can automate assumption checking and then automate transformations or other fixes should we find major violations. Those would be noted in the output. Such software would likely be a boon to scientists and science.

Increasingly, I'm thinking that we need to recognize that for most researchers, statistics is a tool. They are doing their science, and they need an answer to progress their work. They are not interested in statistics beyond that. So here's my idea: We need to think about statistics the way other tool makers think about the tools they make. We need to figure out metrics for what makes a tool good in this context and then evaluate how we are doing. I fear that, if we evaluate current statistical practices by any reasonable standard used to evaluate tools, we will not do well. Currently, we believe that someone must spend 15 to 30 weeks (at least) to have even a marginal chance at using the most basic of statistical tools. That's horrible. If a hallmark of good design is ease of use, then, Houston, we have a problem. I suspect some of this relates back to the fact that we teach/design/implement statistics *the way we like to think about it*. And we are people who like to think about it, as opposed to the vast majority of people in our classes, who don't want to think about it. They just want it to work and be easy to use. It would be bad enough if statistics was relatively rare in science, but it is increasingly obligatory.

I know there are interesting epistemological issues related to statistics. I've spent much of the past year reading about them. However, I don't think your average user needs to know anything about them most of the time. I think we, the folks who think the most about these tools, need to make a concerted effort to produce a better product. It should be robust, straightforward, and transparent. Robust in the sense that the user doesn't have to know every little thing about running the analysis. We have advanced to the point where we can get software to drive a car, but we are still asking researchers to do their own assumption checking before running a model? Straightforward in the sense there should be few, if any, options available to the user. The more options there are the higher the potential for confusion or, even worse, malfeasance of some kind. Transparent so we all know what's going on. That's just good science. I am not a fan of black boxes, but I am increasingly becoming a fan of transparent ones. I want everyone to be able to see what's going on, but I think the world would be a better place if people had fewer choices when it came to statistics.

The title of this section came from watching some talks about teaching statistics. On more than one occasion, someone derided "cookbook statistics." I don't blame them—I have done this myself on repeated occasions. But then I did something I hadn't done before: I actually thought about it. What's wrong with cookbooks? Cookbooks are freaking amazing. They allow people, with minimal training in a few basic skills, to consistently prepare a mind-boggling array of dishes. They have worked for millennia. The fact that there are cookbooks—and the unquestionably simplified steps that the format sometimes requires—does not mean there cannot be Michelin-starred chefs.[18] It does not mean that experts, with years of training, are not free to explore flavors and preparations and textures to the limits of their skills. But people need to eat, and cookbooks are a time-tested way of robustly, straightforwardly, and transparently sharing knowledge about how to prepare dishes. I suspect our problem with the idea of cookbook statistics is twofold. First, I think we are elitists, and we think it degrades something we are passionate about. That's a bad outcome from a less-than-bad place. We can work on that. Second, I think we are not very good at writing cookbooks. Many of us (but not all—there are notable exceptions) struggle to describe even the most basic statistical analysis with the clarity one finds regularly in even the most mundane cookbook. Imagine if you wanted to know how to make Hollandaise sauce and, rather than handing you a page or two on how to do it, I told you that you needed to take a 15-week course. No one loves eggs Benedict that much. You would just skip it. Except in many sciences, that's no longer an option. Just because we have a captive audience doesn't mean we should ignore their goals.

Two last points before I wrap things up. First, one of the reviewers of this chapter pointed out that this section seemed disconnected from the rest of the chapter. He was completely right. I will try to fix that a little bit now. To some extent, this idea *is* a bit disconnected from everything else. What it has in common with what preceded it is that I started thinking about this idea after reading a bunch of philosophy of science and trying to understand why scientists were using statistics. Are the statistics an end in themselves? A simple means to an end? Or a mixture of those? I then thought about how I viewed statistics and got to thinking about how my understanding of statistics might differ from my students' understanding of statistics. This led, slowly, to the idea described earlier. The second point, raised by the same astute reviewer, was that what I've said could be taken as an argument for *not* including philosophy of science in quantitative courses. My intention was the opposite. I thought that if I was going to argue we should spend time in quant/methods courses talking about philosophy of science, I should have a suggestion for what we should take out or, more broadly, how the courses could change to accommodate the addition of new material. I then thought about some of the things I often covered in my courses that might be of dubious utility, which led me to thinking about other ways to (perhaps) gain some efficiency. So, put a much shorter and simpler way, my basic idea is that if we build better tools, we can focus less on the mechanics and minutiae of the tools and more on what they can help us learn.

The End

I realize the future I am suggesting looks substantially different from current practice. I think that's good. I don't know if we'll get there, and I'm not even convinced we should try to, but it has been rewarding to question basic premises about teaching statistics and imagine changes that might make things better. It has caused me to rethink my job as a teacher of statistics, and I have already begun making course corrections (pun intended). I hope that in writing this chapter, I have said something that sparks your curiosity. I hope it leads you to think more deeply and critically about our responsibilities to our students as well as to the larger scientific enterprise.

Notes

1. Two of my favorite academic quotes concern validity. Thissen and Wainer (2001, p. 11) explain reliability and validity as follows: "In casual terms, we can define validity as measuring the right thing, and reliability as measuring the thing right." Simple but spot-on. The other is from Markus and Borsboom (2013, p. xii), "In contrast to test theory as a whole, test validity represents the least mathematical specialization within the most mathematical sub-field of less mathematical disciplines." I wish I had written that.
2. I'll say more about this later, as well as defining realism and constructivism.
3. *The Logic of Scientific Discovery* (Popper) was originally published in 1935 but first appeared in English in 1959. *The Structure of Scientific Revolutions* (Kuhn) was originally published in 1962.
4. Sorry for the morbid turn. I haven't had enough coffee yet today, which always makes me think about death.
5. If I *had* consumed enough coffee, I would probably say something about how deeply problematic this way of thinking is, since the odds are very good that any inferential model we use is so simple when compared to the complexity of the cosmos that believing there is a "true" analog in the population seems pretty daft.
6. I mention this mostly because it was a bit surprising to me. I thought Popper was all falsification, all the time. Turns out he *preferred* falsification but wasn't unaware that repeated failures to falsify something should probably not be ignored.
7. Popper was quite clear that falsified theories should be discarded without mercy. In my experience, that isn't how scientists work, but let's not let reality ruin a good discussion about theory.
8. I've been thinking about what we should call a collection of fit measures. You know, like a gaggle of geese or a murder of crows. I suggest: a folly of fit measures.
9. https://xkcd.com/1539/
10. Antirealist always sounds like an insult to me, so I'll use constructivist.
11. I have these on a pretty regular basis, so these are not inherently a realist experience.
12. There is a chapter by Chalmers in the Curd et al. (2013) edited book. It is very similar to chapter 12 in Chalmers (2013), so either works if you want to learn more.
13. I can hear you asking, "Well, why didn't you just do it?" I might break down and do it at some point, but I've made it this far in my career without having to collect data.
14. Except falsifiability and paradigms.
15. Now my sample size is two. Any less and I'm just talking to myself, right? Well, for what it's worth, I do talk to lots of colleagues who are at other universities, and this trend seems widespread. Also, several of my colleagues have done research on these topics (Aiken, West, & Millsap, 2008), and what I'm saying is consistent with what they have found.
16. I mean quantitative psychologists here, but also folks who are into the same stuff: statisticians, biostatisticians, econometricians, overly eager social psychologists, "data scientists," etc.
17. I opened up version 24 of SPSS on my desktop, and a quick count reveals more than 30 checkbox options when doing an ANOVA (and more once you get deeper into the options).
18. One complexity I am dodging is that, in the real world, we train our quantitative doctoral students in many of the same classes as the students concentrating in other substantive areas.

References

Achinstein, P. (2013). Explanation v. prediction: Which carries more weight? In M. Curd, J. A. Cover, & C. Pincock (Eds.), *Philosophy of science: The central issues* (2nd ed., pp. 439–450). New York: W. W. Norton & Company.

Aiken, L., West, S. G., & Millsap, R. (2008). Doctoral training in statistics, measurement, and methodology in psychology: Replication and extension of Aiken, West, Sechrest, & Reno's (1990) survey of PhD programs in North America. *American Psychologist*, *63*, 32–50.

Cartwright, N. (1983). *How the laws of physics lie*. New York: Oxford University Press.

Cartwright, N. (2013). Do the laws of physics state the facts? In M. Curd, J. A. Cover, & C. Pincock (Eds.), *Philosophy of science: The central issues* (2nd ed., pp. 871–882). New York: W. W. Norton & Company.

Chalmers, A. F. (2013). *What is this thing called science?* (4th ed.). Indianapolis, IN: Hackett Publishing Company.

Curd, M., Cover, J. A., & Pincock, C. (Eds.). (2013). *Philosophy of science: The central issues* (2nd ed.). New York: W. W. Norton & Company.

Feyerabend, P. (2010). *Against method* (4th ed.). New York: Verso.

Godfrey-Smith, P. (2003). *Theory and reality: An introduction to the philosophy of science*. Chicago, IL: University of Chicago Press.

Howson, C., & Urbach, P. (2005). *Scientific reasoning: The Bayesian approach* (3rd ed.). La Salle, IL: Open Court.

Klosterman, C. (2014). *I wear the black hat*. New York: Scribner.

Klosterman, C. (2016). *But what if we're wrong?* New York: Blue Rider Press.

Kuhn, T. S. (2012). *The structure of scientific revolutions* (4th ed.). Chicago, IL: University of Chicago Press.

Markus, K. A., & Borsboom, D. (2013). *Frontiers of test validity theory*. New York: Routledge.

Mayo, D. (1996). *Error and the growth of experimental knowledge*. Chicago, IL: University of Chicago Press.

Mayo, D. (2013). A critique of Salmon's Bayesian way. In M. Curd, J. A. Cover, & C. Pincock (Eds.), *Philosophy of science: The central issues* (2nd ed., pp. 550–564). New York: W. W. Norton & Company.

Okasha, S. (2016). *Philosophy of science: A very short introduction* (2nd ed.). New York: Oxford University Press.

Popper, K. (2002). *The logic of scientific discovery*. New York: Routledge Classic.

Popper, K. (2013). Science: Conjectures and refutations. In M. Curd, J. A. Cover, & C. Pincock (Eds.), *Philosophy of science: The central issues* (2nd ed., pp. 3–10). New York: W. W. Norton & Company.

Quine, W. V. (1953). *From a logical point of view*. Cambridge, MA: Harvard University Press.

Rodgers, J. L. (2010). The epistemology of mathematical and statistical modeling: A quiet methodological revolution. *American Psychologist*, *65*, 1–12.

Salmon, W. C. (2013). Rationality and objectivity in science *or* Tom Kuhn meets Tom Bayes. In M. Curd, J. A. Cover, & C. Pincock (Eds.), *Philosophy of science: The central issues* (2nd ed., pp. 518–549). New York: W. W. Norton & Company.

Thissen, D., & Wainer, H. (2001). *Test scoring*. Mahwah, NJ: Lawrence Erlbaum Associates.

van Fraassen, B. C. (2013). Arguments concerning scientific realism. In M. Curd, J. A. Cover, & C. Pincock (Eds.), *Philosophy of science: The central issues* (2nd ed., pp. 1060–1082). New York: W. W. Norton & Company.

Widaman, K. F. (2007). Common factors versus components: Principals and principles, errors and misconceptions. In R. Cudeck & R. C. MacCallum (Eds.), *Factor analysis at 100: Historical developments and future directions* (pp. 177–203). Mahwah, NJ: Lawrence Erlbaum Associates.

Chapter 3

Optimizing Student Learning and Inclusion in Quantitative Courses

A. T. Panter, Viji Sathy, and Kelly A. Hogan

Training scientists and quantitative scholars is of national interest (PCAST, 2012a; PNSTC, 2018; Mervis, 2018). For several years, the two largest professional associations in psychology, American Psychological Association (APA) and the Association for Psychological Science (APS), advocated that psychological science *writ large* and the rigorous scientific study of the human should be included as a core component within the broader category of science, technology, engineering, and mathematics (STEM) fields (APA Presidential Task Force on the Future of Psychology as a STEM Discipline, 2010; National Science Board, 2018). According to the 2010 Psychology as a STEM Discipline Task Force report, psychological science's exclusion from the STEM core cluster has led to significant challenges and missed innovation opportunities due to (1) inconsistent STEM-focused federal grant dollars and other investments; (2) lack of incentives for psychology to build collaborative networks with other STEM fields; and (3) widespread negative perception, including by members of the field, that undermine psychology's connections to STEM fields.

Quantitative Psychology as a STEM Field

Quantitative psychologists never seemed to doubt their STEM status. Scholars, researchers, and teachers develop and apply new methods in research design, measurement, statistical modeling, and reporting for studies of all sizes and complexity, involving human abilities, individual differences, and behavior. Historically, Division 5 (now called Quantitative and Qualitative Methods; www.apa.org/about/division/div5) was one of the earliest APA divisions, established almost 75 years ago. Many of the first 20 Division 5 presidents also served as APA presidents as well and were pioneers in theories and applications of the overall field of psychology, including learning, psychophysics, and psychometrics, psychological and educational measurement, statistics, research design, industrial/organizational psychology, program evaluation, and assessment (Robertson, 2009).[1]

Quantitative psychologists, secure in their STEM status, expressed other sorts of worries. These included how to (1) increase, or at least maintain, the production rate of new doctorates; (2) counteract the graying of the field's members; (3) include scholars with different backgrounds in discipline and life experience; and (4) train top scholars in state-of-the-art methodologies for academic, government, industry, nonprofit, and other settings in the face of downsizing pressures by academic departments (APA Task Force for Increasing the Number of Quantitative Psychologists, 2009; Aiken, West, & Millsap, 2008). Currently, 50 doctorates graduate each year in the specific National Science Foundation category called "quantitative and psychometrics," a twofold increase over the last 10 years (National Science Foundation Survey of Earned Doctorates, 2017).[2]

The Task Force for Increasing the Number of Quantitative Psychologists report (2009) suggested that quantitative psychology could address its relative invisibility and small footprint by: (1) increasing outreach about the discipline to high school students and undergraduates; (2) documenting existing, research active quantitative doctoral programs; and (3) offering workshops on quantitative methods more frequently and to broader audiences.[3] Two important articles (Aiken et al., 2008; Aiken, West, Sechrest, & Reno, 1990) documented the relative scarcity of required and elective quantitative courses at the undergraduate and graduate levels. Nationally accredited psychology doctoral programs were shown to require just 1.6 years of coursework, inclusive of the common "first-year statistics sequence." This low commitment to quantitative coursework was present even at our nation's most selective doctoral programs and over two decades. The Quantitative Pipeline Task Force report and Aiken et al. (1990, 2008) were focused on who would be available to teach and curriculum as it existed.

Yet in all of the discussions about training the next generation of quantitative psychologists, the APA Quantitative Pipeline task force report and articles did not seriously address how undergraduate and graduate students are actually taught in quantitative psychology. They never discussed (1) re-thinking pedagogical approaches; or (2) training quantitative graduate students who intend to be future faculty members how to enhance undergraduate student learning through intelligent pedagogical design. Focusing mainly on research and scholarship, graduate students are not formally taught pedagogical principles and often must "learn by doing" in their teaching assistant roles for undergraduate statistics courses (following the lead of the instructor). Importantly, both graduate students and faculty members are not taught how to (1) use state-of-the-art STEM pedagogy that encourages inclusive excellence in their teaching; (2) design courses to improve student learning; or (3) use their expertise in measurement to assess teaching at the undergraduate and graduate levels.

In the last decade, several institutions, including our own, shifted their teaching culture, the culture of diversity and inclusion in the sciences and beyond, and how we articulate intended student learning within courses. In this chapter, we review how psychology, and specifically quantitative psychology, has not yet matched STEM-type education in higher education institutions. We believe that some quantitative psychologists, along with their colleagues in educational measurement in their university's graduate school of education, with their expertise in statistics, measurement, assessment, individual differences, design, data visualization, program evaluation, and reporting, are particularly equipped to contribute to the research and scholarship on STEM teaching and learning. They can foster the creation of tools to aid in institutional change pertaining to STEM education, and in many cases, their background makes them particularly effective influencers to produce institutional change pertaining to STEM education on their campuses.

STEM Education in the 21st Century

Significant change has been afoot in STEM education in P–12 grades, as well as in colleges and universities across the nation (Wieman, 2017; Weaver, Burgess, Childress, & Slakey, 2015; Felder & Brent, 2016; Leshner, 2018). This change is so significant and far reaching that scholars have identified current pedagogical approaches as "education reform" (Wieman, 2017; Mulnix, 2016) and "the second generation of science education" (Eddy & Hogan, 2014, p. 453). For professionals who dedicate their lives to quantitative training of undergraduate students and in university settings for graduate students, it is important to consider the specific choices instructors make through their in-class and out-of-class assignments, assessments, and materials to generate student learning. Some rationales would be weak arguments for demonstrating student learning ("I learned it this way in graduate school; current students should also learn it this way"). But what types of evidence would demonstrate student learning? In the field, direct measures, such as student work on a poster, results section, an annotated set of findings, as rated by trained others on prespecified dimensions, might serve as appropriate evidence of learning. In addition, research shows that indirect measures of self-reported student learning (e.g., "I enjoyed this lecture," "I feel like I learned a lot from this lecture," "The instructor was effective at teaching," "I wish all my [STEM] courses were taught this way") are not related to actual student learning in randomized experimental design (Deslauriers, McCarty, Miller, Callaghan, & Kestin, 2019). Rather, intelligent program and course design—in which desired program outcomes are specified first and specific instructional activities within a course are closely tied to these outcomes—are considered state of the art in the STEM scholarship of teaching and learning.

Well-designed curricula, intentional course design focusing on specific outcomes that undergraduate and graduate students should know and be able to do, and the adoption of specific STEM pedagogy course characteristics, such as accountability, structure, and asynchronous practice (i.e., opportunity to engage in low-stakes practice outside of the classroom), positively affect whether or not students engage and learn (e.g., Freeman, Haak, & Wenderoth, 2011). Some important additional outcomes of student-centered design include increased enrollments (sometimes followed by increased institutional allocation of resources and rankings), better student performance, and higher participation in the field by underrepresented groups.

In his 2017 book, *Improving How Universities Teach Science: Lessons From the Science Education Initiative*, Nobel Prize winner and Stanford professor Carl Wieman discussed past decades of STEM education, especially at the undergraduate level, noting that STEM pedagogy has overrelied on "haphazard, unplanned" models that are "poorly matched to modern educational needs" (p. 6). He pointed to five major changes that have driven significant educational STEM reform: (1) needs in the modern economy; (2) student demographics including increased educational access and opportunity, especially for higher education; (3) landscape in higher education, particularly with respect to faculty roles and responsibilities at research universities; (4) expertise about how people learn science; and (5) the state of education-related technology.

In the next sections, we review two main areas, academic design and teaching, feedback, and assessment, where Wieman (2017) identified major discrepancies in how universities currently operate with respect to STEM education ("actual") versus how they optimally or ideally could operate ("ideal"). To underscore the importance of his insights in relation to quantitative teaching, we reproduced two tables and discuss the "actual" versus "ideal" concepts he identified and discuss how quantitative psychology, in particular, can benefit from this type of careful thought and design. We then provide a few specific examples of how the authors have implemented some of these ideas at our own institution. It is important to consider one's own current educational context, space, undergraduate students, graduate students, and faculty when thinking through how education design steps can be made. Last, we include recommendations for how members of the quantitative community can contribute to these efforts.

Academic Design

As shown in Table 3.1, an essential component of STEM education reform involves the use of backward design to determine the primary educational goals of an academic degree program as well as the primary student learning outcomes for each course within that degree program.

Table 3.1 Current Versus Optimized Universities: Academic Design

Current	Optimized
Each academic program has a series of courses that are required. These requirements are set rather idiosyncratically and revised intermittently when someone in the department feels the inclination.	Each academic program has a clearly delineated set of educational goals that encompass the full set of skills, knowledge, and ways of thinking that are part of an education. These goals are created collectively by the faculty in consultation with other stakeholders, such as industry, educational systems, and government.
The department offers a set of courses defined by a list of topics. These choices largely reflect faculty teaching interests and history.	Each academic program has a series of courses that are carefully aligned and sequenced to progress toward the program goals. Each course is defined by explicit and detailed learning goals that identify the full set of student knowledge and competencies provided by the course.
Faculty work in isolation to set their own agendas and goals.	These learning goals explicitly relate to the program goals and are established by a consensus of the department faculty members. They are maintained, regularly reviewed, and updated as part of the normal functioning of academic departments.
When students enter a program or even just a course, their background preparation is largely unknown and underdetermined. Faculty members routinely spend time unnecessarily teaching known material while also leaving large gaps in coverage of important items. Prerequisites are often poorly matched to what is needed.	The backgrounds of the students in each course will be known and conveyed to the instructor.

Source: Reproduced from Wieman, C. (2017). *Improving how universities teach science: Lessons from the Science Education Initiative*, Table 1, p. 18.

In other words, an instructor or group of instructors could determine in advance what specific capacities they wanted their students to learn as a result from the lessons on particular days. They would start with the student learning they would like to observe and then work backward to design class activities and assignments that directly correspond to that desired outcome. Using backward curricular design requires a high level of discipline by the instructor(s) to state precisely the intended learning outcomes and design all aspects of the course that come to mind. Wieman (2017) discussed how this work requires great care and investment by faculty members who are able to take a long, broad view of student learning. Such a view requires intentionality to ensure that each educational goal and student learning outcome is tied directly to activities within the course, course sequence, or degree program.

Faculty members developing curricula have often fixated on content representation or topic coverage rather than focus on developing educational experiences requiring a set of portable capacities or transferrable skills that students will acquire and be ready to use as a result of the work (Wieman, 2017; Sireci, 1998). Specifying student learning outcomes and the curricular activities that it takes to achieve this learning requires considerable thought. When a department rushes to meet a last-minute instructional need and asks a faculty member to step in to teach a quantitative course not in their typical portfolio of courses, these actions can jeopardize student learning. Wieman also noted that no single person can or should make final decisions about what an academic program should be. Rather, a panel of faculty members with disciplinary knowledge, in consultation with key stakeholders inside and outside of the academy, should be able to state clearly what degree program graduates should know and be able to do. The achievement of student learning outcomes can be best viewed in terms of the expectations for what follows in the immediate and long-term future, as a student progresses to the next set of courses, to graduate school, toward the achievement of additional degree-related milestones, and/or in terms of future workforce expectations.

At the same time, the curriculum needs to be designed recognizing that students, upon entry into course work or a degree program, arrive with different levels of preparedness and deserve opportunities to learn in settings that are well aligned to their level. When academic program components are well designed, faculty members can optimize their teaching by ensuring that they are well aware of student preparedness upon arrival to a set of courses to avoid a student x level mismatch. These are concepts that are quite familiar to teachers in quantitative methods.

Implications for Quantitative Psychology

Fortunately, quantitative faculty members come to the academic design task with critical expertise and competencies that make them very well positioned to conduct this type of backward-design curricular work. For example, psychologists who work in test development are well-versed in discussions of individual differences, validity, and test specification and design, which match very closely with principles in the Testing Standards, for example (The Standards for Educational and Psychological Testing, 2014; see Part 2, Operations: Test Design and Development). Psychologists trained in program evaluation are also well versed in the preparation of logic models outlining outputs and inputs (Shadish, Cook, & Leviton, 1990).

Additionally, due to the nature of quantitative courses in the curricula for undergraduate and graduate degrees, those who teach quantitative courses are uniquely positioned to espouse these effective methods to impact large numbers of students at key points during their training. For example, faculty for quantitative courses typically teach the required statistics courses for undergraduate students or often one of several "service courses" within the larger department for graduate students (e.g., first-year ANOVA-regression sequence). This breadth of background and treatment presents a unique opportunity to invite students with varying interests to the merits of quantitative approaches as well as to provide students models of effective teaching pedagogy in STEM courses.

However, despite quantitative psychologists' unique expertise they bring to the academic design task, other unique challenges exist for quantitative curriculum development. First, both quantitative psychology faculty and doctoral programs are relatively few. Other than certain documented quantitative psychology programs in the country, quantitative faculty members in psychology departments are typically alone or with very few others, sprinkled among other faculty members with non-quantitatively oriented interests (Aiken et al., 2008). As a result, faculty with quantitative expertise can be the lone, sometimes overshadowed voice in curricular discussions regarding the importance of quantitative education of undergraduate students or graduate students among departmental instructional committee peers. Being one of a few quantitative faculty members adds extra administrative burden to engage fully in curricular discussions and often comes with little perceived institutional reward and little actual institutional reward, especially for early-career faculty members. Sometimes heeding the service call to "fix" the quantitative training or the curriculum can cost a faculty member their position when they are hired into a university with a strong research focus. While one could argue that a faculty member's most important function is the serious curricular work described here, this work comes with significant burden and responsibility for quantitative psychologists.

An opposite phenomenon is that other department faculty members may feel "out of their element" and leave all of the curricular decision-making to a single quantitative faculty member. This situation, too, presents a significant challenge to curricular development, because department faculty have disengaged from the discussion, do not provide their diverse perspectives about how quantitative methods are used in their areas, and, by handing it off to others, in a sense are making quantitative psychology invisible and a side interest.

In addition, low numbers of quantitative faculty members within departments can add instability to a department's ability to offer regular courses within a curricular sequence. To help address the stability issue at the undergraduate level, within the past decade, many psychology departments at many universities have added teaching professors (contract faculty with these titles), whose primary responsibilities are to teach large sections for main curricular offerings, such as gateway courses including statistics and research methods. Thus, a department may have faculty from different ranks teaching different sections of the same course. Yet if different sections of a quantitative course differ in student learning outcomes and pedagogical approach (Table 3.1, row 3), student learning may not be optimized. To align across sections, groups of faculty members (hired with different purposes by the university) need to coordinate to work together in planning the curricula for these courses. At the graduate level, small quantitative programs are subject to more haphazard offerings (e.g., research and study leaves, administrative assignments, and so on). This reality increases the chances that a department administration does not anticipate quantitative curricular holes, leading to staffing decisions by instructors with less central quantitative expertise and incomplete curricular coverage for certain students.

In terms of the designed curricular experiences, quantitative psychologists have been challenged by their long history of being particularly "topic focused" rather than specifying clear competencies that they expect their students to exhibit/demonstrate. The field tends to conceptualize knowledge domains, such that students will be prepared once they have completed a course, a section of a course on a topic, or smaller chunks of topics in introductory statistics courses, for example, a certain statistical test or a concept (e.g., multilevel models, quasi-experimental designs, sampling, item response theory, the independent groups t-test, chi-square test, calculating between-groups sums of squares). But at what level, specifically, does a student achieve competency within an area? For example, is it the ability to (1) know, use, and contrast underlying formulae by hand; (2) understand at a conceptual level the formulae and assumptions; (3) identify under what conditions within a research agenda the procedure is warranted; (4) use a widely popular computer program to perform a test and write about findings; and/or (5) develop hypotheses within a research context, carry out an analysis, and write findings according to our field's standards? At the graduate level, the overarching competency focus for student learning may be to improve the methodological contribution in applications of psychological research. Undergraduate and graduate textbooks in statistics and quantitative methods are remarkably stable in terms of covered topics. The APA Quantitative Pipeline Task Force report (2009, Appendix F) outlined a topics-based, not learning outcome-based, table of contents for a potential new undergraduate textbook on quantitative psychology.[4] Panter (2000) observed that there was essentially no variation in topic coverage when she reviewed more than 40 introductory psychology statistics textbooks on the market. Rodgers (Chapter 8, this volume) discussed a review of current-day undergraduate statistics textbooks mirror classic texts such as Kirk (1968) showing the same general topics in the same order.[5] Aiken et al. (2008) provided the quantitative topic list for doctoral programs nationally and identified some areas where curricular innovation and uptake seemed to have occurred (e.g., structural equation modeling) and was spurred by new, accessible textbooks and computer programs.

Wieman (2017) noted that a curricular program can be negatively affected by individual faculty members who are peripherally engaged in curricular discussions, hold idiosyncratic views based on nostalgia, or are overly invested in their particular niche, agenda, and teaching history. Because quantitative faculty lines, retirements, and transitions are so rare, topics covered within a single course or a course sequence (with their specified student learning outcomes) need to be carefully scheduled and planned, often in collaboration with other programs that have interest in the curriculum that is being offered. Quantitative programs vary in their ability to conduct long-term planning of their courses. In quantitative graduate program curricular planning, the offerings to students can be driven by departmental need, a faculty member's research program, research and study leave schedule, grant funding course releases, administrative buyouts, and offerings in other quantitative spaces in the department and university. Undergraduate curricular planning of quantitative courses can be affected by the availability of tenured/tenure-track faculty after the graduate course needs are filled, with teaching faculty with varying degrees of quantitative expertise filling in the instructional holes. Quantitative faculty members believe that there is a set of capacities that students should achieve for expertise in the field and for postgraduation opportunities. It is important to recognize that as faculty members contribute to the larger curriculum, some may work on their own courses, without collaboration of teaching with others, in silos, and consider standardization of outcomes across courses within a curricular program to be an imposition on their academic freedom.

We believe that quantitative psychologists can "borrow strength" from their colleagues around the country by conducting curricular design, as a collective, as advocated by Wieman. Writing and facilitated discussions within the field, such as seen in this volume, could allow for broader, more balanced discussions of academic design and quantitative learning outcomes for particular types of the academic program. Professional organizations in quantitative psychology such as APA Division 5 or the Society of Multivariate Experimental Psychology, with input from other stakeholders not in quantitative psychology, could lead such efforts. These efforts could provide clear guidance about student learning, examples for faculty using open-source approaches, and evidence about learning at the undergraduate and graduate levels. As is the case with nonpsychology natural science fields, contributions to these curricular designs and STEM pedagogy teaching resources in quantitative coursework could be recognized as valuable contributions to the scholarship of teaching and learning.

At Our Own Institution

The authors teach at a highly selective, leading global research university with a very strong public mission and commitment to access ("Of the public, for the public"; Chancellor's Strategic Plan, 2017). Over the past decade, individual faculty members have become increasingly familiar with the students we serve, especially at the undergraduate level.[6] While there is still a long way to go, regular reporting of summary information about the students in our programs and courses helps us tailor our curricular materials and activities to the preparation of the students and ensure that students can develop skills in required foundational areas through technology, additional coursework, or individualized attention. There is inefficiency, as Wieman notes, in teaching material that is a repeat for some and completely out of reach for others.

AAU STEM REDESIGN GRANT

A large course redesign initiative was launched in 2013. AAU awarded UNC a grant to conduct course redesigns in the Departments of Biology, Chemistry, and Physics. The university provided in-kind support for this grant. The goal was to redesign all gateway STEM courses in these departments through a mentor–apprenticeship model and faculty learning communities (Krumper, McNeil, & Crimmins, 2015). The mentor–apprenticeship model involved the most skilled instructors in high-structure active learning (often teaching assistant professors) teaching faculty members who did not yet have those skills (often tenured professors). It was a dynamic that was not typically seen, yet the goals were training faculty members with state-of-the-art methods and institutionalizing new approaches. One component of the individual course redesign effort within each STEM department involved, as a collective faculty, identifying student learning outcomes for each course (common across sections) as well as a consideration of the undergraduate curriculum overall within each department. Department faculty worked together to think about what they specifically wanted their graduates to achieve (program outcomes) and what courses it would take for students to get there. Significant normalized learning gains were made in each of these departments at the undergraduate level. Most important was a shared vision that these introductory courses were "owned" by departments and were not to be changed at the whim of an individual instructor.

DATA ANALYTIC TOOLS AND DASHBOARDS TO UNDERSTAND STUDENTS BEING TAUGHT

To help departmental faculty become more knowledgeable about the students they teach, the authors designed a new suite of data analytic tools and approaches for all academic departments and university leadership. In partnership with our university's Office of Institutional Research and Assessment (OIRA), all of the directors of undergraduate studies at the university, and university counsel, we designed a department profile dashboard to shed light on basic attributes of student preparation, course taking, engagement with desired high-impact educational practices that are of value to our department (e.g., semester-long mentored research, internship, study abroad, honors). We created additional dashboards for individual instructors to mine their course grades over time matched to institutional student background data, helping faculty uncover where achievement gaps may exist and for administrators to examine program-level grading patterns (e.g., consistency of grading distributions across sections of introductory-level courses; division-level patterns).[7] These data analytics tools are like holding up a mirror, allowing us to see how our students navigate through college, curricular-level trends, and where improvement in teaching and learning may be necessary.

CURRICULUM DEVELOPMENT USING STEM PEDAGOGY

Incorporating STEM pedagogy innovations is a university priority. In the STEM departments most instructors incorporate these methods. The university has forwarded curricula through our Quality Enhancement Plan (directed by the third author), which has required pan-university course submissions, reviewed by pan-department experts in STEM pedagogy. For example, to incorporate course-based undergraduate research experiences (CUREs) into the curriculum, proposals are collected once a year and a panel of faculty review whether the course adheres to the characteristics of authentic research that will be sustainable, impactful, and supported by the departmental chair. Funds awarded include a stipend to participate in a yearlong faculty learning community where faculty further refine their ideas, peer review one another's learning goals and lesson plans, plan assessments, and perform class observations. As one highlight of collaboration and curricular change, the work of a lab director, an internationally renowned organic chemist, and other STEM colleagues led to the development of a robust CURE for about 1,000 organic chemistry lab students every year.

RELIANCE ON THE APA GUIDELINES FOR THE UNDERGRADUATE PSYCHOLOGY MAJOR (2013)

Within our Department of Psychology and Neuroscience, our multiyear assessment plan of the undergraduate major, required by our accrediting body, relies on the learning goals (Knowledge Base in Psychology, Scientific Inquiry and Critical Thinking, Ethical and Social Responsibility in a Diverse World, Communication, Professional Development) and the student learning outcomes within those goals. For example, for Scientific Inquiry and Critical Thinking, after completing the psychology curriculum for the major, students should be able to: (1) use scientific reasoning to interpret psychological phenomena; (2) demonstrate psychology information literacy; (3) engage in innovative and integrative thinking and problem-solving; (4) interpret, design, and conduct basic psychological research; and (5) incorporate sociocultural factors in scientific inquiry. However, in our department, the curriculum design and the individual courses have not used these student learning outcomes as recommended by Wieman (2017). At the undergraduate level, quantitative concepts are barely mentioned. Quantitative faculty could contribute to APA's consensus on the undergraduate major. At the graduate level, the quantitative field could benefit from collaborative work and design to articulate academic design and coursework for quantitative graduate work at the doctoral level. This approach would contrast with the very program-specific approach that depends on the specific quantitative program, the specific faculty members present at the time, and the specific time period. However, we must acknowledge that with a small faculty size and specific areas of expertise, adjustments have to be made when even a single faculty member departs the university and departmental needs shift.

Teaching, Feedback, and Assessment

> Bloodletting was the medical treatment of choice for 2,000 years. It is the same thing. . . . Look at the impact, though: You let some blood out, and go away and watch them, and they get well. . . . You give people lectures. And they go away and they learn the stuff. But it wasn't because they learned it from the lecture. They learned it from homework, from assignments.
>
> (Wieman, 2016)

As seen in Table 3.2, Wieman (2017) describes how specific courses can be designed within an academic curriculum according to the "actual" versus "ideal" STEM pedagogy that facilitates student learning. Each course can be designed using backward design to develop instructional approaches, materials, and technologies, select placement and diagnostic measures, obtain regular feedback from students, provide regular individualized and group feedback, and appropriately assess the quality and amount of student learning within a course setting.

In the modern university (Dean & Clarke, 2019), faculty member roles are increasingly multi-faceted, requiring skills about which they feel ill prepared, experience discomfort, and/or choose

Table 3.2 Current Versus Optimized Universities: Teaching, Feedback, and Assessment

Current	Optimized
Faculty use whatever teaching methods they prefer, usually traditional lecture.	In each class, the students encounter pedagogical approaches, materials, and technology based on careful research and measurement of results. Research-based interactive engagement teaching techniques are used extensively, with ongoing feedback provided to students (individually and collectively) during class.
Faculty members occasionally ask students which topics they have learned. A few develop review materials for the students based on their best guesses as to what some students lack that is important.	Before a course starts, students complete a detailed diagnostic examination that accurately measures their preparation. This examines their content and conceptual knowledge of the subject and the subjects that the course builds upon, such as mathematics and related science disciplines. It also diagnoses their attitudes and epistemologies about the subject and how it is best learned.
Many faculty members spend several class periods rapidly reviewing the knowledge they think the students need. The students who already know the material are bored and find this a waste of time and often become overconfident as to the level of challenge of the course. The students who are less prepared don't benefit because the review is too rapid to learn from.	Before a student has ever seen an instructor, the instructor has a profile of his or her strengths and weaknesses, and the computer has already flagged serious deficiencies. If these deficiencies are widespread, the student is guided to enroll in a more appropriate course.
	When deficiencies are localized and not severe, the computer provides the student with feedback and suitable exercises to complete that remedy these deficiencies. This ensures that the course will begin with all students at roughly the same level of knowledge and competence.
	The instructor uses the profile of the class to suitably tailor the learning environment.
The frequency of evaluation of the students is determined by the instructor and typically includes only graded homework (although often does not), one or two midterm exams, and a final exam. Due to a lack of faculty expertise, many homework problems and faculty-created exams primarily practice and test memorized factors and procedures. Feedback from these evaluations is usually delayed by one to two weeks and provides little to the students beyond a score showing the fraction of questions answered incorrectly.	There are regular ongoing evaluations of the student's thinking and learning throughout the course. These evaluations are linked to targeted timely feedback to both student and instructor. Information technology is used widely to support this ongoing evaluation and feedback, including online homework systems that include intelligent grading and tutoring systems.
Typically, technology is developed and used for its own sake, often provides little educational value, and is seldom evaluated as to its effectiveness.	Technology is chosen by looking carefully at how it can enhance learning by supporting good pedagogical design, enhance the capabilities of the instructor, and improve instructional efficiency.

Current	Optimized
Collaborative learning by students is discouraged by curve grading and relies on informal student arrangements. Communication and teamwork skills are usually not part of regular science courses.	The full benefits of collaborative learning are realized by building such collaboration into the structure of the classes, assignments, and grading. This also improves students' teamwork and communication skills.
Faculty teaching evaluations are based on student course evaluations. These have little correlation with learning and none with the use of effective teaching methods.	Faculty teaching evaluations are linked to good measures of student learning and the use of the most effective teaching practices.

Source: Reproduced from Wieman, C. (2017). *Improving How Universities Teach Science: Lessons From the Science Education Initiative*, Table 1, p. 18.

to ignore. Because new faculty positions are rare, especially in quantitative psychology, faculty hiring of teaching professors and tenured-tenure-track faculty are highly competitive. Hiring committees may prefer candidates with experience teaching particular courses of particular sizes but give scant attention to evidence of the candidate's promise to and/or ability to maximize student learning outcomes or effectiveness of teaching.

In other words, the hiring process can be similar to the academic design: focused on coverage rather than quality of teaching experience or potential to do so effectively. Hiring may also be focused primarily on an individual's ability to generate knowledge. Little to no attention is devoted to understanding how one collaborates with students and colleagues, counsels students on careers, is active in campus efforts, leads center or administrative units, and considers themselves a life-long learner. An individual's approach to designing their courses, consulting the literature in the scholarship of teaching and learning, or collaborating with colleagues in professional organizations pertaining to teaching are rarely considered. Some institutions garner billions of dollars of sponsored research (our institution = $1.1B in 2018), yet relatively little is expended on sponsorship of teaching practices or training.

Faculty often ask: "If not the traditional lecture, what is the alternative?" The alternative in STEM pedagogy is called high-structure active learning (HSAL; e.g., Haak, HilleRisLambers, Pitre, & Freeman, 2011), Deboeck, Chapter 12; Eddy & Hogan, 2014; Sathy, 2018; Sathy & Moore, Chapter 13, this volume; Wieman, 2017). HSAL is aimed at (1) clearly specifying student learning outcomes for a given topic; (2) maximizing accountability for student learning by ensuring that adequate preparation is conducted prior to a class meeting; (3) providing multiple touchpoints to provide formative feedback to students so both students and the instructor can check comprehension of specific concepts; (4) offering multiple, low-stakes practice opportunities—before, during, and after class; and (5) optimizing actual class time so that students, faculty, and other instructional support staff, working together, may engage in some of the more challenging conceptual areas of the course.

For a given HSAL course, well-selected course content is shifted for students to complete outside of class time, prior to meeting and after meeting. Instructors design engaging small-group activities for the classroom that stimulate critical thinking and devote class time to higher-level problem-solving. These activities keep both student and instructor accountable for preparation. This approach also maximizes educational capital of peers within a classroom through peer instruction, collaboration, and communication. This shifts from traditional lecture with students who watch, listen, and take notes (Felder & Brent, 2009) to an environment that involves students "doing things and thinking about the things they are doing" (Bonwell & Eison, 1991, p. 2). Such methods can encourage instructors to engage in practices such as "just-in-time teaching" (JiTT), which allows instructors to receive feedback from students about where students are struggling or have questions (Novak, Patterson, Gavrin, & Christian, 1999), and scientific teaching, where the approach to teaching is treated as having the same rigor as conducting science itself (Handelsman, Miller, & Pfund, 2006). Instructors can provide mini-lectures delivering content when it is most needed, after a question has been posed or when it is needed to complete the next step. It also allows the achievement of higher cognitive processing levels on Bloom's Taxonomy, such that students generate, create, analyze, and apply knowledge rather than simply understand, recall, and remember (Anderson et al., 2001; Bloom, Engelhart, Furst, Hill, & Krathwohl, 1956). They can practice under the guidance of peers and instructional staff who are present and ready to facilitate rather than via a homework assignment, where students may unduly struggle without guidance.

These research-based HSAL approaches demonstrated improved STEM learning gains (Freeman et al., 2014; Theobald, Hill, Tran, Agrawal, Arroyo, et al., 2020) as well as produced a reduction in achievement gaps (Eddy & Hogan, 2014). Furthermore, failure rates decline, allowing more students to pass into subsequent coursework. In quantitative fields, this is especially helpful in shifting mindset related to math and ability to succeed with motivation and interest improving with HSAL (Sathy, this volume; Latulipe, Rorrer, & Long, 2018). All of these are vital to broadening the pool of students who may be interested in pursuing quantitative fields.[8]

But challenges exist on multiple fronts. First, adopting pedagogical "business as usual" approaches hurts science training and hinders participation. Lecture is defined as continuous exposition by a speaker to an audience whose members we assume have the intention and motivation to learn. Students generally have one encounter with the lecture and the transmission of information. Research shows that lecture itself does not necessarily promote thought, change attitudes, or inspire interest (Bligh, 2000) and overall leads to little student learning (Wieman, 2016, 2017). All of us may have excellent, memorable examples of lectures that we experienced from our educational histories that profoundly affected our views of an area, taught us about an important concept within our field, or modeled for us how to present a difficult concept to others.[9] Science students learn best when they are held accountable for their learning with clear assignments that are due and graded at relatively small intervals, can frequently practice and get feedback on course concepts and approaches on their own while not being graded (i.e., under low-stakes conditions), and have opportunities to engage in activities that mirror what scholars and scientists do in their field when they conduct their work (i.e., are authentic). The traditional lecture is not consistent with new approaches in science learning and the development of scientific identity through sustained work with personal ownership (Corwin, Runyon, Robinson, & Dolan, 2015).

Table 3.3 High-Structure Active Learning

Course Structure	Graded Preparatory Assignments e.g., reading quiz	Student in-Class Engagement e.g., clicker questions, worksheets, case studies	Graded Review Assignments e.g., practice exam, problems
Low: Traditional Lecture	None; <1 time per week	Students talk <15% of course time	None; <1 time per week
	1 per week	Students talk 15%–40% of course time	1 per week
High	≥1 per week	Students talk >40% of course time	≥1 per week

Source: Reproduced from Eddy and Hogan (2014). *Getting Under the Hood: How and for Whom Does Increasing Course Structure Work?*, p. 455, Table 1.

One second challenge to adopting HSAL has been training for faculty members on how to use active learning in their own discipline and how to observe it. Identifying HSAL courses can be a challenge. As seen in Table 3.3, some metrics involving classroom sound levels (single voice instructor vs. multiple voices students vs. silent thinking time) have been used to define HSAL classrooms. Also, promising new methods have described the level and extent of active learning in a classroom through sound and work to help instructors establish goals toward a more HSAL classroom (Owens et al., 2017). By its very nature, HSAL rejects the unidirectional "sage on the stage"/"profess" approach toward a bidirectional, facilitative approach ("guide on the side"; "cognitive coach"). This approach has the added benefit of helping students cultivate ownership in their learning rather than relying simply on the instructor to transmit information. Designing activities and material to the appropriate desirable difficulty and scaffolding learning experiences can take some time to learn and master.

Implications for Quantitative Psychology

By virtue of the quantitative field, faculty members have become accustomed to teaching undergraduate and graduate courses either to students who are required to be there (undergraduates) and/or who vary considerably in their quantitative background (undergraduates, graduate students). Faculty members rarely know very much about their students when they enter their course unless they teach in a very small program and have past experience with a particular student in a course or on a research project. Wieman (2017) has identified this lack of understanding about the students one teaches and their preparedness to be a major area of improvement for science instructors.

Some faculty develop their own methods to get around their lack of knowledge about their students by developing their own presurveys to understand better the range of student backgrounds and quantitative experience within their classroom or program. Despite every institution offering an undergraduate psychology degree requiring a statistics and/or methodology course, for example, very few standard presurveys exist or are used widely (an exception is the Survey for Attitudes Towards Statistics; Schau, Stevens, Dauphinee, & Vecchio, 1995). Without this information, quantitative faculty teach to students with varying quantitative backgrounds and skills, and it is not until the instructor looks at descriptive information from the first assessments that these variations are observed formally.

In a sense, it is not surprising that our students at the undergraduate and graduate levels do not persist in science at higher rates and lack diversity. As undergraduates, students may be exposed to large gateway science classes with an instructor at the front of the classroom and teaching assistants sitting in the wings where seats are fixed, interactions with classmates are limited, and classroom engagement is nominal. "Discussion" is limited to relying on what are often a few brave students willing to speak in a room of hundreds. Instead of thinking of these introductory courses as an opportunity to welcome individuals into the field, cultivate appreciation or curiosity to study it further, or simply be equipped with key principles in the event this is the only course one takes in this area of study, many are still subjected to "the look to the left, look to the right" weeding-out process. Faculty may hold notions of the purpose of these introductory courses to allow the "cream to rise to the top." In fact, faculty may engage in practices that limit the number of students who can earn top grades, such as norm-based grading (curved) instead of performance- or standards-based grading, thereby limiting the number of students interested or able to advance to subsequent coursework. In such environments, collaborative learning is discouraged.

Poor facilitation and course design can result in exacerbating student achievement differences by enabling students who know how to approach college and have strong note-taking and study skills to do well, whereas students who are less knowledgeable or experienced suffer and are potentially turned off to further study in the area.

In a time of so many open-source educational tools and courses, at the undergraduate level, for example, we regularly ask what is the value added to bringing many students, drawn together by academic interest, to a class where most of a class session involves watching a professor work problems? Graduate students learn to teach these courses via "on-the-job-training" opportunities as teaching assistants. In rare cases, they serve as teaching fellows with sole responsibility for a course and have a mentor who may or may not be engaged with the pedagogy, student learning outcomes, and assessments. Their graduate curricula do not usually allow for formal study about what is needed to maximize student learning within a course or pedagogy more broadly. Nor is sufficient attention paid to how students learn, despite advances in the literature by cognitive psychology and learning sciences colleagues (Greene, 2018).

At Our Own Institution

At UNC-Chapel Hill, we significantly invested in multiple ways to train and support faculty members to become expert in STEM pedagogy.

1. *Course Redesign Grants and Hiring.* Current faculty can improve teaching practices through course redesign grants and participation in faculty learning communities (FLCs). Faculty participate

in FLCs through a variety of initiatives provided by the university and/or external funding agencies: large course redesign grants, teaching with HSAL methods, teaching Course Undergraduate Research Experience (CURE) courses, and integrated curriculum courses. FLCs are structured opportunities for faculty to meet, troubleshoot specific aspects of a course, practice lesson planning via backward design, and so on and are facilitated by experienced faculty and staff. The FLC concept is now very familiar to university faculty, and faculty members participate knowing that it will be an opportunity for dedicated time to discuss their teaching approaches and engage in course development/redesign. In addition, as seen in Table 3.4 showing a STEM pedagogy position description, the university committed to hiring faculty who excel in these areas. The teaching professor career track at our large public university includes a schedule for promotions from teaching assistant professor to teaching associate professor to teaching professor. Titles for this employment track were changed within the past few years by vote of the university's Faculty Council and were subsequently approved by the Board of Trustees. Note that the word "permanent" in the job add does not mean that this is a tenured/tenure-track position, but rather the position is "not temporary" and includes discrete contracts after each formal promotion.

2. *Training in HSAL.* As mentioned, the AAU grant involved a model in which faculty members with more experience using active learning within large science lecture courses (often early-career teaching faculty member) mentored and trained another faculty member (often later career tenure-track faculty member) as they co-taught the class. Faculty learning communities were also used to provide support to faculty as they transformed their teaching. Twelve STEM gateway courses were transformed, learning gains increased, and more than 6,000 students are now impacted beneficially by these transformed courses each year.

3. *Finish Line Project (FLP).* In 2014, Panter was awarded a U.S. Department of Education grant focusing on the experiences of first-generation college students as well as the institutional programs and supports that can increase students' progress to degree. A grant component included a case study with Department of Mathematics ($n = 11$ faculty members) and a randomized controlled trial with STEM faculty recruited through email messages from the eight departments within

Table 3.4 Example Language for a Teaching Professor Position With STEM Pedagogy Expertise

The [*Department*] at [*University*] seeks applicants for a permanent 9-month teaching professor position, effective [*date*]. The position involves assisting with innovative science, technology, engineering, and mathematics (STEM) course redesign of introductory [*STEM*] courses and **teaching 2–3 classes per semester** in courses such as [*list of courses*].

The successful candidates will also contribute to the implementation and evaluation of programs to bring evidence-based teaching methods to introductory courses, collaborate with faculty conducting [*discipline*] education research, and work closely with tenure-track faculty in their discipline. Applicants should have a PhD in [*discipline*] or science education with at least one semester of full-time college teaching as instructor of record. **Candidates should have clearly demonstrated a commitment to using evidence-based teaching methods in the classroom and have strong interdisciplinary content knowledge**.

the natural science and mathematics division of the College of Arts and Sciences ($n = 22$ faculty members). All participants in FLCs were provided with a stipend of $5,000 upon completion of the FLC. For the randomized controlled trial, the study was open to faculty members who had not taken part in an FLC or had large course design grants in the past. Participants had to be the instructor of record for the course section being redesigned. The study drew equal numbers of tenured/tenure-track faculty and some teaching professors. In the case study in mathematics, we created a faculty learning community (FLC) that engaged much of the department over two semesters, provided reasonable incentives for participation, involved faculty across a range of career stages, and relied on a strong and respected group of four facilitators to lead the group through professional training (a teaching assistant professor who excelled in HSAL, a tenured professor who cared deeply about teaching, a facilitator from the university Center for Faculty Excellence, and the third author). FLC members were trained to think systematically about ways (1) to redesign their gateway quantitative courses, (2) to enhance active learning, and (3) to focus on student learning outcomes rather than teaching tradition. Training occurred in group settings, through specialized one-on-one coaching sessions with consultants and FLC facilitators who focused on current evidence-based scholarship on STEM pedagogy and learning science. FLC members also were encouraged to conduct systematic peer observations of successfully redesigned STEM classrooms. Finally, each FLC member was responsible for applying concepts to their own courses with outcomes ranging from complete course redesigns to restructuring of assessments, specific out-of-class assignments, and class time. Course instructors in quantitative psychology methods were not part of these FLCs, yet computer scientists, ecologists, mathematicians, and statisticians were. More generally, it would be desirable to observe participation of quantitative psychologists in these STEM-related activities and collaborative discussions, including curricular redesigns to maximize student learning through low-stakes practice and accountability, opportunities for peers to collaborate in a structured way, authentic data science projects that maximize student ownership, and assessments that are tied to the prespecified learning outcomes. The products of such innovative efforts could then be shared so that a broader discussion could exist within the field.

4. *Leveraging Technology.* Faculty may be tempted to employ technology or specialized apps in their courses. Often, technology is developed and used for its own sake, often provides little educational value, and is seldom evaluated as to its effectiveness. At UNC, many gateway courses employ classroom response systems (CRS) such as Poll Everywhere or Pearson's Learning Catalytics as a means of providing frequent formative feedback to large numbers of students. In quantitative courses, these tools double as a means to instantly collect data for immediate analysis. As noted in Sathy and Moore's chapter (Chapter 13, this volume; see also Deboeck, Chapter 12), instructor-produced screencasts can provide a means of content delivery at a pace and time best suited for students. For example, students can rewatch a video on calculating standard deviation, employ closed-captioning, or simply hit pause to work a problem alongside the instructor. Leveraging technology to improve learning outcomes will be an important feature of STEM education reform. Furthermore, educational technology should be designed with the aim of facilitating student success, and one size will not fit all classrooms.

5. *Summer Science Institute.* Incoming faculty can receive training through the teaching center (Center for Faculty Excellence), and more recently, starting in 2017, all incoming STEM faculty were invited by the dean of Arts and Sciences to participate in the Summer Institute for Scientific teaching (http://summer-institute.unc.edu/). Faculty members who are invited are new to the university. Some may be new to teaching overall, while others are seasoned instructors who are moving to the university. This five-day training is a replicate of the National Summer Institutes model (www.summerinstitutes.org/) and is hosted locally by the College of Arts and Sciences and the Summer School. Workshop participants work in small groups to develop one of their lesson plans using backward design, practicing writing student learning objectives as well as assessment methods. They deliver the lesson to peers for feedback. Faculty often cite it as one of the first times they become aware of HSAL. Most new faculty members move to campus around July, with the semester opening in late August. Over the years, we have tried to choose a time when faculty members would have enough time to make changes before the semester begins.

    Center for the Integration of Research, Teaching and Learning (CIRTL): Graduate students can learn about teaching by serving as a teaching assistant and can partake in certification efforts in STEM education via the CIRTL national network CIRT. Our institution joined the CIRTL network in 2017, and as such, students can participate in training remotely with other trainees across the country and receive credit toward different levels of certification: Associate Level, Practitioner, and Scholar (www.cirtl.net).

6. *Administrative Structural Changes.* In 2014, the College of Arts and Sciences established an Office of Instructional Innovation staffed by a Director of Instructional Innovation (third author). Since then, the position has been elevated to associate dean, and the office serves to connect administrators, faculty development opportunities, and faculty in a variety of ways. At the department level, the associate dean works with chairs to help them think about hiring teaching faculty and more holistic ways to evaluate teaching effectiveness and has a liaison in each department that passes along news related to teaching and learning. The office has served to connect the nearly 200 teaching faculty in the college by calling meetings each semester to discuss administrative policies and professional development and build community. At a curricular level, the office has tasked faculty to look at solutions for curricular problems, such as quantitative literacy, and has been involved in helping to shape and implement a new general education curriculum. Individual faculty have interfaced with the office through specific professional development opportunities such as classroom observation, consulting, workshops, and community-building events.

7. *Creation of Peer Visits Program.* As an outgrowth of the first cohort of faculty in a large-course FLC, faculty members (including the authors) identified a need to have opportunities to learn from peers through classroom observations. At that time, the only opportunities for faculty to be observed teaching were for tenure, promotion, or renewal of contracts—all high-stakes in nature with very little by way of feedback on instruction. This FLC felt strongly that more classrooms needed to be opened up for faculty to visit and to see various teaching methods and technologies used. The program, administered through the university's Center

for Faculty Excellence, has grown to include a large number of faculty who are willing to have anyone attend a class session.

8. *Measurement Research on Student Evaluations of Teaching (SETs)*. Finally, considerable research emerged in the last five years about differential ratings for student, instructor, and course-level factors on student evaluations of teaching (SETs) in end-of-term administrations (Linse, 2017; Uttl, White, & Gonzalez, 2017). Specifically, in quantitative fields evidence shows that SETs can yield lower ratings for instructors of underrepresented backgrounds such as women and minorities (Uttl & Smibert, 2017). Yet SETs continue to be the predominant assessment method used to describe student learning and the effectiveness of faculty teaching. In collaboration with colleagues at University of California at Los Angeles (Cai, Sturm, Sathy, & Panter, 2018), the authors are examining responses from SETs recognizing their structure with multilevel, item-level factor analyses by discipline over multiple years. We evaluate SETs as a function of student characteristics (e.g., gender, underrepresented minority status, first-generation status, financial need, course performance, evaluation completion), instructor characteristics (e.g., gender, URM), and course characteristics (course size, SET response rate, nature of course as an introductory gateway, upper level, or course-based research related, and division). Additionally, we are connecting these quantitative analyses with the qualitative evaluation through natural-language processing of the open-ended comments of SETs as a function of the student, instructor, and course variables. By identifying overall themes, sentiment, and attributes of the comments, we hope to enrich our understanding of student ratings as a high stakes assessment method across STEM and other disciplines.

Conclusion

When the President's Council of Advisors on Science and Technology (2012a) declared its first national priority was to increase STEM retention of majors to generate additional STEM degrees, they recognized that STEM pedagogy was no longer going to be "business as usual." STEM instructors in the higher education space were expected to move beyond class periods being the time, for example, for students to gather to watch an instructor transmit knowledge and work problems. Rather, through STEM pedagogy, they called for serious engagement with the material before, during, and after class through low-stakes practice, accountability, authentic activities, and structured interactions with classmates and outside of the classroom related to course learning outcomes. This alternative course form has shown superior student learning in the sciences, including psychology (Freeman et al., 2011).

In this chapter, we discussed how quantitative psychology, as a STEM field, is just as well suited to use these approaches to academic design and teaching, feedback, and assessment as mathematics, physics, chemistry, biology, statistics, or another science within the STEM cluster. These approaches can improve student learning in quantitative psychology courses at both the undergraduate and graduate levels. At our own university, the L. L. Thurstone Psychometric Laboratory and quantitative program was placed in the Department of Psychology [now, and Neuroscience] by Lyle V. Jones when Dorothy Adkins was department chair, with the understanding that if the department were ever not an appropriate home, alternate plans would be made. Years ago, a forward-thinking department chair, Bernadette Gray-Little, when given the option, decided that psychology should be assigned to the division of Natural Sciences and Mathematics (rather than in the Social Sciences) in the College of Arts and Sciences because she understood that greater university resources would come to this division. At the undergraduate level, quantitative psychology is at the table. For example, the three chapter authors were on a small design team for "IDEAs in Action," the university's new general education curriculum, which received a positive vote by the faculty in spring 2019 and is in the implementation phase. The new general education curriculum affects the 5,000+ incoming undergraduates per year and includes (related to this chapter) (1) a redesigned quantitative literacy and quantitative reasoning requirement; (2) a new required data science component of an interdisciplinary course; and (3) a new required high-impact research and discovery experience such as mentored research and CUREs. In addition, the second author works with the system office to design different math pathways for all universities and community colleges in the North Carolina system. Finally, the university is planning to create a School of Data Science from the existing School of Information and Library Science school. The first author works on a planning committee related to the undergraduate curriculum for that school as well as managing planned significant increases in overall undergraduate enrollment that will be required to fund such a school (enrollment dollars). At the graduate level, our quantitative faculty members have some voice on key university committees, where their expertise in curriculum design and research are needed, but some efforts, such as the development of a new School of Data Science, have weak representation, as compared to other quantitative departments across the university such as computer science, statistics and operations research, mathematics, and biostatistics.

Despite challenges in creating high-quality quantitative programs within psychology departments and consistently teaching all sections in such a way as to maximize student learning, quantitative faculty members are particularly well-suited to help guide and inform the discussion around effective teaching. Many of the issues in STEM pedagogy, after all, are related to test design, measurement, and research design: How do we assess constructs of an effective instructor or an effective course? How do we document student learning? What are some common items that help document preknowledge in a course? What evidence is required to document and determine where effective teaching is occurring in the university? Our unique training can and should be used not only to advance the improvement of statistics teaching but to help further the efforts of effective STEM education more broadly.

Not discussed in depth in this chapter is the considerable savings of faculty and student time that results when faculty invest time in advance to design their programs and courses to align their activities and exercises with their specific student learning outcomes (Wieman, 2017). Faculty members save time by collaboratively designing their courses, ensuring that continuous improvement mechanisms are "baked into" the cycle of course offerings and thus not needing to conduct their design work separately, in silos, de novo.

Setting clear learning goals and using evidenced-based approaches to teach optimizes student learning and preparation. Additionally, graduate student teaching assistants and undergraduate learning assistants develop a good understanding of how to address student difficulties and scientific teaching expertise for future faculty and K–12 educators. The chapter authors are in agreement that using these approaches optimizes faculty and student efficiency and serves as excellent training opportunities for future educators.

Our chapter outlined the importance of curricular design, collective discussion and agreement on student learning outcomes for programs and courses, course redesign tied to STEM pedagogy, and taking time to understand the individual differences of the students being taught. Colleges and departments can do the following to move STEM pedagogy forward (Bradforth et al., 2015). They can:

- **Communicate the importance and value of effective teaching** through promoting the academic design ideas discussed in this chapter, rewarding faculty who work to improve their teaching through time, resources, and promotion, and encourage learning through peers.
- **Train their PhD students differently** by providing teaching training aligned to career goals, such as future faculty fellows programs or participation through a network such as CIRTL. These efforts should create opportunities for graduate students to teach undergraduates using high-structure active learning approaches. Graduate students can and should work in partnership with faculty teaching courses to discuss course design.
- **Train faculty differently** by encouraging faculty development opportunities and learning communities devoted to student learning and STEM pedagogy. As we learned from the grants at our university, the format of these learning communities can be within department, across departments, and/or across faculty ranks. There should be stated incentives and rewards in place for faculty members who meaningfully contribute to the creation of a curriculum or course redesign, even for tenure-track assistant professors. These rewards can be communicated as a value in requests for external letters for personnel decisions, in departmental tenure guidelines, and/or through stipends and consultant support. Good teaching can be celebrated and help break down rank and hierarchy barriers that may exist in a department.

Assess Teaching Differently by Expanding Beyond the Usual Inputs

There are many rubrics to evaluate different dimensions of teaching in person and through course design. However, most reviews of teaching only take the form of very few inputs, usually: a teaching statement, a classroom observation, and student evaluations of teaching. Often little time or effort is spent deciding who is evaluating the teaching (what kind of record with student learning?) and how effective teaching will be evaluated. Effective teaching should encompass the entire set of resources and structures in place to facilitate student learning in a course. As with students and learning, formative feedback for faculty regarding teaching by trained observers who may be peers and quality rubrics is ideal and serves as important diagnostic information for a faculty member. Such information requires an institutional commitment starting with hiring and continuing through the promotion of the faculty member. At many major research universities, such a model would be a significant modification of values and current practice. Senior administration should recognize and reward good teaching to encourage faculty buy-in at the individual and departmental levels. Data should be available to departments and faculty to evaluate the impact of their teaching.

To train the next generation of quantitative psychologists to solve significant human and societal challenges, we can devote time and collaborative energy to articulate the learning outcomes that we expect for the successful achievement of quantitative training. And then we can take all of this important work one step farther by aligning the specific program and course activities that we expect of our students to these outcomes. In this way, we would be "holding up a mirror" for our field and ensuring that we are truly teaching and preparing our students in the way that we intend.

Notes

1. The first 20 Division 5 presidents of the American Psychological Association are: L. L. Thurstone (1946; APA President in 1933); J. P. Guilford (1947; APA President in 1950), Robert L. Thorndike (1948), Paul Horst (1949), Harold Gulliksen (1950), Quinn McNemar (1951; APA President in 1964), Dorothy C. Adkins (1952), Edward E. Cureton (1953), Lee J. Cronbach (1954; APA President in 1957), Herbert S. Conrad (1955), John C. Flanagan (1956), George K. Bennett (1957), Clyde H. Coombs (1958), Allen L. Edwards (1959), Lloyd G. Humphreys (1960), Ledyard R. Tucker (1961), Jane Loevinger (1962), Lyle V. Jones (1963), Louis L. McQuitty (1964), Anne Anastasi (1965; APA President in 1972). Retrieved from: www.apadivisions.org/division-5/leadership/past-presidents/index.aspx
2. Scholars with quantitative expertise from other disciplines in psychology (e.g., industrial/organizational, clinical, developmental, social, neuroscience) are not included in these figures.
3. The first author was a member of the 2009 APA Task Force for Increasing the Number of Quantitative Psychologists, chaired by Leona Aiken.
4. The topic coverage included: introduction, history of quantitative psychology, experimental design and methodology, applied statistics, psychometric theories, measurement and assessment, evaluation, and examples of research conducted using elements taught in prior sections.
5. A potential interesting exception is reflected in the shift in approach used by Maxwell and Delaney (1990) for the first time for quantitative graduate programs around the country when a "model-based" approach to regression was used.
6. For example, our undergraduate students represent a broad set of highly selective undergraduate students, primarily from the state (82%), as required by the North Carolina Constitution. They are also diverse in their level of need-based aid, with 44% qualifying for need-based aid in 2018. More than 13% of entering students were living 200% below poverty level and were admitted as Carolina Covenant scholars with an institutional promise to graduate debt-free. More than 20% of undergraduates are first generation college students, and 44% of enrolled students transferred from a community college in the state (Office of Institutional Research and Assessment, 2019). These students are highly engaged and motivated and have similar five-year graduation rates as their peers (87% vs. 90%).

   Our graduate students come from all over the world and comprise 28% of the student body (UNC-CH Graduate School, 2019). Psychology graduate students come from a variety of institutions and programs, with many having postbacc or master's degrees in related areas. The quantitative psychology program currently has 13 doctoral students, a smaller number compared to programs such as clinical psychology and behavioral neuroscience.
7. Our institution practice related to Family Educational Rights and Privacy Act (FERPA) protections is not to report data for cell sizes that reflect five or fewer students.
8. In fact, it is through such engagement in an introductory statistics course that at least one author discovered and pursued a degree in psychometrics!
9. For example, the first author thanks Jon Levenson for a riveting description of the structure of the Bible, Robin Akert for inspiring research on ways to assess one's ability to decode nonverbal communication, and J. S. Tanaka for showing that certain humans can actually think in multidimensional space. Thanks also to the editor of this volume for raising this point about certain memorable and effective lectures.

References

Aiken, L. S., West, S. G., & Millsap, R. E. (2008). Doctoral training in statistics, measurement, and methodology in psychology: Replication and extension of the Aiken, West, Sechrest, and Reno (1990) survey of PhD programs in North America. *American Psychologist, 63*, 32–50.

Aiken, L. S., West, S. G., Sechrest, L. B., & Reno, R. R. (1990). Graduate training in statistics, methodology, and measurement in psychology: An international survey. *American Psychologist, 45*, 721–734.

American Psychological Association. (2009). *Task force for increasing the number of quantitative psychologists.* Retrieved from www.apa.org/science/leadership/bsa/quantitative/report.pdf.

American Psychological Association. (2010). *Presidential task force on the future of psychology as a STEM discipline.* Retrieved from www.apa.org/pubs/info/reports/stem-report.pdf.

American Psychological Association. (2013). *APA guidelines for the undergraduate psychology major.* Retrieved from www.apa.org/ed/precollege/about/psymajor-guidelines.pdf.

Anderson, L. W., Krathwohl, D. R., Airasian, P. W., Cruikshank, K. A., Mayer, R. E., Pintrich, P. R., . . . Wittrock, M. C. (2001). *A taxonomy for learning, teaching, and assessing: A revision of Bloom's taxonomy of educational objectives* (Complete ed.). New York: Longman.

Bligh, D. A. (2000). *What's the use of lectures?* San Francisco: Jossey-Bass.

Bloom, B. S., Engelhart, M. D., Furst, E. J., Hill, W. H., & Krathwohl, D. R. (1956). *Taxonomy of educational objectives: The classification of educational goals. Handbook I: Cognitive domain.* New York: David McKay.

Bonwell, C. C., & Eison, J. A. (1991). *Active learning: Creating excitement in the classroom. ASHE-ERIC Higher Education Reports.* Washington, DC: Association for the Study of Higher Education.

Bradforth, S. E., Miller, E. R., Dichtel, W. R., Leibovich, A. K., Feig, A. L., Martin, J. D., . . . Smith, T. L. (2015). University learning: Improve undergraduate science education. *Nature, 523*, 282–284. https://doi.org/10.1038/523282a

Cai, L., Sturm, A., Sathy, V., & Panter, A. T. (2018). A multilevel item response model of student evaluations of teaching: Effects of student-, instructor-, and course-characteristics. Manuscript in preparation.

Corwin, L. A., Runyon, C., Robinson, A., & Dolan, E. L. (2015). The Laboratory Course Assessment Survey: A tool to measure three dimensions of research-course design. *CBE Life Science Education, 14*(4), ar37. https://doi.org/10.1187/cbe.15-03-0073

Dean, J. W., & Clarke, D. Y. (2019). *The insider's guide to working with universities: Practical insights for board members, businesspeople, entrepreneurs, philanthropists, alumni, parents, and administrators.* Chapel Hill: University of North Carolina at Chapel Hill Press.

Deslauriers, L., McCarty, L. S., Miller, K., Callaghan, K., & Kestin, G. (2019). Measuring actual learning versus feeling of learning in response to being actively engaged in the classroom. *Proceedings of the National Academy Sciences, 116*(39), 19251–19257. https://doi.org/10.1073/pnas.1821936116

Eddy, S. L., & Hogan, K. A. (2014). Getting under the hood: How and for whom does increasing course structure work? *CBE Life Science Education, 13*, 453–468.

Felder, R. M., & Brent, R. (2009). Active learning: An introduction. *ASQ Higher Education Brief, 2*, 4–9.

Felder, R. M., & Brent, R. (2016). *Teaching and learning STEM: A practical guide.* New York: Jossey-Bass.

Freeman, S., Eddy, S. L., McDonough, M., Smith, M. K., Okoroafor, N., Jordt, H., & Wenderoth, M. P. (2014). Active learning increases student performance in science, engineering, and mathematics. *Proceedings of the National Academy of Sciences, 111*(23), 8410–8415. https://doi.org/10.1073/pnas.1319030111

Freeman, S., Haak, D., & Wenderoth, M. P. (2011). Increased course structure improves performance in introductory biology. *CBE Life Science Education, 10*, 175–186.

Greene, J. (2018). *Self-regulation in education.* New York: Routledge.

Haak, D. C., HilleRisLambers, J., Pitre, E., & Freeman, S. (2011). Increased structure and active learning reduce the achievement gap in introductory biology. *Science, 332*, 1213–1216.

Handelsman, J., Miller, S., & Pfund, C. (2006). *Scientific teaching.* New York: W.H. Freeman.

Kirk, R. (1968). *Experimental design: Procedures for behavioral sciences.* Belmont, CA: Brooks/Cole.

Krumper, J., McNeil, L. E., & Crimmins, M. T. (2015). Advancing evidence-based teaching in gateway science courses through a mentor-apprentice model. In G. C. Weaver, W. D. Burgess, A. L. Childress, & L. Slakey (Eds.), *Transforming institutions: Undergraduate STEM education for the 21st century* (pp. 77–89). West Lafayette, IN: Purdue University Press.

Latulipe, C., Rorrer, A., & Long, B. (2018). Longitudinal data on flipped class effects on performance in CS1 and retention after CS1. *Proceedings of the 49th ACM Technical Symposium on Computer Science Education*, 411–416. https://doi.org/10.1145/3159450.3159518

Leshner, A. I. (2018). Student-centered, modernized graduate STEM education. *Science*, 969–970.

Linse, A. R. (2017). Interpreting and using student ratings data: Guidance for faculty serving as administrators and on evaluation committees. *Studies in Educational Evaluation*, 54, 94–106.

Maxwell, S. E., & Delaney, H. D. (1990). *Designing experiments and analyzing data: A model comparison perspective*. Belmont, CA: Wadsworth/Thomson Learning.

Mervis, J. (2018, March 30). Congress gives science a record funding boost. *Science*, 359(6383), 1447–1448. https://doi.org/10.1126/science.359.6383.1447

Mulnix, A. B. (2016). STEM Faculty as learners in pedagogical reform and the role of research articles as professional development opportunities. *CBE Life Sciences Education*, 15, es8.

National Science Board. (2018). *Science and engineering indicators 2018 digest*. NSB-2018-2. Alexandria, VA: National Science Foundation. Retrieved from www.nsf.gov/statistics/digest/

National Science Foundation, National Center for Science and Engineering Statistics. (2018). *Doctorate recipients from U.S. universities: 2017*. Special Report NSF 19–301. Alexandria, VA: National Science Foundation. Retrieved from https://ncses.nsf.gov/pubs/nsf19301/.

Novak, G., Patterson, E. T., Gavrin, A. D., & Christian, W. (1999). *Just-in-time teaching: Blending active learning with web technology*. Upper Saddle River, NJ: Prentice Hall.

Owens, M. T., Seidel, S. B., Wong, M., Bejines, T. E., Lietz, S., & Tanner, K. D. (2017). Classroom sound classifies teaching practice. *Proceedings of the National Academy of Sciences*, 114, 3085–3090.

Panter, A. T. (2000, August). *The next generation of quantitative psychology: Teaching undergraduate statistics*. Paper presented at the symposium (Beins, Dunn, & Panter), Teaching Statistics: Before and After APA's Task Force on Statistics, American Psychological Association Meetings, Washington, DC.

President's Council of Advisors on Science and Technology (PCAST). (2012a). *Engage to excel: Producing one million additional college graduates with degrees in science, technology, engineering, and mathematics*. Retrieved from https://obamawhitehouse.archives.gov/sites/default/files/microsites/ostp/pcast-engage-to-excel-final_2-25-12.pdf.

President's Council of Advisors on Science and Technology (PCAST). (2012b). *Engage to excel: Producing one million additional college graduates with degrees in science, technology, engineering, and mathematics*. Executive Office of the President. Retrieved from files.eric.ed.gov/fulltext/ED541511.pdf

President's National Science and Technology Council. (2018). *Charting a course to success: America's strategy for STEM education*. The White House Office of Science and Technology Policy. Retrieved from www.whitehouse.gov/wp-content/uploads/2018/12/STEM-Education-Strategic-Plan-2018.pdf.

Robertson, G. J. (2009). Division 5 past presidents: A closer look (Part 1). *The Score*, 3–5.

Sathy, V. (2018, April). Charting a new course: Fixing my broken statistics class with high structure active learning. *The Score*. Retrieved from www.apadivisions.org/division5/publications/score/2018/04/active-learning.

Schau, C., Stevens, J., Dauphinee, T. L., & Del Vecchio, A. (1995). The development and validation of the Survey of Attitudes toward Statistics. *Educational and Psychological Measurement*, 55, 868–875.

Shadish, W. R., Cook, T. D., & Leviton, L. D. (1990). *Foundations of program evaluation: Theories of practice*. Newbury Park, CA: Sage.

Sireci, S. G. (1998). The construct of content validity. *Social Indicators Research*, 45, 83–117.

Theobald, E. J., Hill, M. J., Tran, E., Agrawal, S., Arroyo, E. N., Shawn B., Chambwe, N., Laboy Cintrón, D., Cooper, J. D., Dunster, G., Grummer, J. A., Hennessey, K., Hsiao, J., Iranon, N., Jones II, J., Jordt, H., Keller, M., Lacey, M. E., Littlefield, C. E., Lowe, A., Newman, S., Okolo, V., Olroyd, S., Peecook, B. R., Pickett, S. B., Slager, D. L., Caviedes-Solis, I. W., Stanchak, K. E., Sundaravardan, V., Valdebenito, C., Williams, C. R., Zinsli, K., and Freeman, S. (2020). Active learning narrows achievement gaps for underrepresented students in undergraduate science, technology, engineering, and math. *Proceedings of the National Academy of Sciences*, 117, 6476–6483; DOI: 10.1073/pnas.1916903117.

Uttl, B., & Smibert, D. (2017). Student evaluations of teaching: Teaching quantitative courses can be hazardous to one's career. *PeerJ*, *5*, e3299. https://doi.org/10.7717/peerj.3299

Uttl, B., White, C. A., & Gonzalez, D. W. (2017). Meta-analysis of faculty's teaching effectiveness: Student evaluation of teaching ratings and student learning are not related. *Studies in Educational Evaluation*, *54*, 22–42.

Weaver, G. C., Burgess, W. D., Childress, A. L., & Slakey, L. (2015). *Transforming institutions: Undergraduate STEM education for the 21st century*. West Lafayette, IN: Purdue University. Retrieved November 27, 2018, from Project MUSE database.

Wieman, C. (April 14, 2016). *A Nobel laureate's education plea: Revolutionize teaching*. Washington, DC: National Public Radio.

Wieman, C. (2017). *Improving how universities teach science: Lessons from the science education initiative*. Cambridge, MA: Harvard University Press.

Chapter 4

Not the What of Quantitative Training but the Who

Leona S. Aiken

Changing curriculum has been likened to moving a graveyard (Cobb, 2015). By this Cobb meant that curricular reform occurs in the context of (a) the particular existing curricular structure of each academic department and (b) the idiosyncratic teaching portfolios of all faculty who might be involved in and/or affected by curricular change. Thus any consideration of reform in the teaching of undergraduate statistics and research methods must address the faculty who teach these courses and the curricular structure of departments of psychology. To this end, I have summarized both the sheer magnitude of the number of psychology departments and psychology majors in the U.S. and the existing quantitative methods curriculum in undergraduate departments of psychology. I then focus much of this chapter on the new generation of faculty currently being hired into departments of psychology. Given the long, arduous, and often meandering road to curricular reform, it is to these currently new faculty members that much responsibility for the delivery of innovative quantitative training at the undergraduate level may well fall.

Joseph Lee Rodgers (Chapter 8) opened the question of need for curricular reform with the observation that the undergraduate introductory statistics curriculum has hardly changed for essentially seven decades, while the field of quantitative methods has made massive strides during this same period. Rodgers articulated, for example, the central importance of exploratory versus confirmatory methods, since much current psychological research involves the specification and confirmation of complex models. Rodgers further mused on the possibility of moving statistical modeling to the foreground of statistics instruction, while null hypothesis significance testing moves to the background. Novel work in graphics opens and enlivens the world of data exploration and visualization, providing a clarifying window on our data. Yet our teaching of undergraduate statistics hardly reflects the richness of exploratory data analysis methods and of confirmatory thinking.

As Rodgers points out, textbooks have very much the same content now as they did many years ago. Writing this chapter and confessing my advanced age, I opened the first statistics textbook from which I took two semesters of undergraduate statistics in the 1960s, that is, J. P. Guilford's *Fundamental Statistics in Psychology and Education*, published in 1956. I compared it to a current representative introductory statistics text that enjoys wide adoption. My old book has the standard chapters on frequency distributions, central tendency, variability, normal curve, correlation, hypothesis testing with z- and t-tests, one-factor ANOVA, chi square, plus two chapters on regression analysis (one predictor and multiple regression analysis). Reflecting the great contributions of J. P. Guilford to measurement, it also has chapters entitled "Cumulative Distributions and Norms," "Reliability and Significance of Statistics," "Special Correlation Methods and Problems," "Reliability of Measurements," "Validity of Measurements," and "Test Scales and Norms." The new book, in comparison, has three chapters on the t test, and two chapters on ANOVA (including two-factor and one-factor repeated measures ANOVA). Reflecting on the time my old book was written, I note that the article introducing computation of sums of squares for interactions in ANOVA appeared in *Psychometrika* in 1950 (Edwards & Horst, 1950). The classic book that introduced a complete treatment of ANOVA to psychology, that is, B. J. Winer's *Statistical Principles in Experimental Design*, was not published until 1962.

In all, we've come a long way in quantitative psychology in 70 years. Our teaching of undergraduate statistics has not.

Magnitude of the Task of Improving Undergraduate Statistics Training: A Look at the Numbers

It comes as no surprise that psychology is among the four most popular undergraduate majors in the United States; it is the fourth-highest discipline in awarding baccalaureate degrees and also the fourth highest in awarding associate degrees. In 2017, a total of 116,861 baccalaureate degrees were awarded in psychology (U.S. Department of Education, 2018). In 2016, an additional 117,000 associate degrees were awarded in psychology (National Center for Educational Statistics, 2018). Introductory statistics is at the core of the undergraduate psychology major, whether students enter the major in an associate or a baccalaureate program.

There are almost 3,000 departments of psychology cataloged in the Carnegie Foundation for the Advancement of Teaching database of postsecondary educational institutions (2010).[1] The distribution of these departments by type of institution is summarized in Table 4.1 (Norcross et al., 2016). We (Norcross et al., 2016) examined the undergraduate curriculum in psychology in a stratified sample of one-third of the departments of psychology ($n = 972$) in the Carnegie Foundation 2010 data base. The strata of institutions employed in sampling of institutions and response rate by stratum in our survey are given in Table 4.1. The overall response rate was 45%.

The offerings in quantitative methods are summarized in Table 4.2 for all baccalaureate-granting programs (Norcross et al., 2016). Among baccalaureate programs, research methods and statistics are essentially universally taught and are required; half of all introductory statistics courses include an associated laboratory section. Upward of half of all baccalaureate departments also offer an advanced undergraduate statistics course. According to Norcross et al., (2016), fully 50% of associate degree programs teach statistics, required by 61% of these programs. In addition, 41% of associate degree programs teach research methods, required

Table 4.1 Number of Departments of Psychology in the U.S., Organized by Highest Degree Granted.

Program Strata	Total Number of Institutions	Invitations to Participate in Study of Undergraduate Curriculum	Response Rate by Stratum
Associate degree only	1,076	354	29%
Associate dominant with bachelor's degree	98	30	23%
Bachelor's degree only	807	221	48%
Bachelor's degree plus master's degree	718	253	56%
Bachelor's degree plus doctoral degree	289	114	70%
Total	2,988	972	45%

Sources: Data are taken from Table 1 of Norcross, J. C., Hailstorks, R., Aiken, L. S., Pfund, R. A., Stamm, K. E., & Christidis, P. (2016). Undergraduate Study in Psychology: 2014. *American Psychologist.* 71(2), 89–101 http://dx/doi/org/10.1037/a0040095. Published by American Psychological Association; adapted with permission.

Table 4.2 Quantitative Methods Courses Offered in Baccalaureate Programs in Psychology

Course	2014 Course Alone or With Lab	Lab Included	Required Versus Elective, When Offered		
			Required	Chosen Among Group	Elective
Baccalaureate Degree-Granting Departments of Psychology					
Research methods	100%	65%	98%	1%	1%
Psychological testing/assessment	67%	11%	13%	43%	44%
Statistics	95%	48%	96%	2%	2%
Statistics (advanced undergraduate)	39%	20%	31%	15%	54%

Sources: Data are taken from Tables 2 and 3 of Norcross, J. C., Hailstorks, R., Aiken, L. S., Pfund, R. A., Stamm, K. E., & Christidis, P. (2016). Undergraduate Study in Psychology: 2014. *American Psychologist.* 71(2), 89–101 http://dx/doi/org/10.1037/a0040095. Published by American Psychological Association, adapted with permission.

by 72% of these programs. Many major public institutions of higher education that grant the baccalaureate degree have articulation agreements with associate degree-granting institutions. These articulation agreements specify course equivalences between courses taught in associate versus baccalaureate programs; statistics courses are among the foci of articulation. Such agreements serve the many students who transfer to baccalaureate from associate degree programs. Consequently, how quantitative methods are taught in associate degree programs is part of the domain of curricular reform consideration.

Hiring of Faculty to Teach Undergraduate Statistics and Research Methods

It is indeed informative to consider the nature of faculty currently being hired into faculty positions in which at least a portion of their teaching responsibility is undergraduate statistics. To this end, I examined the Association for Psychological Science (APS) database of all faculty position announcements posted by APS during the 2017–2018 academic year.[2] The database contained 764 position announcements. I eliminated from the 764 positions all postdoctoral positions, research positions, administrative positions (including department chairs, deans, center directors, lab managers, and the like), and all non–university-based positions. The remaining 499 positions included teaching as a tenure-track or tenured professor, lecturer, instructor, visiting professor, or visiting instructor. The position announcements of 83 of the 499 positions identified statistics as part of the teaching portfolio; I eliminated those 4 of the 83 that were wholly devoted to graduate teaching. The remaining 79 positions (10% of the 2017–2018 positions) became the focus of my analysis; all these positions identified undergraduate statistics as part of the required or potential teaching portfolio. Among the 79 positions, 59% (n = 47) were in departments that offered only baccalaureate degrees; another 18% (n = 14) offered both baccalaureate and masters' degrees; 23% (n = 18) offered the baccalaureate through PhD degrees.

Substantive Areas in Positions Involving Undergraduate Statistics Teaching

Not surprisingly, only six of the 79 positions were for a quantitative psychologist per se; the remaining 73 job postings (92%) named at least one substantive area of specialization. These specializations are summarized in Table 4.3; where a position announcement mentioned multiple specializations, all specializations are included. "Hard science" substantive psychology positions predominated. Neuroscience (including cognitive neuroscience and behavioral neuroscience) was the most often identified specialty, followed by cognitive. Clinical/counseling, developmental, and social were each mentioned in slightly over 10% of job announcements. Of interest, five of the six stand-alone quantitative methods positions were mentioned by PhD-granting departments; the sixth, by a Master's level department. Three other position announcements mentioned quantitative methods as secondary to designation of one or more required substantive areas (two PhD and one baccalaureate institution).

Teaching in One's Specialty and Contributing to the Core, Including Statistics

The dominant theme in position postings was that individuals hired would focus on their substantive areas in teaching—they would teach multiple undergraduate (and graduate) courses in their particular substantive areas and often contribute more specialized courses and seminars in

Table 4.3 Identified Specializations of Faculty Positions in Which Undergraduate Statistics Is Included in the Teaching Portfolio Across the 79 Advertised Positions in the APS 2017–2018 Database. All specialties mentioned are included (percentages are of 78 positions).

Specialty	Number of Positions Mentioning Specialty	Percentage of Positions Mentioning Specialty
Neuroscience	16	20%
Cognitive	12	15%
Clinical/Counseling	11	14%
Developmental	11	14%
Social	8	10%
Experimental	7	9%
Quantitative (only specialty mentioned)	6	8%
Quantitative (secondary mention)	3	4%
Biological/Physiological	4	5%
Industrial/Organizational	3	4%
Health	3	4%
Applied	2	3%
Personality	2	3%
Diversity Science	2	3%
General	2	3%
Other (each mentioned once: animal, engineering, community)	3	4%
Open, unspecified	12	15%

Note: All specializations mentioned in a position announcement are included; percentages therefore sum to greater than one.

their substantive areas as well. In addition, they would contribute to undergraduate (and graduate) research experiences. The teaching of undergraduate statistics was often characterized in terms of contributing to core department courses including introductory psychology, statistics, and/or research methods, over and above the substantive area for which individuals were hired. Selected quotations from position announcements that reflect the idea of contributing to the common core by teaching statistics are given in Table 4.4, with italics added for notable phrases with regard to teaching statistics and research methods. The impression sometimes given is that basic classes including statistics and research methods have to be taught and that this is a shared responsibility rather than a matter for individuals highly specialized and/or particularly interested in teaching these subjects. In sum, the prevailing model of faculty whose teaching portfolios include undergraduate statistics is that these are substantive-area hires with a substantive focus in their work.

Table 4.4 Position Announcements Indicating Faculty Contribution to Undergraduate Statistics Instruction Beyond Substantive Area Specialization (italics added; APS database, 2017–2018)

Specialty Area of Position	Highest Degree	Narrative Concerning Teaching of Statistics
Behavioral Neuroscience	BA/BS	"successful candidate will also be expected to occasionally *join the teaching rotation* for our departmental methods and statistics laboratory course."
Diversity Science	BA/BS	"particularly encourage applications from candidates who can *alternate with other instructors* in teaching the research methodology and statistics sequence"
Industrial-Organizational, Developmental	BA/BS	"be qualified to teach courses in their area of interest. Applicants must also be qualified to *teach departmental core courses* (research methods, statistics, history and systems, senior seminar)"
Cognitive Neuroscience	BA/BS	"teaching courses in biological and/or cognitive psychology, advanced practicum and seminar courses in the candidate's specialty area, a *contribution to our required courses*, such as introductory psychology, psychological statistics, research methods"
Human Neuroscience	BA/BS	"teach general Psychology classes such as Introductory Psychology, Research Methods, and Statistics *as departmental need arises*"
Clinical	Master's	"two specialized courses in their area of expertise (seminar and advanced research methods), and *one service course* (research methods, statistics, or introductory psychology)"
Cognitive	PhD	"teach courses in cognitive psychology and area of specialization; teach a course in Introductory Psychology, Statistics, or Research Methods"

Teaching of Undergraduate Statistics by Quantitative Faculty

Faculty hired into positions in major quantitative programs have substantial teaching and mentoring responsibilities in quantitative methods. These responsibilities may go beyond those of faculty in substantive areas. The reason is simple: Quantitative faculty members are often expected to collaborate with and provide statistical consulting for colleagues and doctoral students beyond the confines of the quantitative program. Nevertheless, in most quantitative PhD programs in North America, quantitative faculty members do contribute to teaching undergraduate statistics.

Teaching by Tenure/Tenure-Track Faculty Versus by Teaching Faculty (Lecturers, Instructors), and Visiting Faculty

Among the 499 positions, a total of 97 (19%) were designated for lecturers (35 in all), instructors (22 in all), and visiting faculty (40 in all). Both lecturers and visiting faculty were overrepresented among the 79 positions that specified teaching of statistics. In all, 14% of the 79 statistics-relevant positions were for lecturers; this was so for only 6% of the 421 positions focused wholly on substantive teaching. For visiting faculty, the corresponding percentages were 13% versus 7%, for statistics relevant versus substantive-only positions, respectively.

Teaching Loads of Faculty in Positions Involving Undergraduate Statistics

In all, teaching loads were stated in the position advertisements of 35 of the 79 statistics-relevant positions (45% of positions); all data reported here are based on these 35 institutions. The annual teaching load of faculty, transformed to the common metric of number of 3-credit one-semester courses, ranged from 4 to 10 courses per academic year. The modal annual teaching load was six courses (median = 6.08; mean = 6.43). The nature of the institutions with the lowest teaching loads (i.e., 4 or 5 courses per year; n = 10 reporting) was homogeneous. With the exception of two PhD-granting institutions, the remainder was comprised of small, mostly private liberal arts colleges with student–faculty ratios ranging from 8:1 to 11:1. These undergraduate institutions placed heavy emphasis on extensive student–faculty interaction in the form of small seminars, one-on-one meetings, individual research project supervision, senior theses, and research internships. In brief, these institutions are hardly representative of the major public institutions in which there is need to provide statistics training for large numbers of psychology majors, which may number in the thousands. In contrast, 11 of the reporting departments had course loads of 8 to 10 courses per year. Of the 11 departments with these high teaching loads, seven were advertising for an instructor, lecturer, or visiting assistant professor for the position involving teaching of statistics.

Teaching Faculty Positions With Focus Including Undergraduate Statistics and Research Methods

Thus far, I have discussed the many faculty positions that seek individuals who will teach in their designated substantive specializations and will also contribute to teaching core introductory courses, including undergraduate statistics, as I documented in Table 4.3. In contrast, a small number of teaching faculty positions has been created with the express responsibility for the delivery of undergraduate statistics and, to a lesser extent, research methods. I identified seven such position announcements during an approximately 2.4-year time frame of the APS database, from fall 2016 to January 2019. I do not claim that this is the universe of such existing position advertisements in all sources during this time frame.

While there is a notable focus on undergraduate statistics, full responsibilities vary by position. The seven academic institutions with these positions are PhD-granting institutions. Six are in the United States; the seventh is in Canada. Five of the six U.S. universities have the Carnegie classification "very high research activity"; the sixth is classified "high research activity." Each university has created its own administrative structure and status for the position. These positions provide potential models for how innovative undergraduate instruction in statistics and research methods might be delivered by individuals devoted to innovative curriculum. Given the novelty and variety of these positions, I have summarized them in Table 4.5, with information quoted from publicly available position announcements.

The University of Oklahoma Department of Psychology teaches introductory statistics to 1,300 students per year in more than 30 individual sections within psychology and across the

Table 4.5 Announcements of Faculty Teaching Positions Devoted to Undergraduate Quantitative Methods (fall 2016–January 2019)

Institution	Academic Year Advertised	Position Title	Status of Position	Teaching Responsibilities (quoted from position announcement)
Duke University	2016–2017	Assistant Professor of Practice	Non–tenure-track; initial three-year contract, eligible for extensions	"contribute to a wide range of undergraduate instructional needs, including research methods and statistics as well as more specialized courses"
University of Oklahoma	2016–2017	Master Teacher of Introduction to Applied Statistics	Tenured or tenurable at the associate professor level	"lead and coordinate the department's efforts in introductory statistics instruction at the undergraduate level … 1200 per year in introductory statistics"
Pennsylvania State University	2016–2017	Lecturer	Initial one-year contract, multiple yearly renewable depending on funding	"teaching undergraduate research methods courses, possibly also introductory statistics, and courses in clinical, cognitive
Simon Fraser University (Canada)	2016–2017	Lecturer in Research Methods	Continuing lecturer, permanent non–tenure track	"core and service courses in statistics, research methods (quantitative, qualitative, mixed methods)"
University of California, Santa Barbara	2017–2018	Lecturer	Lecturer with Potential for Security of Employment (LPSOE), permanent position	"Teaching responsibilities will include undergraduate courses in statistics and research methods, and may also include quantitative courses at the graduate level as well as courses in the candidate's and department's areas of expertise"
Florida Atlantic University	2017–2018 2018–2019	Instructor	Permanent, non–tenure-track position	"primary responsibility for this position is teaching undergraduate and graduate courses in experimental design and statistics"
New York University	2018–2019	Clinical Assistant Professor	Non–tenure track	"teaching research methods and statistics in the master's and undergraduate psychology programs"

Note: Position postings for all universities except Simon Fraser were given in the 2016–2017 or 2017–2018 APS jobs posting database. The Simon Fraser announcement was individually circulated.

College of Arts and Sciences. Oklahoma provides the most extreme example of vesting in a single individual responsibility for leading and coordinating the introductory statistics curriculum. The Oklahoma position is the only position of the seven that grants professorial (rather than instructor or lecturer) status and the potential for tenure at the associate professor level. This position requires supervision of all instructors of individual sections to insure homogeneity of curriculum and quality of instruction; in addition, it involves teaching undergraduate statistics and developing technical teaching materials (personal communication, Professor Robert Terry, University of Oklahoma, January 23, 2019). The Oklahoma model may afford the opportunity for important curricular modernization and innovation in the teaching of undergraduate statistics, particularly because the individual who was hired into the position is, in fact, a quantitative psychologist. The same is true of Simon Fraser University, which recently hired a quantitative psychologist into a permanent lecturer position. This individual teaches both undergraduate research methods and statistics, and, in addition, has offered a specialized quantitative course taken by both doctoral and undergraduate students (personal communication, Professor Rachel T. Fouladi, January 24, 2019). While I discuss new positions here, this class of positions is not new. For example, at University of Washington, a lecturer has been teaching undergraduate statistics in psychology for more than a decade (personal communication, Professor Liliana Lengua, January 26, 2019).

While the positions I have described thus far focus on undergraduate statistics and research methods, other similar positions have broader portfolios. The Pennsylvania State University position is distinct in that it identifies research methods rather than undergraduate statistics as the focus; the position description lists a number of courses in substantive areas beyond statistics that may be included in the teaching portfolio. As a final note, this class of positions, with their focus on teaching at the university level, is not unique to quantitative methods. For example, Duke University has several faculty members with the title Professor of Practice whose teaching efforts are devoted to other areas of psychology. Such positions may provide models for new positions focusing on quantitative methods at the undergraduate level.

Faculty With Quantitative Expertise Across Departments of Psychology

Having faculty in substantive areas with notable quantitative expertise and interest may provide a resource for enhancing the teaching of undergraduate courses in quantitative methods. To this end, I sought evidence of the hiring of such faculty by departments of psychology.

Hiring of Faculty to Teach Advanced Doctoral-Level Quantitative Courses

First, let us consider faculty specifically hired to teach advanced doctoral-level quantitative courses; these individuals could be a resource for enhancing quantitative training. Aiken, West, and Millsap (2008) surveyed all PhD-granting departments in the U.S. and Canada to assess the quantitative training of PhD students across substantive areas of psychology. We asked each department to characterize the preferred quantitative versus substantive research foci of faculty hired

Table 4.6 PhD-Granting Departments' Preferences for Research Program of Faculty Hired to Teach Advanced Quantitative Courses Beyond the First-Year Doctoral Quantitative Sequence (*n* = 201 programs, 86% response rate)

Research Area Requirement or Preference	Percent of Doctoral Programs
Department requires person to have a substantive research program	43%
Department prefers person to have a substantive research program	32%
Department has no preference for quantitative versus substantive research program	19%
Department prefers person to have a quantitative research program	4%
Department requires person to have a quantitative research program	2%

Source: Data are drawn from Aiken et al. (2008).

to teach quantitative courses beyond the first-year doctoral sequence. Table 4.6 summarizes our findings. The vast majority of departments hiring faculty to teach advanced doctoral-level quantitative courses required or preferred that these individuals have a substantive research program. This suggests that beyond departments with quantitative emphases or programs, most, if not all, faculty responsible for doctoral-level training in advanced quantitative methods will be specialists predominantly in a substantive area rather than in quantitative methods per se.

Recent job announcements for quantitative faculty reflect a "twofer" or "two for the price of one" view (Aiken et al., 2008). We refer to faculty positions that seek faculty who have two responsibilities: (a) contribute to advanced teaching and research mentoring in their substantive specialty area and (b) teach advanced graduate-level quantitative methods courses and also provide quantitative consulting with faculty and doctoral students. For example, one recent advertised position seeks an expert in advanced quantitative methods who both can contribute to the existing graduate quantitative program and has expertise in a specific substantive area beyond quantitative psychology. Serving two masters is not a propitious circumstance for productivity that pleases both masters. Thus, we have observed that early-career faculty hired into such positions historically have had difficulty achieving tenure.

Substantive Position Announcements in 2017–2018 APS Database Mentioning Quantitative Rigor/Excellence

Here I focus on the 487 positions in the APS 2017–2018 database specifically for hires in substantive areas, setting aside all quantitative positions. About 8% of the substantive position announcements mentioned interest in hiring individuals with notable quantitative skills. Regardless of the substantive area of the position, the recurrent theme was that individuals have strong quantitative skills and excellence in the application of advanced quantitative methods in their research. Departments sought candidates with the following characteristics in addition to the specific disciplinary focus: "a research program that uses rigorous computational and/or mathematical modeling methods" (cognitive); "expected to use multiple methods, including ecologically valid approaches and utilize advanced statistics in their program of research" (social/personality, developmental), "innovation and excellence in the application of modeling techniques" (human perception or cognition), "use advance quantitative or computational approaches" (aging); "apply computational science methods to behavioral science problems" (industrial-organizational); "strong knowledge of and primary focus on quantitative-based clinical research designs" (clinical/counseling); and "competence in quantitative methods of research, statistics/biostatistics and research design" (health). This emphasis on great strength in modern methodologies among substantive faculty certainly brings ambient quantitative strength to departments of psychology. It is noteworthy that position announcements for these substantive positions, with few exceptions, mention both graduate and undergraduate teaching, yet none mentions undergraduate statistics as a possible course. The focus appears to be substantive at both the graduate and undergraduate levels.

Tiny Numbers of Quantitative Faculty, Potential Reformers

Broad curricular reform in undergraduate statistics will require the commitment and driving force of quantitative psychologists who have a broad grasp of the modern field of quantitative methods and a commitment to quantitative training. Yet there are very few quantitative faculty who might undertake the task. The number of quantitative doctoral programs in the U.S., broadly defined, is fewer than 30, compared to almost 300 psychology PhD programs (see Table 4.1). Furthermore, quantitative programs typically have small faculties. The American Psychological Association Report of the Task Force for Increasing the Number of Quantitative Psychologists (2008), which task force I chaired, documented the number of individuals receiving the PhD in quantitative psychology between 1978 and 2006 based on the National Science Foundation Survey of Earned Doctorates (www.nsf.gov/statistics). Estimates of numbers of degrees granted in accredited United States academic institutions hovered around 20 per year during the period from 1978–2006. Counts from 2007 through 2017 suggest growth in number of graduates over time; the specific NSF counts[3] are given here: 35, 23, 29, 36, 35, 34, 44, 33, 48, 49, and 51, respectively per year, from 2007 through 2017 (www.nsf.gov/statistics/2018/nsf18304/datatables/tab13.htm; https://ncses.nsf.gov/pubs/nsf19301/assets/data/tables/sed17-sr-tab013.pdf Accessed Feb. 5, 2019).

We Are Not Alone in the Universe: American Statistical Association (ASA) Curricular Reform Considerations

The American Statistical Association has great concern about the way in which statistics is taught on its own turf to undergraduate students studying to be statisticians. "Approaches and materials once considered standard are being rethought. The growth that statistics has undergone is often not reflected in the education that future statisticians receive. There is a need to incorporate more meaningfully into the curriculum the computational and graphical tools that are so important today." This quote is from deliberations in the field of statistics not recently but in 1992 by Committee on Applied and Theoretical Statistics (CATS), 1994, quoted in Horton and Hardin

(2015, p. 259). The ASA has had another recent round of considerations of reform, put forth in the November 2015 issue of *The American Statistician*. I share another quote from this issue that I found both stunning in its clarity and remarkable in its consistency with presentations by Charles S. Reichardt, Pascal R. Deboeck, Robert Terry, and William Revelle at the conference held at Vanderbilt University, March 24, 2017, entitled "Teaching Statistics and Quantitative Methods into the 21st Century." Presentations at this conference, which was organized by Joseph Lee Rodgers, may be accessed at http://peabody.vanderbilt.edu/events/teachingstat-mini-conf.php.

> In the humanities, students in a first course engage with original sources. You do not just *prepare* your students to read Austen; they *read* Austen. You do not just *prepare* your students to hear Bach; they *hear* Bach. Our statistics curriculum should follow those examples. Our job is not to *prepare* students to use data to answer a question that matters; our job is the help them to use data to *answer* a question that matters. In short, *teach through research*.
>
> (Cobb, 2015, p. 276)

Quite amazing to me, Cobb, himself a named professor emeritus of statistics, highlighted the teaching of Professor Lisa Dierker, not a statistician but rather a psychology professor at Wesleyan University. She teaches introductory undergraduate statistics for psychology majors, as well as for students from the natural and social sciences. Professor Dierker is a developmental psychologist with a strong quantitative background. In her introductory statistics class, each student carries out an individual research project by which he or she learns statistics. First, Professor Dierker introduces her students to multiple large databases, for example, the General Social Survey (GSS). Students generate hunches about relationships among variables and turn to literature searches to generate hypotheses they will test. The remainder of the semester is focused on learning statistical methods from which they select those appropriate to answer their research questions and carry out data analysis. The course culminates in the students making poster presentations about their work and findings; this poster plus presentation constitutes their final examination. Professor Dierker's course development has been funded by a National Science Foundation grant entitled Passion Driven Statistics: A Multidisciplinary Project-Based Supportive Model for Statistical Reasoning and Application (2013–2017). The title speaks clearly to her pedagogical goals.

A Zeitgeist of Curricular Reform

The strategies employed by Professor Dierker to teach what she terms "passion-driven statistics" resonate with examples of curricular reform presented at the Vanderbilt Conference. In his presentation, Charles S. Reichardt highlighted the richness of the General Social Survey and, furthermore, the ease of its use with the available Survey Documentation and Analysis interface (also see Chapter 9, this edited book, for a written treatment of Reichardt's presentation). He demonstrated ways in which the GSS could be used effectively to teach quantitative literacy in psychology classes including but hardly limited to undergraduate statistics. The hypothesis-generation and literature search steps of Professor Dierker's classes mirror ideas in the presentation by William Revelle as well (see Chapter 14 of this edited book). Revelle's undergraduate students carry out simulations of psychological models with simulation software he developed. Students base the relationships and their effect sizes to be simulated from reviews of psychological literature. Pascal R. Deboeck (see Chapter 12 of this edited book) flips his graduate classroom so that studying goes on outside class while the classroom time is spent on analysis of data sets that he creates to challenge students (e.g., a data set with a binary outcome that has complete separation on the predictors). Robert Terry (see Chapter 10 of this edited book) integrates modern graphical displays that engage non-mathematically oriented students in acquiring quantitative literacy. These resemblances suggest the rumblings of Zeitgeist of reform in early progress.

Curriculum Reform and Local Institutional Structure

Professor Dierker's innovative curriculum is carried out in a small, elite private institution with just under 3,000 undergraduates. Her class enrollment is capped at 19 students, far smaller than the size of many undergraduate statistics classes. Sections at major public universities may run into the hundreds of students per large lecture section. These vast differences in the teaching environment harken to the critical point made by Cobb (2015) that curriculum reform is carried out locally within particular academic structures and existing faculties.

My academic home, Arizona State University, the largest university in the U.S. based on undergraduate enrollment, has a total of 100,000 students on five campuses (about 60,000 undergraduates). Our campuses operate independently in creating course content for courses that bear the same course number, for example, undergraduate statistics in psychology. Section sizes of our undergraduate statistics course in psychology have different enrollment caps on different campuses. Textbook choices vary by faculty member within and across campuses. On the main campus, our undergraduate psychology introductory statistics classes are taught predominantly by lecturers to sections of 50 students; each section has a 20-hour-per-week teaching assistant. I share that one impressive lecturer who teaches eight courses per year has created a statistics course in which she has made videos of all her lectures that students view outside class. They discuss the videos in class and then spend the majority of class time working together in groups on analyzing data with the support of the lecturer and her teaching assistant (see also Sathy, this volume, for an example).

The psychology department at University of Oklahoma, as I described before, teaches more than 30 sections of undergraduate statistics per year, taught by doctoral students. Instructors are now supervised by a recently hired specialized tenured associate professor whose focus is this course; one current textbook that provides students with substantial additional online support is employed in all sections.

Summary of Observations on the Teaching Workforce in Academia for Undergraduate Quantitative Methods

1. The audience for undergraduate statistics in psychology is enormous, with about 3,000 psychology departments in the U.S. and upward of 300,000 students per year receiving baccalaureate and associate degrees in psychology.

2. A review of position advertisements for psychology faculty is informative with regard to human resources for teaching undergraduate statistics.

    a. The vast majority of new faculty positions that include teaching of undergraduate statistics have substantive areas of specialization.
    b. Teaching undergraduate statistics is viewed by departments as part of contributing to the core curriculum by individuals whose primary teaching focus is in their substantive areas (e.g., social psychology, neuroscience, developmental psychology).
    c. Lecturer and visiting faculty positions are advertised at twice the rate for teachers of undergraduate statistics as for teachers of substantive courses.
    d. A third of positions seeking to hire individuals who will teach undergraduate statistics have teaching loads of 8 to 10 courses per year.
    e. New positions are being created in psychology departments at research-intensive universities for faculty whose focus is the undergraduate statistics course; these are predominantly lecturer positions.
    f. The vast majority of PhD-granting departments hiring a quantitative faculty member prefer or require that the faculty member have a substantive research program in addition to quantitative psychology.

3. There are very few quantitative faculty being produced in North America.
4. Any curricular reform must take place in the context of the structure of departments and the faculty of those departments.
5. A zeitgeist for curricular reform in teaching undergraduate statistics appears to exist among psychology faculty who are exceptionally skilled in quantitative methods and who are thus capable of curricular innovation.

Some Musings on Curricular Reform in Teaching of Undergraduate Statistics

First and foremost, if we want to undertake curricular reform, we need to articulate what we envision as reform. Needless to say, the quantitative community has to formulate a vision of what curricular reform should involve. Reformers need to be acutely aware of the quantitative capabilities, interests, and work demands of those to whom actual implementation of reform will fall, the faculty who teach undergraduate quantitative methods. I have attempted to characterize that population in this chapter. It is clear that most faculty members being hired to teach introductory statistics have substantive and not quantitative foci. These faculty members have a first responsibility for implementing curriculum in their substantive areas; many have heavy teaching loads. Teaching undergraduate statistics appears from current position announcements to be viewed not as a priority it its own right but rather as *shared responsibility among faculty to contribute to basic core department curriculum needs*. Reformers will need to convince the academic psychology community that reform in the ubiquitous introductory statistics course is critically important both for student learning and for psychology. Reformers will need to provide a new generation of teaching materials to make the vision of the reform clear and accessible. They will need to teach the teachers of undergraduate statistics in psychology new ways of thinking about quantitative methods, for example, data exploration on the one hand and model specification and confirmation on the other. For those of us who are concerned about reforming teaching, the elephant in the room is us, that is, whether we ourselves are willing to set aside aspects of our careers to engage in the process of reform.

Notes

1. The Carnegie Foundation for the Advancement of Teaching (2010) database on which Norcross et al. (2016) based the sampling of institutions is no longer accessible under the URL we used in 2013. In 2014, the Carnegie Commission transferred responsibility for the Carnegie database to Indiana University School of Education. (http://archive.news.indiana.edu/releases/iu/2016/02/carnegie-classification-institutions-of-higher-education.shtml; accessed February 5, 2019).
2. The APS position announcement database was furnished by Christina Garneski, Director of Marketing and Communications of the Association for Psychological Science. I am most grateful for her willingness to provide both the 2016–2017 and the 2017–2018 databases.
3. The coding of quantitative methods in the NSF Survey of Earned Doctorates changed between 2003 and 2004. Prior to 2004, there were two separates codes: 630, psychometrics; 633 quantitative psychology; in 2004, the codes were collapsed into one category: 633, psychometrics and quantitative psychology.

References

Aiken, L. S., West, S. G., & Millsap, R. E. (2008). Doctoral training in statistics, measurement, and methodology in psychology: Replication and extension of the Aiken, West, Sechrest, and Reno (1990) survey of PhD programs in North America. *American Psychologist, 63*(1), 32–50. https://doi.org/10.1037/0003-066X.63.1.32

American Psychological Association. (2008). *Task force for increasing the number of quantitative psychologists.* Leona S. Aiken, chair. Retrieved January 27, 2019, from www.apa.org/science/leadership/bsa/quantitative/index.aspx

Carnegie Foundation for the Advancement of Teaching. (2010). *Carnegie classification file, May 2013.* Retrieved from classifications, carnegie-foundation.org/methodology/ugrad_program.php.

Cobb, G. (2015). Mere renovation is too little, too late: We need to rethink our undergraduate curriculum from the ground up. *The American Statistician, 69*(4), 266–282. https://doi.org/10.1080/00031305.2015.1093029

Edwards, A. L., & Horst, P. (1950). The calculation of sums of squares for interactions in the analysis of variance. *Psychometrika, 16*(1), 17–24.

Guilford, J. P. (1956). *Fundamental statistics in psychology and education.* New York: McGraw-Hill.

Horton, N. J., & Hardin, J. S. (2015). Teaching the next generation of statistics students to "Think With Data": Special issue on statistics and the undergraduate curriculum. *The American Statistician, 69*(4), 259–265.

National Center for Educational Statistics. (2018). *The condition of education.* Chapter 2. Programs, courses, and completions: Undergraduate degree fields. Retrieved January 24, 2019, from https://nces.ed.gov/programs/coe/

Norcross, J. C., Hailstorks, R., Aiken, L. S., Pfund, R. A., Stamm, K. E., & Christidis, P. (2016). Undergraduate study in psychology: 2014. *American Psychologist, 71*(2), 89–101. http://doi/org/10.1037/a0040095

U.S. Department of Education. (2018). *National Center for Education Statistics, Higher Education General Information Survey (HEGIS), "Degrees and Other Formal Awards Conferred" surveys, 1970–71 through 1985–86; Integrated Postsecondary Education Data System (IPEDS), "Completions Survey" (IPEDS-C:91–99); and IPEDS Fall 2000 through Fall 2017, Completions component.* Retrieved January 24, 2019, from https://nces.ed.gov/programs/digest/d18/tables/dt18_322.10.asp?current=yes

Winer, B. J. (1962). *Statistical principles in experimental design.* New York: McGraw-Hill.

Chapter 5

Is Methodological Research Moving Into Practice? The Critical Role of Formal Methodological Training

Jessica K. Flake, Ian J. Davidson, and Jolynn Pek

Introduction

In psychology, norms are shifting as publishing policies and incentives change. Journals are requiring statements on sample size determination and statistical power (Cowan, 2018; Eich, 2014), acknowledging and encouraging preregistration (Nosek, Ebersole, DeHaven, & Mellor, 2018), and offering new publishing formats, such as registered reports (Hardwicke & Ioannidis, 2018). These shifts in our publishing policies are changing *how* we do our research, in particular how we plan and carry out our statistical analyses. These reforms are aimed at addressing a crisis of confidence in psychological science, which followed from a series of failed replications (Open Science Collaboration, 2015) and demonstrations of entrenched flaws in our standard statistical practices (Gelman & Loken, 2013; Simmons, Nelson, & Simonsohn, 2011; Wagenmakers, Wetzels, Borsboom, & van der Maas, 2011).

We welcome these reforms that promote transparency and support refining and improving the implementation of statistical analyses in our research, but we also see a need to extend these reforms more broadly beyond current researchers to bring about change for students who are training to become psychological scientists. The purpose of this chapter is to raise awareness about poor methodological practices beyond statistics to those that have been ignored in discussions and connect those practices to a critical challenge we face: the deficiency of methodological training, broadly defined, for students and early-career researchers in psychology. In this chapter, we start by briefly reviewing current methodological reform efforts and their emphasis on statistical practices. Then we transition to describing metascience research that illustrates the extent to which poor practices span beyond statistical analyses. Finally, we discuss how current reform efforts have mainly focused on the practice of statistics while neglecting the importance of methodology more broadly. We conclude that training in methodology is essential for collecting high-quality data that is necessary for strong scientific conclusions.

A Crisis of Confidence and the Reform Movement

In the early 2010s, the conduct of psychological science came under scrutiny because of controversial findings. Bem (2011) published a paper purporting the existence of extrasensory perception, a large study focused on replicating a 100 well-known psychological studies reported a low rate of replication (Open Science Collaboration, 2015), and Diederik Stapel was caught in a massive data-fabrication effort, ultimately resulting in dozens of retracted papers (58 per reactionwatch. com; Verfaellie & McGwin, 2011). To say we began a process of self-reflection is a euphemism for what followed. A critical eye was cast on individual researchers (e.g., Amy Cuddy; Dominus, 2017), research paradigms (e.g., ego depletion; Hagger et al., 2016; facial feedback; Wagenmakers et al., 2016), and questionable statistical practices (how analytical flexibility produces false positive results; e.g., Gelman & Loken, 2013; Simmons et al., 2011). A theme emerged from this self-reflection: misrepresenting exploratory statistical analyses as confirmatory (e.g., analyzing data until significance is achieved, fitting more models to data than reported, and processing the data in multiple ways but reporting a single approach) is a common practice that results in a noncumulative literature with high rates of false-positive findings.

Despite the lack of consensus regarding the scope and severity of these issues (Gilbert, King, Pettigrew, & Wilson, 2016; Lindsay, 2015; Van Bavel, Mende-Siedlecki, Brady, & Reinero, 2016), publishing policies are changing to encourage transparency and nudge psychological scientists into adopting recommended practices. As an example, the journal *Psychological Science* has adopted badges as an incentive for authors to engage in transparent practices (Eich, 2014). A badge, formalized as a part of the Transparency and Openness Promotion (TOP) guidelines by the Center for Open Science (Nosek et al., 2015), is an icon that features prominently on an article and can signal any combination of three transparent practices: open data, open materials, and preregistration. The open data and open materials badges are featured on an article when the authors have made accessible to readers their data (open data badge) or materials (open materials badge) used to conduct the study. The preregistration badge is featured on an article when the authors provide evidence, such as a link to a time-stamped document, which specifies their hypotheses, design, and methodologies for investigating them before data collection and/or analysis (Nosek et al., 2018).

These policy changes are influencing how psychologists conduct their research. Kidwell et al. (2016) report that previous to the introduction of badges in 2014, 3% of the papers in *Psychological Science* had open data, and in the year after, 23% did, which was followed by an upward trend in the following years. In the issue published during the writing of this chapter (October 2018), 12 research articles were published in *Psychological Science*, with over half featuring an open data badge and a quarter a preregistration badge. There has also been a shift toward requiring authors to make explicit statements regarding sample size determination and statistical power within submitted manuscripts. For example, recent editorials from the prominent journals *Journal of Personality and Social Psychology*, *Journal of Experimental Psychology: General*, and *Psychological Science* recognize the value in justifying sample sizes and encourage, if not require, power analyses (see editorials by Cooper, 2016; Cowan, 2018; Kitayama, 2017; Lindsay, 2015).

These incentives promote rigor in that they provide requisite information necessary for evaluating published results. When researchers share their data and materials, the community can more readily reproduce and replicate their work. When researchers disclose all statistical tests conducted, explicitly state which of those were planned a priori, and justify their sample sizes, we can thoroughly review their methodology and rule out selective reporting as a competing explanation for the findings (Simonsohn, Nelson, & Simmons, 2014). Indeed, reform of statistical practices is desperately needed to limit the apparent widespread practice of conducting analyses many ways for the purpose of obtaining statistical significance (Head, Holman, Lanfear, Kahn, & Jennions, 2015; Simonsohn et al., 2014). However, even if we are transparent in the research process, and even if we are not *p*-hacking, our methodology can continue to be flawed such that our results lack validity.

The purpose of the current chapter is to focus on methodological practices that underlie and complement statistics, particularly research design and measurement. Rigorous statistical practice cannot remedy a botched manipulation in an experiment or address poor reliability of a scale. Given the interest in methodological reform and willingness of our community to scrutinize our current practices, we aim to emphasize pervasive poor practices during the phases of study design that are antecedents to statistical analysis. Specifically, we discuss our methodological research involving systematic reviews of common design issues in the use of scales and mediation analysis. From these reviews, we will underscore the grave challenges we face as a field to improve these practices in a climate of limited teaching resources to address them.

Pervasive Poor Practices: The Case of Measurement and Mediation

Here we share the results of our own work that reviews the published literature in psychology, focusing on the use of item-based scales for psychological measurement and mediation analysis. We highlight these two areas of practice because they address issues that precede statistical practice: measurement and research design. In the first subsection, we provide a succinct review of the construct validation process for psychological measurement. Then we share results from systematic reviews, which pinpoint poor practices that are common in the literature. In the next subsection, we focus on mediation analysis. We briefly review the rationale of mediation and the importance of research design for this specific analysis. Then we describe the results of a systematic review of practice in mediation analysis and offer ways to emphasize research design when teaching mediation.

Construct Validation Practices and Scale Use

The social sciences, including psychology, differ from the physical and natural sciences in that we often wish to study phenomena that are impossible to directly measure. For example, psychologists created the constructs of self-concept and satisfaction as a means of understanding aspects of the human condition. To employ these latent constructs in research, the onus is on psychological scientists to define them, provide evidence that they exist, and develop a method of measuring them. When a number is calculated to represent a person's standing on the construct, it is assumed that this number is meaningful. A person with a higher score on our measure of self-concept indeed possesses more self-concept relative to another person with a lower score. The validity of that claim, similar to the validity of any claim from a scientific study, requires evidence. Construct validation is the process by which we gather and integrate evidence to support such claims. Cronbach and Meehl (1955, p. 290) described construct validation as necessary whenever "an investigator believes that his instrument reflects a particular construct, to which are attached certain meanings."

What counts as evidence to support the validity of constructs and their associated measures is vast, and can take on diverse forms. Modern validity theory and the official *Standards for Educational and Psychological Testing* (American Educational Research Association, American Psychological Association, & National Council on Measurement in Education, 2014) purports that it is not the measure itself that requires validation but how the score from it will be interpreted and used. Stated differently, the validation process does not validate a measure but the application of scores generated from the measure. An important consequence of this approach to validation is that the same measure requires ongoing validation, as the measure can be used in different contexts or for different purposes. Stated differently, the validity of a score is context dependent and has to be evaluated across different research contexts.

There are philosophical, theoretical, and methodological debates in the field of psychological measurement regarding what counts as validity evidence and the best approaches for obtaining that evidence. A thorough review of those debates and methodologies is beyond the scope of this chapter, and we refer readers to comprehensive texts (e.g., Bandalos, 2018; Crocker & Algina, 1986; Markus & Borsboom, 2013; McCoach, Gable, & Madura, 2013; Raykov & Marcoulides, 2011; Slaney, 2017). Here, we briefly discuss some of the common approaches to construct validation, organized using Loevinger's (1957) phases of validation: substantive, structural, and external.

Substantive

In the substantive phase, one gathers evidence that supports the theoretical foundation of a measure and the content used to create the scale (see Gehlbach & Brinkworth, 2011, for a didactic overview). This begins with a review of the previous literature and incorporating it to define the construct and determine its breadth and depth. When developing scales, researchers then write items purported to measure the construct. The performance on tasks can also be treated as responses to items (e.g., eye tracking, key strokes, reaction time, etc.). Investigations of response processes can also be included in this phase (Embretson, 2016; Zumbo & Hubley, 2017). For example, one could conduct a qualitative study to understand the cognitive processes respondents engage in when reading items. Information garnered from such qualitative studies can then be used to define constructs and to write and refine items. Once the content has been developed to measure the theorized aspects or components of a construct, one can evaluate content validity by enlisting experts to sort items into their theorized components (Dawis, 1987; Sireci, 1998).

Structural

After developing the substantive foundation for a construct and the content for the measure, one would progress to the structural phase. In the structural phase, results from quantitative analyses provide empirical evidence for the theoretical construct developed in the substantive phase. There are many quantitative methodologies that could be utilized in this phase, though factor and reliability analyses are most common in scale development studies (Shear & Zumbo, 2014). These psychometric methodologies include but are not limited to exploratory and confirmatory factor analysis, item response theory, latent class and profile analysis, psychometric network models, principal and structural components analysis, reliability analyses, and tests of measurement invariance or differential item functioning. These methodologies are conveyed in various comprehensive texts (e.g., Millsap, 2011; Raykov & Marcoulides, 2011).

External

In the final, external phase, researchers gather evidence for how the construct and the corresponding measure operates in a nomological network of constructs (Cronbach & Meehl, 1955). Common evidence reported in validation studies from this phase is relationships to other variables (Campbell & Fiske, 1959; Shear & Zumbo, 2014), and many research questions in psychology could fit in this phase. Examples are the extent to which a measure predicts a critical outcome (i.e., predictive validity), does not relate to a measure of a different construct (i.e., discriminant validity), and does relate to similar measures in expected ways (i.e., convergent validity).

An important consequence of these three phases is that they progress sequentially. If one advances to investigating the factor structure of a scale (structural phase, 2), before having defined the construct and reviewed the items used to measure it (substantive phase, 1), the results of the factor analysis have limited use (see Maul, 2017). Similarly, if someone sets out to predict an outcome using a construct (external phase, 3) without establishing the reliability of the scale (structural phase, 2), the results are likely indefensible, because unreliability of measures biases estimates.

Construct Validation in Practice

A number of older and recent studies across an array of areas in psychology (e.g., counselling, social, personality, and educational psychology) find that a nontrivial percentage of scales is utilized without any reported validity evidence. Percentages range from 95% of scales (Meier & Davis, 1990) to nearly half (Barry, Chaney, Piazza-Gardner, & Chavarria, 2014; Flake, Pek, & Hehman, 2017; Hogan & Agnello, 2004; Qualls & Moss, 1996) having no reported validity evidence when used in a published article. In regard to the reporting of reliability coefficients, the results of systematic reviews of practice are mixed. Some reviews observe that reliability is reported for less than or approximately half of scales (Meier & Davis, 1990; Qualls & Moss, 1996; Vacha-Haase & Thompson, 2011; Willson, 1980; Zientek, Capraro, & Capraro, 2008); whereas other reviews observe a large majority of scales with reported reliability coefficients calculated from the current sample (Barry et al., 2014; Flake et al., 2017; Hogan & Agnello, 2004). Because these reviews were conducted in different subdisciplines of psychology (e.g., social, health, counselling), they likely demonstrate different norms for reporting reliability coefficients.

As scales are used for different purposes, the goal of ongoing construct validation is to ensure that their validity evidence supports that use. One cannot assume a scale's reliability or validity evidence holds in new contexts or populations. Vacha-Haase, Kogan, and Thompson (2000) devised the term *reliability induction* to describe the practice of referencing previous reports of a scale's reliability with the assumption that the previous reliability coefficient extends to its current use. Consistent with *The Standards*, they reiterate the notion that reliability (and also validity) are properties of test scores and interpretations, and not stable properties of tests by showing that reliability is highly variable for commonly used scales (e.g., the Rosenberg Self-Esteem Scale). This inappropriate practice of induction is reported as common in two recent reviews (Barry et al., 2014; Flake et al., 2017). Barry et al. observed that a minority of previously developed scales was reported with a sample specific reliability and validity evidence. Flake et al. (2017), found that though sample specific reliability was commonly reported for previously developed scales (78%), sample specific validity evidence, such as a factor analysis (exploratory or confirmatory) was less common (21%). It appears that the central assertion from modern validity theory and *The Standards*, that scales require ongoing validation, is largely ignored in nonmethods research.

Additionally, we should not assume that most of the scales used in published literature have undergone previous validation. A number of these reviews note a high prevalence of scales, ranging from 30 to 44%, which have not undergone previous validation (Barry et al., 2014; Flake et al., 2017; Qualls & Moss, 1996). Importantly, it is common for such "on-the-fly" scales, ones that the researchers appear to have created for the study at hand, to be utilized without any supporting reliability or validity evidence. Two recent studies note that at least half of these scales had no apparent source, reliability, or validity information (Barry et al., 2014; Flake et al., 2017).

As Slaney (2017) describes, because there is such limited research on how psychologists use measures in their research, these reviews do not provide a complete picture. Taken together, they do suggest that measurement practices are inconsistent with *The Standards* and vary between sub-disciplines of psychology. Scale development and psychometric literature have provided comprehensive methods for initial scale construction, but we lack a clear set of best practices for scale use. Clearly poor measurement practices, such as using the reliability coefficient alpha without any evaluation of its assumptions or using on-the-fly scales with no evidence of validity, are common and persist (Barry et al., 2014; Flake et al., 2017; Schmitt, 1996). Poor measurement practices beget indefensible findings that are unlikely to replicate. Beyond focusing on the application of statistics to address concerns about replication, an obvious solution, which is informed by this review, is to develop a set of guidelines to encourage better measurement practices while teaching researchers how to conduct construct validation and incorporate it into their research programs. Increased education in psychological measurement is particularly crucial, as much of our discipline depends on the assumed measurability of purported but invisible qualities. Neglecting psychological measurement as a complex, difficult, and tentative process threatens the foundation on which our field stands. For example, reputable social psychologists who publish experimental research that disregards ensuring fundamental psychometric qualities send a strong and incorrect signal to students and early-career researchers: our tools are stable, boring, and ready-to-use; the real stuff is in the Results section.

Mediation Practices and Research Design

Mediation analysis is one of many mathematical formulations of the fundamental philosophical question about underlying cause (MacKinnon, 2008). Because of its promise of identifying and unpacking a causal relationship, statistical mediation is an extremely popular method in

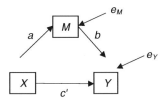

Figure 5.1 Path diagram of simple mediation. The observed variables are depicted in rectangles where X is the predictor, Y is the outcome, and M is the mediating variable. Endogenous or dependent variables have arrows pointing toward them, and exogenous or independent variables have arrows emerging from them.

psychological science and its allied disciplines. Papers on how to test mediation with statistical procedures are extremely highly cited (according to Google Scholar in October 2018, at least 79,500 times for Baron & Kenny, 1986; almost 18,000 times for Preacher & Hayes, 2004; and more than 4,300 times for MacKinnon, Lockwood, & Williams, 2004).

Statistical procedures for mediation provide empirical evidence in support of a theorized causal process where an independent variable (X) is purported to cause a response in a dependent variable (Y) by way of an intervening or mediating variable (M). When the indirect pathway from X to Y through M is significant (i.e., the product of a and b; see Figure 5.1), M is often considered to have explained the relationship between X and Y (Baron & Kenny, 1986; Judd & Kenny, 1981; see also Pek & Hoyle, 2016). Figure 5.1 depicts simple mediation in a path diagram.

Figure 5.1 implies that the direct pathway from X to Y (often represented by c and not presented) is mediated by M, which is represented by the relation of X to M (i.e., a) and the relation of M to Y, adjusted by X (i.e., b). The residuals of M and Y are denoted by e_M and e_Y, respectively; and the intercepts of the model are not shown for parsimony. Statistical approaches to test and quantify mediation have a long history of quantitative methodological development (e.g., see MacKinnon, Lockwood, Hoffman, West, & Sheets, 2002) and continue to be refined and extended to more complex systems of variables (e.g., Hayes, 2015; Lachowicz, Preacher, & Kelley, 2018). Our focus, however, is on the fundamental aspects of research design essential for strong evidence in support of a causal process formulated as a mediation.

Essential Design Aspects

Suppose that the intent is to establish a causal effect of X on Y and identify the mediator M as an underlying mechanism. Here, M is taken to explain the directional effect of X on Y as depicted in Figure 5.1. Significant results from statistical procedures of inference are necessary to suggest the presence of a mediated and causal effect (e.g., the indirect effect carried by a and b, typically evaluated as $a*b$, is significant). Stated differently, the data supports a hypothesized mediation (i.e., signal), which is unlikely due to sampling variability (i.e., noise). Statistical significance, however, is not enough to claim a causal process. Specific design elements are necessary to eliminate alternative explanations of significant statistical findings, especially in the presence of equivalent models. Briefly, models are equivalent when they are mathematically identical to one another in terms of goodness of fit despite having distinct parameterizations and theoretical implications (MacCallum, Wegener, Uchino, & Fabrigar, 1993). As such, the collected data can support alternative explanations despite observing statistical significance for key effects of a researcher's preferred parameterization (e.g., see MacKinnon, Krull, & Lockwood, 2000; Pek & Hoyle, 2016; Thoemmes, 2015, for details and examples of equivalent models in simple mediation).

Three study design elements can eliminate the plausibility of competing equivalent models associated with mediation analyses: (a) randomization in an experiment, (b) temporal precedence, and (c) longitudinal measurement. Randomization of levels in X (the manipulation) ensures the directionality of $X \rightarrow Y$ and that X causes Y because randomization eliminates alternative explanations attributed to potential confounders or omitted variables by chance (Shadish, Cook, & Campbell, 2002). Temporal precedence is embodied in mediation whereby X precedes M and M precedes Y (i.e., $X \rightarrow M \rightarrow Y$). As such, X, M, and Y should have clear start times distinct from one another (e.g., when X is manipulated) and clear termination times (e.g., Y is no longer changing due to changes in X and M; Davis, 1985, p. 11; see also Gelfand, Messinger, & Tenhave, 2009). For example, it is conceptually reasonable that mother's IQ (X) temporally precedes child's IQ (M), which precedes the child's adult success (Y). Finally, a longitudinal study imposes the concept of temporal precedence by ensuring that the data collected incorporates the passing of time in measures of X, M, and Y. A longitudinal design thus allows the expected causal process to unfold and points to the requirement of timely measurements of M and Y, where preceding influences of X and M, respectively, have occurred (Cole & Maxwell, 2003; Gollob & Reichardt, 1991).

Taken together, defensible claims about causal mediation require the three elements of research design as well as statistical significance of the mediated effect. In what follows, we describe past reviews on mediation and report on results of a systemic review we conducted on the practice of mediation analysis. Results from past reviews and our own highlight aspects of research involving mediation analysis that could be improved for more defensible conclusions.

Mediation in Practice

Background

Gelfand et al. (2009) conducted a systematic review of papers published in 2002, which were identified by using the search term "mediation" and citing Baron and Kenny (1986).[1] 410 papers met their selection criteria, and a random sample of 50 was drawn and coded on the design elements of randomization and longitudinal measurement. They found that only 24% of the articles involved experiments with randomization, and 21% involved some form of longitudinal measurement. The majority of studies was found to be cross-sectional (54%), suggesting that strong evidence for mediation as a causal process was lacking. In a related review, focused specifically on longitudinal design, Maxwell and Cole (2007) examined five American Psychological Association journals most likely to have published research using mediation analysis in 2005. They reported that 53% of studies were cross-sectional and 38% were *half-longitudinal*. Half-longitudinal designs have the characteristic of time elapsing either between X and M or M and Y but not both (Cole & Maxwell, 2003).

Method

We examined peer-reviewed publications listed in the PsycINFO database, which were published in English from 2002 to 2012, had "mediation" anywhere, and cited Baron and Kenny (1986) to be consistent with reviews conducted by Gelfand et al. (2009) and MacKinnon, Fairchild, and Fritz (2007). A total of 1,749 articles met the search criteria, where 1,597 were empirical articles and the remaining 152 articles were conceptual or methodological papers. Next, we drew a stratified random sample (by year) of 160 empirical articles (about 10% of the finite population of 1,597 empirical articles) and coded them for information pertaining to the three aspects of research design described. Two coders independently coded the articles, and discrepancies were resolved by discussion to arrive at a single consistent data file. In total, 168 studies were reported within the 160 selected articles, and 1,089 tests of mediation were conducted.

Results

Similar to Gelfand et al.'s (2009) findings, less than half of the 1,089 tests of mediation were part of a study with an experimental manipulation (18.5%). Evidence of temporal precedence, which did not necessarily accompany a longitudinal design, was observed for 35.1% of the tests of mediation. Similar to Gelfand et al. (2009), and Maxwell and Cole (2007), a large proportion of mediation analyses (63.1%) was based on a cross-sectional study. Only 26.2% of the tests of mediation involved longitudinal measurement; and of these tests based on longitudinal data, close to half of them involved half-longitudinal measurement (43.2% of the original 26.2%). Thus, a mere 11.3% of coded studies made use of a proper longitudinal design (i.e., time elapsing between X, M, and Y). These reported percentages are marginal, and only 17.1% of the 1,089 tests of mediation were based on studies incorporating the three elements of randomization, temporal precedence, and longitudinal measurement. Similar to our observations on the practice of psychological measurement, a majority of study designs involving mediation analyses lack key elements that unequivocally point to a causal effect.

Placing renewed emphasis on the teaching of methodology such as research design in relation to statistical mediation can address aspects of nonreplicable findings apart from statistical reform. For instance, the pedagogy of mediation can be contrasted with moderation (e.g., Baron & Kenny, 1986) to emphasize theoretical distinctions between the two approaches. Moderation highlights the generalizability of the theory (e.g., this effect is present in Western but not Eastern cultures), whereas mediation points to potential underlying mechanisms inherent in the effect of an antecedent variable (X) to an outcome (Y). Additionally, emphasis should be placed on the need for alignment between theory (e.g., temporal precedence, causality versus cascade effects; see Pek & Hoyle, 2016) and characteristics of the data derived from research design (e.g., cross-sectional, half-longitudinal, longitudinal, experimental) such that results derived from applying statistical models to data are consistent with the theory being researched.

A Methodological Training Crisis

Across the systematic reviews of measurement and mediation practices that we have discussed, an overarching conclusion is that rigorous and current methodological standards are often not reflected in published psychological research. Observed measurement and research design practices are inconsistent with what published standards and methodological literature recommend. Taken together with the high-profile failed replications, which have emphasized persistent and pervasive poor statistical practices (e.g., *p*-hacking and low statistical power), the next step forward is to focus on reform for practice. Some of these reforms are already underway: publishing policies are changing at prominent journals in psychology (e.g., *Psychological Science*) to promote transparency and facilitate the rigor of our statistical analyses. Our reviews indicate that reform is needed on a broader and deeper level that precedes statistical analyses. Although numerous issues need be addressed to improve the quality of psychological research, the most important challenge that requires urgent attention is that early-career researchers and graduate trainees in psychology do not get adequate methodological training to carry out high-quality work.

Aiken and colleagues (Aiken, West, & Millsap, 2008; Aiken, West, Reno, Kazdin, & Sherman, 1986) have conducted two exhaustive reviews of methodological training, broadly defined, in psychology. The most recent, published in 2008, that reports survey results from the late 1990s to early 2000s, indicated that rigorous and comprehensive training in methodology is not required for most psychology PhD programs, and many programs do not offer such training. Though almost all psychology departments require at least one statistics course, a course in measurement is often not required: 64% of counseling psychology programs required a measurement course, whereas less than 20% of programs in cognitive, biopsychology, and social psychology required a measurement course. Relatedly, only one-fourth of the administrators that responded to the survey judged that the students in their program could utilize the methods of construct validation. Though research design courses are offered more routinely across programs, where basic design is offered regularly at 92% of programs, more advanced topics such as quasi-experimental design are less available, with only 66% of programs regularly covering that topic. It is unclear whether basic design courses are aligned with mediation analyses and integrated into statistics more broadly to help students make the connection between statistics, research design, and theory. If averaged across all areas and programs of psychology, the median number of years required for statistics, research design, and measurement courses was 1.2, indicating that a substantial number of psychology PhDs do not get methodological training beyond the first-year statistics sequence. Although Aiken et al.'s (2008) results reflect graduate training in the late 1990s to early 2000s, students from these programs have likely graduated and are now conducting scholarly research. The scrutiny of some of this scholarly research, especially with respect to methodological rigor, seems to point to this less than optimal training experience as reported in Aiken et al. (2008).

Although training in topics such as measurement and advanced research design that is aligned with specific statistical models is not required in psychology, students are nevertheless required to acquire some knowledge in these areas to carry out their research. They likely learn these skills in a piecemeal fashion in their lab from mentors and peers (Latour & Woolgar, 1986). We conducted a survey of training related to mediation analysis as a follow-up to our systematic review of mediation practices in 2016. We solicited responses from psychology listservs of the Society for Experimental Social Psychology and the Society for Personality and Social Psychology, as well as groups on social media such as PsychMAP, the Association for Psychological Science, and the American Psychological Association. In total, 258 respondents completed the survey. Most of the respondents had completed graduate school (66%) and identified as working in the area of social and personality psychology (72%). When asked how respondents learned about the theoretical and statistical concepts related to mediation, the most frequent responses were: on their own by reading books, articles, or visiting webpages. However, when asked how they think mediation *should* be learned, the most frequent responses were in a graduate-level course or in a short course/workshop. Though this informal survey is a mere snapshot, it is consistent with the conclusion of the Aiken et al. (2008) review: psychologists lack formal training in comprehensive methodology.

Conclusion: We Have a Lot to Learn . . . and Teach

Increased scrutiny of research findings in psychology has heightened scrutiny of antecedent research practices. The field is shifting toward transparency to scaffold the rigor of psychological research. Reforms to our publishing policies at influential journals have been effective at motivating researchers to change their practices (Kidwell et al., 2016). As psychologists face these new expectations, they are likely to find themselves feeling uninformed and underprepared. Training in psychology emphasizes content-focused coursework and research in the laboratory, with limited time in the classroom to learn methodology. Despite that, a successful career in psychological science requires advanced and broad knowledge of methodology (quantitative and qualitative) and research design beyond advanced statistical modeling. After a first year in statistics, many graduate students in psychology lack access to courses in the advanced topics they need to conduct their work such as measurement theory and psychometrics, quasi-experimental design, qualitative methodology, and advanced modeling courses. Even at the undergraduate level, where there are usually a handful of mandatory methodology courses, the lessons are unfortunately limited to (often outdated or questionable) rules and procedures. This pedagogical practice affords generations of psychologists learning idiosyncratic perspectives of methodology outside the classroom and passing their knowledge down to their particular students. The status quo is a disservice not only to students but also to the hope of a scientifically rigorous psychology. Current methodological practice yields the opposite of a healthy discipline's desiderata: underpowered and *p*-hacked studies abound (Lebel et al., 2013; Maxwell, 2004), measures are commonly used without validation (Slaney, 2017) and research design inconsistent with (admittedly mutable) best practices (e.g., Cole & Maxwell, 2003; Gelfand et al., 2009).

We do not conclude that these practices are the intentional schemes of nefarious psychologists. However, the unavoidable reality of publications-as-currency and impact-factor-as-credit no doubt tempts many researchers to play the system in a way that most benefits their careers and families (Bakker, van Dijk, & Wicherts, 2012). Instead, we forward that many researchers are oblivious to their foibles and that there is little incentive for those who do know (i.e., those with methodological expertise) to teach those who do not (i.e., those conducting substantive research; e.g., Guttman, 1977). Some psychologists find themselves facing a "crisis of confidence" (Pashler & Wagenmakers, 2012), and for those who endeavor to improve, they are likely to feel they have a lot, maybe even too much, to learn. Of all the barriers we face as a field to improve the quality of our work, changing our approach to training our early-career researchers is an enormous one. We close with some ideas for overcoming this barrier.

Require Methodology Courses

As Aiken and colleagues have reported, available training in methodology varies across institutions, and this makes sense because different areas of psychology have different training needs. Despite these necessary differences, a greater emphasis is needed on formal methodological training for all: early career and beyond. Our graduate students would be better served if our PhD programs required more courses in methodology beyond introductory statistics. Required courses in measurement and research design would allow students to learn those skills from an expert instead of in a piecemeal, adhoc fashion. Different areas of psychology have different methodological tools and foci, but it seems reasonable that all students be required to take a block of methodological courses as a foundational set, even if they can elect which courses to take.

Additionally, funding agencies can take a more active role in ensuring the research they fund is rigorous by contributing to the methodological training at all career stages. For example, the National Center for Education Research in the United States has hosted a summer research training institute, specifically designed to increase the capacity of educational researchers to develop and carryout cluster-randomized control trials of educational interventions. Such opportunities could be routine, and, importantly, become expected activities of early-, mid-, and late-career researchers. The importance of formally supporting these activities to reinforce researchers to develop their methodological skills after graduate school cannot be understated. Though there are training resources available, some at no cost and easily accessible on the internet, for those invested in learning how to improve their methodological practices, there is little time in a full-time research position, academic or otherwise, to take advantage of these resources. Explicit endorsement and support from funding agencies and universities is needed to replace the culture of quick-and-dirty learning in a piecemeal fashion to formal ongoing training from experts. Reforming psychological methodology, through improved statistics or pedagogy, means rehabilitating the engrained and possibly incorrect research protocol of established psychologists.

Bridge the Gap Between Methodological and Substantive Researchers

Knowledge sharing across disciplines is not a new challenge, but it is just as relevant as ever. Methodologists, like researchers in other areas of psychology, face expectations for original developments and novel ideas for hiring and promotion. However, there is a wealth of methodological advancements that lack utilization by the research communities they were developed to serve (Sharpe, 2013). Scholarly communication that translates these developments in an accessible way and utilizes them to answer important psychological research questions should be valued by hiring and promotion committees. We are encouraged by recent editors making efforts to support this kind of methodological research by having special calls for tutorials in respected outlets (e.g., *Psychological Methods* under the editorship of Lisa Harlow) and the new Association for Psychological Science journal, *Advances in Methods and Practices for Psychological Science*, the stated aims and scope of which is for methodological work that is accessible to all psychologists (Simons, 2018). But only a fraction of psychological researchers attend to these venues, as there is little incentive, or time, to keep up to date with methodological developments in one's later career. Both quantitative methodologists and substantive research psychologists are responsible for enhancing the robustness of scientific results by providing pedagogical support for and engaging in learning recommended statistical and methodological practice. The economic reality: If we can support this work and value its impact on the field when hiring and promoting psychologists, we will go some distance in bridging the gap between the methodological practices put forth by methodologists and the ones that actually end up in practice by psychologists at large. Researchers need incentives to upgrade their methodological journey from a few courses in their past to a career-long learning process.

Integrating the availability of formal training in methodology with incentives to communicate methodological research in an accessible manner has the added benefit of supporting the development of methodological mavens. Mavens are trusted experts in a field who pass on knowledge to others (Sharpe, 2013). Sharpe discusses many of the barriers to bridging the gap between the methodological and substantive research communities but argues that mavens have a particularly important role to play. Mavens of methodology are aware of innovations and recommend them to substantive researchers, which Sharpe argues is why some advances catch on more than others. Mavens also author prescriptive articles that illustrate statistical methods, and such useful articles are the most cited from methodological journals (e.g., Baron & Kenny, 1986). Recognizing their work as important contributions and supporting their development through training, hiring, and promotion is a part of addressing the lack of uptake of best practices.

Summary

Calls for statistical reform, such as emphasizing replicable research findings, have been at the forefront in disciplinary healing. Providing new guides or rulebooks to reform our statistical practices does not guarantee a stronger and reflective scientific discipline. Metascientific reviews of published research practice provide essential information about the health of our discipline and indicate that measurement and research design practices are not consistent with standards.

Methodological improvements can be incorporated into the discipline as neutered and mechanized rules that suggest objectivity while impeding reflection (Davidson, 2018). We need to reform the teaching of psychological science and its methods to promote rigor at the beginning of one's research career. Curricula need to be expanded for graduate students such that they have access to comprehensive methodological training. Additionally, we need to incentivize the ongoing training of later-career researchers by supporting formal training and methodological scholarship that is accessible to psychology at large. By deepening and broadening our pedagogy, we can build a bridge between the methodological and substantive research communities and improve the quality of our work.

We recognize these are not new suggestions, and in these discussions we find ourselves asking, "Why haven't we done this yet?" or "Who can make these changes?" But we can capitalize on the larger changes and discussions going on in psychology right now. We can revisit these issues with renewed urgency. As a student, you can tell your advisors you want more training and courses. As a faculty member who teaches and serves on hiring, promotion, and curriculum planning committees you can make methodological training and rigor a priority. If we can reform in other areas, we can reform our pedagogy.

Note

1. Omitting Baron and Kenny (1986) as a citation would include papers on mediation and conflict resolution.

References

Aiken, L. S., West, S. G., & Millsap, R. E. (2008). Doctoral training in statistics, measurement, and methodology in psychology: Replication and extension of Aiken, West, Sechrest, and Reno's (1990) survey of PhD programs in North America. *American Psychologist*, *63*(1), 32–50. https://doi.org/10.1037/0003-066X.63.1.32

Aiken, L. S., West, S. G., Sechrest, L., Reno, R. R., Roediger III, H. L., Scarr, S., . . . Sherman, S. J. (1990). Graduate training in statistics, methodology, and measurement in psychology: A survey of PhD programs in North America. *American Psychologist*, *45*(6), 721–734. doi: 10.1037/0003-066X.45.6.721

American Educational Research Association, American Psychological Association, & National Council on Measurement in Education. (2014). *Standards for educational and psychological testing*. Washington, DC: Joint Committee on Standards for Educational and Psychological Testing.

Bakker, M., van Dijk, A., & Wicherts, J. M. (2012). The rules of the game called psychological science. *Perspectives on Psychological Science*, *7*, 543–554. https://doi.org/10.1177/1745691612459060

Bandalos, D. L. (2018). *Measurement theory and application for the social sciences*. New York: Guildford Press.

Baron, R. M., & Kenny, D. A. (1986). The moderator–mediator variable distinction in social psychological research: Conceptual, strategic, and statistical considerations. *Journal of Personality and Social Psychology*, *51*, 1173–1182. https://doi.org/10.1037/0022-3514.51.6.1173

Barry, A. E., Chaney, B., Piazza-Gardner, A. K., & Chavarria, E. A. (2014). Validity and reliability reporting practices in the field of health education and behavior. *Health Education & Behavior*, *41*(1), 12–18. https://doi.org/10.1177/1090198113483139

Bem, D. J. (2011). Feeling the future: Experimental evidence for anomalous retroactive influences on cognition and affect. *Journal of Personality and Social Psychology*, *100*(3), 407–425. https://doi.org/10.1037/a0021524

Campbell, D. T., & Fiske, D. W. (1959). Convergent and discriminant validation by the multitrait-multimethod matrix. *Psychological Bulletin*, *56*(2), 81–105. https://doi.org/10.1037/h0046016

Cole, D. A., & Maxwell, S. E. (2003). Testing mediational models with longitudinal data. Questions and tips in the use of structural equation modeling. *Journal of Abnormal Psychology*, *112*, 558–577. https://doi.org/10.1037/0021-843X.112.4.558

Cooper, M. L. (2016). Editorial. *Journal of Personality and Social Psychology*, *110*(3), 431–434. https://doi.org/10.1037/pspp0000033

Cowan, N. (2018). Editorial. *Journal of Experimental Psychology: General*, *147*(4), 459–461. https://doi.org/10.1037/xge0000439

Crocker, L. M., & Algina, J. (1986). *Introduction to classical and modern test theory*. New York: Holt, Rinehart and Winston.

Cronbach, L. J., & Meehl, P. E. (1955). Construct validity in psychological science. *Psychological Bulletin*, *52*, 281–302. https://doi.org/10.1037/h0040359

Davidson, I. J. (2018). The ouroboros of psychological methodology: The case of effect sizes (mechanical objectivity vs. expertise). *Review of General Psychology*, *22*(4), 469–476. https://doi.org/10.1037/gpr0000154

Davis, M. D. (1985). *The logic of causal order*. Beverly Hills, CA: Sage.

Dawis, R. V. (1987). Scale construction. *Journal of Counseling Psychology*, *34*(4), 481–489. https://doi.org/10.1037//0022-0167.34.4.481

Dominus, S. (2017, October). When the revolution came for Amy Cuddy. *New York Times*.

Eich, E. (2014). Business not as usual. *Psychological Science*, *25*(1), 3–6. https://doi.org/10.1177/0956797613512465

Embretson, S. E. (2016). Understanding examinees' responses to items: Implications for measurement. *Educational Measurement: Issues and Practice*, *35*(3), 6–22. https://doi.org/10.1111/emip.12117

Flake, J. K., Pek, J., & Hehman, E. (2017). Construct validation in social and personality research: Current practice and recommendations. *Social Psychological and Personality Science*, *8*(4), 1–24. https://doi.org/10.1177/1948550617693063

Gehlbach, H., & Brinkworth, M. E. (2011). Measure twice, cut down error: A process for enhancing the validity of survey scales. *Review of General Psychology*, *15*(4), 380–387. https://doi.org/10.1037/a0025704

Gelfand, L. A., Messinger, J. L., & Tenhave, T. (2009). Mediation analysis: A retrospective snapshot of practice and more recent directions. *The Journal of General Psychology*, *136*, 153–178. https://doi.org/10.3200/GENP.136.2.153-178

Gelman, A., & Loken, E. (2013). *The garden of forking paths: Why multiple comparisons can be a problem, even when there is no "fishing expedition" or "p-hacking" and the research hypothesis was posited ahead of time*. Department of Statistics, Columbia University. https://pdfs.semanticscholar.org/b63e/25900013605c16f4ad74c636cfbd8e9a3e8e.pdf

Gilbert, D. T., King, G., Pettigrew, S., & Wilson, T. D. (2016). Comment on "Estimating the reproducibility of psychological science". *Science*, *351*(6277), 1037. https://doi.org/10.1126/science.aac4716

Gollob, H. F., & Reichardt, C. S. (1991). Interpreting and estimating indirect effects assuming time lags really matter. In L. M. Collins & J. L. Horn (Eds.), *Best methods for the analysis of change: Recent advances, unanswered questions, future directions* (pp. 243–259). Washington, DC: American Psychological Association.

Guttman, L. (1977). What is not what in statistics. *Journal of the Royal Statistical Society, Series D*, *26*(2), 81–107. https://doi.org/10.2307/2987957

Hagger, M. S., Chatzisarantic, N. L., Alberts, H., Anggono, C. O., Batailler, C., Birt, A. R., . . . Zwienenberg, M. (2016). A multilab preregistered replication of the ego-depletion effect. *Perspectives on Psychological Science*, *11*(4), 546–573. https://doi.org/10.1177/1745691616652873

Hardwicke, T. E., & Ioannidis, J. P. A. (2018). Mapping the universe of registered reports. *Nature Human Behaviour*, *2*(11), 793–796. https://doi.org/10.17605/OSF.IO/FZPCY

Hayes, A. F. (2015). An index and test of linear moderated mediation. *Multivariate Behavioral Research*, *50*, 1–22. https://doi.org/10.1080/00273171.2014.962683

Head, M. L., Holman, L., Lanfear, R., Kahn, A. T., & Jennions, M. D. (2015). The extent and consequences of P-Hacking in science. *PLoS Biology*, *13*(3), 1–15. https://doi.org/10.1371/journal.pbio.1002106

Hogan, T. P., & Agnello, J. (2004). An empirical study of reporting practices concerning measurement validity. *Educational and Psychological Measurement*, *64*(4), 802–812. https://doi.org/10.1177/0013164404264120

Judd, C. M., & Kenny, D. A. (1981). Process analysis estimating mediation in treatment evaluations. *Evaluation Review*, *5*, 602–619. https://doi.org/10.1177/0193841X8100500502

Kidwell, M. C., Lazarević, L. B., Baranski, E., Hardwicke, T. E., Piechowski, S., Falkenberg, L. S., . . . Nosek, B. A. (2016). Badges to acknowledge open practices: A simple, low-cost, effective method for increasing transparency. *PLoS Biology*, *14*(5), 1–15. https://doi.org/10.1371/journal.pbio.1002456

Kitayama, S. (2017). Editorial. *Journal of Personality and Social Psychology*, *112*(3), 357–360. https://doi.org/10.1037/pspa0000077

Lachowicz, M. J., Preacher, K. J., & Kelley, K. (2018). A novel measure of effect size for mediation analysis. *Psychological Methods*, *23*(2), 244–261. https://doi.org/10.1037/met0000165

Latour, B., & Woolgar, S. (1986). *Laboratory life: The construction of scientific facts*. Princeton, NJ: Princeton University Press.

Lebel, E. P., Borsboom, D., Giner-Sorolla, R., Hasselman, F., Peters, K. R., Ratliff, K. A., & Smith, C. T. (2013). PsychDisclosure.org: Grassroots support for reforming reporting standards in psychology. *Perspectives on Psychological Science*, *8*(4), 424–432. https://doi.org/10.1177/1745691613491437

Lindsay, D. S. (2015). Replication in psychological science. *Psychological Science*, *26*(12), 1827–1832. https://doi.org/10.1177/0956797615616374

Loevinger, J. (1957). Objective tests as instruments of psychological theory. *Psychological Reports*, *3*, 635–694. https://doi.org/10.2466/pr0.1957.3.3.635

MacCallum, R. C., Wegener, D. T., Uchino, B. N., & Fabrigar, L. R. (1993). The problem of equivalent models in applications of covariance structure analysis. *Psychological Bulletin*, *114*, 185–199. https://doi.org/10.1037/0033-2909.114.1.185

MacKinnon, D. P. (2008). *Introduction to statistical mediation analysis*. New York: Lawrence Erlbaum Associates.

MacKinnon, D. P., Fairchild, A. J., & Fritz, M. S. (2007). Mediation analysis. *Annual Review of Psychology*, *58*, 593–614. https://doi.org/10.1146/annurev.psych.58.110405.085542

MacKinnon, D. P., Krull, J. L., & Lockwood, C. M. (2000). Equivalence of the mediation, confounding and suppression effect. *Prevention Science*, *1*, 173–181. https://doi.org/10.1023/A:1026595011371

MacKinnon, D. P., Lockwood, C. M., Hoffman, J. M., West, S. G., & Sheets, V. (2002). A comparison of methods to test mediation and other intervening variable effects. *Psychological Methods*, *7*, 83–104. https://doi.org/10.1037/1082-989X.7.1.83

MacKinnon, D. P., Lockwood, C. M., & Williams, J. (2004). Confidence limits for the indirect effect: Distribution of the product and resampling methods. *Multivariate Behavioral Research*, *39*, 99–128. https://doi.org/10.1207/s15327906mbr3901_4

Markus, K. A., & Borsboom, D. (2013). *Frontiers of test validity theory: Measurement, causation, and meaning*. New York: Routledge.

Maul, A. (2017). Rethinking traditional methods of survey validation. *Measurement: Interdisciplinary Research and Perspectives*, *15*(2), 51–69. https://doi.org/10.1080/15366367.2017.1348108

Maxwell, S. E. (2004). The persistence of underpowered studies in psychological research: Causes, consequences, and remedies. *Psychological Methods*, *9*(2), 147–163. https://doi.org/10.1037/1082-989X.9.2.147

Maxwell, S. E., & Cole, D. A. (2007). Bias in cross-sectional analyses of longitudinal mediation. *Psychological Methods*, *12*, 23–44. https://doi.org/10.1037/1082-989X.12.1.23

McCoach, D. B., Gable, R. K., & Madura, P. J. (2013). *Instrument development in the affective domain: School and corporate applications*. New York: Springer.

Meier, S. T., & Davis, S. R. (1990). Trends in reporting psychometric properties of scales used in counseling psychology research. *Journal of Counseling Psychology*, *37*(1), 113–115. https://doi.org/10.1037/0022-0167.37.1.113

Millsap, R. E. (2011). *Statistical approaches to measurement invariance*. Florence, KY: Routledge.

Nosek, B. A., Alter, G., Banks, G. C., Borsboom, D., Bowman, S. D., Breckler, S. J., . . . Yarkoni, T. (2015). Promoting an open research culture: Guidelines for journal could help to promote transparency, openness, and reproducibility. *Science*, *348*(6242), 1422–1425. https://doi.org/10.1126/science.aab2374

Nosek, B. A., Ebersole, C. R., DeHaven, A. C., & Mellor, D. T. (2018). The preregistration revolution. *Proceedings of the National Academy of Sciences*, *2017*(15), 201708274. https://doi.org/10.1073/pnas.1708274114

Open Science Collaboration. (2015). Estimating the reproducibility of psychological science. *Science*, *349*(6251), aac4716–aac4716. https://doi.org/10.1126/science.aac4716

Pashler, H., & Wagenmakers, E. J. (2012). Editors' introduction to the special section on replicability in psychological science: A crisis of confidence? *Perspectives on Psychological Science*, *7*(6), 528–530. https://doi.org/10.1177/1745691612465253

Pek, J., & Hoyle, H. H. (2016). On the (in)validity of tests of simple mediation: Threats and solutions. *Social and Personality Psychology Compass*, *10*(3), 150–163. https://doi.org/10.1111/spc3.12237

Preacher, K. J., & Hayes, A. F. (2004). SPSS and SAS procedures for estimating indirect effects in simple mediation models. *Behavior Research Methods, Instruments, & Computers*, *36*, 717–731. https://doi.org/10.3758/BF03206553

Qualls, A. L., & Moss, A. D. (1996). The degree of congruence between test standards and test documentation within journal publications. *Educational and Psychological Measurement*, 209–214. https://doi.org/10.1177/0013164496056002002

Raykov, T., & Marcoulides, G. A. (2011). *Introduction to psychometric theory*. New York: Routledge.

Schmitt, N. (1996). Uses and abuses of coefficient Alpha. *Psychological Assessment*, *8*(4), 350–353. https://doi.org/10.1037/1040-3590.8.4.350

Shadish, W. R., Cook, T. D., & Campbell, D. T. (2002). *Experimental and quasi-experimental designs for generalized causal inference*. Boston, MA: Houghton Mifflin.

Sharpe, D. (2013). Why the resistance to statistical innovations? Bridging the communication gap. *Psychological Methods*, *18*(4), 572–582. https://doi.org/10.1037/a0034177

Shear, B. R., & Zumbo, B. D. (2014). What counts as evidence : A review of validity studies in educational and psychological measurement. In B. D. Zumbo & E. K. H. Chan (Eds.), *Validity and validation in social, behavioral, and health sciences*. Switzerland: Springer.

Simmons, J. P., Nelson, L. D., & Simonsohn, U. (2011). False-positive psychology: Undisclosed flexibility in data collection and analysis allows presenting anything as significant. *Psychological Science*, *22*(11), 1359–1366. https://doi.org/10.1177/0956797611417632

Simons, D. J. (2018). Introducing advances in methods and practices in psychological science. *Advances in Methods and Practices in Psychological Science*, *1*(1), 3–6. https://doi.org/10.1177/2515245918757424

Simonsohn, U., Nelson, L. D., & Simmons, J. P. (2014). P-curve: A key to the file-drawer. *Journal of Experimental Psychology: General*, *143*(2), 534–547. https://doi.org/10.1037/a0033242

Sireci, S. G. (1998). The construct of content validity. *Social Indicators Research*, *45*(45), 83–117. https://doi.org/10.1023/A:1006985528729

Slaney, K. (2017). *Validating psychological constructs: Historical, philosophical, and practical dimensions* (J. Martin, Ed.). London: Palgrave Macmillan. https://doi.org/10.1057/978-1-137-38523-9

Thoemmes, F. (2015). Reversing arrows in mediation models does not distinguish plausible models. *Basic and Applied Social Psychology*, *37*, 226–234. https://doi.org/10.1080/01973533.2015.1049351

Vacha-Haase, T., Kogan, L. R., & Thompson, B. (2000). Sample compositions and variabilities in published studies versus those in test manuals: Validity of score reliability inductions. *Educational and Psychological Measurement*, *60*(4), 509–522. https://doi.org/10.1177/00131640021970682

Vacha-Haase, T., & Thompson, B. (2011). Score reliability: A retrospective look back at 12 years of reliability generalization studies. *Measurement and Evaluation in Counseling and Development*, *44*(3), 159–168. https://doi.org/10.1177/0748175611409845

Van Bavel, J. J., Mende-Siedlecki, P., Brady, W. J., & Reinero, D. A. (2016). Contextual sensitivity in scientific reproducibility. *Proceedings of the National Academy of Sciences*, *I*(1), 6454–6459. https://doi.org/10.1073/pnas.1521897113

Verfaellie, M., & McGwin, J. (2011). *The case of Diederik Stapel*. Retrieved from https://www.apa.org/science/about/psa/2011/12/diederik-stapel

Wagenmakers, E. J., Beek, T., Dijkhoff, L., Gronau, Q. F., Acosta, A., Adams, R. B., . . . Zwaan, R. A. (2016). Registered replication report: Strack, Martin, & Stepper (1988). *Perspectives on Psychological Science*, *11*(6), 917–928. https://doi.org/10.1177/1745691616674458

Wagenmakers, E. J., Wetzels, R., Borsboom, D., & van der Maas, H. L. J. (2011). Why psychologists must change the way they analyze their data: The case of Psi: Comment on Bem (2011). *Journal of Personality and Social Psychology*, *100*(3), 426–432. https://doi.org/10.1037/a0022790

Willson, V. L. (1980). Research techniques in AERJ articles: 1969 to 1978. *Educational Research and Evaluation*, *9*(6), 5–10. https://doi.org/10.3102/0013189X009006005

Zientek, L. R., Capraro, M. M., & Capraro, R. M. (2008). Reporting practices in quantitative teacher education research: One look at the evidence cited in the AERA panel report. *Educational Researcher*, *37*(4), 208–216. https://doi.org/10.3102/0013189X08319762

Zumbo, B. D., & Hubley, A. M. (Eds.). (2017). *Understanding and investigating response processes in validation research*. New York: Springer. https://doi.org/10.1007/978-3-319-56129-5

Singletons

Reevaluating Course Objectives When an Introductory Statistics Course Is a Student's Only Statistics Course

Matthew S. Fritz

At a recent interview for a faculty position, I had the opportunity to ask the job candidate which statistics and methods courses they had taken in graduate school. "Both of them" was their response. While those of us who teach statistics, measurement, and research methods courses in psychology might cringe at such an answer, there are others in our field that find this response to be completely reasonable and might even wonder why anyone would need a whole second course in statistics. Without placing blame for this disconnect, the fact that it exists is evidence that those of us who do understand the value of statistics are not effectively communicating to our students and colleagues what the field of quantitative methods is or convincing them of the important role these methods play in psychological research.

The problem, I have come to believe, is a lack of context. The majority of psychology students are required to take a statistics course, but few, if any, are ever told why. Faced with students who are often either fearful or resentful of taking these courses and rarely have any prior research experience, it is understandable why the instructor of an introductory statistics course might be more concerned with teaching students to test a null hypothesis using a *p*-value than providing a broader introduction to the important role of statistics in science. This approach would not be a problem if an introductory statistics course were treated as such—the first in a sequence of statistics and research methods courses that, together with hands-on research experience, provide a deep and nuanced understanding of the process of psychological research. But what if the student does not take any more statistics courses or even a research methods course for that matter? That is, if a student's first statistics course is their only course, what do they actually need to know about statistics?

Do I Need to Memorize This?

I asked myself this question for the first time a few years ago when, 14 weeks into an introductory statistics course, I was discussing the formula for the omnibus *F* statistic in multiple regression, and a student asked, "Do I need to memorize this for the test?" To provide some context, this is a graduate-level introductory statistics course that focuses on the usual topics for such a course: frequencies, measures of central tendency, variability, basic probability, null hypothesis significance testing, *t*-tests, correlations, and simple ANOVA and regression models. The course is designed for graduate students who either did not take introductory statistics as an undergraduate or need a refresher. This course attracts students from a wide variety of disciplines including psychology, the physical sciences, education, architecture, engineering, and even music. At the time, the required textbook was the latest edition of Gravetter and Wallnau (2013), and the students' final grades were based on eight homework assignments, all of which required hand calculations and the use of statistical software, and three exams comprised of short-answer questions and a numerical example they had to work through.

What concerned me about the student's question was not that they asked it but that it indicated the students were more concerned with memorizing equations for the exams than understanding what the equations represented or why we were using them. As I thought more about this, I realized I had never been completely satisfied with the course, because while students might be able to compute a few simple statistics when the course was over, they did not seem to be able to hold a conversation about statistics or even state why they had been required to take the course in the first place. At the next class meeting, I informally polled the students and asked what other statistics and research methods courses they had or were planning to take, hoping to hear a long list of additional courses. The majority, however, indicated that my introductory course was not only the sole statistics course they would take but the only methods course of any kind. Given this harsh reality, I realized that I needed to reevaluate my objectives for the course. What follows is a personal case study of how I redesigned my introductory statistics course in an effort to give the students a more comprehensive overview of the role of statistics in psychological research and the broader scientific method.

Peer Review of Teaching Project

The Peer Review of Teaching Project (PRTP; https://peerreview.unl.edu/) is a program at the University of Nebraska–Lincoln (UNL), started in 1994, designed to provide faculty with a framework for critically evaluating their courses. As part of the PRTP, faculty identify a specific course for which they (a) articulate new key learning objectives and how those differ from any existing learning objectives, (b) identify appropriate instructional strategies to achieve the new objectives, (c) create assessments to determine if these strategies are successful, (d) create measures of student learning, and (e) reflect on practices that worked and those that need further revision. Instructors then receive critical feedback from other faculty in the program. The PRTP culminates with a written teaching portfolio that documents this process; my complete portfolio can be downloaded here: http://digitalcommons.unl.edu/prtunl/80/.

Using my introductory statistics course as the focal point for the PRTP, my initial analysis revealed that while my original three learning objectives (Table 6.1) included theory, implementation, and interpretation, the course lectures, assignments, and exams were focused primarily on the computation of statistics. When I really thought about what I wanted the students to take away from the class, I realized that my primary goal was for the students to become critical consumers of statistics so that when they read a statistic in a research article or the press, they could

Table 6.1 Original and Revised Learning Objectives

Original Learning Objectives	Revised Primary Learning Objectives	Subobjectives
1. Theory—learn the theory behind basic descriptive and inferential statistics.	1. Become a critical consumer of statistics in published research and the popular press.	1.a. Correctly interpret reported statistics in order to evaluate the conclusions of the author.
2. Implementation—learn how to compute basic descriptive and inferential statistics.		1.b. Understand the questions that need to be answered about the statistics in order to make this evaluation.
3. Interpretations—learn how to interpret basic descriptive and inferential statistics.	2. Know which statistics are appropriate for different types of data and/or studies.	2.a. Be able to state whether a specific statistic is appropriate to answer a specific research question and whether that question can be answered with the existing data.
		2.b. Understand the assumptions that accompany a specific statistical method and the consequences of violating those assumptions.
	3. Be able to compute and interpret basic descriptive and inferential statistics using data.	3.a. Be able to compute basic statistics by hand and by computer.
		3.b. Be able to answer questions about the data based on the computed statistics.
	4. Understand the importance of statistics in research.	4.a. Understand the role of statistics in the scientific method.
		4.b. Develop self-efficacy with regard to statistics.

not only determine whether the statistic supported the author's conclusions but also know what questions needed to be answered about the statistics in order to make this determination. Knowing whether the author is using the correct statistics requires the students to know which statistics are appropriate for different data, what hypotheses different statistics test, and how those statistics are affected when assumptions are violated. Since many students are going to conduct their own research at some point, they also needed to become critical producers of statistics, able to compute the appropriate statistics and make conclusions based on the results. Finally, the students needed the 'lay of the land' to understand statistics as a field and develop the self-efficacy to take ownership of their methods training.

Additional Readings

To achieve these new learning objectives, I decided to have the students read a series of articles and chapters, approximately one per week, and to discuss the readings in class. To make sure the students did the readings and focused on the most important points, they were required to answer five short questions for each reading. These questions formed the basis for the in-class discussions and students were allowed to revise their answers as part of the discussion. Since the course is taught by multiple instructors and is a prerequisite for other courses, however, none of the existing topics could be eliminated to provide this discussion time. Instead, in order to gain enough time to discuss the new readings, I made the difficult decision to drop the exams and accompanying review sessions, which freed up an extra 25 minutes of class time per week for the discussions. The other change was to move from 8 biweekly statistical assignments to 15 weekly assignments, which allowed each assignment to be shorter while including more contextual questions about each topic.

There is a large number of well-written and insightful pieces about the role of statistics in science, the potential pitfalls of using statistics, and the state of methodological training in psychology. Selecting readings that were accessible to students new to statistics, provided context for the course, matched up with the statistical techniques being covered that week, and fit into the allotted time was challenging, and many excellent pieces had to be excluded. In the end, I selected the following 14 additional readings, each introducing at least one important contextual idea; Table 6.2 provides a complete list of additional readings, including the order and the corresponding statistical topic being covered when the reading was discussed.

I.   *Statistics Are Only One Piece of the Scientific Method*

As the old adage states, it is best to start at the beginning, so the first reading is Alan Kazdin's (2003) "Methodology: What It Is and Why It Is so Important." Kazdin defines methodology as "the overarching term that encompasses diverse principles, procedures, and practices related to the conduct of research" (p. 9) including research design, assessment, and data evaluation, both quantitative and qualitative, as well as ethics. With regard to why it is important, Kazdin notes that methodology is a common language for advancing scientific knowledge in a way that is cumulative and adheres to the four key characteristics of scientific knowledge. That is, following the scientific method (a) results in the most parsimonious viable explanation, (b) eliminates other plausible rival hypotheses, (c) produces findings that can be replicated, and (d) promotes caution and precision in thinking.

The point of this reading is to make the students understand that statistics are just one piece of the scientific method, an idea that is driven home by having the students compare the table of contents of a research methods book (Cozby, 2009), which has two chapters on the use of statistics in research, with the table of contents of their introductory statistics book (Gravetter & Wallnau, 2013). Since statistics are tools to quantitatively evaluate observed data, the goal of computing a statistic should never be statistical significance, but what the significance or nonsignificance of a particular statistic tells us about our original research question. Kazdin also cautions against trying to infer more from a statistic than what the statistic can provide based on the design of the study, such as using caution in making causal inferences with observational data.

Table 6.2 Order of Statistical Topics and Associated Additional Readings

Statistical Topic	Additional Reading
1. Data and frequency distributions	Kazdin, A. E. (2003). Methodology: What it is and why it is so important. In A. Kazdin (Ed.), *Methodological issues and strategies in clinical research* (3rd ed., pp. 5–22). Washington, DC: APA.
2. Central tendency	Best, J. (2001a). The importance of social statistics. In *Damned lies and statistics* (pp. 9–29). Berkeley, CA: University of California Press.
3. Variability	Best, J. (2001b). Soft facts: Sources of bad statistics. In *Damned lies and statistics* (pp. 30–61). Berkeley, CA: University of California Press.
4. The standard normal distribution and z-scores	American Psychological Association. (2010). *Publication manual* (6th ed., pp. 29–36). Washington, D.C.: APA.
5. Probability	Best, J. (2004). Toward statistical literacy? In *More damned lies and statistics* (pp. 171–182). Berkeley, CA: University of California Press.
6. The distribution of sample means and standard errors	Aiken, L. S., West, S. G., & Millsap, R. E. (2008). Doctoral training in statistics, measurement, and methodology in psychology. *American Psychologist, 63,* 32–50.
7. Significance testing and z-tests	Belkin, L. (2002). The odds of that. *New York Times Magazine, 32.*
8. One-sample *t*-tests	Tversky, A., & Kahneman, D. (1971). Belief in the Law of Small Numbers. *Psychological Bulletin, 76,* 105–110.
9. Independent groups *t*-tests	Cozby, P. C. (2009). Generalizing results. *Methods in behavioral research* (10th ed., pp. 268–281). Boston, MA: McGraw-Hill.
10. Repeated-measures *t*-tests	Thompson, B. (1999). If statistical significance tests are broken/misused, what practices should supplement or replace them? *Theory & Psychology, 9,* 165–181.
11. One-factor ANOVA	Cowles, M., & Davis, C. (1982). On the origins of the .05 level of statistical significance. *American Psychologist, 37,* 553–558.
12. Two-factor ANOVA	Salsburg, D. (2001). *The lady tasting tea: How statistics revolutionized science in the twentieth century.* New York: W. H. Freeman and Comp. (pp. 25–29, 41–51).
13. Correlations	Stigler, S. M. (2005). Correlation and causation: A comment. *Perspectives in Biology and Medicine, 48,* S88–S94.
14. Multiple regression	Cohen, J. (1990). Things I have learned (so far). *American Psychologist, 45,* 1304–1312.

2. *Every Statistic Must Be Evaluated by Asking Who, Why, and How*

The second reading, from Joel Best's (2001a) book *Damned Lies and Statistics*, notes that social statistics are created for two (not always unrelated) reasons: to accurately provide a true description of the world and to support a particular viewpoint. While the notion that statistics are an objective tool for increasing scientific knowledge is a nice idea, the reality is that people create statistics to serve specific purposes. Best states, "People use statistics to support particular points of view, and it is naïve simply to accept numbers as accurate, without examining who is using them and why" (p. 13). Hence, in order to evaluate the credibility of any statistic, regardless of the source, the student *must* ask: who created the statistic, why did that person create the statistic, and how did they create the statistic? This is an extremely difficult lesson for many students to accept as they want to believe that statistics published in scientific journals and the media are completely accurate and unbiased. To illustrate this lesson, I ask them to find a statistic quoted in the media and answer who, why, and how. The majority cannot answer all three questions for their selected statistic.

Best suggests that what exacerbates this issue is that many of us suffer, to some degree, from *innumeracy*, which is the inability to understand and apply basic mathematical ideas (Paulos, 1988). One example is that many people have an inability to truly differentiate between large numbers. When asked to estimate the number of stars in a photo of the night sky, someone might say, "a billion" when the answer is really closer to 50,000. Another example is failing to understand that a 5% chance of an event occurring means there is a 95% chance the event does not occur.

3.   42% of All Statistics Are Made Up—17% of All People Know That

The third reading is also from Best (2001b) and focuses on several sources of bad statistics. The *dark figure* refers to the difference between the number of recorded events (e.g., the number of people in the U.S. diagnosed with HIV reported to state health boards by doctors) and the actual number of events (e.g., all people in the U.S. actually infected with HIV). By necessity, the dark number is an estimate, but not all estimates are created equal. Provided we know the statistic is an estimate and how it was created, we can evaluate it. The larger problem is *number laundering*, in which an estimate gains credibility just by being reported. A perfect example is the (I hope) obviously made up statistic that serves as the heading for this section.

Perhaps the most important point that Best raises is how two statistics can be dramatically different yet both equally valid, depending on how the creator operationally defined the construct of interest. For example, what constitutes a person being classified as homeless? If one researcher includes any person who has ever spent a single night in a homeless shelter, while another researcher only includes people who have been without shelter for 14 consecutive days in the past month, the estimated total number of homeless individuals will be very different, though neither is necessarily wrong. The issue of measurement is especially tricky in psychology when dealing with latent constructs such as fatigue or extraversion. Knowing how someone defined a specific variable is vitally important to determining the credibility of a statistic, but this information is often not provided outside of scientific journals.

4.   The Burden of Proof Rests With the Author, Not the Reader

The question then becomes, why do scientific journals include, for the most part, the information needed to evaluate a statistic? Is it just serendipity? The fourth reading comes from the American Psychological Association's publication manual (APA, 2010) and focuses on the information authors are required to provide when writing a scientific research article. Specifically, the students are asked to focus on what information is required in a Methods section (participant characteristics, sampling procedures, sample size/power/precision, measures and covariates, research design, and manipulations/interventions), a Results section (recruitment, participant flow, statistics and data analysis, manipulation fidelity, baseline data, and adverse effects), and a Discussion section (support or nonsupport for hypotheses, consequences, alternative explanations, and study/analysis limitations).

The students are then asked to consider two critical-thinking questions. First, why is this information required? The answer is that APA requires the information necessary for a peer reviewer or a reader to evaluate the reported statistics. That is, the author must provide the information to answer who, why, and how. Second, does requiring this information guarantee that the reader will be able to evaluate the reported statistics completely? This question is tougher, because the answer often depends on what purpose the reader has for using the statistic. The students are also asked to identify the reporting standards for their discipline. While many use the APA or similar standards (e.g., Modern Language Association), distressingly, some students state that their fields have no reporting standards.

5. Statistical Literacy Is Important (Even If Someone Else Is Calculating Your Statistics . . .)

The fifth reading focuses on statistical literacy and comes from Best's (2004) follow-up book called *More Damned Lies and Statistics*. Specifically, Best asks with whom the responsibility of ensuring statistical literacy lies: the student, parents, K–12 teachers, institutions of higher education, the institution's Department of Statistics, a student's primary academic department, a student's research adviser, etc. When polled, the students in my courses tend to provide a variety of answers, though most take a holistic view, placing responsibility with all of these sources. When asked what the biggest obstacle is to their own statistical literacy, the students identify a lack of time to take additional classes, but more importantly, a lack of communication from their departments and advisers with regards to the importance of statistical and methodological training. That is, many students have been told they are required to take a statistics course but nothing about why these courses are required or when enrolling in these courses would be most beneficial. This is the primary reason so many students wait to take methods courses until they are already working on their theses and dissertations.

Another important question I ask the students about statistical literacy is whether it is more common in their respective fields for researchers to compute their own statistics or hire statistical consultants to compute statistics for them. For those who plan to hire consultants, the question I pose is: If you are not statistically literate, how can you communicate to your consultant what you want them to do or make sure that what they actually did was correct? This is a major issue considering that the primary author is taking full responsibility that all of the information in the write-up of the study is correct.

6. . . . Yet Most Psychologists Are Required to Take Very Few Statistics Courses

When asked how their respective degree programs address statistical literacy, the majority of the students report only being required to take one or two statistics courses. Despite most students agreeing that statistical literacy is important, a puzzling blind spot for many students is that they seem to believe that the psychologists publishing research articles must have a large amount of statistical

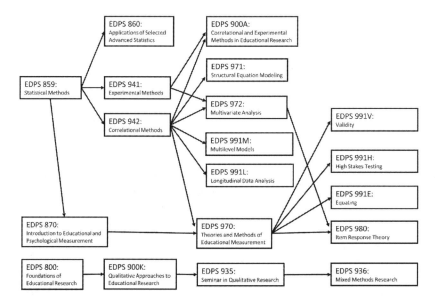

Figure 6.1 Statistics road map for psychology.

and methods training, even if they themselves are only required to take a single course. The general lack of quantitative methods training in psychology is driven home by having them read Aiken et al.'s (2008) review of 201 psychology doctoral programs—a must read for anyone who teaches quantitative methods courses in psychology—which found the mean number of years of required statistics courses to be approximately 1.0, with the exception of quantitative methods PhD programs.

The other takeaway from the Aiken et al. article is that statistics is not a single course but an entire field. It is important that students know about the variety of different statistics and methods courses that are of interest to psychologists, as well as whether these courses are offered by the student's institution, as early as possible during their training so they can find adequate time to take courses relevant to their research. To this end, I developed a handout for the students in my course called the Statistics Road Map for Psychology (Figure 6.1) to help the students know what methods courses are offered by my department and provide a general recommendation for the order in which the courses should be taken.

7.   *Humans Are Not Good at Making Decisions Based on Probability*

At this point in the course, the standard normal distribution, standard errors, and null hypothesis significance testing are being introduced. Given that inferential statistics rely on probability, the next two readings take a closer look at how people interpret and use probability in everyday life.

The seventh reading (Belkin, 2002) is titled "The Odds of That" and illustrates how humans often find patterns where there are none, such as when several unrelated but low-probability events occur in a short amount of time or geographically small area. The example given is the death of 11 "bioterrorism researchers" in a four-month period following the September 11 terror attacks in the U.S. While there has never been any evidence connecting these deaths and several of these individuals had only tenuous connections to bioterrorism research, reporting by individuals on the Internet and then in the mainstream media connected these deaths.

There are two main takeaways from this article. First, when there are a large number of opportunities for an event to occur, even very low-probability events, such as being struck by lightning or winning the lottery, can occur with some frequency. When unrelated rare events occur in a relatively short time span or small geographical area, this is called a *coincidence*. But most humans are uncomfortable with coincidence, instead seeking to relate unrelated events, no matter how convoluted the connection, in order to help make sense of and gain a measure of control over the world. Though it's not assigned as a required reading, Carl Sagan writes about this phenomenon at length in his book *The Demon-Haunted World* (1995), which is even more remarkable given that it was published before the growth of the Internet exacerbated the issue.

Second, there is a large difference between the *actual probability* of an event occurring and the *perceived probability* of an event occurring. A fun exercise to illustrate this point is to have the students compute the probability of flipping a fair coin 10 times and alternate between getting heads and tails with each flip (i.e., HTHTHTHTHT) compared to the probability of flipping the same coin 10 times and getting heads each time (i.e., HHHHHHHHHH). The probability of both sequences is the same, 1/1024 or 0.097%, but getting 10 heads in a row just *feels* less likely to most people (including myself, who knows better). There is also the issue that many students mistakenly think this exercise is comparing the probability of getting all heads (1/1024) to the probability of getting at least one tail (1023/1024).

8. No, Really, Humans Are Not Good at Making Decisions Based on Probability

Tversky and Kahneman (1971) examine a different issue related to the perception of probability. Most introductory statistics courses discuss the Law of Large Numbers, which is the idea that "very large samples will indeed be highly representative of the population from which they are drawn" (p. 106). The problem is that many people believe the Law of Large Numbers applies to small samples as well. This would be true if probability was self-correcting, but since it is not, the so-called Law of Small Numbers is false. An obvious example of this is the *gambler's fallacy*, wherein a gambler who has lost money on several bets in a row believes they are more likely to win money on the next bet because they are *due* or that after winning several bets in a row, they are more likely to win the next bet because they are on a *streak*. Unfortunately for the gambler, if the game is fair, then the cards and dice have no memory.

Tversky and Kahneman also discuss how the probability of finding a true effect in a study is related to statistical power and describe how Jacob Cohen came up with his cutoffs for small, medium, and large effects. This presents an excellent opportunity to point out to students that (a) large effects are not necessarily more important than small effects, as large effects are just those that explain more variance than small or medium effects, and (b) unless the student is conducting abnormal social psychology research in the 1960s, the cutoffs for small, medium, and large effects need to be recalibrated for their variables and populations of interest.

9. Maybe the Problem Is Not Bad Samples but Overgeneralization

Debunking the Law of Small Numbers leads some students to believe that small samples can never be representative of a population. While the Law of Large Numbers states that large samples are more likely to be representative than small samples, small samples can be representative. A more useful way to think about this issue is that all samples are representative of some population, just possibly not the population to which the researcher wants to generalize. Cozby (2009) illustrates this issue by discussing the problems with generalizing research on college students to all adults, generalizing findings from one culture to another culture, and generalizing results from laboratory settings to nonlaboratory settings. The point of this discussion is not to suggest we completely stop conducting laboratory research with U.S. college students but to stop overgeneralizing the results from these studies to all adults across the world. Instead, psychologists need to be better at identifying the populations that are actually represented by their samples.

I give the following example in my course: suppose we are interested in determining whether participation in a STEAM (science, technology, engineering, arts, and mathematics) preparatory course for seventh-grade girls in the U.S. increases the number of women who earn a college degree in a STEAM field. If we can take a random sample of 1,000 seventh-grade girls in the U.S., we would have no problem generalizing our results to all seventh-grade girls in the U.S. If we instead take a random sample of 25 seventh-grade girls from a single middle school in Lincoln, NE, we can easily generalize our results to all of the seventh-grade girls at that middle school. In order to generalize the results from those 25 girls to all seventh-grade girls in the U.S., however, we first have to make the case that the girls from that middle school are representative of all seventh-grade girls in Lincoln, NE, then make the case that seventh-grade girls in Lincoln, NE are representative of all seventh-grade girls in Nebraska, and that seventh-grade girls in Nebraska are representative of all seventh-grade girls in the U.S. This does not mean that the smaller, local sample cannot give us valuable information, only that researchers need to be realistic about the representativeness of their sample and their generalizations.

10. Statistical Significance Tests Can Be and Often Are Misused

In February of 2015, the journal *Basic and Applied Social Psychology* banned the use of significance testing, including *p*-values and confidence intervals, instead requiring authors to focus only on descriptive statistics and effects size measures using very large samples. The rationale for this ban was the general misuse of significance tests by psychologists, including the misinterpretation of *p*-values. Thompson (1999) lists three ways in which *p*-values are most often misinterpreted and explains why these interpretations are incorrect. First, using *p*-values as measures of effect size is wrong because two studies with identical effects but different sample sizes will have different *p*-values. Second, many psychologists mistakenly believe that 1 minus the *p*-value represents the probability of replicating the effect in a second study.

Third, *p*-values cannot provide information about the relative importance of an effect. Statistical significance testing involves a dichotomous decision to reject or fail to reject the null hypothesis, so ascribing degrees or levels of significance (e.g., *highly significant*) is nonsensical. For example, using a Type I error rate of .05, two effects with *p*-values of .01 and .001, respectively, would both be statistically significant, but the effect with the *p*-value of .001 is not more significant than the other effect and may actually be the less important effect. This also brings up the common practice of describing effects with *p*-values slightly larger than .05 (e.g., .06) as *marginally significant* or *trending toward significance*. In addition to the fact that the *p*-value provides absolutely no information about trends, talking about nonsignificant effects as if they were significant defeats the purpose of using significance testing in the first place. If all effects with *p*-values of .10 or less are important enough to discuss, then why not just use a Type I error rate of .10 to begin with?

Thompson recommends five practices to provide the information not provided by *p*-values. First, researchers should always report effect size measures that are not dependent on the sample size. Second, researchers should choose effect sizes that can be interpreted in a meaningful way and then actually interpret them. Third, echoing Tversky and Kahneman, researchers should recalibrate what small, medium, and large effect sizes mean for specific variables and populations. Fourth, researchers should provide actual information about the likelihood of replication. Finally, researchers should always report confidence intervals around parameter estimates and effect size measures, although if confidence intervals are only used to test for statistical significance, their inclusion adds limited value at best.

11. Alpha = .05 and Power = .80 Are Conventions Adopted by Psychology, not Laws of Statistics

Considering that many students new to statistics still seem to come into the course knowing "alpha = .05" and "power = .80," it is surprising how few have ever considered why. Cowles and Davis (1982) trace the origin of the .05 statistical significance level back to Sir R. A. Fisher, who stated, "It is convenient to take this point as a limit . . . [d]eviations exceeding twice the standard deviation [*error*] are thus formally regarded as significant" (p. 553, italics added). In my opinion, Fisher is saying that only differences between groups that are at least two standard errors apart have practical implications for the variables that he was studying (i.e., soil and crops) and are therefore worthy of his attention. If the differences are normally distributed, then a little more than 5% of all differences are larger than two standard errors apart, so a cutoff of 5% is convenient. Logically, this would also indicate that 5% might be wholly unsuitable, either too large or too small, when used with other variables or in other situations. Cowles and Davis note that other famous statisticians seem to support this view including Kendall, who states it is "a matter of personal taste" (p. 553), and Cochran, who believes that Fisher was fairly casual about .05 "as the words *convenient* and *prefers* have indicated" (p. 553).

If .05 is not a law, then why have psychologists set .05 as the de facto minimum bar for publication instead of some other standard? After all, there is the famous line by Rosnow and Rosenthal (1989), "[S]urely, God loves the .06 nearly as much as the .05" (p. 1277). At this point, one reason is simply that there is a precedent; we can cite other psychologists' work who have also used .05. But Cowles and Davis pose an interesting question:

> The fundamental questions that remain are straightforward and simple: Do people, scientists and nonscientists, generally feel that an event that occurs 5% of the time or less is a rare event? Are they prepared to ascribe a cause other than chance to such infrequent events?
>
> (p. 557)

My question for the students is: given the depth and breadth of the problems psychologists are studying, do they believe that a single α level, regardless of whether it is .05 or some other number, is equally suited to all situations? Interestingly, the students are usually evenly divided on this question and provide different rationales for their answer, but at least they are making a conscious choice about how willing they are to make a Type I error.

What Cowles and Davis's discussion misses entirely, however, is that the selection of a value for α is not based solely upon our willingness to make a Type I error but also on our willingness to make a Type II error (β). In general, when everything else is held constant, as α decreases, β increases, so these two values need to be balanced to meet our needs; otherwise, we would just set α to some ridiculously small value and be done with it. Statisticians have understood this trade-off between Type I and Type II error for years. For example, Scheffé (1959) writes that he used α levels of .10 or even .20 if he was worried about missing an effect. Though Jacob Cohen is rightly credited with raising awareness of statistical power in psychology, psychologists seem to have reduced his work to a single dictum: statistical power should be .80. What is so bizarre about students believing that they should always set $\alpha = .05$ and power $= .80$ is that when asked whether it is worse to make a Type I or a Type II error, students often say these errors are equally bad. Yet, these same students are nonplussed when I point out that when they use these values, they are four times more likely to make a Type II error than a Type I error.

12. Most Statistics Were Created to Answer Real-World Questions

Another strange belief among many students is the idea that new statistical techniques spring fully formed from the minds of statisticians who then look for situations in which the new techniques can be applied. While this might be true for some statistics, Salsburg's (2001) *The Lady Tasting Tea* makes the case that the majority of statistics were created by researchers who had questions that could not be satisfactorily answered by existing methods. While the entire book is worth reading, limited time forces us to discuss only two examples: Gosset's development of the *t*-test in order to improve consistency at the Guinness brewery and Fisher's development of analysis of variance in order to study the impact of soil type and weather on crop yields.

13. Correlation Does Not Equal Causation, but Neither Does Multiple Regression

"Correlation does not equal causation" is an axiom that many students come into their first statistics course already knowing. For example, when Stigler (2005) states that there is a statistically significant positive correlation between the U.S. economy and sun spots, the students are quick to point out that the correlation does not give us any information about the direction of the causal effect or even guarantee this relationship is causal. The students do not apply the same amount of caution to interpreting the results from multiple-regression models, however, even though multiple regression is based solely on correlations. Students need to understand that the issue of causation and correlation extends beyond multiple regression to all statistical techniques, even structural equation modeling, which was specifically developed to model causal relationships. That is, the issue is not the statistical technique being used but the way in which the data were collected that prevent us from being able to conclude causality. Specifically, making causal conclusions based upon cross-sectional and/or observational data requires meeting a large number of implausible assumptions in order for us to rule out other possible reasons for the relationship such as measurement error and spurious correlations. Causal conclusions from true experiments are stronger, since meeting these assumptions is more tenable when cases are randomly sampled and randomized to conditions.

14. Good Statistics Will Never Make Up for Bad Research Questions or Designs

The final reading for the course is the aptly named "Things I Have Learned (So Far)" (Cohen, 1990) and nicely summarizes the course as a whole. In the paper, Cohen makes six reflections on research in psychology. First, "some things you learn aren't so," such as a sample size of 30 being adequate in all situations (which I believe is a misinterpretation of the Central Limit Theorem), so always question the origin of conventions such as using a Type I error rate of .05. Second, Cohen states that "less is more," which I interpret as: good statistics will never make up for bad research hypotheses or designs. Third, "simple is better" takes "less is more" a step further by reminding us not to overlook simple things like histograms and scatterplots. Fourth, "the Fisherian legacy" makes the point that the dichotomous choice required by null hypothesis significance testing makes a lot of sense when trying to make a decision about whether more potatoes are grown with fertilizer X compared to fertilizer Y but may not work as well when developing scientific theories about psychological constructs. Fifth, "the null hypothesis tests us" reminds us that the point of our research is not simply to achieve statistical significance and that statistical significance alone does not tell us whether an effect is important. Finally, "how to use statistics" implores researchers to explore their data, to plan their research in advance including conducting power analyses, to focus on effects sizes instead of p-values, and most importantly, to remember that the specific methods we use often matter less than the reasons these specific methods were used in the first place. In general, these are lessons all psychologists need to be reminded of from time to time.

Did It Work?

Evaluating the effectiveness of the additional readings and discussions in achieving the revised learning objectives is tricky as the exams were removed to provide time for the discussions and, since this is a graduate-level class, there has never been that much variability in final grades, with most students earning A's and B's. The quality and depth of the students' contributions to the in-class discussions indicate that they are doing the readings, but are they becoming critical consumers of statistics? Multiple pieces of evidence suggest yes. First, the before- and after-class conversations have changed from the students discussing other courses and weekend plans to discussions of statistics and research. Second, the questions the students ask during the lectures have changed from whether they need to memorize an equation for the exam to how the topic relates to what we discussed the previous week and whether we need to use a different statistic in situation X. Third, a large number of students now bring in published articles they are reading for other courses or for their thesis and dissertation and say, "OK, I've read this three times and I do not think the authors' conclusions match their results" or "Look, the authors did not provide information on Y, so how can we trust their results?" That is, the students are demonstrating their ability to critically think about and discuss statistics, which they were not able to do in the previous version of the course.

Perhaps more importantly, the students are learning the importance of statistics in science and developing the self-efficacy to take ownership of their statistical literacy as evidenced by more students from the introductory course now enrolling in additional methods courses. Many of these students have also decided to pursue a minor or certificate in quantitative or mixed methods. This indicates a belief that every additional methods course is another tool in their research toolbox and that better methods training leads to better science. Therefore, the real objective of an introductory course in statistics is not to teach students all of the statistics knowledge they will ever need but to motivate these students to continue their statistical training after the first class is over.

Additional Thoughts

As with any case study, generalizing the results from my class to other introductory statistics courses is not without challenges. The readings I selected are by no means complete or even necessarily the best treatment of each topic, but they did fit my needs; one colleague was enthusiastic about the idea of the additional readings but stated they would assign an entirely different set of readings emphasizing the role of research design on statistical analysis decisions. Also, my course is a relatively small (fewer than 25 students) graduate course, not a 60- or 100-student undergraduate course. In addition to the logistical problems of trying to have a discussion with that many students, undergraduates would likely benefit from the motivation provided by having exams. Removing the exams was initially a tough decision, but it is striking how relaxed the atmosphere of the class became when the anxiety of an impending exam was removed. In addition, the students seemed happy to actually do more work (i.e., the additional readings and additional statistical assignments) provided this work did not include exams. Finally, I am a faculty member in a quantitative and mixed-methods psychology PhD program that offers a large number of methods courses on a regular basis (Figure 6.1). This allows me some latitude in what I cover in my introductory course, because if a student is interested in learning a specific statistical technique I did not cover, it is likely covered in another course we offer. Introductory statistics teachers in other departments are often not as lucky. But that does not mean we, as a field, cannot always strive to be better and come up with innovative ways to teach and motivate students in our statistics courses.

Acknowledgments: I wish to thank all of the instructors who motivated my interest in statistics and quantitative methods over the years as well as the students who have taken my courses and continually motivate me to improve my own teaching.

References

Aiken, L. S., West, S. G., & Millsap, R. E. (2008). Doctoral training in statistics, measurement, and methodology in psychology. *American Psychologist*, *63*, 32–50.

American Psychological Association. (2010). *Publication manual* (6th ed.). Washington, DC: American Psychological Association.

Belkin, L. (2002). The odds of that. *New York Times Magazine*, *32*.

Best, J. (2001a). The importance of social statistics. In *Damned lies and statistics* (pp. 9–29). Berkeley, CA: University of California Press.

Best, J. (2001b). Soft facts: Sources of bad statistics. In *Damned lies and statistics* (pp. 30–61). Berkeley, CA: University of California Press.

Best, J. (2004). Toward statistical literacy? In *More damned lies and statistics* (pp. 171–182). Berkeley, CA: University of California Press.

Cohen, J. (1990). Things I have learned (so far). *American Psychologist*, *45*, 1304–1312.

Cowles, M., & Davis, C. (1982). On the origins of the .05 level of statistical significance. *American Psychologist*, *37*, 553–558.

Cozby, P. C. (2009). Generalizing results. In *Methods in behavioral research* (10th ed., pp. 268–281). Boston, MA: McGraw-Hill.

Gravetter, F. J., & Wallnau, L. B. (2013). *Statistics for the behavioral sciences* (9th ed.). Boston, MA: Cengage.

Kazdin, A. E. (2003). Methodology: What it is and why it is so important. In A. Kazdin (Ed.), *Methodological issues and strategies in clinical research* (3rd ed., pp. 5–22). Washington, DC: American Psychological Association.

Paulos, J. A. (1988). *Innumeracy: Mathematical illiteracy and its consequences*. New York: Hill and Wang.

Rosnow, R. L., & Rosenthal, R. (1989). Statistical procedures and the justification of knowledge in psychological science. *American Psychologist*, *44*, 1276–1284.

Sagan, C. (1995). *The demon-haunted world: Science as a candle in the dark*. New York: Ballantine Books.

Salsburg, D. (2001). *The lady tasting tea: How statistics revolutionized science in the Twentieth Century*. New York: W. H. Freeman and Comp.

Scheffé, H. (1959). *The analysis of variance*. New York: Wiley.

Stigler, S. M. (2005). Correlation and causation: A comment. *Perspectives in Biology and Medicine*, *48*, S88–S94.

Thompson, B. (1999). If statistical significance tests are broken/misused, what practices should supplement or replace them? *Theory & Psychology*, *9*, 165–181.

Tversky, A., & Kahneman, D. (1971). Belief in the law of small numbers. *Psychological Bulletin*, *76*, 105–110.

## Chapter 7

When Statistical Assumptions Are Interesting Outcomes Instead of Nuisances—Looking Beyond the Mean

Rachel T. Fouladi

Traditional textbooks and curriculum in undergraduate and introductory graduate statistics courses consider the primary research questions of interest in terms of patterns of means. Consequently, the focus is typically on comparisons of means, whether this be in a between-group, within-group, or between/within-groups data analysis context. Most of the analytic strategies presented in commonly used textbooks deploy parametric data analytic strategies; some underlying assumptions discussed include distributional normality, homogeneity of variances, or covariance structures for between-group univariate or multivariate analysis of variance or assumptions of sphericity for analyses where at least one factor is a within-subjects factor. Findings of violations of these assumptions are typically presented as nuisances. Although such analyses and findings of assumption violations are indeed nuisances to what may be the usual and primary analysis of interest, the analyses can yield interesting findings. Consider for example a randomized controlled clinical trial on an intervention comparing a control group versus intervention group where the intervention yields a difference in the variances on the primary outcome rather than a difference in the means. With scenarios such as these and others in mind, I argue that an updated pedagogical approach is advisable.

As quantitative psychologists engaged in the teaching of statistics at the undergraduate and graduate level in our programs, three of the key things that we cover with our students include: (a) a review of statistical procedures to address specific research questions and the fundamental assumptions on which the inferential statistical procedures are based, (b) the procedures by means of which to assess the tenability of these assumptions, and (c) the procedures available to address violations of these particular assumptions. These vary, of course, as a function of the specific procedure that we are reviewing or specific models that we are considering with our students. The approach that I advocate be brought to the teaching of statistics in psychology is that the assessment of the tenability of statistical assumptions should *not* be considered as a nuisance, an annoyance, or an obstacle. Indeed, I argue that we should teach that the assessment of the tenability or violation of an assumption can, in many cases, be framed as a research question of value in and of itself.

If we agree that, in some circumstances, the assessment of an assumption violation can be framed as a research question of value, it follows, then, that a violation of fundamental assumptions is *not*, in these circumstances, simply something that needs to be overcome, in the sense that if we obtain an assumption violation, we simply need to identify the appropriate robust statistical procedure. Rather, if we obtain an assumption violation, then we may have an opportunity to learn something more about the variables, groups, or case under study. It presents for us the idea that, perhaps, we can be starting out with a consideration of these types of queries as viable research questions in the first place, and if not, then we can at least appropriately discuss (address) findings of "assumption violations", why they may have occurred, and the possibility that their finding may open up new lines of research.

This chapter is structured to build an argument and provide resources for a revised pedagogy regarding "assumption violations" and research questions "beyond the mean" in our regular introductory undergraduate and graduate statistics curriculum in psychology. The first major section of the chapter provides an overview of coverage of assumption violations and varied distributional conditions, with a focus on literature in which "assumption violations" are considered common/expected and interesting. In the second section, I argue that, although they are helpful to our teaching, current innovative textbooks and software are not enough. In the following section, I provide a classroom strategy to promote broader and more creative thinking on these topics; key to this strategy is reference to exemplar articles and the provision of scenarios highlighting (a) the "full" distribution of variables and (b) compelling research questions "beyond the mean". I close with a chapter summary and my hopes for an updated curriculum.

Coverage of Assumption Violations and Distributional Conditions

Correct and complete description of fundamental assumptions is appropriate in any coverage of parametric statistical procedures. In the context of tests on means, these include but are not limited to assumptions regarding distributional form and variance/covariance structure. Common treatments include some variations of statements regarding an expectation of normality or multivariate normality (e.g., normality of conditional distributions) and an expectation regarding the variance/covariance structures (e.g., homogeneity of variance of conditional distributions, sphericity, equality of covariance matrices). Although there is a variety of flexible approaches for the analysis of mean structures, the introductory coverage in statistics courses in the behavioral sciences, particularly in psychology, is focused on a small set of standard procedures. The current section provides an overview of discussions in the literature on (a) assumption violations and varied distributional conditions as common or expected and (b) assumption violations and distributional conditions as informative. I provide this overview as key evidence for the need for revised treatment of assumption violations and varied distributional conditions in our traditional curriculum but also as material to which an instructor who is seeking to revise their curriculum can refer.

Assumption Violations as Common

Although some of us were trained with textbooks with memorable quotes such as, "God loves a normal curve" (Hopkins & Glass, 1978, p. 95), the idea that assumption violations are *common, expected,* or *normative* is not new. In his classic book of *Psychometric Theory*, Nunnally wrote, "Strictly speaking, test scores are seldom normally distributed" (Nunnally, 1978, p. 160). More recently, in a special-topics textbook on methods for the analysis of event-related potential (ERP) data, Luck (2012) highlights the prevalence of non-spherical data and heterogenous covariances in ERP studies. Although non-normality is acknowledged by some as common, with a few exceptions (e.g., Wilcox, 2017a), most introductory statistics textbooks directed at undergraduate or graduate psychology curriculum bypass these views.

Many teachers of statistics in psychology departments recognize that within certain disciplines, there is a high prevalence of assumption violations. Although some instructors are trained as quantitative psychologists and read key quantitative methods literature, in many departments, the teaching of statistics courses is by instructors with different areas of expertise, e.g., cognitive psychology (see Aiken, Chapter 4 of current volume). As is well known to many quantitative psychologists but may be less well known by the broader set of instructors engaged in the practice of teaching statistics in psychology departments, a number of review articles and editorial pieces in psychology journals have highlighted the prevalence of varied distributional conditions that commonly constitute "assumption violations" (e.g., nonnormality and heteroscedasticity; Micceri, 1989; Ruscio & Roche, 2012). Reference to these articles by an instructor in the course of developing teaching materials or directly referring students to these articles can be a useful strategy to bring awareness to the possibility, if not commonality, of the occurrence of varied assumption violations across the different areas of psychology. The following provides a brief overview of some of these reviews with regard to distributional nonnormality, between-group heteroscedasticity, and covariance structures.

Distributional Nonnormality

Researchers in certain domains within psychology have long been aware of distributional nonnormality in some of their key variables of interest, e.g., reaction time in cognitive tasks, survival data from clinical trials, substance use in drug abuse research. Recent reviews by Blanca, Arnau, López-Montiel, Bono, and Bendayan (2013) and Bono, Blanca, Arnau, and Gomez-Benito (2017) provide a variety of examples from different literatures including psychology. According to Micceri (1989), however, historically, the prevalence of nonnormality has largely been unacknowledged or ignored in other areas of psychology: "today's literature suggests a trend toward distrust of normality; however, this attitude frequently bypasses psychometricians and educators" (p. 157).

Micceri's *Psychological Bulletin* article was instrumental in bringing to the foreground that nonnormality may be more common across a broader range of variables of interest in psychology and education than previously accepted (1989). Micceri provided a review of nonnormality in the educational and psychological variables (number of variables = 440) drawn from data sources including journal articles and national and regional sources. Micceri's well-cited review illustrated that distributional shapes that are not normal are not unusual and are more common for certain types of variables/domains of research than others. More recently, Blanca et al. (2013) reviewed 693 datasets in terms of skewness and kurtosis and found that only 5% of the distributions were close to expected values under normality. Bono et al. (2017) conducted a review of abstracts of 262 articles in health, education, and social science journals, which reported the distributions of the response variable; they identified common nonnormal distributions as including gamma, negative binomial, multinomial, binomial, lognormal, and exponential distributions. Cain, Zhang, and Yuan (2017) examined univariate and multivariate data for 1,567 univariate distributions and 254 multivariate distributions for articles published in two major journals in psychology and education; from their review of the datasets, they found more than half of the distributions differed from either univariate (74%) or multivariate (68%) distributions. Based on their findings, Cain, Zhang, and Yuan argued that "it is time to routinely report skewness and kurtosis along with other summary statistics such as means and variances" (p. 1716)—a recommendation with which I fully agree.

Between-Group Heteroscedasticity

With regard to reviews highlighting the prevalence of between-group heteroscedasticity, a couple of articles published in psychology and education journals stand out. In reviews of between-group heteroscedasticity, a commonly used metric is the magnitude of the variance ratio (VR), i.e., the ratio of the variance in one group versus the variance in a separate group (c.f., Ruscio & Roche, 2012). In an examination of the statistical practices of educational researchers using ANOVA, MANOVA, and ANCOVA, Keselman et al. (1998) considered results on 86 variables and found a mean VR of 2.0 and VRs up to a magnitude of 23.8. In a 2008 *American Psychologist* article, Erceg-Hurg and Mirosevich reviewed 28 studies from two issues of two experimental psychology journals that used ANOVA techniques and noted that between-group differences in sample variances yielded magnitudes of VRs that "suggest that it is not unusual for the homoscedasticity assumption to be violated" (p. 592). In *Methodology*, Ruscio and Roche (2012) reviewed a series of 455 experimental ($n = 283$) and correlational ($n = 172$) articles across seven key journals in psychology. They showed that VRs exceeded 3 23% of the time, highlighting that heterogeneity of variances between groups was common in the studies they examined. In their abstract, they summarize their findings thus: "Sample variances differed, often substantially, suggesting frequent violation of the assumption of equal population variances" (p. 1).

"Undesired" Covariance Structures

Commonly described multivariate analysis of means structures procedures, including standard repeated measures analyses, MANOVA, and MANCOVA procedures, make assumptions regarding the underlying multivariate distribution having a specified covariance structure in a single group analysis or with regard to equality of covariance structures in a multiple independent groups analysis. Although no corresponding published literature or data synthesis project was identified regarding the prevalence of assumption violations with regard to covariance structures, in certain areas of psychology (e.g., psychophysiology), the possibility of or the regular occurrence of covariance structure relevant assumption violations is largely recognized.

In 1987, the journal *Psychophysiology* published an editorial statement (Jennings, 1987) that the issue of sphericity in repeated measures "must be" acknowledged for publication in that journal.

Jaccard and Ackerman (1985) wrote, "It is unlikely that applications in clinical psychology meet sphericity assumptions" (p. 426); although they did not back up their claim with specific examples from the literature, they provided several hypothetical research scenarios as exemplary. Bathke, Schabenberger, Tobias, and Madden (2009) wrote that by the time of writing of their 2009 paper, the 1959 work of Greenhouse and Geisser, which offers a well-known strategy to address violation of an assumption of sphericity, had already been cited more than 1,000 times in psychology and neurosciences and more than 2,000 times overall across a variety of disciplines (Google Scholar overall citation count: 4,500, January 2019).

Luck (2012), in an introductory textbook to ERP analysis, recognizes both the prevalence of lack of sphericity within a single covariance matrix as well as the possibility of heterogeneity of covariance structures between groups. Advances in covariance structure analysis including structural equation modeling have seen a burgeoning of direct inquiries with regard to similarity/difference of covariance structures between groups, with increasing instances in the literature regarding the lack of equivalence (at least on some parameters between groups); however, as with the prevalence of nonspherical structures, to date, no literature review synthesis has documented the prevalence of dissimilar covariance structures in multigroup analyses. That said, a recent paper by Putnick and Bornstein (2016) did conduct a survey of papers published over a period of a year, which were indexed in the APA PsycNet database, regarding examinations of measurement invariance. Although measurement invariance can be examined within-group (e.g., across time points, related informants), it is commonly applied in between-group contexts. In the one-year period of review, they identified 126 papers that attempted to directly evaluate the tenability (or lack thereof) of levels of measurement invariance; although the methods of "testing" measurement invariance may be critiqued, and the papers do not simply assess equality/inequality of covariance structures, the literature surveyed by Putnick and Bornstein does suggest that inequality of covariance structures *is not rare*.

Assumption Violations as Informative

The commonality of assumption violations is appropriate justification for methodological research (e.g., Arnau, Bendayan, Blanca, & Bono, 2012, 2013, 2014), including my own (e.g., Fouladi, 2000; Fouladi & Yockey, 2002), in the quest for data analytic solutions that are robust to these data conditions. Indeed, I confess to have forged a primary research line into examining performance characteristics (e.g., Type I and II error control) of procedures under varied distributional conditions. However, while we make headway in the area of developing more robust data analytic techniques, assumption violations are typically presented as an obstacle. While extremely useful in advancing statistical practice, titles such as "Managing Heteroscedasticity in General Linear Models" (Rosopa, Schaffer, & Schroeder, 2013) and "Comparing Correlations: Dealing with Heteroscedasticity and Non-normality" (Wilcox, 2009) illustrate this common perspective.

Although somewhat rare in the literature, the idea that finding assumption violations, e.g., heteroscedasticity, *informative* is not a novel conceptualization and has been incorporated in some research areas in psychology. This is actually an area in which the content researcher teaching statistics may be at an advantage over the quantitative psychologist. Whoever the instructor, reference to review articles on the prevalence of assumption violations and literature where assumption violations are informative will increase an instructor's understanding/appreciation of the importance and possibilities of an expanded frame with which to consider research and data analysis. These in turn can inform the coverage of materials and the types of examples discussed in class. The following provides a brief overview of some potential resources for instructors to reference, with primary focus on literature regarding heteroscedasticity and covariance structures.

Importantly, even though Rosopa et al. (2013) present heteroscedasticity as something to be managed, they also acknowledge that "the careful analysis of heteroscedasticity may play an important role in psychological research" (p. 339). Articles that invite new ways of looking at data, such as "Moving Beyond the Mean in Studies of Mental Chronometry: The Power of Response Time Distributional Analysis" (Balota & Yap, 2011) and "Treatment Effects Beyond the Mean: A Practical Guide Using Distributional Regression" (Hohberg, Pütz, & Kneib, 2017), are valuable pieces in the advancement of different research frames. Although I can point to Jaccard and Ackerman (1985), Bryk and Raudenbush (1988), and Grissom (2000) as articles highlighting the informativeness of heteroscedasticity, I do not know of any similar key papers in psychology or education targeting a broad readership highlighting the informativeness of other data conditions that are commonly seen as constituting assumption violations—although perhaps the increased interest in evaluating measurement equivalence (or lack thereof) serves as an interesting exception (e.g., Putnick & Bornstein, 2016).

In their treatment of assumptions underlying traditional repeated measures ANOVA data analysis strategies, Jaccard and Ackerman (1985) speak to the commonality of correlation and variance structures that can combine to constitute violation of sphericity assumptions.

> It is unlikely that applications in clinical psychology meet sphericity conditions. One frequent design has a longitudinal structure, in which a client's responses are observed over numerous occasions. In such designs, it is common to find that successive or adjacent measurement occasions are more highly correlated than nonadjacent measurement occasions, with the correlation between these measurements decreasing the further apart the measurements are in the series. . . . A second common experimental plan assesses client responses in a before-during-after treatment design, in which the responses are measured r times before the treatment, during each of p treatment sessions, and at some time after cessation of the treatments. Treatments frequently have impact on group variances as well as on group means. For example, after several initial treatment sessions, the variance of scores may reduce and stabilize in later treatment sessions.
>
> (p. 426)

Although the examples speak to the informativeness of inspection of the correlations and variances with regard to the data-generating scenario, the authors present lack of sphericity as an obstacle to overcome in the analysis of the mean structures through recommended application of appropriately modified data-analytic procedures.

Published shortly after the Jaccard and Ackerman (1985) paper, the 1988 *Psychological Bulletin* paper by Bryk and Raudenbush, entitled "Heterogeneity of Variance in Experimental Studies: A Challenge to Conventional Interpretations", is exemplary on the topic of between-group differences in variances as informative. It emphasizes methods by means of which to query heterogeneity of variances and proceed with primary analyses of interest in the case of heterogeneity of variances. Bryk and Raudenbush provide a couple of excellent examples with regard to the informativeness of analyzing variances; the following is an excerpt from their article regarding a secondary data analysis of previously published findings:

> In this study . . . the treatment had an effect on the variance that went unrecognized in the original investigation . . . reanalysis . . . reveals substantial differences in the residual variance in the experimental and control groups. . . . the treatment apparently exerts a disequalizing effect. . . . Specifically, the residual variance in the experimental group . . . was significantly larger than the residual variance in the control group.
>
> (p. 400)

The 2000 *Journal of Consulting and Clinical Psychology* article by Grissom, entitled "Heterogeneity of Variance in Clinical Data", is also exemplary in providing a very clear statement; indeed, a section heading is titled "Variance Is More Than Just a Nuisance Parameter". Regretfully, however, after providing several examples of between-group heterogeneity of variance, the paper only briefly reviews procedures available to assess homo- or heteroscedasticity, and states, "some applied statisticians de-emphasize tests of homoscedasticity, maintaining that researchers should proceed directly to heteroscedastic methods" (p. 157). Thus the emphasis again, in this style of discourse, comes down on the side of heteroscedasticity as an obstacle to be overcome.

Grissom (2000) and Bryk and Raudenbush (1988) are to be recognized for clearly taking a position (e.g., through section headings) that heteroscedasticity is worthy of study. Although Grissom outlines some ways heteroscedasticity can be informative, the detailed examples provided by Bryk and Raudenbush are particularly illuminating of the missed opportunities when heteroscedasticity is not noted, and the finding is not given its due consideration.

Current Textbooks and Software as a Way Forward?

Even in the current period of rapid dissemination of research through online journal publications, as useful as articles are, unless they are widely cited, their impact in the short term is small. I was once told it takes 20 to 40 years for a statistical practice to take hold—I know I cannot wait that long.

Improved textbooks, currently largely lacking at the introductory statistics level in general psychology curriculum (Rodgers, Chapter 8 of current volume), are an important way forward. Wilcox has been instrumental in trying to advance statistics education in the behavioral and social sciences, with his textbooks introducing standard as well as alternative data analytic practices. His classic book, *New Statistical Procedures of the Social Sciences: Modern Solutions for Basic Problems* (Wilcox, 1987), and his more recent books, *Fundamentals of Modern Statistical Methods Substantially Improving Power and Accuracy* (Wilcox, 2010), *Modern Statistics for the Social and Behavioral Sciences: A*

Practical Introduction (Wilcox, 2017b), *Introduction to Robust Estimation and Hypothesis Testing* (Wilcox, 2017a), and *Understanding and Applying Basic Statistical Methods Using R* (Wilcox, 2017c), are all part of this project. Even though much of Wilcox's work can be read as advocating the use of robust strategies where assumption violations are normative nuisances to be overcome, the fourth edition of his book *Introduction to Robust Estimation and Hypothesis Testing* (Wilcox, 2017a) is exemplary in its organizational structure, placing inferential procedures regarding different measures of location alongside procedures regarding different measures of scale—with the layout suggesting little hierarchy of values. Instructor reference to if not use of books, such as Thode (2002) and Wilcox (2017a), with coverage of assessment of parameters other than those emphasized in traditional introductory curriculum would go a long way in updating our teaching.

With the advent of open-source statistical software options, innovative statistical analysis options that were not and still are not implemented in large-scale packages are becoming more readily available. However, we need to be careful about the source of the software. We also need to be careful not to tie our teaching to specific software. In the absence of excellent accompanying readable documentation describing the technical details of relevant procedures, the black-box approach to improving data analytic practice is not one I endorse. Although promoting the practice of checking assumptions and use of robust techniques is good, we need to change attitudes toward data and research questions such that "assumption checking" and "assumption violations" are not nuisances to be overcome.

In the Classroom: A Way Forward With Pedagogy Reframed

If we are to bring teaching of statistics to the 21st century, we must find ways to encourage broader ways of thinking of research questions and data in our students. As quantitative psychologists and/or educators of statistical methodology in psychology, we are well positioned to change data analytic practice and attitudes, starting in our classrooms, through the use of varied examples and different research frames. Data analytic strategies are or can be quite varied across different domains of psychology. Although I agree that we all need to teach the basics, it is important to provide examples of different ways of looking at data and the variety of research questions that may be posed in psychology. Our examples of research scenarios and questions should include questions not just about means but also about other distributional parameters. By providing different examples and showing students how to generate novel research questions in which assumption violations are or may be informative, we encourage new ways of thinking and creativity in research. These examples can be drawn from or inspired by the literature, or we can make up our own. Specifically, we must go beyond the typical introductory textbook and typical introductory curriculum. This is an opportunity to be creative.

In this section on bringing innovation into the classroom, I provide a strategy by which to promote a broader perspective on data and research questions. This approach (a) highlights the "full" description of the distribution of different types of variables within and between groups, and (b) illustrates research questions "beyond the mean". For each of these, I discuss the use of exemplar research articles and scenarios—including some of my favourite "beyond the mean" research scenarios in which interventions are designed to impact parameters other than the mean!

The "Full" Distribution

In our teaching, we need to increase our emphasis on the full reporting of summary statistics, including univariate or multivariate skewness and kurtosis as appropriate. Indeed, we must emphasize the necessity of inclusion of figures to illustrate the full distribution of the variables—at least univariately. Although reporting guidelines for journals have page/word limits, if we are to bring our teaching of statistics to the 21st century, we must provide the course content, structure, and environment for our students to learn data analysis and communication skills, which include full and succinct communication supplemented with informative graphical displays.

Reporting practices regarding distributional characteristics are typically limited to means and variances or standard deviations. Cain et al. (2017), in a survey of researcher reporting practices, contacted 124 researchers publishing in a select set of journals; out of 124 researchers contacted, Cain et al. found only 3 reported skewness and kurtosis in their articles. Cain et al. conjectured that underreporting of normality or lack thereof may include (a) lack of awareness of prevalence and influence of nonnormality, (b) lack of familiarity with measures of skew or kurtosis and their interpretation, (c) extra analytic burden to compute measures of skewness and kurtosis, and (d) concern regarding consequences of reporting large values of skewness and kurtosis. Importantly, Cain et al.'s paper also includes a figure of a random sample of 20 univariate distributions (for 1,567 univariate distributions and 254 multivariate distributions mentioned previously) illustrating a vast variety of empirical distribution shapes (see Figure 7.3 at https://link.springer.com/article/10.3758%2Fs13428-016-0814-1). Cain et al. emphasized the necessity of better reporting practice and providing tools to improve reporting practice of skew and kurtosis; however, the issue "that there is no common shape that explains skewness and kurtosis" (p. 1721) points to the importance of use of graphical tools to illustrate empirical distributions.

In the following, I provide a brief overview of an example paper that broadly reported summary statistics of the type one might refer to in classroom examples. I follow this with a set of example scenarios of the type an instructor can use to discuss varied distributional characteristics and the informativeness of looking at the full distribution of a variable.

A recent paper (Whisman & Judd, 2016) published in *Psychological Assessment* probing cross-national differences in older adults from three countries on a commonly used 5-item satisfaction-with-life scale, provides a simple table of means, variances, univariate skewness, and kurtosis, along with complete reporting of the Pearson-product moment correlations among the items, for each sample. Although the authors report values of "Mardia multivariate kurtosis indices for the data collected for each country", no values for multivariate skewness are provided. Importantly, even without this additional index, the authors are to be credited for extensive reporting of summary statistics to provide a better understanding of the distributional characteristics of the multivariate data being analyzed. That said, although nonnormality was observed and reported, like most papers in psychology, the multivariate nonnormality was presented as an obstacle to be overcome. As a reader of the article, I noted that some of the values of indices of nonnormality were at least as sample statistics somewhat different from each other between groups (e.g., multivariate kurtosis values of 13.52 vs. 35.99, univariate kurtosis values 2.48 vs. -0.12); if making a cross-national comparison, would it not be interesting to query whether the distribution shapes are plausibly similar to/different from one another in a substantive way? Would it not have been interesting to have a substantive interpretation of the phenomenon (and/or measurement system) in the context of the distributions of scores that were observed? I certainly would be interested; this interest or type of query is one I can share with my students.

Scenario Set: Considering Distributional Form of Scores on a Questionnaire

One of my areas of interest is how people respond to questionnaires. The questionnaire on which I have been focusing over recent years is the Center for Epidemiologic Studies—Depression Symptoms Scale (CES-D: Radloff, 1977), a commonly used questionnaire in health psychology, behavioral medicine, and epidemiology. Items are scored 0 to 3, with higher scores reflective of greater levels of depressive symptomology. The composite CES-D score is typically reported as a sum across appropriately recoded items, with a theoretical minimum of zero, theoretical maximum of 60. For purposes of illustration, the following section provides figures, based on analyses for the current chapter, of public-use datasets of the CES-D (total/subscale/item-level CES-D scores from the random digit dialing (RDD) sample for the Midlife Development in the United States survey (MIDUS-2: Ryff, Seeman, & Weinstein, 2010); and total CES-D scores from the Well Elderly Project (c.f., Wilcox, 2017c).

Composite-Level Examination of Scores

Figure 7.1 illustrates the frequency distribution of scores on the CES-D for the overall RDD sample of the US MIDUS-2 dataset. The figure clearly depicts a distribution that does not approximate a normal distribution. With consideration of the distribution of CES-D scores from the MIDUS-2

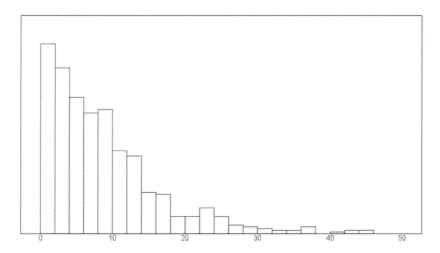

Figure 7.1 Histogram of total CES-D scores from RDD sample of MIDUS-2 survey.

sample, we get a better understanding of the samples' reporting of depressive symptoms, with the most common pattern response being reporting no or minimal symptoms in the previous week, with a steady decrease of the proportion of individuals endorsing higher levels of symptoms, with substantially fewer individuals reporting the higher levels of depressive symptomology—this is something that would have eluded us with reporting of mean, median, mode, trimmed mean, etc. With careful inspection of the distribution graphically and considering the varied parameter estimates, we can make informed decisions as to whether additional measures of central tendency, dispersion, or shape will enhance our data description.

Composite Score Distributions—Separated by Groups

In the case of two or more groups, such as might occur with gender categories, it is important to ritualize the provision of graphics separated by major categories. Depending on the dataset, there may be no major differences; nonetheless, it is important to convey that information. In the

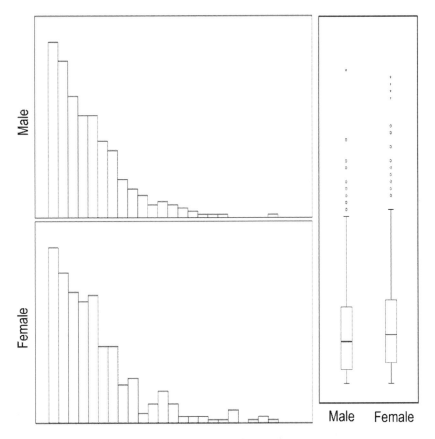

Figure 7.2 Histograms and boxplots of total CES-D scores from RDD sample of MIDUS-2 survey, separated by dichotomous gender category.

MIDUS-2 dataset, if we break down the responses in separated histograms by dichotomous gender category (male, female), we see the general trend of positive skew for both groups. By examining the distribution, we can see that although there is a general similarity to the distribution shapes, there are a few more cases in the tail of the distribution for women as compared to the men. For this dataset, the histograms and box plots show tremendous similarity between the two distributions except for the occurrence of extreme values. There are a number of different strategies to compare distributions based on independent groups. In this case, the separate distributions are mostly indistinguishable from one another on most parameters.

Wilcox has also utilized the CES-D in his work, referring to it for the purpose of examples in articles and in textbooks (e.g., Wilcox, 2017c). For educational purposes to supplement his textbook, he has included several datasets to which he refers in his examples, including some for total scores on the CES-D on his website: https://dornsife.usc.edu/labs/rwilcox/datasets/. In order to emphasize the importance of considering differences between groups, in this case between separate study samples but also in terms of providing a full understanding of the data in a given sample, I provide a boxplot illustration of the difference in the distribution of total scores on the CES-D for the RDD MIDUS-2 sample versus the Well Elderly sample (see Figure 7.3). Table 7.1 provides simple summary statistics for CES-D total scores based on the two publicly available datasets considered here.

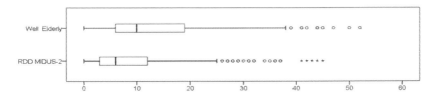

Figure 7.3 Boxplots of total CES-D scores by publicly available dataset.

Table 7.1 Descriptive Statistics for CES-D Total Scores in Two Public Use Datasets

Sample	Well Elderly	RDD MIDUS-2
N	328	637
Minimum	0	0
Maximum	52	45
Mean (SE)	13.49 (0.59)	8.35 (0.31)
5% Trimmed Mean	12.66	7.53
Median	10	6
Std. Deviation	10.68	7.88
Range, IQR	52, 13	45, 9
Skewness (SE)	1.10 (0.13)	1.66 (0.10)
Kurtosis (SE)	.84 (0.27)	3.42 (0.19)

Item-Level and Subscale-Level Examination of Distributions

If we look at CES-D item and subscale scores, we see a variety of distributional forms. Using RDD MIDUS-2 sample data, Figure 7.4 provides histograms for example item-level and subscales-level scores (DA: Depressed Affect, PA: Positive Affect, SC: Somatic Complaints, IP: Interpersonal Problems), with two example items provided for each subscale. The first two rows of histograms in Figure 7.4 illustrate different item-level distributional shapes. It is important to note these do not represent a random sample of item frequency distributions for the RDD sample. I purposefully selected sample items that depict the most extreme discrepancy for this dataset. Examining the item-level histograms, we can see the overwhelming endorsement of the lowest response option for some items contrasted with the overwhelmingly strong endorsement of the highest response option for other items; these patterns sharply contrast with the more gradual stepped frequency distributions for other example items. The bottom row of Figure 7.4 illustrates the shapes of the data from the RDD-MIDUS-2 subscale composites (without reverse coding the PA items), highlighting differences/similarities of shapes at the subscale level. By showcasing an example such as this CES-D example, I highlight that there is a variety of nonnormal distributional forms that may be present in scores (total, subscale, and item-level), even within just one questionnaire. There are many other examples that we can deploy in our teaching.

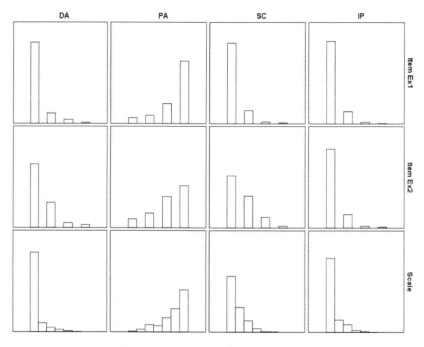

Figure 7.4 Histograms for 2 example items and subscale scores for each of the 4 scales on the CES-D in the RDD MIDUS-2 dataset.

Research Questions Beyond the Mean

Typical introductory statistics texts have a large focus on examination of and comparisons of the means across groups. In the independent groups case, the typical reliance is on the assumption of normality of the variable of interest within each group. As is the case in the single group scenario, textbooks include statements regarding robustness to nonnormality when samples sizes for the groups are large; additionally, statements of robustness to heterogeneity of variances under equal sample sizes are also commonly included. Wilcox (2010) cites research, highlights these statements as "problematic" (2010, p. 9), and advocates for use of robust statistics. Whether problematic or not, the statements and robust data analytic strategies are primarily used to bypass examination of the tenability of the corresponding assumptions. I argue that although comparing location properly is important, the assessment of the "nuisance" assumptions should not be bypassed and is interesting.

As mentioned previously in the "Assumption Violations as Informative" section, treatment of findings of what would constitute "assumption violations" in a typical analysis of means framework, e.g., heteroscedasticity and nonnormality of conditional distributions, dissimilarity of distributional conditions, as informative has been incorporated in some research areas in psychology. The papers by Bryk and Raudenbush (1988) and Grissom (2000) are suggestive of dissimilarity in parameters other than the mean resultant from experimental manipulations as well as existing groups. Although the examination (and "explanation") of gender differences in ability testing has a contentious history, the chronological list of sample titles in Table 7.2 exemplifies research in which statistical findings of what would typically constitute "assumption violations" are considered informative.

In the following, I provide an overview of an example paper from the literature on sex differences in personality of the type that can serve as an exemplar in classroom discussions. This is followed by a set of scenarios I use in my teaching to draw attention to research questions about parameters other than the mean.

Table 7.2 Examples With Between-Group Differences in Variances or Shape as Informative

Year	Title	Authors
1992	Sex differences in variability in intellectual abilities: A new look at an old controversy	Feingold
1995	Sex differences in mental test scores, variability and numbers of high-scoring individuals	Hedges & Nowell
2006	Sex differences in variance of intelligence across childhood	Arden & Plomin
2011	Gender differences in variance and means on the Naglieri Nonverbal Ability Test: Data from the Philippines	Vista & Care
2016	Gender differences in variability and extreme scores in an international context	Baye & Moneur
2016	Sex differences in the right tail of cognitive abilities: An update and cross-cultural extension	Makel, et al.

The recent paper by Borkenau, McCrae, and Terracciano (2013) stands out in its examination of "Do Men Vary More Than Women in Personality: A Study of 51 Countries". It is noteworthy as a recent paper examining heteroscedasticity directly. In their introductory comments, the authors provide a review of the small but growing literature in personality research examining sex differences in variances. They describe one paper as finding greater variability in each of six examined samples in talkativeness (specifically on the index of estimated number of words uttered daily) in men than in women (even though the original authors had not found mean differences in talkativeness). A second cited paper was a meta-analysis examining impulsivity indices, which reported finding gender differences on variances on only one facet of a sensation-seeking scale, specifically, that of disinhibition. Borkenau, McCrae, and Terracciano's own examination found greater variability in personality ratings of male targets than of female targets, greater variability among female raters than male raters, as well as between culture differences in variability. They described their findings in the context of cultural variation in societal norms, providing a clear discussion of what, in an analysis of means context, would have been "assumption violations" as "informative". Use of an exemplar paper such as this in classroom discussions illustrates that research questions of parameters other than the mean are being utilized in the discipline and how one might structure an explanation of findings.

Scenario Set: Illustrative Comparisons of Groups/Conditions on Varied Parameters

Many of the examples that I give in class are scenarios in which interventions are compared. *All of the following scenarios can be considered as between-group as well as within-group designs.* For each example scenario that follows, I provide a figure with a pair of graphical displays (note: in each example depicted, the intervention is "successful"). If the intervention study is considered to have been conducted using a randomized independent groups design, the graphical pairing represents the control group (on the left) and the "successful" intervention group (on the right); if considered as having been conducted using a repeated measures design, the graphical pairing represents the preintervention data (on the left) and the "successful" postintervention data (on the right). With these examples, my goal is to illustrate that research need not be just about location, it can be about other aspects of the distribution. If we highlight these kinds of examples to students and to our colleagues, and if we write about them in our textbooks, we can shift away from what is primarily central location, mean focused, pedagogy and analyses.

INTERVENTION DESIGNED TO CHANGE LOCATION AND SHAPE

Let us consider an intervention in which the goal is to reduce negative/destructive behaviors/ attitudes. Example 1 in Figure 7.5 provides the hypothetical histograms for engagement in negative/destructive behaviors without intervention (on the left) and with "successful" intervention (on the right). In this example, our "successful" intervention is changing more than just the central location (e.g., mean) of the distribution; we are changing the shape, if not also the variance. If this scenario were posed as a randomized study, the distribution for the control group would be framed as the histogram on the left, and the postintervention data of the intervention group would be framed as the histogram on the right. If this scenario was posed as a repeated measures within-subjects design, the left represents preintervention data, and the right represents those cases' postintervention data. Clearly if the variable of interest is occurrences of negative behaviors, perhaps self-harm, the goal of a successful intervention is for people to not be engaging in self-harm behaviors. Our ideal is that zero self-harm behaviors would be performed. Thus, in the minimum, we want a pattern similar to the one depicted on the right (actually, we would probably want a pattern more extreme than that).

Let us consider a different intervention in which the goal is to increase positive/constructive behaviors/attitudes or increase knowledge/skill. Let Example 2 in Figure 7.5 represent the hypothetical histograms for positive behaviors (e.g., skill) without intervention (on the left) and with

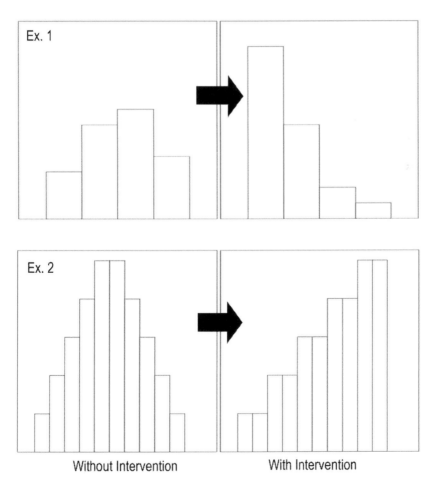

Figure 7.5 Histogram pairs for two examples of hypothetical between- or within-group scenarios for interventions designed to change location and shape.

"successful" intervention (on the right). In this scenario, I am imagining that we are starting with a somewhat normal, at least symmetric, distribution of skill in the control group (or preintervention). If the goal is to produce mastery of skill and if our intervention is somewhat "successful", we might easily have postintervention data that are negatively skewed distribution. As in Figure 7.5-Ex.1, if these data were from a randomized study, the control group data are illustrated on the left and the postintervention group data illustrated on the right. If this intervention study were conducted with a within-subjects design, the histogram on the left represents the preintervention data, and the right is the postintervention data of those cases.

INTERVENTION DESIGNED TO CHANGE VARIANCE

Let us consider an intervention that is intended to reduce variability, indeed to bring scores within an acceptable range. In this example, we are not interested in changing the mean, nor does our intervention change the mean. Imagine that people, on average, have acceptable blood pressure; however, we have some people who have low blood pressure and some whose blood pressure is far too high. We want an intervention that reduces the variability, i.e., we want to bring everybody's blood pressure into an acceptable range. Let Figure 7.6 illustrate the example for an imagined "successful" intervention, with the distribution of scores without intervention on the left and the distribution of scores with/after the "successful" intervention on the right. Again, as with the preceding graphical pairs, this figure can be considered in the context of a between-groups or a within-group design.

INTERVENTION DESIGNED TO CHANGE CORRELATION

Let us consider an intervention in which the goal is to "break" the association between variables. Let us consider a scenario in which without intervention, individuals who have low test anxiety

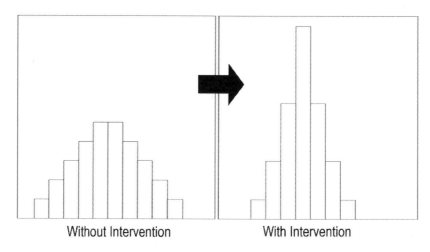

Without Intervention   With Intervention

Figure 7.6 Histogram pair for example hypothetical between- or within-group scenario for an intervention designed to change variance.

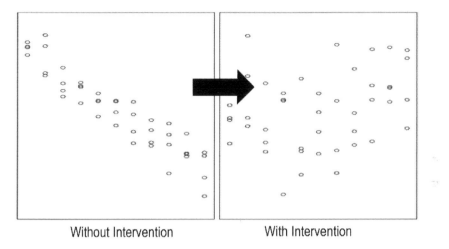

Figure 7.7 Histogram pair for example hypothetical between- or within-group scenario for an intervention designed to change correlation.

perform well on tests and those with high test anxiety have low levels of test performance. Perhaps we want to reduce (indeed eliminate) the association between test anxiety and test performance. The pair of scatterplots in Figure 7.7 depict the hypothetical control group or preintervention scatterplot on the left (negative linear association) and the hypothetical postintervention scatterplot on the right (no linear association) presuming an intervention that has achieved the goal. Again, as with the preceding graphical pairs, this figure can be considered in the context of a between-groups or a within-group design.

Conclusion: Closing Comments

Looking at "assumption violations" as interesting and informative involves looking "beyond the mean". Although they are often neglected or treated as annoying diagnostic strategies in articles, textbooks, and software programs, we have a variety of statistical data analytic strategies that we can use to look at parameters other than those of central location. We have viable techniques to examine distributional form (between and within groups), to assess homogeneity or heterogeneity of variances (between and within groups), and between and within-groups homogeneity and heterogeneity of covariance and correlation matrices. Importantly, we have techniques that are viable under different distributional conditions and sample sizes.

In this chapter, I have argued that "assumptions" need not be nuisances and indeed can be addressed as interesting research questions in and of themselves and have provided resources to advance a pedagogical shift. I illustrated that there is a wide variety of literature in which "assumption violations" are normative and are considered informative. I discussed the status of innovative textbooks and software as teaching resources. I provided multiple examples for expanded class-room teaching practices that include interesting research questions that promote thinking about distributional parameters in ways which are not typically addressed in most introductory statistics textbooks and courses in psychology.

To move our teaching of statistics and quantitative methods in psychology forward, we need to incorporate thinking about parameters other than those of location explicitly in our pedagogy. We need to place the teaching of strategies to assess these other parameters at a higher level of impor-tance. We need to provide students of all levels with corresponding resources that are readable and user friendly, to encourage use of these techniques that are not widely available, because ultimately until these techniques are made more obvious in their utility to their outcomes by addressing fun-damental research questions, they will continue to be seen merely as tedious diagnostic strategies to address assumption violations; and findings of assumption violations will continue to be seen as "nuisances" to be overcome. The increased awareness of robust data analytic strategies and incor-poration of these techniques in the literature, in textbooks, and in software is a clear improvement. However, I really do think we can do better. It is my hope that the variety of examples from the literature and exemplar scenarios considered in the current chapter will be inspiring and promote different ways of thinking and teaching.

References

Arden, R., & Plomin, R. (2006). Sex differences in variance of intelligence across childhood. *Personality and Individual Differences*, *41*, 39–48.

Arnau, J., Bendayan, R., Blanca, M. J., & Bono, R. (2012). Effect of the violation of normality and sphericity in the linear mixed model in split-plot designs [Article in Spanish]. *Psichotherma*, *24*, 449–454.

Arnau, J., Bendayan, R., Blanca, M. J., & Bono, R. (2013). The effect of skewness and kurtosis on the robustness of linear mixed model. *Behavioral Research Methods*, *45*, 873–879.

Arnau, J., Bendayan, R., Blanca, M. J., & Bono, R. (2014). Should we rely on the Kenward-Roger approximation when using linear mixed models if the groups have different distributions. *British Journal of Mathematical and Statistical Psychology*, *67*, 408–429.

Balota, D. L., & Yap, M. J. (2011). Moving beyond the mean in studies of mental chronometry: The power of response time distributional analysis. *Current Directions in Psychological Science*, *20*(3), 160–166.

Bathke, A. C., Schabenberger, O., Tobias, R. D., & Madden, L. V. (2009). Greenhouse-Geisser adjustment and the ANOVA-type statistic: Cousins or twins? *The American Statistician*, *63*, 239–246. https://doi.org/10.1198/tast. 2009.08187

Blanca, M. J., Arnau, J., López-Montiel, D., Bono, R., & Bendayan, R. (2013). Skewness and kurtosis in real data samples. *Methodology: European Journal of Research Methods for the Behavioral Sciences*, *9*, 78–84. http://doi.org/10.1027/1614-2241/a000057

Bono, R., Blanca, M. J., Arnau, J., & Gomez-Benito, J. (2017). Non-normal distributions commonly used in health, education, and social sciences: A systematic review. *Frontiers in Psychology*, *14*. https://doi.org/10.3389/fpsyg. 2017.01602.

Borkenau, P., McCrae, R. R., & Terracciano, A. (2013). Do men vary more than women in personality? A study in 51 cultures. *Journal of Research in Personality*, *47*, 135–144.

Bryk, A., & Raudenbush, S. (1988). Heterogeneity of variance in experimental studies: A challenge to conventional interpretations. *Psychological Bulletin*, *104*, 396–404.

Cain, M. K., Zhang, Z., & Yuan, K. H. (2017). Univariate and multivariate skewness and kurtosis for measuring nonnormality: Prevalence, influence and estimation. *Behavior Research Methods*, *49*, 1716–1735. https://doi.org/10.3758/s13428-016-0814-1

Erceg-Hurn, D. M., & Mirosevich, V. M. (2008). Modern robust statistical methods: An easy way to maximize the accuracy and power of your research. *American Psychologist*, *63*(7), 591–601.

Feingold, A. (1992). Sex differences in variability in intellectual abilities: A new look at an old controversy. *Review of Educational Research*, *62*, 61–84.

Fouladi, R. T. (2000). Performance of modified test statistics in covariance and correlation structure analysis under conditions of multivariate nonnormality. *Structural Equation Modeling*, *7*, 356–410. https://doi.org/10.1207/S15328007SEM0703_2

Fouladi, R. T., & Yockey, R. D. (2002). Type I error control of two-group multivariate tests on means under conditions of heterogeneous correlation structure and varied multivariate distributions. *Communications in Statistics—Simulation and Computation*, *31*, 375–400.

Greenhouse, S. W., & Geisser, S. (1959). On methods in the analysis of profile data. *Psychometrika*, *32*, 95–112.

Grissom, R. (2000). Heterogeneity of variance in clinical data. *Journal of Consulting and Clinical Psychology*, *68*(1), 155–165. http://doi.org/10.1037/0022-006X.68.1.155

Hedges, L. V., & Nowell, A. (1995). Sex differences in mental test scores, variability, and numbers of high-scoring individuals. *Science*, *269*, 41–45. http://doi.org/10.1126/science.7604277

Hohberg, M., Pütz, P., & Kneib, T. (2017). *Treatment effects beyond the mean: A practical guide using distributional regression*. Göttingen, Germany: University of Göttingen. Retrieved from www.uni-goettingen.de/de/20_Hohberg_10_2017/574017.html

Hopkins, K. D., & Glass, G. V. (1978). *Basic statistics for the behavioral sciences*. Englewood Cliffs, NJ: Prentice-Hall.

Jaccard, J., & Ackerman, L. (1985). Repeated measures analysis of means in clinical research. *Journal of Consulting and Clinical Psychology*, *53*, 426–428.

Jennings, J. R. (1987). Editorial policy on analyses of variance with repeated measures. *Psychophysiology*, *24*, 474–475.

Keselman, H. J., Huberty, C. J., Lix, L. M., Olejnik, S., Cribbie, R. A., Donahue, B., . . . Levin, J. R. (1998). Statistical practices of educational researchers: An analysis of their ANOVA, MANOVA, and ANCOVA analyses. *Review of Educational Research*, *68*, 350–386.

Luck, S. J. (2012). *An introduction to the event-related-potential technique* (2nd ed.). Cambridge, MA: MIT Press.

Makel, M. C., Wai, J., Peairs, K., & Putallaz, M. (2016). Sex differences in the right tail of cognitive abilities: An update and cross-cultural extension. *Intelligence*, *49*, 8–15.

Micceri, T. (1989). The unicorn, the normal curve, and other improbable creatures. *Psychological Bulletin*, *105*, 156–166.

Nunnally, J. C. (1978). *Psychometric theory* (2nd ed.). New York: McGraw-Hill.

Putnick, D. L., & Bornstein, M. H. (2016). Measurement invariance conventions and reporting: The state of the art and future directions for psychological research. *Developmental Review*, *41*, 71–90.

Radloff, L. S. (1977). The CES-D Scale: A self-report depression scale for research in the general population. *Applied Psychological Measurement*, *1*, 385–401. https://doi.org/10.1177/014662167700100306

Rosopa, P., Schaffer, M. M., & Schroeder, A. (2013). Managing heteroscedasticity in general linear models. *Psychological Methods*, *18*, 335–351.

Ruscio, J., & Roche, B. (2012). Variance heterogeneity in published psychological research. *Methodology*, *8*, 1–11. https://doi.org/10.1027/1614-2241/a000034

Ryff, C. D., Seeman, T., & Weinstein, M. (2010). *National survey of Midlife Development in the United States (MIDUS II): Biomarker project, 2004–2009 (ICPSR29282-v6)*. Ann Arbor, MI: Interuniversity Consortium for Political and Social Research [Distributor]. http://doi.org/10.3886/ICPSR29282.v6

Thode Jr., H. C. (2002). *Testing for normality*. New York: Marcel Dekker, Inc.

Vista, A., & Care. E. (2011). Gender differences in variance and means on the Naglieri Non-Verbal Ability Test: Data from the Philippines. *British Journal of Educational Psychology*, *81*, 292–308. https://doi.org/10.1348/000709910X514004

Whisman, M. A., & Judd, C. M. (2016). A cross-national analysis of measurement invariance of the Satisfaction with Life Scale. *Psychological Assessment, 28*, 239–244. http://doi.org/10.1037/pas0000181

Wilcox, R. R. (1987). *New statistical procedures for the social sciences: Modern solutions to basic problems.* Hillsdale, NJ: Lawrence Erlbaum Associates, Inc.

Wilcox, R. R. (2009). Comparing Pearson correlations: Dealing with heteroscedasticity and nonnormality. *Communications in Statistics—Theory and Methods, 38*, 2220–2234. https://doi.org/10.1080/03610910903289151

Wilcox, R. R. (2010). *Fundamentals of modern statistical methods: Substantially improving power and accuracy* (2nd ed.). New York: Springer, Inc.

Wilcox, R. R. (2017a). *Introduction to robust estimation and hypothesis testing* (4th ed.). London, UK: Academic Press/Elsevier Inc.

Wilcox, R. R. (2017b). *Modern statistics for the social and behavioral sciences: A practical introduction.* Baton Rouge, FL: CRC Press/Taylor & Francis Group.

Wilcox, R. R. (2017c). *Understanding and applying basic statistical methods using R.* Hoboken, NJ: Wiley Press.

Chapter 8

Teaching Introductory Statistics to Applied Researchers in the 21st Century

A Dialectic Examination

Joseph Lee Rodgers

This chapter is about the curriculum in introductory statistics courses. Though treating the curriculum might at first introduction appear dull and mundane, it most certainly is not. A teaching revolution is upon us, one that has the potential to radically and fundamentally change statistics pedagogy, to move it "forward into the future."

I begin the introduction to this chapter with three simple and straightforward statements about typical textbooks, syllabi, and the field of statistics in relation to both the undergraduate and graduate level (with emphasis on the former). First, most introductory textbooks and syllabi have hardly changed in the past 50 years (perhaps longer). Second, during the time that the textbooks and syllabi have been remarkably stable, the field of statistics, and more broadly of quantitative methods, has undergone a remarkable transformation. Most of the important advanced courses into which introductory statistics courses naturally flow were not even in existence 50 years ago. Examples include structural equation modeling (SEM), multilevel modeling (MLM), categorical data analysis methods, and hazards modeling, among many others. Third, there is not even an inkling of these more advanced methods that shows up in the standard introductory teaching curriculum used in 2018, when this chapter is being written.

The revolution in statistical and mathematical modeling referred to is underway (see Rodgers, 2010a, for documentation and discussion). The goal in this chapter is not to create the revolution, or even to provide much stimulation; that has and will occur completely separately from publication of this chapter. Rather, the goal is to suggest some orienting strategies to help manage the revolution in relation to statistical pedagogy. The past strategy—to ignore the revolution and continue teaching using a "business as usual" approach—is no longer viable. The goal of developing orienting strategies will be introduced by creating several "dialectic challenges."

Dialectics involves discussing the truth of an opinion. It is a concept drawn from the field of philosophy that focuses on debate and dialog; it emphasizes discussion and evaluation of opposing ideas (see the writing of Hegel and Fichte, in particular, for the original stimulation of the dialectic challenge). A dialectic dialog involves stating a thesis, a basic position; an antithesis, a conflicting position; and a synthesis, a summary or resolution emerging from careful examination of the conflicting opinions. Several dialectical challenges associated with statistical pedagogy will be presented and examined, and in each case, a conclusion will be offered by the author. Obviously, in each case, other legitimate interpretations exist as well.

I note an apt analogy, one that may strike statisticians/methodologists as especially germane to the current discussion. In the context of a null hypothesis significance testing (NHST) setting, one could easily view the null hypothesis as having similar status to the thesis of a dialectic argument. The alternative hypothesis is a natural antithesis to the null hypothesis. And the result of a statistical analysis placing these mutually exclusive hypotheses in competition could be viewed as the synthesis. In other words, NHST is already a natural setting for dialectic examination.

The chapter will begin with documentation of the problem referred to earlier; the (lack of) growth, change, and development in the introductory statistics curriculum will be described, and a few important efforts to effect change will be noted and reviewed. Then two broad dialectic challenges will be presented, discussed, debated, evaluated, and acted upon. These actions will stimulate the next section, in which several proposed revisions in the "standard approach" to teaching statistics will be presented and illustrated, with reference to the author's efforts to apply them in his own teaching. Those include new and modern approaches to teaching sampling distributions; to teaching about degrees of freedom; and to teaching about test statistics (especially the F statistic) in an NHST paradigm. Finally, in conclusion, a last dialectic challenge will be presented, discussed, debated, evaluated, and synthesized.

The Problem: Stasis in Teaching Introductory Statistics

A careful inspection of introductory statistics textbooks (e.g., at major conferences such as American Psychological Association or American Educational Research Association) shows substantial similarity among the major textbooks on the market. That is not so surprising because of the market value of an excellent statistics textbook, and (thus) the safety of relying on the "standard dogma" in developing a statistics textbook. What is a bit more surprising, given the potential for gradual change/evolution in such textbooks, is that the typical standard introductory text is very similar to ones used in the 1970s. There exists an apparent formula for producing a table of contents (TOC) that includes two major sections, descriptive statistics and inferential statistics (with slight variations on those names). Within the first are chapters on research design; measurement; graphical methods; basic descriptive statistics; estimation; and regression and correlation. Within the second are chapters on probability; sampling distributions; general issues in hypothesis testing; z-tests and t-tests; simple ANOVA; and higher-way ANOVA. Of course, most texts slightly adjust this basic formula and often claim innovation. Some expand on graphical procedures. Some include interesting and varied data examples. Some include counting techniques (permutations and combinations) in the section on probability, and some do not. Some treat measurement level in the introductory material, and some do not. The important point to emphasize is that at the broad level, this TOC formula has been virtually unchanged for 50 years. The author of this chapter taught introductory statistics for the first time in 1980; the textbook (McCall, 1970) was only slightly different in organization compared to the one used during the fall 2018 semester (in 2018, more than 38 years later, by Moore, Notz, & Fligner, 2017; note the 47-year gap in copyrights).

The modern textbook is much richer in data examples and rather broader in treatment of graphical methods. But the TOC is surprisingly similar. Further, there is no treatment in my current textbook—written by a former president of the American Statistical Association—of the new/modern methods noted earlier.

Excellent reasons exist to explain this stasis. First, the topics in the formula TOC described are the basic core topics that any introductory statistics course necessarily needs to cover. They feed into the next set of statistics and quantitative methods courses. Without facility/basic understanding of estimation, sampling distributions, and the basic approaches to hypothesis testing, students will flounder in following courses or will be judged not competent in relation to the basic starting material. Second, at an economic level, authors and book publishers make a great deal of money from selling introductory statistics textbooks; using the formula is safe, and if a competent book is written and effectively marketed, then positive sales are highly likely. Third, the formula TOC described obviously "works"; in other words, there has apparently been little call from teachers of introductory statistics to adjust this 50-year-old formula.

One of the few slightly consistent changes from 1970 textbooks to 2018 textbooks occurs in the domain of graphical presentations. For example, most textbooks now include treatment of graphical displays such as stem-and-leaf diagrams and boxplots, reflecting the exploratory data analysis (EDA) paradigm shift successfully promoted by John Tukey (1977). But Tukey's effort was to introduce a whole new way of thinking about statistics (including but certainly not limited to emphasis on graphical methods); to follow Tukey's advice, textbooks would be fairly radically different now from those used in the 1970s. In August 2018, the author of this chapter inspected around 20 modern introductory undergraduate statistics texts at exhibits at APA. However, only two included either "Tukey" or "exploratory data analysis" in the index (though treatment of the stem-and-leaf diagram and boxplot, typically without reference to Tukey, was virtually universal). It appears that the standard formula was able to absorb some new graphical methods but stopped short of implementing anything more innovative or radical (or modern).

Having discussed the remarkable 50+-year stability of the organizational structure of the textbooks used in psychological (and other applied) statistics courses, I note that innovation does exist (though it is often difficult to find in statistics textbooks at APA). The introductory chapter and other chapters in this volume include treatment of several efforts to improve pedagogy in introductory statistics courses. In the next sections, I will examine the different sides of issues related to pedagogy in introductory statistics courses, and I will propose some apparent and obvious (though not universal) opinions about where we should go from here.

Dialectic Challenge #1

The first dialectic challenge is the root challenge, the question of whether introductory statistics teaching should have changed in the past and whether it should change in the future.

Thesis: The reason that there has been so little change in the TOCs of statistics textbooks over the past 50 years is that the foundational material itself hasn't changed and doesn't need to change.

This position proposes that the (lack of) development, transition, and evolution in the material covered in introductory statistics courses is logical, sensible, and the natural result of thoughtful and even planned (lack of) development by teachers and textbooks authors. This position is entirely defensible! The core topics described in the earlier paragraph—estimation, sampling distributions, ANOVA, and regression—have themselves changed relatively little during the past 50 years, at least at the basic introductory level. Even if the structure that sits on top of the foundation has become more technical and sophisticated, the foundation itself needs to remain on solid and stable ground. Thus, even if SEM and MLM now exist and didn't exist 50 years ago (at least not in their current form), that's of no relevance to the authors/teachers of introductory statistics material; a sampling distribution is still a sampling distribution, the significance level, α, is still α.

> Antithesis: The introductory material should be changing as the targets to which they are ultimately directed—the sophisticated extensions of those methods—develop and evolve.

This position proposes that the introduction should contextualize the target at which it is aimed. Even if sampling distributions still have the same definition as they did 50 years ago, the nature of a sampling distribution needs to be more flexible if it is to handle hypothesis testing and model comparisons that have become much more sophisticated. Further, it is a misnomer to claim that sampling distributions have and should always remain the same. Sampling distributions defined using the bootstrap, for example, which are based on resampling theory that creates empirical sampling distributions, are now powerful and broadly applied across statistics and applied research. Those are virtually never treated in introductory textbooks, though they are simple to teach and students enjoy learning about them; the author of this chapter has been teaching resampling theory in introductory statistics courses for more than 20 years, and it actually works. In other words, a sampling distribution is now substantially more than it was 50 years ago. The same is true of many foundational concepts. And finally, at the very least, we should have become more effective at teaching foundational material after doing it for 50 years; aren't there any new teaching approaches that should infuse our statistical pedagogy, based if for no other reason on our teaching experience and new teaching methods?

> Synthesis: Both of these positions have advocates, but only the latter provides stimulation for moving statistical pedagogy forward. The former is defensible but is also overly conservative and supports thoughtless and weak pedagogy.

It is likely obvious by now that the author believes—strongly, even at times passionately—in the antithetical position. I have occupied that position—often with frustration—for many years. I have waited for years for the first wave of modern textbooks to be published. Judd and McClelland (1989) did contribute a modern textbook and deserve credit for both their innovation and their courage. Maxwell and Delaney (2004) and Cohen, Cohen, West, and Aiken (2003) wrote two others, though hardly at the introductory level. What is out there in the world of textbooks is hardly a new wave, hardly even a trickle in 2018.

As noted, only the thesis of the dialectic argument is represented strongly in the world of introductory textbooks. That is the momentum position, and both inertia and financial incentives will continue to carry that until teachers of statistics actively intervene and say, "enough is enough." But we need reasons and approaches to support doing that.

Dialectic Challenge #2

The second dialectic challenge emerges naturally from the first. If the standard traditional teaching model will continue until there is substantial effort otherwise, then it falls to those (like myself and others) who believe that it is past time to develop a new pedagogical model (or several new submodels). The second dialectic challenge assumes the author's answer to the first challenge, that new curricula, new approaches, and new textbook TOC organizational structures are past due.

> Thesis: If the basic pedagogical model to teach introductory statistics should change, it should change at the level of the details.

This starting point in the dialectic challenge suggests that the way teaching and textbooks have changed is the way they should have changed. There have been changes at the detail level, including the development of new graphical methods (stimulated by but seldom attributed to Tukey's 1977 book). Slight shifts in how power is treated, and the substitution of p-values for critical values, represent two other subtle shifts that can be found in modern textbooks.

> Antithesis: If the basic pedagogical model to teach introductory statistics should change, it should be developed as a fundamental and philosophical shift in how statistics is taught.

This antithetical argument involves a complete reframing of how the field of statistics is taught. There are different versions for how this reframing could be developed, though the author will propose pieces of a perspective that emerge from recent writing (by himself and others). The reframing—which will be developed in more detail in the next section—involves three steps. First, null hypothesis significance testing (NHST) should be moved into the background rather than occupying the central epistemological status within the framework of hypothesis testing. A de-emphasis on NHST is certainly not new, in fact, it is a very old argument; it is the starting point for the current argument. Second, what should be used to replace NHST is an orientation toward statistical and mathematical modeling. That orientation has surely existed for some time but has not occupied primacy within either teaching or research practice. Finally, the third pillar in this reframing is the argument that statisticians have for much too long taught statistics as though it is a computational, procedurally driven enterprise. Most students in introductory statistics courses—especially those heading for research careers—are neither as computationally oriented (or talented) as the statisticians/methodologists who teach their courses. Requiring students to learn how to compute within and between sums-of-squares to computationally define the F-ratio is a striking example (among many others). Rather, future researchers should be learning how to define and develop models—statistical or mathematical models—to explain and predict real-world phenomena. It is notable, even critical, that NHST does not in any sense disappear within this framework; in fact, it is still an important component. But it moves from being the orienting principle to being a part of the framework.

> Synthesis: Although the details are important, they cannot carry curricular change. Only a broad and overall philosophical reorganization of the introductory statistics curriculum will be sufficient to provide pedagogical reform that will actually make a difference.

Any statistics teacher or scholar who believes—as the current author does—that the maturity of psychology as a science can support the development of models of psychological/behavioral phenomena will recognize the value of moving statistical pedagogy in a new and modern direction. Currently, NHST focuses on the null hypothesis; it is either rejected or not rejected. Ironically, the researcher's hypothesis, the alternative, is not acted upon within the current framework. From a model comparison perspective, each model has status and is in competition to explain empirical data. That simple statement motivates the value of the antithetical position, which moves into the synthesis. It is a true synthesis, however, because NHST maintains its role as an important element of this framework.

Three Examples to Help Fuel the Pedagogical Revolution (There Are Others!)

In this section, I will consistently use the first person to facilitate a description of three specific teaching approaches – innovations – that I have used in my own introductory statistics classes that are consistent with the synthesis statements given. Those three teaching approaches include treatment of degrees of freedom, teaching sampling distributions using resampling theory, and teaching ANOVA as a model-comparison approach. These particular examples I chose for several reasons. First, none have any status in existing introductory textbooks. Second, I have been using these in my own introductory statistics classrooms (obviously without text support) for many years, in some cases for 20 to 30 years. Third, these methods are characteristically *non-procedural* and rather are oriented toward student understanding. Fourth, these methods are focused on students in introductory statistics courses as *future researchers* rather than as future statisticians. Fifth, these methods much more naturally lead into more sophisticated courses in quantitative methods devoted to structural equation modeling, multilevel modeling, hazards modeling, etc.

Teaching Degrees of Freedom as a Measure of Statistical Capital

It is possible that the important (critical!) concept of degrees of freedom is the worst-taught core concept in statistics. It may be the worst-taught core concept in any STEM discipline. Whole encyclopedic textbooks never define degrees of freedom (e.g., Statistics, 1988, by William Hays). I've collected several dozen quotes from textbook authors explaining how difficult it is to teach this concept and thus why they are avoiding deep explanatory treatment (see Rodgers, 2019).

At its mathematical level, degrees of freedom is indeed difficult to understand. Degrees of freedom is the rank of a quadratic form, the dimensionality of a constrained data space, or the result of applying a set of formulas to specific research design settings, each of which adjusts the overall sample size by a count of the number of estimated independent parameters. Each of these perspectives is either mathematically or computationally challenging (even for sophisticated statisticians, including many/most introductory textbook authors).

Degrees of freedom is also a concept often linked to the complexity of a model as a measure of parsimony. This conceptualization is more pedagogically natural. If models are defined appropriately (e.g., the mean is a model in the same sense as the regression equation or the linear ANOVA model), then degrees of freedom have a beautiful interpretation that introductory statistics students can easily understand and quickly master.

Degrees of freedom is a count of the flow of statistical money into and out of a conceptual statistical bank. Degrees of freedom corresponds to the numbers on a statistical balance sheet. When data are collected, each data point is deposited into a statistical bank, and each data point represents one piece of "statistical money." (Some teachers/researchers refer to each data point as a "bit of information," although technically a bit refers to a "binary digit.") Degrees of freedom provides the summary of how many pieces of "statistical money" there are in the bank. It literally and simply counts the number of data points that have been collected, and then tracks their status as the data points (statistical money) are used up in the conduct of statistical analysis. If the heights of 83 students are obtained, there are 83 degrees of freedom in the bank at this point. The statistician/researcher can "spend" the statistical money in the bank to "buy" valuable statistical commodities. These commodities are generally "estimated parameters;" the sample statistics are used to estimate the value of population parameters, which, when combined, provide predictions that are obtained from a statistical model. To estimate a model requires statistical money. How much do we have? Consult the degrees of freedom. How much did the model cost? Count the number of independent parameters to be estimated within the model.

Every estimated independent parameter costs the same amount, a single degree of freedom (one unit of statistical money). Thus, to estimate a population mean from a sample mean involves withdrawing a single piece of statistical money, and the remaining degrees of freedom in the statistical bank (often referred to as "residual degrees of freedom") is $df = n - 1$. If instead we estimate a simple regression equation—requiring a slope and intercept estimate—that process involves withdrawing two pieces of statistical money, and the degrees of freedom remaining in the statistical bank are $df = n - 2$.

There are many nuances and expansions of this conceptualization (see Rodgers, 2019), but the basic idea—as described in the previous paragraph—is both simple and powerful. And of particular note, students handle this conceptualization easily. In fact, my teaching experience is that I cannot afford to make a big deal out of this "pedagogical innovation"; it appears too basic and straightforward to treat it as an innovation. Students have asked, "Why doesn't the textbook treat degrees of freedom in this way?" and I respond, "Maybe sometime soon it will."

Teaching Sampling Distributions Through Resampling Theory

If computers had existed in the early 20th century, the t- and F-distributions likely would have never been developed (see Rodgers & Beasley, 2013). Both Fisher and Gosset preferred empirical sampling distributions and used a great deal of their own time to experiment with drawing repeated samples of data written on slips of paper, drawn from a hat (Box, 1978). They developed the theoretical sampling distributions that we call the t- and F-distributions as expedient substitutes for their preferred empirical sampling distributions. These statements create obvious irony in relation to the remarkable reliance our research profession has on t-tests and the ANOVA, using the usual parametric tests developed by Gosset and Fisher. It is the opinion of the current author that they appreciated the empirical version of the sampling distributions because they were more conceptually useful and obvious and required fewer assumptions. Those simple statements are the basis for my own teaching of resampling theory—both as a method to generate a sampling distribution and to teach students what they are.

The distinction between the bootstrap and Fisher/Gosset's Permutation Test (also called the Randomization Test; see Edgington & Onghena, 2007) is unimportant to the current discussion, though I find that resampling using the Permutation Test in the context of the t-test the easiest to teach from a conceptual standpoint. The Permutation Test to generate the sampling distribution of the t-observed test statistic very sharply illustrates how the observed data behave under the null hypothesis. Specifically, in a two-group t-test setting, the line between the two groups is entirely arbitrary, given the null hypothesis. Under H_0, the scores are randomly sorted between the two groups. This simple illustration virtually forces the student to imagine a distribution of the potential values of t-observed scores that would be obtained by switching raw scores back-and-forth across the arbitrary line separating the groups.

I have also found that it is much easier to teach theoretical sampling distributions *after* treating empirical sampling distributions rather than the other way around. With reference to Fisher/Gosset, the instructor can simply state that those early statisticians wanted to develop the distribution empirically, but without sufficient computational resources, they were forced to develop algebraic, theoretical distributions that mimicked the empirical distributions under certain assumptions.

Typically, I present a simple example using five scores per group in a two-independent-t-test design. Students usually understand the two concepts—empirical and theoretical sampling distributions—easily and quickly. As a conclusion, I discuss some of the advances in resampling that computers have allowed, including various types of bootstrapping (which I describe as the Permutation Test, except sampling is done with replacement; see Rodgers, 1999). This presentation typically takes around 30 to 45 minutes of lecture time. I believe that this approach provides students understanding of sampling distributions more deeply for the rest of the semester.

Teaching ANOVA F-Tests Using a Model-Comparison Formula

Rodgers (2010a), among others, proposed that a modeling revolution has occurred, quietly and largely without high-level organizational effort or even very much documentation. The revolution that occurred in the "methodological trenches" reflects the substitution of a statistical/mathematical modeling paradigm for the old NHST paradigm. In a mature science that has enough of an empirical and theoretical basis to justify the development of models and the competition between models, this substitution is fully defensible. In many other settings, ones that are still relatively immature scientifically, the NHST paradigm might be preferable (see Robinson & Levin, 2010; Rodgers, 2010b).

Rodgers (2010a) proposed that teaching students statistics as a competition among scientific models—as a model comparison approach—has many advantages compared to the procedural and computational orientation of teaching through an NHST paradigm. These two paradigms could not be more dramatically and sharply illustrated than by considering Fisher's (1922) Analysis of Variance procedure, supported by the F-test (named after Fisher by Snedecor, 1934, who developed the actual F sampling distribution).

In the NHST approach, the observed F statistic is defined as the ratio of two mean squares (variance estimates), referred to as MS-between and MS-within. The denominator, MS-within, reflects only the overall residual (error) variance; the numerator, MS-between, reflects both the overall residual (error) variance and also variance due to treatment causing population differences among the groups. If the null hypothesis is true, then there is no treatment variance, and the numerator and denominator estimate two separate (statistically independent) versions of the same population parameter, error variance. If the alternative hypothesis is true, then additional variance inflates the numerator, and the null hypothesis is thus rejected for an F statistic larger than the critical value, cutting off alpha under the theoretical F sampling distribution. The description in this paragraph is fairly technical and fairly procedural. If the computational formulas were included as well, it would be clear that the NHST approach is also highly computational, involving computation of multiple types of sums-of-squares and degrees of freedom. To summarize, the test statistic in the NHST approach to ANOVA is:

$$F_{obs} = MS\ between\ /\ MS\ within \tag{1}$$

In the model-comparison approach, the observed F statistic is defined as three different components, which allow the researcher to choose among two competing (nested) linear models. In the numerator of the numerator is the difference in fit statistics between a full and reduced model (in which the reduced model is nested within the full model). The denominator of the numerator is the difference in residual degrees of freedom between the full and reduced model, a measure of how much more complex the full model is compared to the reduced model. These two measures are placed in ratio because of the natural tension within a statistical test between fit and parsimony. The important question in a model comparison is whether the larger full model fits enough better compared to a smaller reduced model to justify the additional complexity, or loss of parsimony, as indexed by the change in degrees of freedom. Finally, the denominator of the overall F statistic is used to scale the numerator and is simply the lack of fit of the larger model divided by the degrees of freedom of the larger model. If we use R^2 as a natural measure of fit and df to abbreviate the residual degrees of freedom, F as the subscript for the full model, and R as the subscript of the reduced model, then

$$F_{obs} = \frac{\left(R^2_F - R^2_R\right)/\left(df_R - df_F\right)}{\left(1 - R^2_F\right)/df_F} \tag{2}$$

When carefully explained, Equation 2 is one of the most elegant and valuable equations in the field of statistics. It is strikingly pedagogical in that it shows exactly how fit statistics behave in a model comparison perspective. The change in R^2s trade off against the change in dfs, reflecting the competition among fit and parsimony as the smaller model competes (with its advantage of parsimony) against the larger model (with its advantage of fitting empirical data).

Of critical importance is that Equations (1) and (2) are identical algebraically (Cramer, 1972). The NHST and the model comparison approaches are identical algebraically; they only differ conceptually. And, importantly, they differ substantially in how a statistics teacher must teach them. Equation (1) is taught as a primarily computational process, with some slight conceptualization like that mentioned related to treatment and error variance. Equation (2) is taught as a scientific exercise, supporting researchers to identify the "winner" of a model comparison competition to choose the model that best fits the empirical data. When embedded within an overall research epistemology, the model comparison approach reflects the process of model development, model competition, and replication.

Conclusion: The Final Dialectic Challenge #3

The thesis of the final dialectic challenge is the following:

> Thesis: If new innovations in teaching statistics were appropriate and necessary, they would already have been implemented by textbook writers and would have been more enthusiastically promoted by statistics teachers.

This position is the "natural evolution" position, suggesting that teachers and textbook writers will always be on the lookout for and will embrace good ideas and teaching innovations that should be implemented.

The antithesis is more pessimistic—even iconoclastic—about the role that textbook writers play in the development of pedagogical innovation and change:

> Antithesis: It is up to leaders in the field of statistics and quantitative methods to promote the value of teaching innovation. Textbook writers and publishers will not break out of their successful and financially lucrative formula until there is external stimulation and motivation from introductory statistics teachers to do so.

There are a number of reasons to expect textbook writers to maintain their standard TOC (as they have for 50 or more years, through several new generations of textbook authors). First, the formula works to sell books and obviously continues to work to sell books. Second, few of the introductory textbook authors are themselves practicing methodologists (many teach at small colleges and universities, and many were not formally trained in quantitative methods, i.e., their PhD focus was in social psychology, I/O psychology, educational psychology, etc.). As a result, it is likely that most are neither aware of nor especially interested in linking undergraduate teaching with more advanced graduate training related to SEM, MLM, hazards modeling, etc. Third, the original development of SEM occurred in the 1960s and later and MLM in the 1980s and later. Past textbook authors have successfully ignored such developments for several decades, and thus have little motivation to account for the ultimate role of methods within a researcher's portfolio of statistical tools at this late date.

> Synthesis: If statistical methods at the introductory level are to be shifted in the direction of modeling (and away from NHST as a foundational, epistemological framework), it is up to leaders of both teaching and practicing statistics to create appropriate channels to facilitate and stimulate that change. The field has already started doing so in certain ways and should become more aggressive and creative in doing so moving into the future.

Many believe that change in the pedagogical model used to teach introductory statistics is both necessary and imminent (and, of course, the motivational spirit of dialectic argumentation embraced in the current chapter also accommodates that some believe otherwise). However, given the arguments, I believe it is clear that change will not emerge from the professional textbook authors. Nor has the extremely wide community of statistics teachers come together to insist on the kind of change that I am promoting in this chapter.

Rather, there are leaders of statistics pedagogy who have been moving the field in the direction that I am promoting as well for many years. The early textbook by Judd and McClelland (1989), who are methodologists, was an early innovation, one that was recently rereleased in its second edition. The Guidelines for Assessment and Instruction in Statistics Education (GAISE College Report; see Wood, Mocko, Everson, Horton, & Velleman, 2018, for discussion), developed at multiple times by the American Statistical Association (see the introductory chapter in this book for details) also reflects the spirit of "change as motivated from the top, through organizational leadership." My direct and immediate interest in these issues emerged from a three-year leadership role as incoming president, president, and past president of the American Psychological Association's Division 5 (Quantitative and Qualitative Methodology). Of course, not incidental to my interest is my 38-year career teaching introductory statistics and methods courses at both the undergraduate and graduate levels.

To conclude, creating positive change is up to us. The "us" to whom I refer are the many scholars involved in the teaching and practice of statistics and quantitative methodology. Statistics pedagogy is not, in my opinion, broken at any deep and fundamental level. Rather, it is laconic, staid, moribund, and in rather immediate need of growth and stimulation. The ideas in this chapter—shared with many others—can help provide an exciting and stimulating future for introductory pedagogy in introductory statistics teaching.

To finally summarize: Introductory statistics teaching should focus on training students how to think about and build models in relation to the empirical world rather than to how to run computational procedures. Introductory statistics teaching should focus on training students to be researchers and to use statistics as the language of research rather than training them to write software to compute test statistics with the facility that quantitative methodologists have for those activities. Introductory statistics teaching should have at its basis the idea that researchers build models, that those models must be evaluated for their goodness of fit and their simplicity, and that statistical procedures should help define an appropriate trade-off of fit and parsimony to help them choose from among a set of plausible behavioral models.

References

Box, J. F. (1978). *R. A. Fisher: The life of a scientist*. New York: Wiley.

Cohen, J., Cohen, P, West, S. G., & Aiken, L. S. (2003). *Applied multiple regression / correlation analysis for the behavioral sciences* (3rd ed.). Mahwah, NJ: Lawrence Erlbaum Publishers, Inc.

Cramer, E. M. (1972). Significance tests and tests of models in multiple regression. *The American Statistician, 26*, 26–30.

Edgington, E., & Onghena, P. (2007). *Randomization tests*. New York: Chapman & Hall.

Fisher, R. A. (1922). Studies in crop variation. I. An examination of the yield of dressed grain from broadbalk. *Journal of Agricultural Science, 11*, 107–135.

Hays, W. L. (1988). *Statistics* (4th ed.). New York: Holt, Rinehart and Winston, Inc.

Judd, C. M., & McClelland, G. H. (1989). *Data analysis: A model-comparison approach*. San Diego, CA: Harcourt Brace Jovanovich.

Maxwell, S. E., & Delaney, H. D. (2004). *Designing experiments and analyzing data: A model comparison perspective* (2nd ed.). Mahwah, NJ: LEA.

McCall, R. B. (1970). *Fundamental statistics for Psychology*. New York: Harcourt, Brace, & World.

Moore, D. S., Notz, W. I., & Fligner, M. A. (2017). *The basic practice of statistics* (7th ed.). New York: W. H. Freeman.

Robinson, D. H., & Levin, J. R. (2010). The not-so-quiet revolution: Cautionary comments on the rejection of hypothesis testing in favor of a "causal" modeling alternative. *Journal of Modern Applied Statistical Methods, 9*, 332–339.

Rodgers, J. L. (1999). The bootstrap, the jackknife, and the randomization test: A sampling taxonomy. *Multivariate Behavioral Research, 34*, 441–456.

Rodgers, J. L. (2010a). The epistemology of mathematical and statistical modeling: A quiet methodological revolution. *American Psychologist, 65*, 1–12.

Rodgers, J. L. (2010b). Statistical and mathematical modeling versus NHST? There's no competition. *Journal of Modern and Applied Statistical Methods, 9*, 340–347.

Rodgers, J. L. (2019). Degrees of Freedom at the start of the second 100 years: A pedagogical treatise. *Advances in Methods and Practices in Psychological Sciences, 2*, 396–405.

Rodgers, J. L., & Beasley, W. H. (2013). Fisher, Gossett, and AHST: Bootstrapping multiple correlation alternative hypotheses. In M. Edwards & R. C. MacCallum (Eds.), *Current topics in the theory and application of latent variable models* (pp. 217–239). New York: Routledge.

Snedecor, G. W. (1934). *Calculation and interpretation of analysis of variance and covariance*. Ames, IA: Collegiate Press.

Tukey, J. W. (1977). *Exploratory data analysis*. Reading, MA: Addison-Wesley.

Wood, B. L., Mocko, M., Everson, M., Horton, N. J., & Velleman, P. (2018). Updated guidelines, updated curriculum: The GAISE College Report and introductory statistics for the modern student. *Chance, 31*, 53–59.

Modern Classroom Innovations in Teaching Statistics and Quantitative Methods

Chapter 9

Teaching Quantitative Skills Across the Psychology Curriculum

Charles S. Reichardt

Psychologists can limit the teaching of quantitative skills to courses in statistics and research methods. Or we can teach quantitative skills in a wide variety of substantive psychology courses at the same time we teach the substance of psychology. I show how to do the latter. I show how to teach students to perform and interpret statistical analyses that are relevant to the content of their substantive courses in psychology. In particular, I describe data sets and statistical analyses that can be used with courses in social psychology, clinical psychology, abnormal psychology, personality theory, substance abuse, developmental psychology, human sexuality, gender studies, psychology of religion, cross-cultural psychology, political psychology, and introductory psychology. The resources I describe allow us to teach quantitative literacy across the psychology curriculum using real, high-quality data and easy-to-use statistical software.

The statistical analyses I demonstrate are conducted using one of two statistical interfaces. The first is the Survey Documentation and Analysis (SDA) interface, which was developed by the Computer-assisted Survey Methods Program at the University of California at Berkeley. Students can log onto the SDA interface for free and perform statistical analyses online without downloading either data or statistical software. Hundreds of data sets have been coded so they can be analyzed using the SDA interface. I will show how easy it is to use the SDA interface and describe numerous data sets with which it can be used. The second interface is available at the World Values Survey (WVS) web site. Again, students log onto this interface for free and perform statistical analyses online without downloading either data or statistical software. However, the WVS interface can be used to analyze data only from the WVS. I'll explain how to use the WVS interface when I introduce data from the World Values Survey. But let me start with the more flexible and powerful SDA interface. I will introduce the SDA interface by showing how it can be used to analyze data from the General Social Survey. With the resources I describe, we no longer need to teach statistics using artificial data or complicated statistical software.

General Social Survey

The General Social Survey (GSS) contains results from representative samples of American adults collected almost every other year from 1972 to 2018. The GSS is supported by the National Science Foundation and conducted by the National Opinion Research Center (NORC) of the University of

Chicago. From 1972 to 1974, quota sampling was used to select the individuals in the GSS. Both quota and random sampling were used in 1975 and 1976. Starting in 1977, samples were selected at random. In the early years, about 1,500 people were interviewed in each wave of data collection. In recent years, the sample size has fluctuated between about 2,000 and 3,000 respondents per wave. Across all the years through 2016, the GSS contains data from 62,000 American adults. The data from 2018 became available in 2019.

The GSS contains responses on literally thousands of variables ranging from basic demographics (such as age and years of education) to controversial social attitudes (such as opinions about gun control and abortion). I will give more examples of the available variables as I proceed.

To analyze data from the GSS using the SDA interface, here is all you do:

1.   Log onto http://sda.berkeley.edu/archive.htm
2.   Click on General Social Survey (GSS) Cumulative Datafile 1972–2016

The SDA interface will then appear on your screen linked to the GSS data set. Enter a variable name in the entry for "Row" and click the "Run the Table" button to create a univariate frequency table. Or enter a variable name in the entry for "Row" and a different variable name in the entry for "Column" to create a bivariate frequency table. You can also enter a variable name in the entry for "Control" to create a trivariate frequency table. And, among many other selections, the "Question Text" option provides the text of the question that was asked for each variable. (The SDA interface has been updated over the years, but the general format is likely to stay the same.)

Here is an example of a bivariate frequency table created using SDA and the GSS data. The variable named "EARTHSUN" reports respondents' answers to the question: "Does the earth go around the sun, or does the sun go around the earth?" (Responses to the "EARTHSUN" variable were collected only on waves from 2006 to 2016. Not all variables are collected at every wave.) The "DEGREE" variable asks respondents to report the highest educational degree they have obtained. (Responses to the "DEGREE" variable were collected at each wave of the GSS.) A cross-tabulation of these two variables (summed across years) produces the results in Table 9.1. The last column in Table 9.1 reveals that, overall, 21% of respondents answered the "EARTHSUN" question incorrectly. These respondents believe the sun revolves around the earth. The first column in the table reveals that, for those with less than a high school education, 39% got the answer wrong. The results also show that, even among those with a graduate degree, 7% gave the wrong answer. Note that the sample sizes are reported as fractions because the results have been weighted to adjust for such things as the size of households, given that sampling was performed at the level of the household rather than the individual. But you can also produce results without weights if you desire. To simplify the results in Table 9.1, I also chose to report the percentages without decimal points. But you can report results with decimal values.

If you are interested, you can also use the SDA interface with the GSS data to determine the percentage of American adults who believe humans developed from earlier species of animals (the "EVOLVED" variable) and the percentage of American adults who believe astrology has scientific backing (the "ASTROSCI" variable). (Cross-tabulating these variables by "DEGREE" produces

Table 9.1 Cross-Tabulation of the Highest Educational Degree Obtained and Beliefs About Whether the Earth Revolves Around the Sun or the Sun Revolves Around the Earth

Frequency Distribution

Cells contain: —Column percent —Weighted N		*DEGREE*					
		0 *LT HIGH SCHOOL*	*1* *HIGH SCHOOL*	*2* *JUNIOR COLLEGE*	*3* *BACHELOR*	*4* *GRADUATE*	*ROW TOTAL*
EARTHSUN	1: Earth around sun	**61**	**77**	**79**	**89**	**93**	**79**
		573.3	2,821.3	483.7	1,245.4	689.0	5,812.7
	2: Sun around earth	**39**	**23**	**21**	**11**	**7**	**21**
		359.4	866.4	128.3	149.7	48.6	1,552.5
	COL TOTAL	*100*	*100*	*100*	*100*	*100*	*100*
		932.7	3,687.7	612.0	1,395.2	737.7	7,365.3

interesting results.) You can also ask a variety of other questions about scientific knowledge (Reichardt, 2016). (You can find the variable names for science questions by searching for "Sci Knowledge" using the SDA search function. You can also find names for GSS variables, grouped by substantive categories, using the web site https://gssdataexplorer.norc.org/variables/vfilter.) Students might also be interested to see how the distribution of educational degrees has changed over the years. If you enter the variables "DEGREE" and "YEAR," you will find that the percentage of Americans with less than high school educations has declined precipitously (from 39% in 1972 to 12% in 2016), while the percentage of Americans with graduate degrees has greatly increased (from 3% in 1972 to 10% in 2016). These results suggest that competition for high-paying jobs is much stiffer for current students than it was for their parents when they were the same age.

It is easy to recode data using the SDA interface. A frequency table with the variable "AGE" (which has values ranging from 18 to 89 and over), for example, would be unmanageable. But it is a simple matter to collapse the "AGE" variable into categories. Instead of entering "AGE" into the SDA interface, enter "AGE(c: 10, 20)," and the SDA interface will produce a table in which the variable "AGE" is collapsed into groups by decade starting with 20-year-olds. A similar recoding can be used with categorical data. For example, the variable "POLVIEWS" reports respondents' political views in seven categories ranging from "extremely liberal" to "extremely conservative." To recode the "POLVIEWS" variable into just the three categories of liberals, moderates, and conservatives, replace "POLVIEWS" with "POLVIEWS(r: 1–3 "Liberal"; 4 "Moderate"; 5–7 "Conservative")." You can use the "Select Filter(s)" option to select ranges of scores on variables (including filtering by "YEAR" to obtain results for specific time periods). Or you can enter a range of scores to be selected by adding the range after a variable's name. For example, if you want to examine only those between 20 and 29 years old, you could replace "AGE" with "AGE(20–29)." The SDA interface supplies easy-to-use help files to describe other options for recoding and entering variable names.

The SDA interface will easily produce tests of statistical significance and confidence intervals using one or two simple options. Indeed, the default option in cross-tabulations is to supply color codes for cells in the table to indicate which cells deviate statistically from the values in marginal distributions. I have found that even if students have taken required courses in statistics and research methods, they still need additional practice in performing and interpreting tests of statistical significance and confidence intervals. Students can easily obtain such practice with the SDA interface.

The SDA interface will also easily produce graphs of data. For example, you can have the SDA interface produce the line graph in Figure 9.1 by entering "FEPOL" as the row variable and "YEAR" as the column variable, then doing no more than selecting "Chart Options" and "Line Chart." The "FEPOL" variable asks respondents whether they agree or disagree with the statement: "Most men are better suited emotionally for politics than are most women." Notice how the percentages of those agreeing and disagreeing, as displayed in Figure 9.1, were the same in the mid-1970s but have diverged strongly since then so that, by 2016, the vast majority of respondents disagree with the statement. Creating and interpreting graphs are other important quantitative skills for students to practice.

The SDA interface can also calculate means of variables in addition to producing frequency tables. Figure 9.2 presents a plot of the mean years of education (the variable "EDUC") over time (the variable "YEAR") separately for whites and African Americans (the variable "RACE(1,2)"). Notice how whites have more education on average than African Americans at each year but that both races show steadily increasing trends in educational attainment over time, with the gap between whites and African Americans slowly decreasing from 1972 to 2016.

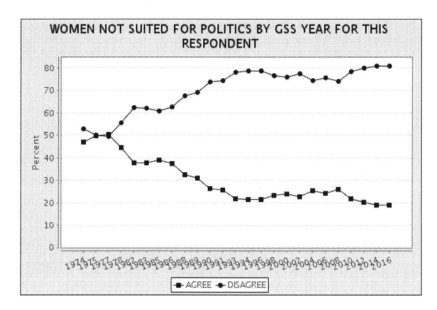

Figure 9.1 An SDA-interface figure plotting beliefs that women are not well suited for politics by year.

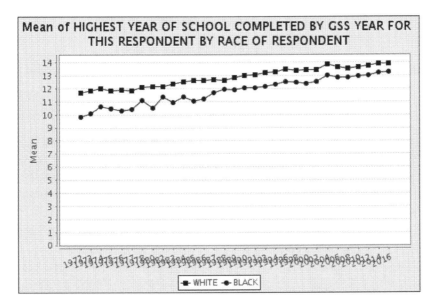

Figure 9.2 An SDA-interface figure plotting the mean years of education for whites and African Americans by year.

In addition to producing frequency tables and calculating means (as well as correlations), the SDA interface will also perform multiple regression. For example, the SDA interface will perform a multiple regression of the data in Figure 9.2 if you select the "Regression" option, then enter "EDUC" as the dependent variable and "YEAR," "RACE(1,2)," and "YEAR*RACE(1,2)" as independent variables. The results show that all three effects (year, race, and the interaction of year and race) are statistically significant. The slopes of the regression lines are .05 and .07 for whites and African Americans, respectively. This means that the mean years of education has increased, on average, by .5 and .7 years per decade for the two races. The SDA interface will also perform logit and probit analyses. And the SDA interface will let you easily download data on select variables along with command files that allow you to read the data into SAS, SPSS, or STATA should you prefer to use those statistical programs rather than the SDA interface.

World Values Survey

The WVS contains the results of nationally representative samples from a wide selection of countries from around the world. The WVS has collected data in six waves, starting with a first wave in 1981 to 1984 and ending with a sixth wave in 2010 to 2014 (N roughly $= 1,000$ to $4,000$ per country per wave). A seventh wave began in January 2017. Future waves are scheduled for every five years. The first wave of the WVS contained data from only 10 countries (including the U.S.). More recent waves have added nations for a total of 60 countries in the sixth wave. The data set contains answers from respondents on hundreds of variables. Questions asked on the surveys cover demographics as well as attitudes about a wide range of topics including religion, gender equality, and well-being.

The interface for analyzing the data at the WVS web site is not nearly as flexible as, and has many fewer options than, the SDA interface. But the WVS interface still allows users to create cross-tabulations of any variable with any other variable, including the variable of wave to reveal how responses change over time. You have to log onto the WVS web site at www.worldvaluessurvey. org/WVSOnline.jsp. At this web site, you select a wave of the WVS and the countries you want to examine. Then you select the survey question of interest, which can be accessed either from a complete list or by substantive categories. Clicking the "Show" button produces a univariate frequency table for the variable for each country selected. You can then create cross-tabulations with any other variable in the data set. By selecting the "Time Series" option, the WVS interface will create bivariate frequency tables by wave.

Other Data Sets

If the thousands of variables available in the GSS and the WVS are not adequate for your purposes, you can find hundreds of other data sets that can be analyzed using the SDA interface (though not using the WVS interface, which is restricted to the WVS data). The SDA archive at the http://sda. berkeley.edu/archive.htm web site contains a number of additional data sets. But the single largest source of data sets that are available for analysis with the SDA interface is the Inter-university Consortium for Political and Social Research (ICPSR) at the University of Michigan. Not all of the thousands of data sets maintained at the ICPSR are linked to the SDA interface, but hundreds are. (And those data sets that are not coded for analysis with the SDA interface can usually be downloaded in formats such as R, STATA, SPSS, and SAS.) The one drawback to using data from the ICPSR is that your institution must be a member of the organization to access some (but not all) of the data sets. But the ICPSR has 776 members, and it is possible your institution is already one of them. If not, your organization can join for a yearly fee.

The data sets (including the GSS data set) that are available from the ICPSR can be found at the following web site: www.icpsr.umich.edu/icpsrweb/ICPSR. (If you want you can click on "Lists of studies for which online analysis is available" and then search for data sets by name.) In what follows, I will mention a few of the SDA-linked data sets that are available for teaching both quantitative skills and substantive content in psychology courses, but there are many, many more data sets than the ones I mention.

Data Analysis in Courses in Social Psychology

Both the SDA and WVS interfaces can be used to teach quantitative skills while also teaching content in courses in social psychology. For example, prejudice is a classic topic in social psychology and can be addressed using the GSS data set with the SDA interface.

The GSS data set has numerous questions about prejudice against both women and African Americans. I have already mentioned the "FEPOL" variable, which asks whether most men are better suited emotionally for politics than are most women. Another variable (named "FEFAM") that assesses prejudice against women asks:

> "Please tell me whether you strongly agree, agree, disagree, or strongly disagree with. . . . It is much better for everyone involved if the man is the achiever outside the home and the woman takes care of the home and family."

Other variables in the GSS data set that assess prejudice against women include "FEPRES," "FEHOME," "FEWORK," and "FEHELP." One of the variables ("RACOPEN") that assesses prejudice against African Americans asks:

> "Suppose there is a community-wide vote on the general housing issue. There are two possible laws to vote on: a. One law says that a homeowner can decide for himself whom to sell his house to, even if he prefers not to sell to (negroes/blacks/African-Americans). b. The second law says that a homeowner cannot refuse to sell to someone because of their race or color. Which law would you vote for?"

Other variables in the GSS data set that assess prejudice against African Americans include "RAC-PUSH," "RACMAR," "RACSEG," "RACDIF2," and "RACDIF4."

You can use the GSS data set to investigate four theories of the causes of prejudice (against either women or African Americans). The first theory is that prejudice springs (at least in part) from an authoritarian personality. As Eliot Aronson (1984, p. 252) explained:

> Basically, authoritarian personalities have the following characteristics: They tend to be rigid in their beliefs; they tend to possess "conventional" values; they are intolerant of weakness (in themselves as well as in others); they tend to be highly punitive; they are suspicious; and they are respectful of authority to an unusual degree.

A number of variables in the GSS assess such authoritarian traits including the variables named "OBEY," "IFWRONG," "OBEYTHNK," "SPANKING," "TWOCLASS," and "PUNSIN." A second theory is that prejudice is caused by feelings of inferiority. Variables in the GSS that assess feelings of inferiority include "WRTHLESS," "WORKLIFE," and "FAMLIFE." A third theory is that prejudice is caused by economic competition for jobs. The variables named "JOBLOSE," "RDISCAFF," and "WORRYJOB" are relevant to worries about losing one's job. The fourth theory is that prejudice is due to displaced aggression, which has been called the scapegoat theory of prejudice. The variable named "HIT" is directly related to aggression.

If any of these theories correctly predict the causes of prejudice, cross-tabulations should reveal relationships between variables that represent prejudice and variables that assess the causes of prejudice. If the cross-tabulations show no such relationships between prejudicial attitudes and potential causes of prejudice, the theories of the causes of prejudice would be unsupported by the data. On the other hand, if the cross-tabulations show such relationships, the theories are supported by the data. For example, consider the cross-tabulation of the variables "FEPOL" and "OBEYTHNK".

The "OBEYTHNK" variables asks respondents which is more important for preparing children for life: "to be obedient or to think for themselves." Of those respondents who report being obedient is more important, 35% agree that "most men are better suited emotionally for politics than are most women." In contrast, of those respondents who report teaching children to think for themselves is more important, only 16% agree that "most men are better suited emotionally for politics than are most women." These differences are statistically significant and support the authoritarian theory of prejudice. Interestingly, the GSS data supports some of the four theories of prejudice more than it does others.

The WVS also has variables related to prejudice against women. For example, variable "V51" asks respondents if they believe men make better political leaders than women do. Other variables that tap into prejudice against women include variables "V45," "V52," and "V53." These variables can be used to explore cross-cultural differences in prejudice.

Data Analyses Relevant to Other Psychology Courses

The GSS and the WVS data sets can be used to study any number of other topics besides prejudice. In addition, there are a good number of data sets that can be analyzed with the SDA interface that are relevant to other psychology courses besides courses in social psychology. In this section, I consider nine other psychology courses.

Clinical Psychology and Abnormal Psychology

The GSS contains a number of items related to mental health that could be used in courses in clinical and abnormal psychology. For example, the GSS could be used to test two theories of depression (where depression can be assessed by the variable "SHAKEBLU"). The first theory is that learned helplessness is a contributing cause of depression. The hypothesis is that to the extent people believe they have little control over important outcomes in their lives, they will tend to feel depressed. Several variables in the GSS that concern a person's feelings of control over one's life are "BADBRKS," "LITCNTRL," "MOSTLUCK," and "NOPLAN." The second theory is that repressed anger is a contributing cause of depression. A GSS variable related to repressed anger asks respondents if they let people know when they are angry (variable "SHOWANGR"). Cross-tabulations reveal that only the theory of learned helplessness is well supported by the data.

Other data sets beside the GSS that are relevant to courses in clinical psychology, abnormal psychology, and mental health can be found at the ICPSR web site and assessed with the SDA interface. (Unless noted otherwise, the data sets described in the text are available at the ICPSR web site and linked to the SDA interface.) The National Comorbidity Survey (NCS) Series consists of four nationally representative samples of the U.S. population. Each used a structured psychiatric interview to assess the prevalence, risk factors, and consequences of mental disorders. The NCS Baseline study ($N = 8,000$) was conducted between 1990 and 1992. The NCS Reinterview study ($N = 5,000$) reinterviewed the baseline sample between 2001 and 2002. The NCS Replication study ($N = 7,000$) was conducted in 2001 to 2003 in conjunction with the Reinterview study.

The NCS Replication Adolescent Supplement study focused on adolescents and was conducted in 2001 to 2004 (but this data set is not linked to the SDA interface). The Collaborative Psychiatric Epidemiology Surveys are a compilation of three adult population surveys that also assess the distribution and correlates of mental disorders. The Collaborative Psychiatric Epidemiology Surveys merges the NCS Replication study with two other surveys that focus on minorities. Also consider the three waves of the Midlife in the United States Survey ($N = 7,100$) that were conducted from 1995 to 2013. These surveys assessed differences across the ages of 25 to 74 in both physical and mental health.

Personality Theory

In 2006, the GSS asked two questions for each of the big five personality traits ($N = 1500$, variables "BIG5A1" to "BIG5E2"). These items can be cross-tabulated with demographic and other characteristics. Such cross-tabulations could be put to use in a course on personality theory.

Substance Use

The GSS asks a few questions about drug use: for example, should marijuana be legalized ("GRASS") and do we spend too much money on drug addiction ("NATDRUG"). But several SDA-linked data sets available at ICPSR are far more relevant to courses dealing with substance use. The National Survey on Drug Use and Health (formerly called the National Household Survey on Drug Abuse) has been conducted most years from 1979 to 2014 ($N = 55,000$ in 2014 alone). The survey documents prevalence and correlates of drug use (and includes measures of mental disorder) for those aged 12 and over. The Treatment Episode Data Set is divided into two parts: admissions data and discharge data. Both contain national census data on characteristics of people admitted to and discharged from substance abuse treatment facilities. The admissions data extends from 1992 to 2012 ($N = 1,700,000$ in 2012). The discharge data extends from 2006 to 2011 ($N = 1,700,000$ in 2011). The Monitoring the Future surveys have been conducted yearly from 1975 to 2018. The surveys assess 12th-grade students and, starting in 1991, 8th-and 10th-grade students for a total, each year, of approximating 50,000 students (with about 1,400 variables). The data contain questions on drug use as well as "attitudes toward religion, changing roles for women, educational aspirations, self-esteem, exposure to drug education, and violence and crime (both in and out of school)," among other variables. An interesting exercise might be to compare results from across data sets, asking students why different data sets (with different wordings of questions) might yield somewhat different answers.

Developmental Psychology

Courses in developmental psychology could make use of a variety of data sets that are linked to the SDA interface at the ICPSR web site. The Early Head Start Research and Evaluation Study ($N = 3,000$) used an experimental design to assess the effects of the Early Head Start program on children from birth to elementary school (over the years 1996 to 2010) on cognitive, social-emotional and physical development. Also see the Head Start Impact Study 2002–2006. The National Center for Early Development and Learning Multistate Study of Pre-Kindergarten, 2001–2003 ($N = 1,000$) assessed prekindergarten programs in six states. The purpose of the study was to describe the early-educational experiences of children and assess relationships between those experiences and outcomes in later schooling. The Marital Instability Over the Life Course / Work and Family Life Study was a national longitudinal study comprising six waves of data from 1980 to 2000 on married couples from 18 to 55 years of age (Ns = hundreds to thousands). The purpose of the study was to "identify the causes of marital instability throughout the life course." The Longitudinal Study of Generations ran from 1971 to 2005 and examined intergenerational relationships and same stage-of-life comparisons across four generations ($N = 300$ in 1971). As mentioned before, the three waves of the Midlife in the United States Survey ($N = 7,100$) assessed differences across the ages of 25 to 74 in both physical and mental health, as well as on a range of other variables. These data could well support comparisons of longitudinal versus cross-sectional analyses.

Human Sexuality

The GSS data set contains a wealth of information about sexual practices and attitudes that could be examined in courses on human sexuality. Questions asked about sexual practices include questions about sexual frequency ("SEXFREQ"), marital infidelity ("EVSTRAY"), condom use ("CONDUM"), pick up sex ("PIKUPSEX"), and the sex of one's sexual partners ("SEXSEX"). Questions concerning attitudes about sexual practices include questions about homosexual relationships ("HOMOSEX") and premarital sex ("PREMARSX"). Changes in sexual behaviors and attitudes could be assessed over time, and questions about sex could also be cross-tabulated with other variables (such as sex, religion, and age) in the GSS data set. Here are two examples. Figures 9.3 and 9.4 present the results for attitudes about premarital sex and homosexual sex, respectively, cross-tabulated with year. The figures show that attitudes about the acceptability of premarital sex and homosexual sex have increased dramatically from the early 70s to 2016. The National Couple Survey ($N = 2,000$ individuals) was conducted in 2005 to 2006 and contains data on contraceptive decision-making by couples. The Social Justice Sexuality Project, 2010 National Survey contains a sample ($N = 5,000$) of LGBT people of color. The survey assesses a wide range of experiences in these populations and covers topics such as sexual orientation, gender identity, religion, mental health, and family dynamics.

Gender Studies

Both the GSS and the WVS include a variable for a respondent's sex (named "SEX" in the GSS and "V240" in the 2011–2014 wave in the WVS). Most other data sets described in this chapter also

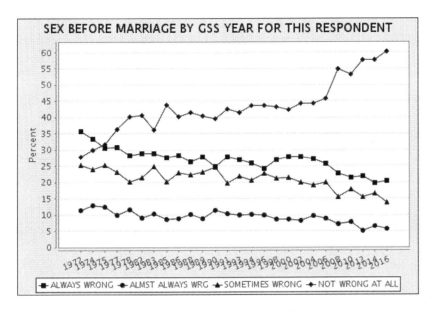

Figure 9.3 An SDA-interface figure plotting attitudes about premarital sex by year.

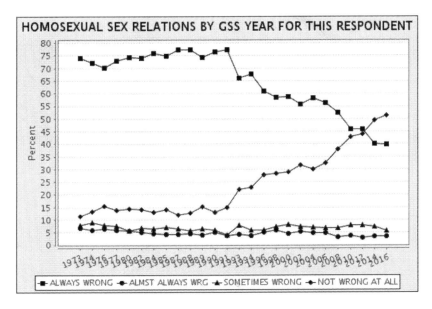

Figure 9.4 An SDA-interface figure plotting attitudes about homosexual relations by year.

contain a variable for respondent's sex. These sex variables can be cross-tabulated with any other variables in the data sets to explore gender differences in courses dealing with that topic.

Psychology of Religion

The GSS data set contains numerous items about religion that could be explored in a course on the psychology of religion. For example, there are questions that ask about the respondent's religious affiliation ("RELIG") as well as items about attendance at religious services ("ATTEND"), strength of religious beliefs ("RELITEN"), beliefs about the bible ("BIBLE"), and beliefs about God ("GOD"). Students could explore how responses to these items have varied over time as well as how items are related to the many background variables and attitudes assessed in the GSS. The WVS also contains a wealth of data on religious beliefs.

Reichardt and Saari (2015) and Reichardt (2018) present interesting results using questions about religion from the GSS.

Cross-Cultural Psychology

The WVS data set provides fertile ground for courses in cross-cultural psychology. I've already mentioned how prejudice against women can be explored cross-culturally using the WVS data set. The WVS data set contains both basic background demographics and hundreds of opinion items on which to compare nations both contemporaneously and over time.

Political Psychology

Courses in political psychology could make use of the American National Election Study ($N = 4,300$ for 2016), which is available in the archives at the SDA Berkeley web site and is described (at the ICPSR web site) thusly:

> The American National Election Study (ANES), begun in 1948, is the oldest continuous series of survey data investigating electoral behavior and attitudes in the United States. The focus of the survey includes voter perceptions of the major political parties, the candidates, national and international issues, and of the importance of the election. Also explored are voter expectations about the outcome of the election, degree of voter interest in politics, political affiliation and voting history, as well as participation in the electoral process. ANES interviews are conducted before and after presidential elections and after national congressional elections. Post-election interviews include questions on actual voting behavior and voter reflections about the election outcome.

Tests of Astrology

In this section, I show how to conduct tests of the validity of astrological predictions using the SDA interface and the GSS data set. Such investigations could be used to teach the process of theory testing with an example that is engaging to a general audience. Or such an investigation could be used to debunk the theory of astrology (Culver & Ianna, 1988; Hines, 2003). In either case, the investigations could be relevant to several different psychology courses. But perhaps such an investigation might be most welcome in a course in personality theory or introductory psychology.

An instructor can easily find predictions of astrologers that can be tested using the GSS data set. Or an instructor could consult Reichardt (2010), who provided a number of predictions. To test the predictions of astrology, an instructor cross-tabulates respondents' zodiac sign (variable "ZODIAC") with the GSS variables relevant to a given astrological prediction. Here is an example.

The web site www.astrology-online.com/persn.htm says people with different zodiac signs have traits that should be related to the likelihood they engage in marital infidelity. For example, those born under the sign of Aquarius are said to be "faithful to [their partners] for life" and those born under the sign of Pisces are "intensely loyal and home-loving and will remain faithful." In contrast, those born under the sign of Leo:

> may have numerous love affairs for their love of pleasure and beauty is liable to drive them from one attractive partner to another. They are very much inclined to deceive. Their marriages may fail for the same reason.

Note, too, that different signs are said to have traits that would lead to the prediction that those born under different signs should have different proclivities to be married.

The preceding astrological characterizations of individuals born under different signs can be assessed by cross-tabulating whether individuals have had extramarital affairs (the "EVSTRAY" variable) with zodiac sign. The results are presented in Table 9.2. Even though the results are highly stable because the sample size is huge ($N = 28,000$), none of the entries across the columns differ to any substantial degree. Nor are any of the entries statistically different from the entries in the marginal distribution. In particular, those born under the signs of Aquarius, Pisces, and Leo show no tendency out of the ordinary for having extra marital affairs. (Indeed, the trivial differences that exist in the table are in the opposite direction to what is predicted by astrology.) In addition, there are no substantial differences across the zodiac signs in the percentages of those who have never been married, contrary to predictions of astrology.

In looking for differences predicted by astrology, I have never found a cross-tabulation that supported the predictions to any substantive degree. You can find statistically significant differences because of large sample sizes, but the differences are substantively small and don't support the dramatic differences you would expect if the claims of astrologers are correct. The point is that if you want an interesting example with which to teach theory testing and, at the same time, debunk pseudoscience, the GSS data set with the SDA interface provides a powerful example using the variable of zodiac sign.

Table 9.2 Cross-Tabulation of Zodiac Sign and Whether the Respondent Has Had a Premarital Affair

Frequency Distribution

Cells contain:
—Column percent
—Weighted N

| | ZODIAC | | | | | | | | | | | | ROW TOTAL |
EVSTRAY	1 ARIES	2 TAURUS	3 GEMINI	4 CANCER	5 LEO	6 VIRGO	7 LIBRA	8 SCORPIO	9 SAGITTARIUS	10 CAPRICORN	11 AQUARIUS	12 PISCES	
1:YES	**12**	**12**	**12**	**13**	**12**	**13**	**11**	**12**	**13**	**12**	**13**	**13**	**12**
	278.8	172.7	280.5	316.5	310.9	329.2	285.2	265.8	282.4	275.8	314.0	306.9	3,518.7
2:NO	**63**	**63**	**64**	**62**	**62**	**61**	**64**	**63**	**62**	**64**	**61**	**63**	**63**
	1,431.5	1,423.1	1,547.2	1,548.4	1,569.3	1,539.3	1,613.0	1,389.7	1,376.5	1,418.7	1,420.5	1,455.4	17,732.5
3: NEVER MARRIED	**25**	**25**	**25**	**25**	**26**	**25**	**25**	**25**	**26**	**24**	**26**	**24**	**25**
	558.2	576.3	597.4	620.5	665.6	635.8	622.3	560.3	576.0	531.7	595.3	561.0	7,100.5
COL TOTAL	**100**	**100**	**100**	**100**	**100**	**100**	**100**	**100**	**100**	**100**	**100**	**100**	**100**
	2,268.5	2,272.1	2,425.0	2,485.4	2,545.9	2,504.2	2,520.5	2,215.8	2,234.9	2,226.3	2,329.8	2,323.3	28,351.7

Conclusions

There is a long-standing and widespread writing-across-the-curriculum movement (Bean, 2001) on college campuses across the U.S. The point of the movement is to teach writing in all courses and not just in courses that focus on writing (such as general education composition courses). A parallel quantitative-literacy-across-the-curriculum movement involving the teaching of quantitative skills is not as prevalent but should be. That is, quantitative skills should be taught in a variety of courses and not just in those focused on quantitative methods such as courses in statistics and research methods. Like writing, quantitative skills are too important to have their teaching relegated to just a few specialized courses.

I have explained how to teach one set of quantitative skills (statistical analyses) across the psychology curriculum. I have shown how to analyze hundreds of available data sets online without downloading either data or statistical software. The statistical analyses can be performed for free and are remarkably easy to conduct. The data come from high-quality surveys that have psychological content. This allows instructors to easily bring real data analysis into many, if not most, substantive courses in psychology.

The data sets and statistical interfaces I've described could also be used in courses in statistics and research methods. Students need not pay for expensive statistical software and need not spend their time learning complicated instructions for statistical analyses when they take courses in statistics or research methods. The data sets I have described come from real people, which offers many benefits compared to the simulated data so often used in courses and textbooks in statistics and research methods. Real data helps teach students both the joy and sorrows of conducting real research. And real data forces students to deal with the many idiosyncrasies of real research. For example, consider the variable "TVHOURS" in the GSS data set that asks respondents to report the average number of hours spent watching TV per day. A univariate frequency table reveals that the answer some respondents give is 24 hours, which begs for an alternative interpretation. Did the respondents mean how many hours the TV was turned on, whether or not it was being watched? Or did the respondents misinterpret the question to mean how many hours TV was watched per week? Or were the respondents simply being pernicious? In forcing us to ask such questions, real data teaches students some of the nuts and bolts of partaking in real science.

The samples sizes in the data sets I've described are generally quite large and contain results from a wealth of variables. These large Ns allow the instructor to add more and more variables to cross-tabulations (going from bivariate to trivariate to further multivariate frequency tables) without running into tiny cell sizes. The possibility of such detailed analysis allows, even encourages, both instructors and students to probe more deeply into the data. For example, instructors can entice students to wonder if results might differ for sex, race, or age—and then have the answer at one's fingertips. Are women just as prejudiced against women as are men? Are African Americans just as prejudiced against African Americans as are whites? Do either of those comparisons vary over time or by education, political beliefs, or religion? The large data sets that are available make such detailed analyses possible.

The data sets I've described are also sufficiently rich and of sufficiently high quality to support independent projects by students (both in and out of both substantive and methods classes) as well as original research by faculty members. Hundreds of academic publications have already been based on the GSS data set. I'm sure the other data sets I have mentioned have also supported numerous publications in peer-reviewed journals as well—and likely could support more.

The point is that we no longer need to teach statistics using artificial data sets and complicated statistical software nor restrict the teaching of quantitative methods to statistics classes. We can easily teach quantitative skills across the psychology curriculum using real, high-quality data. Real data are more interesting than artificial data. Analyzing real data can deepen students' understanding of substantive content in psychology courses and make classes in statistics and research methods more appealing. The statistical interfaces I've described make analyzing data easy. The real data sets I've described make statistical analyses engaging.

References

Aronson, E. (1984). *The social animal*. New York: Freeman.

Bean, J. C. (2001). *Engaging ideas: The professor's guide to integrating writing, critical thinking, and active learning in the classroom*. San Francisco, CA: Jossey-Bass.

Culver, R. B., & Ianna, P. A. (1988). *Astrology: True or false?: A scientific evaluation*. Buffalo, NY: Prometheus.

Hines, T. (2003). *Pseudoscience and the paranormal* (2nd ed.). Buffalo, NY: Prometheus.

Reichardt, C. S. (2010). Testing astrological predictions about sex, marriage, and selfishness. *Skeptic, 15*, 40–45.

Reichardt, C. S. (2016). Trends in scientific knowledge, education, and religion. *Skeptical Inquirer, 40*, 42–45.

Reichardt, C. S. (2018). Never doubting God: What surveys on belief in God's existence reveal. *Skeptic, 23*, 38–41.

Reichardt, C. S., & Saari, I. A. (2015). When don't the highly educated believe in evolution? The Bible-believer effect. *Skeptical Inquirer, 39*, 42–45.

## Chapter 10

The Eyes Have It

Emphasizing Data Visualization When Teaching Students Meeting a Quantitative Literacy Requirement

Robert Terry and Vincent T. Ybarra

"It isn't what we don't know that gives us trouble, it's what we know that ain't so."

—Will Rogers

Teaching an introductory statistics class to meet general education quantitative literacy requirements involves an everyday close encounter with the wisdom of Will Rogers. Quantitative (statistical) literacy, or numeracy, requires students to develop logical thinking skills and reasoning strategies to apply to everyday activities, leading eventually to increased skills in the domain of decision-making under uncertainty. Although most states now require quantitative literacy skills as part of their general mathematical standards for high schoolers, students in our introductory statistics classes perform quite poorly when pretested upon entering our classes. Using the Statistics Concept Inventory (Allen, Rhoads, Murphy, & Stone, 2004) as a pretest given to students on the first day of class to assess their level of statistical literacy, we consistently find that students on average score barely above chance (Allen, Rhoads, & Terry, 2006). Moreover, students are exceedingly overconfident in areas in which they are the least informed (Allen et al., 2006). This Dunning-Kruger effect (Kruger & Dunning, 1999) indicates a bias in which students of low levels of a relevant skill such as numeracy have illusory confidence in their understanding and mistakenly assess their statistical literacy as greater than it is. Will Rogers, meet Dunning and Kruger!

Yet the imperative to inculcate statistical reasoning in our students has never been greater given their constant exposure to information from a variety of sources, especially the Internet and social media. Making decisions using trustworthy evidence based on data in a time when choices are often overwhelming can be comforting as well as efficient. A course that focuses on statistical reasoning as applied to real-world (and relevant and interesting) problems, rather than a course that merely teaches the methods of statistics, seems timely for our technological age. In this chapter, we describe such a course as currently implemented with the overall goal of increasing the overall quantitative literacy (numeracy) of our students. The desired outcome is teaching students to be informed *consumers* rather than *producers* of statistical analyses.

A useful framework providing guiding principles for our course development is found in the Guidelines for Assessment and Instruction in Statistics Education (GAISE, 2016). Endorsed by the

American Statistical Association in July of 2016, the following six principles (with two instructor additions) serve as guideposts for our course (GAISE, 2016):

1. Teach statistical thinking
2. Focus on conceptual understanding
3. Integrate real data with a context and a purpose
4. Foster active learning
5. Use technology to explore concepts and analyze data
6. Use assessments to improve and evaluate learning.

Following these six principles, two additional goals are to teach statistics as *an investigative process of problem-solving and decision-making* while emphasizing the *central role of variability* in statistical literacy.

In this chapter, we show how the judicious use of data visualizations, collected from real-world case studies easily found via electronic media on the Internet, can be used to satisfy principles 1–4 as well as our two additional goals. The principal idea is to meet students where they currently are in their knowledge, using tools with which they are comfortable (e.g., Googling for information). Rarely will the student actually collect raw data to answer a question of real interest to them; most likely, they will use internet search engines for the answer. Finding trustworthy information and interpreting the data correctly while being aware of the limits of conclusions based on uncertain evidence obtained from samples with both known and unknown variability are the skills we wish our students to acquire in this introductory course.

The rest of this chapter is organized as follows. First, we briefly discuss competing views on data visualization held by computer scientists and statisticians. Next, we discuss some recent literature in graph literacy and why it is an important part of overall numeracy. Finally, we give multiple examples of how we integrate data visualizations throughout the course, through the units on sampling, measurement, design, descriptive statistics, regression, and finally probability and inference.

The Many Goals of Data Visualization

The data science revolution, founded by information (computer) scientists, has resulted in some conflict with data visualization purposes as typically considered by statisticians. Kosara (2007), writing from a computer/data science perspective, suggests three primary goals of the information visualization (InfoVis) revolution as currently practiced. InfoVis developers desire to provide insight into data in an aesthetically pleasing way, to democratize access to data by making it more accessible to nonprofessionals, and to make data analytics faster (e.g., interactive and dynamic). Meanwhile, Gelman and Unwin (2013) suggest that statisticians primarily use graphics to look for patterns and deviations, to effectively display variability, to aim for clarity and transparency, and to stay as close to the data as possible. It is not likely that these sometimes-conflicting goals— what is aesthetically pleasing may be chartjunk to others—will be resolved anytime soon. So, although these competing approaches may differ in these important respects, it does appear that data visualization has at least four common themes: to use visual graphics to tell a story, to communicate results effectively, to assist in evaluating claims, and to aid in decision-making. As part of meeting our GAISE objectives, we are closer in spirit to the Gelman et al. view while mostly emphasizing the commonality between the two views.

Graph Literacy

People who make skilled, informed decisions tend to show a higher prevalence in better economic and social life outcomes (e.g., health, wealth, and happiness; for a review, see *Skilled Decision Theory* by Cokely et al., 2017). This is especially seen with high-risk decisions, as skilled decision makers can evaluate and understand the communicated risks better (e.g., information about health, finance, natural hazards; RiskLiteracy.org) (Cokely, Galesic, Schulz, Ghazal, & Garcia-Retamero, 2012). Unfortunately, individuals with lower decision skills, including many at-risk individuals for poor health outcomes, routinely misinterpret well-intentioned risk communications such as graphical displays of the risk of having a heart attack. This can result in dangerous decision errors like ignoring the common signs of a heart attack (Petrova et al., 2017).

One inclusive way to mitigate these errors is by way of simple-to-understand, transparent, correctly made visual aids (again, such as the graphs seen in this paper; for a review of how to create visual aids, see Garcia-Retamero & Cokely, 2017). Improvements in decision-making tasks when presented with a visual aid can be seen in understanding the risks of medical, lifestyle, and screening treatments (Feldman-Stewart, Kocovski, McConnell, Brundage, & Mackillop, 2000; Paling, 2003; Waters, Weinstein, Colditz, & Emmons, 2007; Zikmund-Fisher, Fagerlin, & Ubel, 2008; Witteman et al., 2015). Further, individuals who understand and apply the graphs to their informed decisions will promote healthier behaviors as seen with the communication of sexual health to young adults (Garcia-Retamero & Cokely, 2011, 2014; Nelson, Hesse, & Croyle, 2009). But perhaps most important is that people tend to understand and recall information more easily if it is presented in a graphical form rather than in a strictly numerical one (Carpenter & Shah, 1998; Feldman-Stewart, Brundage, & Zotov, 2007; Goodyear-Smith et al., 2008; Gaissmaier et al., 2012; Zikmund-Fisher et al., 2014; Okan, Garcia-Retamero, Cokely, & Maldonado, 2015; Tufte, McKay, Christian, & Matey, 1998). One catch to using visual aids is that the benefits only come from having *the skill to understand the graph* (e.g., graph literacy; see Galesic & Garcia-Retamero, 2011 for more). It is estimated that approximately 15% of Americans cannot read the height of a bar chart. This is more than 40 million people (roughly the population of California for analogy). With the ubiquitous use of graphs in risk communication, education, finances, advertisement, and daily life, it makes sense that the training of graphical literacy should be incorporated into an introductory statistics class curriculum.

Some efforts outside academia have been made to help individuals understand graphs such as making the graphs dynamic or creating an online graph literacy trainer (Okan et al., 2015; Woller-Carter, 2015; Ybarra et al., 2017). Dynamic graphs with explanatory labels tended to help those with lower graph literacy, while reflective questions helped all individuals, perhaps due to incited deliberation. The two-hour online graph trainer by Ybarra et al. (2017) showed an improvement in graph literacy (measured pre- and posttest) with an effect size of $d = 1.10$. This is shown to be a most effective, validated graph literacy trainer. One reason for its success is that it breaks down the reading of graphs into the essential cognitive processes. Graphs are perceived in a stepwise fashion in that people first see the visual pattern (e.g., bars of a bar chart), judge the visual features in which the graphical shapes exist (e.g., position and size of the graph shapes, the axis, and the slope or angle of the shapes), and finally apply concepts to the chosen referents (e.g., how do the shapes of the graph compare? Such as judging two sloping lines in a line graph). With these cognitive processes an individual then may be able to make judgements beyond the data (see Figure 10.1). The cognitive processes also may explain how and why someone is tricked by poorly made graphs. For example, graphs leverage ecological heuristics (e.g., "higher equals more" or "steeper means faster"), so when a graph defies these inherent ideals, that person may be "tricked" into being incorrect.

A specific example of how graphs help mitigate making judgement errors from strictly numerical data can be seen in the Okan, Garcia-Retamero, Cokely, and Maldonado (2012) paper, which showed that icon arrays can help people judge medical treatments more proficiently and reduce denominator neglect. Denominator neglect is when an individual gives more attention to the numerator in ratios and incorrectly judges something as riskier (e.g., judging a cancer that kills 1,286 of 10,000 people riskier than a cancer that kills 24.14 of 100 people) (Reyna & Brainerd, 2008). Between-group differences in accuracy saw a 42% to 73% improvement in a denominator neglect problem. Further, in a separate study by Garcia-Retamero, Cokely, and Hoffrage (2015), graphs helped individuals calibrate their overconfidence in a diagnostic medical question. The interpretation of this result is that graphs not only help people understand the information but also help them deliberate upon important, risky decisions. In short, if an individual does not understand how to read a graph, they will be left vulnerable to decision error and overconfident that they made the correct decision. To gain a larger view and historical perspective on how humans use various cognitive processes when presented graphical displays, the interested reader is referred to Kosslyn (1985).

Examples of Graphs Used for Teaching Statistical Concepts

Using graphs to introduce problems while teaching students how to interpret and read graphs using real-world examples is one of the central ideas implemented in our current course offering. Recalling that our students had barely better than chance scores in preclass statistical literacy, offering statistical principles by introducing them graphically—and thus increasing their graph literacy—became the focus of our course.

In practice, in every example that follows, we begin classes with either a visual or a question followed by a visual. Then, while working in small groups, students construct a narrative around the graph, produce questions raised by the graph, and finally either evaluate a claim or state how they would use the information to make a decision. The instructor then spontaneously riffs off the student questions to introduce or reinforce course material. In my experience, it is not always possible to anticipate the direction students may go. A PowerPoint is developed around the graph with relevant material based on anticipating the kinds of questions students tend to ask, yet it is entirely possible the students may wander off into a different concept altogether. Additional exposition required is either done on a whiteboard by the instructor, or—depending on the question—given to the student for extra credit. The latter approach has the value of giving students the chance to find information for themselves and to come up with their own interpretation of statistical information.

Sampling and the 2016 Presidential Election

Nate Silver made his reputation by correctly predicting the 2008 U.S. presidential and Congressional races to a much greater degree of accuracy compared with the political pundits (Stein, 2009), followed by a highly successful encore performance in 2012. By aggregating polls (in a somewhat complex fashion), Silver took on the mantle of expert election prognosticator. In 2016, we had a chance to evaluate in real time his predictions and the aftermath of his actual performance while introducing the idea of sampling and uncertainty to our students. Figure 10.1 presents an adaptation of a graph of selected state-by-state forecasts the day before the election, with Silver predicting that the Republican candidate for president, Donald Trump, had a 29% chance of winning (FiveThirtyEight.com, 2016).

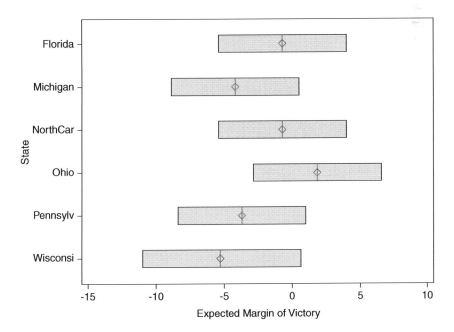

Figure 10.1 Selected state-by-state forecast 2016 presidential election.

Source: Adapted from https://projects.fivethirtyeight.com/2016-election-forecast/.

This graph shows the 80% confidence intervals for the 60 states with close races. Clearly, in these states, the races are so close that it shouldn't be a huge surprise if either candidate came out the victor. This visual can be used to explain the concepts of margin of error, sampling error, what uncertainty means, and why sometimes variability makes strong conclusions impossible. Students were wondering how this translates to a 71% chance of Hillary Clinton winning, and a small computer simulation showing how to combine these estimates with the standard error to get a distribution of electoral votes was presented. The class concluded by suggesting that students look at the early returns for Florida, Pennsylvania, and North Carolina. If all those close races broke for one candidate, it was a good omen for that candidate. Two days later, we had the actual results. Once the election results were in, we discussed, among other things, why it is important to take the margin of error and uncertainty seriously. Students were then given the opportunity to determine what a 29% chance of something happening means in the real world (i.e., among many things, it is the probability that a randomly chosen person over the age of 25 has a college degree). As Silver explains on his Website (FiveThirtyEight.com, 2016), if the sampling and predictive models are properly calibrated, the 29% candidate should win 29% of the time *in the long run*. Silver also mentioned the volatility of the 2016 polls compared to previous elections, the magnitude of undecided voters, and possible last-minute influences (e.g., the Comey effect) as increasing the uncertainty of the prediction. The goal of this visual presentation was to give students a better sense of the uncertainty in the 2016 election and to demonstrate that sometimes there just isn't enough data to reduce the uncertainty in the outcome to level of a high likelihood of having a successful prediction.

Measurement and the MPG Illusion

Fuel efficiency has been increasing in the U.S. vehicle fleet—yet not as fast as many have hoped. The question is how to persuade—or nudge—the U.S. vehicle-buying public into buying more fuel-efficient vehicles. Larrick and Soll (2008) suggested the problem was one of measurement—using miles per gallon (MPG) was misleading buyers as to the actual fuel savings to expect when comparing cars. They called this the MPG Illusion, and it can be demonstrated by the following question given to students:

Consider a decision between two cars—a current vehicle and a new vehicle that is more efficient. Which improvement will save the most gas over 10,000 miles?

A. An improvement from 10 to 11 MPG
B. An improvement from 16.5 to 20 MPG
C. An improvement from 33 to 50 MPG

If you give students just a few seconds to answer this question (in which they will use a heuristic and not do the actual math), nearly every student picks option C. Yet all save the same amount fuel (about 100 gallons). Although one could easily calculate the fuel savings for each option (divide

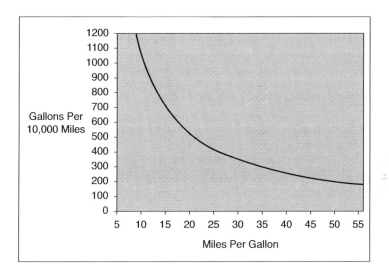

Figure 10.2 MPG illusion and diminishing returns in fuel usage.

Source: Taken from www.mpgillusion.com/p/what-is-mpg-illusion.html.

distance by mpg), why should consumers have to do this? Figure 10.2 shows graphically why one can't simply assume that *equal increases in MPG are equal in gas savings.*

The principle of diminishing returns shows that increases in MPG at higher levels does not translate in the same way as increases in MPG at lower levels. However, using gallons per 10,000 miles makes the comparison easy to do. This reflects a problem of the *construct validity* of measures of fuel efficiency—distance traveled per fuel unit does not meaningfully reflect fuel efficiency as well as fuel used per distance traveled. The MPG Illusion website (found at www.mpgillusion. com) explores the psychology of everyday energy decisions and how using better measures can nudge people toward making better decisions.

Meta-Analysis and the Food–Cancer Association

At the beginning of the semester, a small survey is given, and students' own perceptions of what statistics is about are gathered. A common answer is the Twain/Disraeli quote: "There are Lies, Damn lies, and Statistics." For a health-conscious person, the information overload in the media can be overwhelming and contradictory. Which foods are good/bad for you is a topic many students would like to discuss. Unfortunately, many students have the mindset of the one definitive study to settle the question once and for all. However, even the best of studies (and designs) show more variability from study to study than students imagine—and thus it could be argued that one shouldn't trust a single study. For example, Figure 10.3 shows the results of a meta-analysis of various food groups and risk of cancer (Carroll, 2015).

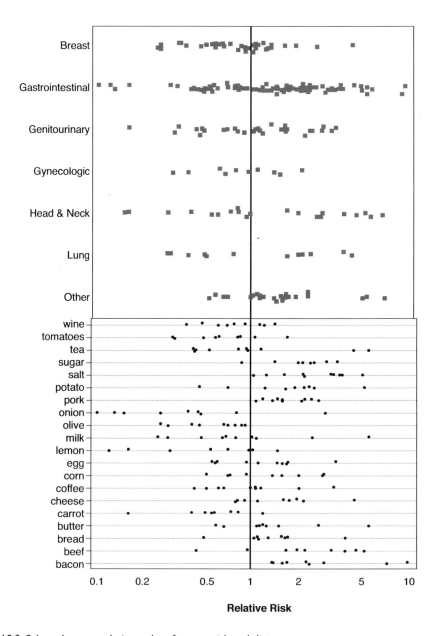

Figure 10.3 Selected meta-analysis results of cancer risk and diet.

Source: Taken from https://theincidentaleconomist.com/wordpress/theres-a-reason-i-use-systematic-reviews-and-meta-analyses/.

Carroll (2015) at the Incidental Economist Website (theincidentaleconomist.com) reports on a study by Schoenfeld and Ioannidis (2013) and suggests reasons we shouldn't believe that exciting new medical study. Once the concept of relative risk has been explained to the students, they mostly are concerned that depending upon which study they happen to read about, they could come to the wrong conclusion. One student could conclude that wine is good for you and another student the opposite. The idea that knowledge is cumulative and ongoing, especially in areas where strong designs are not possible, is difficult for students to grasp. The variation across studies is surprising to most students. They also ask why professors often present studies as if they are the final word. This is indeed an insightful and thought-provoking question, which creates opportunities for instructors to have a conversation on epistemology and the (current) limits of human understanding.

Descriptive Statistics and Survival Curves

Who wants to live forever? Well, maybe not forever, but most of us want to get as many years for ourselves as others do. In 1982, Stephen J. Gould was diagnosed with peritoneal mesothelioma and wrote an article about the experience titled "The Median Isn't the Message." Students are asked to read the article and comment on what his message is and what, if any, graphics could assist cancer patients in understanding a future prognosis. Gould (1985) was told there was a median survival time of 8 months but, recognizing that survival times are almost certainly skewed, focused on the variability of survival times and not the median. Many students focus on his positive attitude as being important and that maybe newer and better treatments extended the time—and few suggest much in the way of a graphic (Gould did not provide any visual information). After class discussion, a survival curve (a survival history of a cohort of patients from the time of diagnosis) is suggested. Figure 10.4 introduces the approximate current (as of 2012) survival curve for peritoneal mesothelioma using the data presented in Faig et al. (2015).

The survival curve for peritoneal mesothelioma suggests a median survival time of about 78 months—quite an extension from 1982. Also, the curve never reaches zero, such that about 43% of diagnosed cancer patients are still alive after 10 years from the time of diagnosis. This is good news, yes, but also is the time to introduce the concept of lead time bias. That is, earlier detection and diagnosis of peritoneal mesothelioma can lead to longer survival times independent of the effects of treatment. Also, many survival curves currently consider many other prognostic factors, such as staging, histology of the cell, age, and sex. Depending upon a person's profile on these moderating factors, a survival curve can vary quite a bit, which suggests to the instructor that this would be a good time to introduce the concept of moderating variables. Finally, many students wonder, all things being equal, where would a person fall on the curve? All things being equal, it is not possible to say, which leads to the final consideration. What, if any, role does sheer good fortune (luck) play in being a member of the 43%?

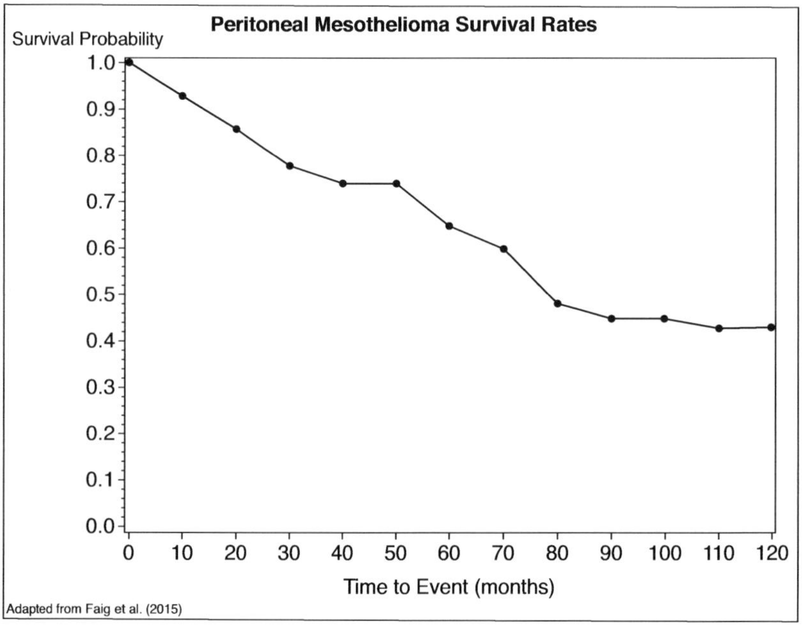

Figure 10.4 Survival curve for peritoneal mesothelioma as of 2012.

Source: Adapted from Faig et al. (2015).

Pie Charts and Health Care Use

Health care systems are a major concern for many of our students, who are health, biology, and psychology students. Comparisons of various health care systems is an exceedingly difficult task—and one we do not take up. Yet, anecdotally, many students express the belief in a preclass survey that many Canadians come to the U.S. for health care (average guess is about 10%) because their single-payer system can't see patients in a timely fashion. Fortunately, Aaron Carroll (2010), writing at the Incidental Economist Blog (found at theincidentaleconomist.com), using data reported by Katz, Cardiff, Pascali, Barer, and Evans (2002), constructed a pie chart representing the estimated proportion of Canadians seeking health care in the U.S. on a yearly basis. Although many statisticians have concluded that pie charts should rarely, if at all, be used because of decoding issues (Cleveland & McGill, 1984), this may be one of those few occasions when a pie chart is the appropriate visual display. Figure 10.5 shows the results.

Surprisingly, the only questions typically pertain to sampling and measurement issues, such as how a study could account for health care use due to the snowbird effect (i.e., Canadians wintering in Florida and Arizona). A more interesting question I pose to them for perspective is how many U.S. citizens either go abroad or get their drugs from other countries (e.g., India, Mexico, or Canada) as medical tourists? The answer is left to the interested reader.

Regression and Climate Change

Although man-made global warming is the current consensus among global warming scientists, one of the issues that students most want from the course is a discussion about the data and the statistics about climate change. Not being a climate scientist, the instructor wondered if there statistical issues that could serve to illuminate data analytic concepts? As it turns out, the so-called Global Warming Hiatus beginning in 1998 (through 2007) provides a wonderful opportunity to present both trend analysis via regression and, surprisingly, the ecological fallacy. Figures 10.6 and 10.7 are presented to the class for discussion.

How many Canadians use the US for health care each year?

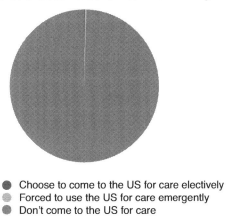

● Choose to come to the US for care electively
● Forced to use the US for care emergently
● Don't come to the US for care

Figure 10.5 Canadian use of U.S. health care.

Source: Taken from https://theincidentaleconomist.com/wordpress/phantoms-in-the-snow/.

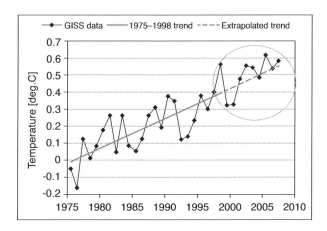

Figure 10.6 Global temperature 1975–2007.

Source: Taken from https://tamino.wordpress.com/2019/01/07/fooled-by-noise/.

Figure 10.6 (Tamino, 2019) shows the global temperatures plotted against year from 1975 through 2007. As Figure 10.6 shows, a regression line was fit through 1998, and then the line was extrapolated from 1998 to 2007. Visually, it certainly appears that the extrapolated regression line fits the data points well. However, if you fit a different regression line, one starting in 1998 through the year to 2007, you will find the line is nearly flat (this graph is regularly shown, but space prevents including it here). So is this indicative of a true change, or is this just a blip in the observed temperature sequence?

Figure 10.7 (Romm, 2012) shows a possible answer to this question. Was 1998 cherry-picked as the starting point, and if so, how can this create the illusion of a pause where there is none? A couple of simple questions can help students draw their own conclusion. If you start in either 1997 or 1999 (the years adjacent to 1998), it is easy to see visually that the trend line would still be positive (if the instructor wishes they could verify this with regression analyses beginning in 1997 and 1999). The goal here is to get students to comprehend why the years on either side matter that much unless 1998 was an outlier. Figure 10.7 shows how by picking your starting and ending points judiciously, you can have a trend line that is decreasing across overlapping intervals of the time period (see the blue lines), yet as indicated by the overall (red) trend line, the trend is actually increasing. This is the ecological fallacy or Simpson's paradox—and suggests we ought to use *all* the data we have when assessing trends. One question that astute students often raise is when we would know if a shift in the current rate of change takes place, the canary-in-the-coal mine

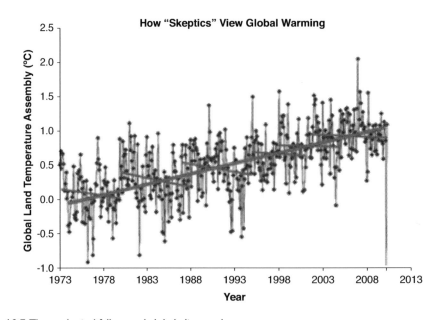

Figure 10.7 The ecological fallacy and global climate change.

Source: Adapted from https://thinkprogress.org/ten-charts-that-make-clear-the-planet-just-keeps-warming-ced872b4918c/.

question. If the instructor has the time, a brief foray into spline-fitting (Schuelke, Terry, & Day, 2013) can at least give the students an introduction to more complex model-fitting ideas.

Inference and Bayesian Thinking

In 2005, John Ioannadis published a paper titled, "Why Most Published Research Findings Are False." Although others working on similar problems had also noted this possibility, this particular paper got a lot of media attention and thus invoked what many have called the replication crisis, particularly in medicine and psychology (Pashler & Wagenmakers, 2012). What do statistics instructors tell our students? We've been telling them sweet little lies all along, and now how do we gently break the news to them?

Finding the Ioannidis (2005) article at much too high a level for our students, finding an easier way to visualize the problem was necessary, which depended minimally upon the usual suspects: alpha, power, the base rate of null hypotheses tested in the real world, and the publication significance filter, all run through a Bayesian filter. Fortunately, Alex Tabarrok in 2005 at the Marginal Revolution Blog (found at marginalrevolution.com) had already developed a simple visualization to convey Ioannidis's ideas. Figure 10.8 shows the visualization.

First, a word on notation. The symbol r here refers to the prior odds that a (null) hypothesis is true. In the situation shown here, the odds across all studies conducted are 1:4 that the null hypothesis is true (which translates into a probability of the null being true of 0.20). The tree then

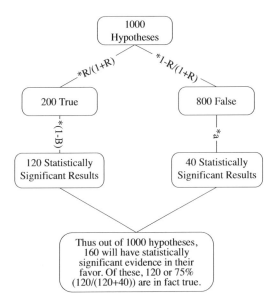

Figure 10.8 Bayesian tree analysis of hypothetical published literature.

Source: Taken from https://marginalrevolution.com/marginalrevolution/2005/09/why_most_publis.html.

presents a simulation of what one should expect in a literature given levels of r, alpha (α), power (1-β), and publication bias toward only significant results.

Start with conducting 1,000 studies, each testing 1 hypothesis. Assume a base rate of 200 of those testing true effects—leaving 800 null effects. Assume the publication significance filter—all statistically significant findings get published, and none of the null findings get published—is applied. With 60% power (quite generous and much higher than in the typical psychology or medical study), 120 "true" effects will get published. With alpha set at 5%, 40 null effects will sneak in. By Bayes logic, 25% of those published findings are false (not 5% as most older textbooks seem to imply). Students, once presented this information in this way, seem to understand the issue better than their pretest answers would indicate, although tying the individual study to the broader scale of an entire literature can be tough to comprehend. For the instructor, once the tree model is established, we can examine changing the prior odds, power, and alpha to different plausible values and see what effects present themselves. Finally, a case where we can use a single tree to see the forest! This discussion then integrates well with the meta-analysis idea introduced earlier of no single study being the definitive study. Further study as to how well students actually retain and act upon this important concept is needed.

Discussion

We began this chapter proposing to develop statistical literacy (numeracy) skills in our students by presenting real-world cases with accompanying data visualizations to better communicate the story. In today's media-intensive, visual world, excelling in the understanding of graphical information (i.e., developing graph literacy) is a skill we consider very useful.

By creating these interactive experiences with students using data visualizations as stimulus material, we hope to show students how statisticians think about problems while working through them in real time interactively with the students. Scores on the postclass SCI show considerable improvement over baseline scores, but without a suitable control group, it is difficult to make causal judgments about the efficacy of the teaching method.

To provide a context for the course, we also do other things more typical of an introductory statistics course. We teach basic ideas of sampling, measurement, and design, with a focus on how to produce (collect) good data. We teach the usual ideas of descriptive measures and show how to construct and evaluate 2 × 2 tables and scatterplots for correlation and regression. We ask students to be able to construct confidence intervals and test statistics to evaluate mean differences and relative risk. Students read and respond to a few target articles containing statistical information and find information themselves on the Web for a few assignments.

We do not emphasize formulas, and we do not ask students to do much in the way of constructing their own graphs using software. Constructing a line plot is much easier than understanding the nuances in evaluating trends, as our examples have shown. Moreover, I stopped doing this several years ago when one of my students enlightened me: "It's all on YouTube. Everything you spent time showing us how to do can be found on a YouTube video." Between "everything we need to find we can Google" and YouTube how-to videos, technology wins out in the end. Fortunately, we humans are still ahead in the reasoning domain.

As much as I am inspired to teach the course using readily available graphics found in numerous places on the Web, this course has a strong human capital investment component that is not for everybody . . . especially novice statistics instructors. As described earlier, this approach works best when the instructor and the students can interact and riff off each other, like a good jazz quartet. This requires the instructor to be comfortable with a variety of statistical practices and to have experience analyzing lots of data and more than passing understanding of the case studies that go along with the data visualizations. John Tukey once told a colleague, "The best thing about being a statistician is that you get to play in everyone's backyard" (Brillinger, 2002, p. 44). But to get to the backyard, you've got to first understand the neighborhood. We showed examples from political science, business, public health, medicine, climate change, health care systems, nutrition, and so on. There are many more examples (32 total for the typical semester-long class) that space prevents discussing. While you don't have to be an expert in any of these fields, you do have to put in the time to get up to speed on the relevant areas if you are to be successful in communicating with the students. The toll in human capital may be too much for novice instructors, who may be more comfortable teaching a step-by-step course.

There is and continues to be considerable disagreement among instructors as to what the purpose of the introductory course should be. The transformation of the course into one focused on statistical and graphical literacy is not for everyone, and it certainly has its detractors. We could not find a single psychology statistics textbook that fits with the overall goal of this course as we envision it. What will best serve your students is likely to vary across contexts. As Tukey also said, "The collective noun for a group of statisticians is a quarrel" (Brillinger, 2002, p. 44).

While the SCI is a generic measure of statistical literacy and has served our purposes for showing increases in statistical literacy in our courses, it cannot answer specific questions related to graphical literacy. It is important for the future to conduct strong, experimentally controlled studies using a measure specifically designed to assess the potential mediating role that graphical literacy may play in increasing statistical literacy.

Finally, the reason we do what we do is because of what we can learn and uncover using the concepts and principles of statistical thinking. To quote Phaedrus, "Things are not always what they seem; the first appearance deceives many; the intelligence of a few perceives what has been carefully hidden" (Plato, 1952). Statistical reasoning can help reveal what has been carefully hidden. We just need to communicate that to our students.

References

Allen, K., Rhoads, T. R., & Terry, R. (2006, October). Work in progress: Assessing student confidence of introductory statistics concepts. In *Proceedings: 36th Annual Conference – Frontiers in Education* (pp. 13–14). Piscataway, NJ: Institute of Electrical and Electronics Engineers (IEEE).

Allen, K., & Rhoads, T. R., Murphy, T., & Stone, A. (2004, June). The statistics concepts inventory: Developing a valid and reliable instrument. Paper presented at 2004 Annual Conference, Salt Lake City, Utah. https://peer.asee.org/13652

Berkson, J. (1942). Tests of significance considered as evidence. *Journal of the American Statistical Association*, *37*(219), 325–335.

Brillinger, D. R. (2002). John W. Tukey: His life and professional contributions. *The Annals of Statistics*, *30*(6), 1535–1575.

Carpenter, P. A., & Shah, P. (1998). A model of the perceptual and conceptual processes in graph comprehension. *Journal of Experimental Psychology: Applied, 4*(2), 75–100.

Carroll, A. (2010, October 11). *Phantoms in the snow*. Retrieved from https://theincidentaleconomist.com/wordpress/phantoms-in-the-snow/

Carroll, A. (2015, March 31). *There's a reason I use systematic reviews and meta-analyses*. Retrieved from https://theincidentaleconomist.com/wordpress/theres-a-reason-i-use-systematic-reviews-and-meta-analyses/

Cleveland, W. S., & McGill, R. (1984). Graphical perception: Theory, experimentation, and application to the development of graphical methods. *Journal of the American Statistical Association, 79*(387), 531–554.

Cokely, E. T., Feltz, A., Ghazal, S., Allan, J. N., Petrova, D., & Garcia-Retamero, R. (2017). Decision making skill: From intelligence to numeracy and expertise. In K. A. Ericsson, R. R. Hoffman, A. Kozbelt, & A. M. Williams (Eds.), *Cambridge handbook of expertise and expert performance* (2nd ed.). New York: Cambridge University Press.

Cokely, E. T., Galesic, M., Schulz, E., Ghazal, S., & Garcia-Retamero, R. (2012). Measuring risk literacy: The Berlin 3570 Numeracy Test. *Judgment and Decision Making, 7*(1), 25–47.

Faig, J., Howard, S., Levine, E. A., Casselman, G., Hesdorffer, M., & Ohar, J. A. (2015). Changing pattern in malignant mesothelioma survival. *Translational Oncology, 8*(1), 35–39.

Feldman-Stewart, D., Brundage, M. D., & Zotov, V. (2007). Further insight into the perception of quantitative information: Judgments of gist in treatment decisions. *Medical Decision Making, 27*, 34–43.

Feldman-Stewart, D., Kocovski, N., McConnell, B. A., Brundage, M. D., & Mackillop, W. J. (2000). Perception of quantitative information for treatment decisions. *Medical Decision Making, 20*, 228–238.

GAISE College Report ASA Revision Committee. (2016). *Guidelines for assessment and instruction in statistics education college report 2016*. Retrieved from www.amstat.org/education/gaise.

Gaissmaier, W., Wegwarth, O., Skopec, D., Müller, A., Broschinski, S., & Politi, M. C. (2012). Numbers can be worth a thousand pictures: Individual differences in understanding graphical and numerical representations of health-related information. *Health Psychology, 31*, 286–296.

Galesic, M., & Garcia-Retamero, R. (2011). Graph literacy: A cross-cultural comparison. *Medical Decision Making, 31*(3), 444–457.

Garcia-Retamero, R., & Cokely, E. T. (2011). Effective communication of risks to young adults: Using message framing and visual aids to increase condom use and STD screening. *Journal of Experimental Psychology: Applied, 17*(3), 270.

Garcia-Retamero, R., & Cokely, E. T. (2014). The influence of skills, message frame, and visual aids on prevention of sexually transmitted diseases. *Journal of Behavioral Decision Making, 27*(2), 179–189.

Garcia-Retamero, R., & Cokely, E. T. (2017). Designing visual aids that promote risk literacy: A systematic review of health research and evidence-based design heuristics. *Human Factors, 59*(4), 582–627.

Garcia-Retamero, R., Cokely, E. T., & Hoffrage, U. (2015). Visual aids improve diagnostic inferences and metacognitive judgment calibration. *Frontiers in Psychology, 6*, 932.

Gelman, A., & Unwin, A. (2013). Infovis and statistical graphics: Different goals, different looks. *Journal of Computational and Graphical Statistics, 22*(1), 2–28.

Goodyear-Smith, F., Arroll, B., Chan, L., Jackson, R., Wells, S., & Kenealy, T. (2008). Patients prefer pictures to numbers to express cardiovascular benefit from treatment. *Annals of Family Medicine, 6*, 213–217.

Gould, S. J. (1985). The median isn't the message. *Discover, 6*(6), 40–42.

Ioannidis, J. P. (2005). Why most published research findings are false. *PLoS Medicine, 2*(8), e124.

Katz, S. J., Cardiff, K., Pascali, M., Barer, M. L., & Evans, R. G. (2002). Phantoms in the snow: Canadians' use of health care services in the United States. *Health Affairs, 21*(3), 19–31.

Kosara, R. (2007, July). Visualization criticism-the missing link between information visualization and art. In *2007 11th international conference information visualization (IV'07)* (pp. 631–636). Piscataway, NJ: Institute of Electrical and Electronics Engineers (IEEE).

Kosslyn, S. M. (1985). Graphics and human information processing: A review of five books. *JASA, 80*, 499–512.

Kruger, J., & Dunning, D. (1999). Unskilled and unaware of it: How difficulties in recognizing one's own incompetence lead to inflated self-assessments. *Journal of Personality and Social Psychology, 77*(6), 1121.

Larrick, R. P., & Soll, J. B. (2008). The MPG illusion. *Science, 320*, 1593–1594.

MPG Illusion Website. (2008). Retrieved from www.mpgillusion.com/p/what-is-mpg-illusion.html.

Nelson, D. E., Hesse, B. W., & Croyle, R. T. (2009). *Making data talk: Communicating public health data to the public, policy makers, and the press.* Oxford: Oxford University Press.

Okan, Y., Garcia-Retamero, R., Cokely, E. T., & Maldonado, A. (2015). Improving risk understanding across ability levels: Encouraging active processing with dynamic icon arrays. *Journal of Experimental Psychology: Applied, 21*(2), 178.

Okan, Y., Garcia-Retamero, R., Cokely, E. T., & Maldonado, A. (2012). Individual differences in graph literacy: Overcoming denominator neglect in risk comprehension. *Journal of Behavioral Decision Making, 25*(4), 390–401.

Paling, J. (2003). Strategies to help patients understand risks. *BMJ, 327*, 745–748.

Pashler, H., & Wagenmakers, E. J. (2012). Editors' introduction to the special section on replicability in psychological science: A crisis of confidence? *Perspectives on Psychological Science, 7*(6), 528–530.

Petrova, D., Garcia-Retamero, R., Catena, A., Cokely, E. T., Heredia Carrasco, A., Arrebola Moreno, A., & Ramírez Hernández, J. A. (2017). Numeracy predicts risk of PreHospital decision delay: A retrospective study of acute coronary syndrome survival. *Annals of Behavioral Medicine, 51*(2), 292–306.

Plato. (1952). *Plato's Phaedrus.* Cambridge: Cambridge University Press.

Reyna, V. F., & Brainerd, C. J. (2008). Numeracy, ratio bias, and denominator neglect in judgments of risk and probability. *Learning and Individual Differences, 18*(1), 89–107.

Romm, J. (2012). *Ten charts that make clear the planet just keeps warming.* Retrieved from https://thinkprogress.org/ten-charts-that-make-clear-the-planet-just-keeps-warming-ced872b4918c/

Schoenfeld, J. D., & Ioannidis, J. P. (2013). Is everything we eat associated with cancer? A systematic cookbook review. *The American Journal of Clinical Nutrition, 97*(1), 127–134.

Schuelke, M. J., Terry, R., & Day, E. A. (2013). Growth spline modeling. In *Proceedings of the 2013 SAS Global Forum Conference.* Cary, NC: SAS Institute Inc.

Silver, N. (2016, November 8). *2016 election forecast.* [Web log post]. Retrieved November 8, 2016, from https://projects.fivethirtyeight.com/2016-election-forecast

Stein, J. (2009). The world's most influential people—The 2009 TIME 100. *TIME.* Retrieved May 8, 2009. http://content.time.com/time/specials/packages/0,28757,1894410,00.html

Tabarrok, A. (2005, September 2). *Why most published research findings are false.* Retrieved from https://marginalrevolution.com/?s=why+most+published+findings

Tamino. (2019, January 7). *Fooled by noise.* Retrieved from https://tamino.wordpress.com/2019/01/07/fooled-by-noise/.

Tufte, E. R., McKay, S. R., Christian, W., & Matey, J. R. (1998). Visual explanations: Images and quantities, evidence and narrative. *Computers in Physics, 12*(2), 146–148.

Waters, E. A., Weinstein, N. D., Colditz, G. A., & Emmons, K. M. (2007). Reducing aversion to side effects in preventive medical treatment decisions. *Journal of Experimental Psychology: Applied, 13*, 11–21.

Witteman, H. O., Chipenda Dansokho, S., Exe, N., Dupuis, A., Provencher, T., & Zikmund-Fisher, B. J. (2015). Risk communication, values clarification, and vaccination decisions. *Risk Analysis, 35*(10), 1801–1819.

Woller-Carter, M. (2015). *Development of the intelligent graphs for everyday risky decisions tutor.* Open Access Dissertation, Michigan Technological University. Retrieved from http://digitalcommons.mtu.edu/etdr/59/

Ybarra, V., Cokely, E. T., Adams, C., Woller-Carter, M., Allan, J., Feltz, A., & Garcia-Retamero, R. (2017). Training graph literacy: Developing the RiskLiteracy. org outreach platform. In G. Gunzelmann, A. Howes, T. Tenbrink, & E. J. Davelaar (Eds.), *Proceedings of the 39th annual conference of the Cognitive Science Society* (pp. 3566–3571). Austin, TX: Cognitive Science Society.

Zikmund-Fisher, B. J., Fagerlin, A., & Ubel, P. A. (2008). Improving understanding of adjuvant therapy options by using simpler risk graphics. *Cancer, 113*, 3382–3390.

Zikmund-Fisher, B. J., Witteman, H. O., Dickson, M., Fuhrel-Forbis, A., Kahn, V. C., Exe, N. L., . . . Fagerlin, A. (2014). Blocks, ovals, or people? icon type affects risk perceptions and recall of pictographs. *Medical Decision Making, 34*, 443–453.

Chapter 11

Low- and Medium-Tech Complements to High-Tech Tools for Teaching Statistics

The Case for Using Appropriate Technology to Implement Cognitive Principles for Teaching

David Rindskopf

Technical advances, especially in computing, have allowed us to do things we could not do before and to do other things better and faster than we could before. We have computer programs for matrix algebra, for finding derivatives and integrals, for function maximization and minimization, for simulations and sampling. We have programs for complex statistical methods and for plotting and graphics. We can typeset complicated equations and compile reference lists for easy insertion into articles in any reference style needed. Email, web sites, Facebook, and other communications programs make many tasks much simpler and less expensive than they used to be.

But just because you CAN do something doesn't mean that you should. When are such high-tech methods appropriate? They are appropriate when they simplify our lives and when they make us more efficient and when they are consistent with psychological principles of effective teaching and communication. On the other hand, high tech can lead instructors to do things they shouldn't, that detract from the learning process. I will describe how low and medium tech can be better than high tech for certain purposes, mostly by encouraging (or forcing) instructors to act in accordance with psychological principles for good learning.

To illustrate one of the advantages of low tech for some purposes, let me first describe one of the most advanced devices available, called the generic word processor, or GWP, introduced by Schrodt (1982). This unique device works as well today as when first introduced. The GWP will write in any font, in any alphabet (e.g., Sanskrit, Phoenician, Cyrillic), and in any font size from extremely small to extremely large. It can also easily be set to write at any orientation (degree of rotation), and will write backward as easily as forwards. As for graphics, it has unlimited capabilities to create any graphics required without complicated commands or settings. Equations are simple and are straightforward to produce in any size and location on the page. The usual facilities for deletion, insertion, and cut and paste are all available.

What is this incredible device? The No. 2 pencil. Who wouldn't rather use this to draw than any computer program? And who wouldn't rather write an equation using the GWP than use Equation Editor or any other system you know (though MathPad is coming close)? As an example, write the equation

$$y_{ij} = \beta_{0j} + \beta_{1j} X_{ij} + r_{ij}$$

first by hand with a GWP and then using any equation editing system; see how many times longer the editing system takes. And who has to read a 500-page manual to learn to use the GWP? When has one ever crashed, or needed an expensive service call? Of course, the article describing the GWP was (mostly) a joke, but it forced readers to think about the technology they were using.

I often use the GWP when I lecture, supplementing it with a device to project what I am writing on the screen. In even lower-tech days, this was known as a "chalk talk," in which the lecturer presented ideas one at a time by writing them on a blackboard. I draw pictures and graphs and develop formulas one step at a time. I believe it makes good psychological sense to build ideas from the ground up, much like a narrative develops. Later, I will illustrate the procedure I use in three different contexts. Before doing so, I will discuss some of the cognitive principles I believe are relevant to this style of teaching.

Cognitive Background for Low-Tech Teaching

Speed kills: Rushing through too much material, too fast, is dangerous. If you ever doubt this, remind yourself of how you felt listening to a conference presentation in which PowerPoint slides went rushing by with too many equations or plots. Admit it: You were lost, or at least struggling. And that's how students feel when we rush through equations too quickly, telling students "and it is easy to see that" and going to the next slide before their eyes have seen the equation, let alone waiting until their brains have processed it. Low tech can help prevent, or at least moderate, this tendency.

We learned from George Miller's (1956) "magical number seven" article that minds are limited in how many items of information they can process at one time. He said seven plus or minus two, and it might be even lower when learning a complex subject such as statistics. A second concept Miller discussed was chunking. As teachers, we have already formed higher-level units from the basic components, so we can take in more information at a time than the students. We see a regression equation, a multilevel model, or a structural equation model, and at a glance we understand it immediately, as one chunk, while students see it as many parts, which they need more time to process than we do.

We are often tempted to present an idea in its most general form, to show all that it can do, but in doing so, we often leave students' minds in a state of confusion. One of my professors, Lloyd Avant, used to say, "Now I'm going to lie to you a little." He meant that he was going to oversimplify an idea so that we wouldn't get overwhelmed by the details. Later on, after we mastered the basics, the details could be understood. (This is similar to Jerome Bruner's [1960] idea of a spiral curriculum.) How do we apply this to low-tech teaching of statistics? If we present a long, complicated equation, then students will be stumped. If we start with a simple equation and add a few items at a time, students can follow the development. In regression, we could start with simple standardized regression, which would emphasize the relationship between correlation and regression, and illustrate where regression got its name (regression to the mean). We could then proceed to simple linear regression, then regression with two predictors, and then many predictors. We could then do a t-test by using a dichotomous predictor, then extend the model to include a several-category predictor. Then we could combine continuous and categorical predictors. To us who know the general linear model, it seems as if we should just introduce the whole system right away, but students cannot possibly understand why we would want to do something so complicated. Developing the model a little at a time helps them realize why the general model is so useful: to combine seemingly separate methods (*t*-test, ANOVA, ANCOVA, regression) into one model.

The same process should be used in developing complicated plots or diagrams. The student does not need to see the whole diagram at once. Start from scratch and build in one part at a time. You can see why a publisher would not like this; rather than one picture, there are five or eight or some other number that drives their printing costs up. But in a classroom, you have no such limitation, either drawing on the board (which forces a step-by-step procedure) or using an overhead projector. It is always tempting to draw the final figure ahead of time and create a perfect drawing using a graphics program, but educational value is sacrificed (as well as the time you spend making it look perfect). To remind yourself of what is lost by having a complex final diagram only, think back to the days when you were learning geometry. So many diagrams are complex; often you don't know where to begin. If they built diagrams up gradually, much of the confusion would disappear.

In teaching, writing or drawing as you go forces you to limit the speed with which new ideas are presented. And you have to slow down enough that the students can actually read what you write. The old-fashioned "chalk talk" and its medium-tech equivalent, writing projected onto a screen by an electronic device, are natural ways to slow the presentation down to a rate that is comprehensible to students, and much less intimidating.

Another psychological principle that is aided (by modeling of behavior) concerns reception versus production. If you passively receive information, it is less likely to be retained than if you are actively involved in some way. As the old New York joke goes, a tourist asked a policeman, "How do you get to Carnegie Hall?" The reply: "Practice, practice, practice." How do we get our students to practice? We do it by modeling the behavior of writing equations and drawing diagrams. If you do it rather than present an already-full screen with all the equations, or all parts of a diagram, the students will be more likely to imitate you. They will notice what the Greek letters look like; where the subscripts go, and which terms have which subscripts; where there should be right angles in a diagram (and where there should not be). By writing equations and drawing diagrams slowly by hand, you enable the students to concentrate on one part of the equation or diagram at a time.

I will illustrate how I use these principles by showing three examples, involving regression, correlation, and multilevel models. Two of the examples are somewhat advanced; one (regression) requires ideas of vector spaces, and another (multilevel models) requires one to think about a group of regressions at the same time. The correlation example could be used with undergraduates and requires no special background. The ideas can be applied at any level, building up from the simplest representation and expanding the complexity a little bit at a time.

Example 1: Simplified Theory of Regression

Students have a difficult time visualizing the vector space representation of regression. I combine visualization with the concrete analogy of a railroad to explain the basic concepts. Figure 11.1 shows a vector that illustrates a person starting out on a trip home; she starts from the origin (O).

The desired journey straight home is the vector Y. But it's a long way home, so she takes the train, which runs along a straight set of tracks shown in the second diagram (Figure 11.2). The direction and unit of measurement along the tracks is X; she can go as far as she wants in this direction, and gets off after going a distance b in that direction, which we denote by bX. Where should she get off

Figure 11.1 Representation of a vector as a route on a trip home.

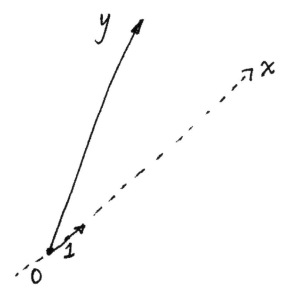

Figure 11.2 Railroad tracks as analogy to predictor variables X.

the train so that the distance remaining (the residual) is as small as possible? The diagram in Figure 11.3 suggests that she should go a distance such that the route home along the residual (e) is at right angles to the railroad tracks. How can we prove this? The fourth diagram, Figure 11.4, shows what happens if she gets out before reaching that point. The remaining distance is now the hypotenuse of a right triangle and therefore must be longer than either of the other two sides, proving

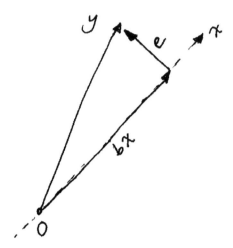

Figure 11.3 Distance travelled on railroad: *bX*. Remaining (residual) distance walked to home: e.

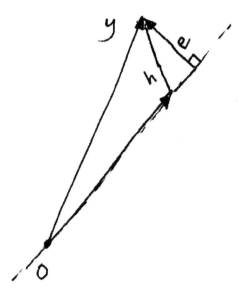

Figure 11.4 If e is orthogonal (at a right angle) to *bX*, it must be the shortest distance to home (*y*), because other places would result in a walk of distance *h*, the hypotenuse of a right triangle, which would be further.

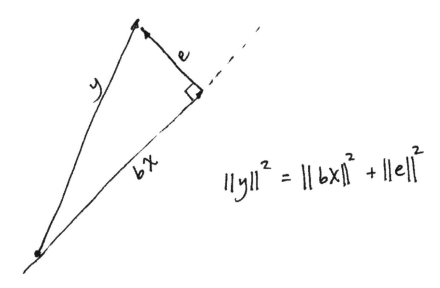

$$\|y\|^2 = \|bx\|^2 + \|e\|^2$$

Figure 11.5 The total sum of squares equals the regression sum of squares plus the residual sum of squares, by the Pythagorean Theorem. At this stage of instruction, we ignore the constant term (mean vector) to maintain simplicity.

that the right angle produces the shortest distance. (The same is obviously true if she goes beyond the right angle.) Pythagoras's Theorem (Figure 11.5) shows that the square of the distance to Y is the sum of the squares of the distance she travels on the railroad (the sum of squares accounted for) and the distance remaining (error sum of squares). We have not mentioned many details and have "lied a little" by omitting the fact that our origin is usually the vector whose elements are the mean of Y, but that is fine; the students have a basis from which to develop their understanding of the geometry of regression.

Example 2: Development of the Concept of Correlation

Most students are taught a formula for correlation without learning the conceptualization behind it. The series of steps needed to develop the concept can be illustrated in a series of drawings. Figure 11.6 shows three plots of points: The first one shows what we would like to call a positive association (points with low values of X generally have low values of Y, and points with high values of X generally have high values of Y). The second plot shows no association (points with low, medium, or high values of X could have any value on Y); the third plot shows a negative association. Our goal is to quantify these qualitative descriptions of relationships.

In Figure 11.7, we show the positive relationship with lines drawn at the middle of the X and Y values. These lines therefore divide points into those above and below the mean on X and Y. For a positive relationship, most points lie in either the upper-right or lower-left quadrant; for no

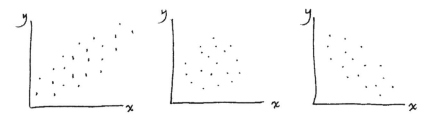

Figure 11.6 Three plots, illustrating positive, zero, and negative relationship.

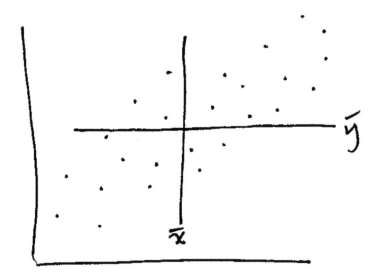

Figure 11.7 Points can be above or below the mean on *x* and *y*. This classifies them as "low" or "high" values.

relationship, they are spread equally over the four quadrants; and for a negative relationship, they are concentrated in the upper left and lower right quadrants.

In Figure 11.8, we calculate the deviation scores, $X - \overline{X}$ and $Y - \overline{Y}$. If a point has a value greater than the mean, the deviation score will be positive; if the point has a value less than the mean, the deviation score will be negative. I then ask the students to consider the product $(X - \overline{X})(Y - \overline{Y})$ for points in each quadrant. In Figure 11.9, we show the signs of the product for points in each quadrant; positive in the upper right and lower left, and negative in upper left and lower right. If we get the sum of these products, called the sum of cross products, we have a quantity that will be positive, zero, or negative for data that have what we want to call positive, zero, or negative association. The students are asked to consider if this is what we need to describe the strength of an association. The next steps, not illustrated here, consider what would happen if the number of

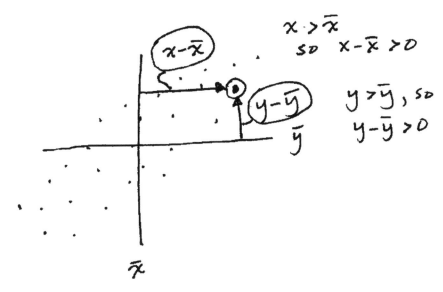

Figure 11.8 The signs of $X - \bar{X}$ and $Y - \bar{Y}$ as a function of whether points are low (below the mean) or high (above the mean).

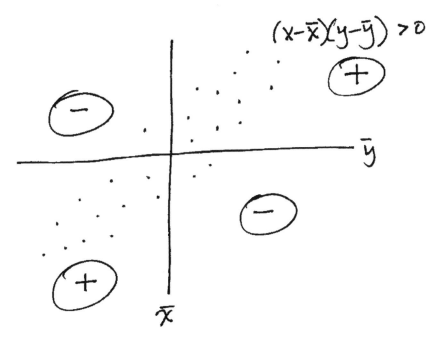

Figure 11.9 The product $(X - \bar{X})(Y - \bar{Y})$ is positive or negative depending on whether $X - \bar{X}$ and $Y - \bar{Y}$ have the same or different signs.

points were doubled (consideration of which leads to dividing by n, or $n - 1$, for an average cross product, or covariance); then to considering a change in scale (examples being feet to inches or pounds to kilos) and adjusting for these by dividing by the standard deviations, leading finally to the correlation.

Example 3: The Representation of Multilevel Models

Multilevel models provide a way to conceptualize a number of situations in which observations are nested within higher-level units. The algebra of such systems is straightforward, but it can seem complicated to students newly exposed to the subject. By drawing plots that illustrate the situation, students can be led through a progressively more complex system, adding one or two concepts at a time rather than having them try to absorb everything at once. Again, I find that drawing data plots and writing equations by hand slows the process down and emphasizes one additional concept at a time, thereby making the whole system less intimidating.

Figure 11.10 illustrates a typical case for a simple regression predicting test score on high school math from student's SES (the example used by Raudenbush & Bryk, 2002, in introducing this model). We note that if the relationship is linear, it is sensible to estimate the intercept, slope, and residual variance. I now tell the class that this was done in one school by a researcher studying that school and that there are researchers in other schools doing the same study, with similar plots and equations (Figure 11.11). We then discuss why the plots (and resulting regression results)

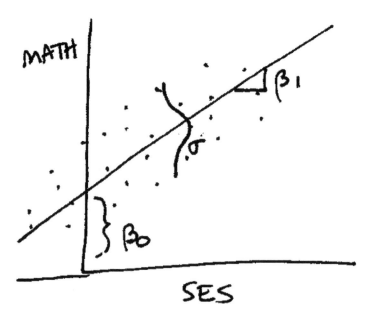

Figure 11.10 Simple linear regression of MATH on SES in one high school, showing the three parameters (intercept, slope, and residual standard deviation).

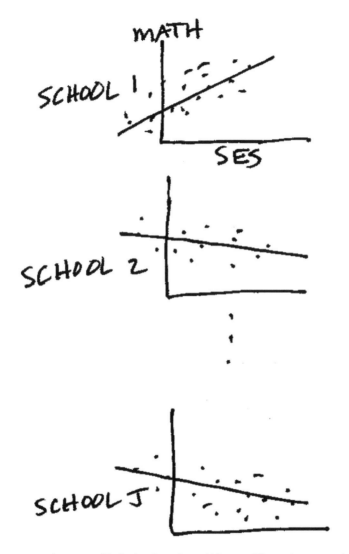

Figure 11.11 The same study repeated in J schools; each could have a different intercept, slope, and residual
standard deviation.

may differ among the schools and conclude that there are reasons to suspect that not all slopes or
intercepts (and perhaps even residual variation) may be the same for all schools.

Next, I ask the class to consider why the slopes and intercepts vary from school to school. It
is obvious at this point that any explanatory variables must be at the school level, not the individual level. I suggest one possibility: the proportion of students at the high school who are in the
academic track. We then examine plots (Figure 11.12) of the intercept and slope as functions of

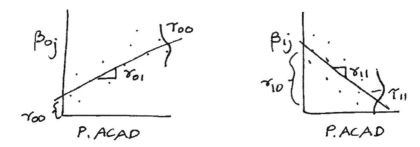

Figure 11.12 School-level plots showing relationship between intercept (left) and slope (right) and a school-level predictor, proportion of students in the academic track at the school.

proportion in the academic track. If the relationship is a straight line, we can describe these by school-level regressions, each of which has an intercept, a slope, and a residual variance. In this way, we develop the notion of level 2 equations.

Note that at this introductory point, we do not consider centering or otherwise transforming the parameters. As important as these are (why would we care about variation in intercepts if they have no important meaning?), again, we use the principle of not piling on too much information at a time but delay for one lecture introducing these concepts.

Discussion

Others have also considered some shortcomings of various high-tech approaches to making presentations. Most notably, Edward Tufte (2003) wrote an influential essay on (problems with) the (default) cognitive style of PowerPoint. He discussed how the very structure of a tool encourages a certain style, which often is suboptimal. His point was not about technology in general but with bad default values for one particular technology. His primary solution is to replace the use of PowerPoint with a handout, specifically an 11 × 17 sheet that can be folded in half to make four pages.

Low tech can be combined with high tech for some purposes. By writing on a graphics pad and recording a presentation, it can be captured for future students to view on YouTube or other media. Some of what I consider the best presentations about mathematics and statistics on the web are done in such a way, including those of Sal Khan (www.khanacademy.org/), Mathematical Monk (www.youtube.com/user/mathematicalmonk/playlists), and Ben Lambert (www.youtube.com/user/SpartacanUsuals/featured).

Note that low tech is often good for the student to use too. Mueller and Oppenheimer (2014) found that students had better recall when they hand-wrote notes rather than using a keyboard. This was true even though they captured much more detailed information using a keyboard. Students evidently process the information better when they have to decide what is worth recording.

I have been asked, "What if my handwriting/drawing is bad?" The first thing I would suggest is to slow down. Any handwriting is made worse by doing it quickly. This will help the students, too:

They can't keep up with fast writing. You're just writing something you know well; they're thinking and writing at the same time.

My low-tech drawings and equations written on paper are supplemented by medium-tech devices that project what I write onto a screen. The technology for doing this is very good today, but the essentials have been available for many decades. For handouts, although high-tech devices are handy for storing copies on computers and transmitting them electronically to students, most prefer the old-fashioned handout produced from a copy machine or printer.

Note that what I am advocating is different in purpose from most of the wonderful work on statistical graphics being done today by people such as Tufte, Wainer, Cleveland, Wickham, and Murrell. They describe methods for more effectively presenting *data*; I am talking about effectively representing *concepts*. Tufte (1997) is the one book of his that emphasizes visualization of explanations rather than purely of data. Perhaps the only source that emphasizes visual explanation in statistics is the book by Farebrother (2002); he cites the few articles doing the same.

I am not making a case for only using low-tech methods but instead for choosing the right method for the right purpose in the right situation. In his book *Small Is beautiful*, Ernst Schumacher (1973) made the case for *appropriate technology*: The largest, most automated system is not always the right one for a particular culture or time or task. His arguments were based on both the dignity of human work and on the greater availability of labor than raw materials and energy sources in some countries. But it also applies to other areas, including teaching statistics. We should use high-tech devices when they are the best for doing a task, but when they are not, we should use whatever is appropriate for the job at hand. Your students will be appreciative; and what would you rather they do to show their appreciation: low-tech applause or high-tech "likes"?

References

Bruner, J. S. (1960). *The process of education*. Cambridge, MA: Harvard University Press.

Farebrother, R. W. (2002). *Visualizing statistical models and concepts*. New York: Marcel Dekker.

Miller, G. A. (1956). The magical number seven, plus or minus two: Some limits on our capacity for processing information. *Psychological Review, 63*(2), 81–97.

Mueller, P. A., & Oppenheimer, D. M. (2014). The pen is mightier than the keyboard: Advantages of longhand over laptop note taking. *Psychological Science, 25*, 1159–1168. https://doi.org/10.1177/0956797614524581

Raudenbush, S. W., & Bryk, A. S. (2002). *Hierarchical linear models: Applications and data analysis methods* (2nd ed.). Thousand Oaks, CA: Sage Publications.

Schrodt, P. (1982, April). The generic word processor. *Byte, 7*(4), 32–36.

Schumacher, E. F. (1973). *Small is beautiful: A study of economics as if people mattered*. London: Blond & Briggs (Hardcover: New York: Harper & Row).

Tufte, E. R. (1997). Visual explanations: Images and quantities, evidence and narrative. Cheshire, CT: Graphics Press.

Tufte, E. R. (2003). *The cognitive style of PowerPoint*. Cheshire, CT: Graphics Press.

## Chapter 12

Hands-on Experience in the Classroom—Why, How, and Outcomes

Pascal R. Deboeck

12.1 Why

The most common course design I have encountered in early and mid-level graduate psychology-taught quantitative courses consists of 3 to 4 hours of weekly lecture, with an additional 1-hour lab session frequently directed by a more senior graduate student teaching assistant (GTA). This seems to be a relatively standard format, although I have not conducted a systematic survey. Instructor styles, techniques, and personalities certainly lend significant variation to the experience and effectiveness of the lecture portion of the course. Common across these differences is that the lecture generally serves as the primary way to convey the course materials and concepts. The lab session frequently serves as a time to practice the analytic methods discussed in the lecture and/or as a review of the critical concepts.

Years later, three reasons for attempting to redesign "Introduction to Categorical Data Analysis" remain prominent. The first reason for redesigning the course was to better address the vast diversity in prior experience and knowledge common to this course. This course was a mid-level graduate quantitative course, typically consisting of 10 to 20 students. At the time, the quantitative courses in psychology at the University of Kansas were known by students in many different departments and colleges across campus. The students were primarily from psychology, but there was a relatively large proportion from education, business, and numerous other departments representing the College of Liberal Arts & Sciences including communication studies and even (once) East Asian studies. The course was expected to be accessible to any student having taken two introductory courses in graduate statistics, which included advanced undergraduates, early through advanced graduate students, and the occasional postdoc. Consequently, some students had just learned the basics of regression/ANOVA, while others could integrate statistical ideas from across a dozen of quantitative courses. A lecturer can incorporate information for segments of a class with differing abilities, but there is fundamentally a bottleneck that occurs with a single speaker. While some portion of the class is working on understanding the fundamentals, another portion will be bored; incorporating something for those coming to the class with more experience may engage one group, but it can confuse other parts of a class. The more diverse a course, the more likely it will be that only some portion of the students are benefiting from the instructor's efforts at any given time.

The second impetus for change came from an article that included an interview with Carl Wieman, a Nobel Prize winner, who was at the time serving as associate director at the White House's Office of Science and Technology Policy (Freedman, 2011). Dr. Wieman highlighted research and his own lecturing experience as to what occurs when students are asked a question about the material presented only minutes earlier during a lecture. For a time following, I experimented with my classes, and I encourage other lecturers to do the same. The experiment was this: Ask a simple or fundamental question about the material presented 15 minutes earlier, and estimate the proportion of students who have understood the concept well. My experience was not unlike that conveyed in the article:

> A University of Maryland study of undergraduates found that after a physics lecture by a well-regarded professor, almost no students could provide a specific answer to the question, "What was the lecture you just heard about?" A Kansas State University study found that after watching a video of a highly rated physics lecture, most students still incorrectly answered questions on the material.
>
> (Freedman, 2011)

One more extreme conclusion that has been drawn from such experiences and related studies is the suggestion to do away with lecturing (Gibbs, 1982). I believe there is value in the lecture format that is not easily replicated. The studies about the effectiveness of lecturing, however, highlight that there is room for improvement in how information is conveyed when using the lecture format. Other chapters in this volume present several ideas for improving lecture-based courses and highlight that "lecturing" is hardly a uniform approach. Still, considering the efficiency and fidelity with which information could be transmitted via lectures was another reason I redesigned my course after five iterations as a lecture-based format.

The third reason for a course redesign came from reevaluating the goals of the course, following my reading of a chapter about "backward design." The chapter does not advocate a specific course design but rather the process by which courses are designed. One salient passage in the chapter states that "many teachers begin [their course design process] with textbooks, favored lessons, and time-honored activities rather than deriving those tools from targeted goals or standards" (Wiggins & McTighe, 2005). An alternative to this approach is that:

> One starts with the end—the desired results (goals and standards)—and then derives the curriculum from the evidence of learning (performance) called for by the standard and the teaching needed to equip students to perform.
>
> (Wiggins & McTighe, 2005, p. 8)

This suggests multiple questions: Beyond defining a course in terms of its content, what are the goals and standards for quantitative training in the 21st century? What are the goals and standards desirable common to all quantitative courses? As instructors of quantitative methods, are we providing students the tools required to meet those goals?

I have no particularly deep or profound answers to these questions. In reading syllabi from several of my courses, however, I could see elements common to many of my quantitative courses. Naturally, every course had fundamental concepts and statistical tools that needed to be conveyed. But there was also an emphasis on students being able (1) to think critically both about their analyses and those of other researchers, (2) to weigh options and make decisions when conducting analyses, (3) to be able to carry out analyses, (4) to think critically about the results presented by the analyses, and (5) to communicate their results. While I was providing many of the essential conceptual pieces reasonably well and introducing new statistical tools, there was more variation in the degree to which students displayed the aforementioned abilities. That is perhaps not surprising, as there is something qualitatively different between seeing an example of an analysis and conducting the analysis oneself. Individuals vary in their ability to extrapolate from class examples to their research. In a lecture-based design, the 1-hour supplemental lab session provided little time for students to practice abilities that seem an essential part of the goals and standards of quantitative training.

12.2   How

12.2.1   Overview

With the reasons in mind for a course redesign, I asked myself the following questions about redesigning a course. How does one change a course to (1) meet the needs of students with a diverse range of experience, (2) more effectively transmit the contents of the course, and (3) provide students with a stronger skill set for performing the analyses discussed in the course? Note that in approaching this redesign, the goals and standards I wanted to ideally achieve, at least broadly, were defined first. Moreover, selecting a course format that would meet these goals was a process that was mostly separate from the selection of the course materials. Multiple paths would address each of these goals. The solution I implemented was a variant of an online class and was what is often characterized as a reversed/flipped classroom. Students were required to watch videos of my lectures before coming to class. The class then consisted of a 3-hour session, with ideally no more than 30 to 45 minutes allocated to highlighting of topics raised in the video, addressing questions about the video contents and administering a short quiz. Afterward, students spent 2.25 hours engaging with several semistructured worksheets in groups. While engaging with the semistructured problems, a GTA and I circulated around the room, addressing questions and ensuring primary conceptual pieces of the problems were understood. The following sections describe how this format met my course goals and provide specific details about implementing this course design.

12.2.2   Meeting Goals

The first redesign goal was to better meet the needs of students with diverse prior experience in quantitative methods and diverse substantive interests. To address this goal, it seemed necessary to find a way to allow the course to be more tailored to individual students. This could be accomplished through individual means (e.g., more individualized feedback, time working with each student) or creating course elements for specific subsets of students (e.g., creating different tracks in the course). In my course redesign, students self-selected into small groups (2–4 students; more on this later) when working on the in-class worksheets. More often than not, these small groups consisted of students with similarities on some dimension, such as similar experience levels or a related area of study.

My interactions with students during class time primarily involved discussions between myself and the small groups. Each group would raise different questions, from questions about specific applications in business for one group, to a question about the likelihood function for another group, and a more fundamental question about reading the output from another. Between these and addressing occasional questions for individuals, there was the opportunity for the instructor to tailor responses to the perspective of much smaller subsets of the class. While it was still necessary to consider the experience and interests of a particular group, it was possible to provide responses tuned to the median of a two- to four-person group, rather than the median of the entire class (or whatever quantile you select). Across 14 sessions of approximately 2.25 hours (> 30 hours) and with around seven small groups, this format allows one to provide much more individualized attention to students. This individual attention was further enhanced by having a GTA simultaneously answering questions.

The second redesign goal was to enhance the effectiveness of the lectures. Having refined the lectures over five iterations, I was unwilling to discard the work that had gone into preparing those materials. In the redesign, recordings of the final year of the lecture format were used to create the videos students were required to watch before class. The 3 hours of lecture time from each week was edited to be a 60- to 75-minute video. These videos and the specifics of the in-class problems ensured a common set of content was required of all students even though there were differences in what students learned based on the small-group and individual questions asked during class time.

While I did little to refine the contents of the lectures, the videos had an unintended consequence. Several students have reported that the "1-hour" videos often take 2 hours to watch. Students were taking the time to stop the video and re-listen to parts they had not initially understood. I had, and have, concerns like many instructors that lecture videos do not allow for the dynamic exchange with students permitted during lecture. What I had not anticipated is that lecture videos, while less dynamic, have an element which allows students to tailor a lecture to their individual needs. For parts of a course that are more structured and primarily involve information being conveyed by the instructor (i.e., less dynamic interactions), videos may be a useful method for improving the transmission of information via lecture because of how students can adjust videos to their own pace.

The final redesign goal was to provide students with a stronger skill set for performing statistical analyses. The last change was inspired by a *Science* article on improving learning in a physics class (Deslauriers, Schelew, & Wieman, 2011). The article discusses a comparison of two out of three sections from a large 850-student required, undergraduate physics class. In the 12*th* week, after measuring multiple factors suggesting approximately equivalent sections in the prior 11 weeks, a variation in teaching style was introduced. The instructor of the control group was a highly rated, experienced instructor who provided a lecture-based presentation. In the experimental group, a trained but comparatively inexperienced instructor provided an instructional approach that required "pre-class reading assignments, pre-class reading quizzes, in-class clicker questions, with student–student discussion, small-group active learning tasks, and targeted in-class instructor feedback" (Deslauriers et al., 2011). Figure 12.1 shows a histogram comparing the scores on a test following the different class styles for the control and experimental groups. It is perhaps not surprising that requiring more participation from students improves their ability to solve problems, but it is a bit more provocative that with some course formats, an inexperienced instructor may achieve notably better results in student achievement than an experienced instructor.

While any single study has its limitations, the *Science* article reminds us of the importance of having students actively engage with new information and the potential this has for improving their analytic skills (Freeman et al., 2014). Repeated engagement with an analysis method allows one to encounter variations due to different data and theoretical questions, challenges, and problems that may occur, and develop or expand one's expertise. As various abilities related to the application of analytic methods were important to my course goals and standards, finding a way to integrate more hands-on experience became essential. It was through repeated hands-on expertise conducting analyses, through carefully constructed exercises, that I planned to improve the ability for students to perform analyses.

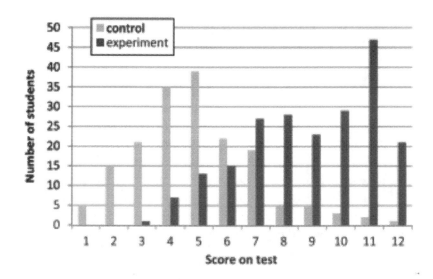

Figure 12.1 Results from comparing two sections of an introductory physics class, one taught using primarily a lecture format (control) and another requiring participation from students both before and during class (experimental). There is a notable amount of missing data (Control 37%, Experimental 21%), but details about the pattern of missing data are not discussed, and thus their impact is difficult to assess.

There are many ways of providing opportunities for hands-on practice. In areas such as physics, engineering, and mathematics, a common experience for students is countless hours toiling over sets of problems outside of the classroom with limited support; while practice is valuable, this can become a frustrating experience for students, particularly students already struggling with the material. While the experience of problem sets is less common in much of the social sciences, practice in applying statistical methods is not unlike the need to practice solving problems in physics, engineering, and mathematics. Moving the problem-solving sessions into the classroom has several advantages for ensuring a more positive experience for students than problems completed outside of class. First, by requiring students to work in groups, it was often only necessary for a single student in each group to understand any particular part of a problem (e.g., appropriate analysis, how to program, how to interpret results, etc.), as working in groups, the students often learned about the material from each other. Second, the presence of an instructor and GTA also allowed for efficient movement past roadblocks, such as programming quirks and errors, which can lead to hours of wasted time and significant frustration. Third, when coming to decision points that would affect the analysis, students could ask questions, the response to which sometimes was the clear message that there was not a single right choice; this was helpful in encouraging certain critical thinking skills where there is not a single answer, but rather a thoughtful decision must be made.

The final class structure was a variant of online classes and what is sometimes called reversed/flipped classrooms. Students interacted with new information prior to class through videos, which seemed to be much more readily adopted by the students than required readings. As with a carefully constructed lecture, the videos allowed the information to be delivered in a way that provides more guidance than readings such as taking time to help students understand how the information fits into a bigger picture. The videos had the unintended consequence of allowing students to tailor their learning of the class information, repeating parts as needed or skipping through some parts faster. The classroom time espoused the idea of "learning by doing," providing students hands-on practice with exercises. Those exercises, as described in a following section, were semistructured rather than constrained and formulaic, in order to provide experiences that closely parallel those that occur when analyzing real data. The presence of experts during this deliberate practice made this type of class starkly different from an online-only class, allowing for hours of ongoing feedback to be provided to individuals and small groups while in the midst of problem-solving. The following sections provide additional details about the class materials and their creation; these "Detail" sections could be skipped in favor of first reading about the "Outcomes" (Section 12.3) of this attempt to bring more hands-on experience to students.

12.2.3   Details: Videos

As described earlier, recordings of my lecture-based course were recorded to create the videos for the redesigned class. At the time my lectures consisted primarily of writing on a whiteboard. Using a writing tablet with my computer, I could project a whiteboard-like lecture while creating a recording of my computer screen (e.g., Figure 12.2. The audio of the course was

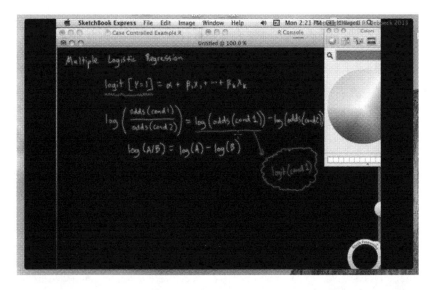

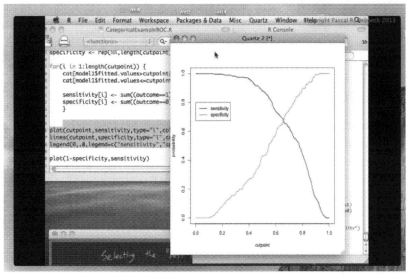

Figure 12.2 Samples of the screen recordings that were used to create the videos for the redesigned course. These videos featured both handwritten whiteboard-like notes (top panel) and examples of analyses in R (bottom panel).

captured both through the computer and with an independent digital voice recorder, as computer audio recordings were sometimes poor (e.g., computer fans, not standing in front of the computer). The screen recordings and audio were then edited to remove time pausing for questions, time when I was writing on the tablet but not speaking, classroom breaks, uncommon questions, time spent recapitulating ideas or the prior class, and conceptual ideas that I would otherwise demonstrate with a classroom problem. It was not unusual for 3 hours of recordings to be reduced to close to the desired 60 to 75 minutes. The use of screen capture was purposeful, as it ensured high enough resolution of the materials being presented, which was prioritized over my physical presence in the videos.

Preparation of the videos was the most time-consuming part of the course redesign. As 3 hours of video had to be reviewed, it was not unusual for a single hour-long video to take 4 to 6 hours of editing time. Ideally, this would be a one-time investment for many years, making early and mid-range quantitative courses more suited to this design than more advanced courses in which the material may evolve relatively quickly. For another class using the same format, I explored recording the videos from scratch. While advantageous from a time perspective, as the videos took half as long to create and edit, the creation of videos without an audience poses its own challenges. It takes some practice to speak in an engaging manner without an audience. Regardless of recording method, it seems prudent to recommend that individuals adopting this approach teach a course several times first to refine the lectures to minimize future re-recording of videos by first identifying explanations of material that resonate well with one's students.

Aside from the lack of dynamic interaction with students, I was also concerned about the potential for a lost sense of connectedness that could occur from removing the lecture portions of the class. Through an editing oversight in one of my videos, I learned that does not always have to be the case. While probably a learned behavior thanks to my students or my kids, it is not unusual for my lectures to include "Dad puns," quotes from movies/music, or other things that make students groan. I either missed or didn't think to remove one of these poor attempts at humor and moreover included a self-deprecating "okay . . . that was a horrible joke." I ended up receiving positive feedback for that, in part because of how it helped to break the pace of the video. It also gave students a chance to jest back at me in class. This is all to say that there is the opportunity for outside-of-class time to be a continuation of experience in-class with an instructor, and the in-class time a continuation of the out-of-class experience with the instructor. Unlike readings, instructors can bring so much more of themselves and their expertise to students even within the constraints of a video, as long as the video is not the sole experience a student has with an instructor.

12.2.4 Details: Class Time and Classroom

The class was scheduled as a single 3-hour session, with the first 30 minutes devoted to providing a short reminder of the video contents and answering any questions about the video. Subsequently, a very short quiz (3 items, 10–15 minutes) was used to ensure that individual students had prepared for class. The quiz questions were not designed to differentiate differences in the understanding of the material but to ensure that the video had been watched somewhat carefully. Topics discussed for at least 10 minutes in the video were often developed into a quiz question and typically asked something very general that demonstrated any learning from the video. For example, "Tell me something from the video about Fisher's Exact Test (e.g., Why do we need this test when we have the chi-square test?)." Students graded each other's papers, which also gave the opportunity to provide a reminder of essential details. Responses were graded generously, such that any demonstration that the video was watched received full credit.

The remaining time was spent on two to three worksheets in self-selected groups of two to four students. From my experience, self-selection seemed to work relatively well. On the positive side, self-selection seems preferable/enjoyable to the students and often results in groups with either common prior experience or substantive interests, which may have contributed to a sense of group cohesion. The only dimension on which I was hopeful heterogeneity would occur would be on experience with statistical programming, which often occurred naturally. I did not, however, explore variations on how to group students, and there is much that could be explored with regard to how to create optimal combinations. Some suboptimal grouping did occur, particularly when a student couldn't find a group in which they fit well, or when a team had multiple members that had difficulty staying on task. But as the majority of the students were clearly invested in their learning, self-selection of groups worked well enough in the first flipped classroom that it was retained the second time the flipped classroom was used.

In creating a class that required a considerable amount of time in small-group interactions, it can quickly become apparent that the design of classrooms and classroom furniture dramatically impacts learning. Classrooms with a relatively flexible space, in which group members can face each other, be relatively close, and maintain personal space, become important. As an example, long tables that are narrower than a customer-service counter can make sitting across from group members an awkward invasion of personal space and are only suited to two people working side-by-side.

12.2.5   Details: Worksheets (Exercises)

The worksheets required several design iterations and were begun as assignments for lab and homework in the lecture renditions of the course. Part of the difficulty was to make the worksheets only semi-structured, rather than narrowly defined problems with clear directions and constrained outcomes. For example, a very constrained problem might ask a student to "Run a logistic regression on these data and report whether x was a significant predictor, including the likelihood ratio statistic and p-value." What I considered an excellent worksheet was one where (1) not all aspects of what needed to be done were explicitly defined, (2) one needed to integrate multiple skill sets (statistical decisions, programming, interpretation, communicating results), and/or materials covered in prior weeks, (3) there were conceptual pieces that were not always immediately apparent from the outset.

Each exercise met these goals to varying degrees. Within the worksheets for any given day, students almost always were required to integrate across a wide range of skills (#2), moving from decisions about which analysis to perform, how to set it up, and implementing it to then produce a short paragraph interpreting the results. Not defining all aspects of the analysis (#1) was perhaps the most difficult for me personally, as for many of those worksheets students could (and would) produce different results in differing groups. It requires relinquishing some control to the students to let them decide whether or not an analysis should be controlling for a particular predictor, whether to report the Wald statistic or Likelihood Ratio test or even how many tests should be run, and which results should be reported. The guiding principle was that by practicing these decisions and taking opportunities to talk with them about decisions while roaming the classroom, students would become better at solving these kinds of problems.

The worksheets also often emphasized specific conceptual lessons (#3). Figure 12.3 shows an example of one worksheet that provided much more explicit steps (does not meet worksheet ideal #1) but was aimed at presenting students a conceptual challenge. In this problem, students need to translate the research question (#1) into a testable model and run that model. They then practice interpreting the odds of survival (#2), which requires them to recall from the prior week that with this model we don't have an identity link function and that the estimate of the regression coefficient must be exponentiated. The third part required calculation of two different p-values,

Class 6 --- Worksheet 2

Goal: the exercise further explores the results produced by logistic regression, and to encourage careful consideration of analysis results

Please use the **Wrksht15_AIDS** dataset for the following questions. These data were generated based on a hypothetical randomized control trial about the effectiveness of a certain AIDS treatment. There are three variables in the dataset: *Survive* [whether the participant survived until 5-year span of the study (=1) or not (=0)]; *WBCC* [the patient's measured white blood cell count at the beginning of the study, in thousands]; and *drug* [whether the patient was assigned to receive the experimental drug treatment (=1) or a placebo (=0)].

1. We would like to know how the drug administered to patients affected their chances of survival, accounting for their base-level of white blood cells. Please code and run this model.

2. How would you interpret the effect of the drug on the odds of survival?

3. What is the Wald p-value for this predictor? And the Likelihood Ratio p-value? What are the AICs for the two models? What do these results tell you?

4. To demonstrate the variance of our estimates, please produce confidence intervals for each beta (the intervals may be either profile likelihood or Wald). What would you conclude based on these confidence intervals?

5. What would you conclude about the drug's effectiveness, given your results?

6. Produce a plot of observed values, with white blood cell count as the x-axis and survival as the y-axis, and a table of observed counts for the number of survivors in each drug condition. What do you observe?

Figure 12.3 Example of a worksheet from the redesigned class. While the individual steps of this worksheet were made very explicit, there is a greater conceptual challenge when the students see that multiplicative effect of the drug on the odds of survival are ridiculously large, the Wald p-value is close to 1, and the Likelihood Ratio test produces a p-value close to 0.

as well as the AIC, and to reconcile what they see; this offers a circulating instructor a chance to see if the students understood from the video the differences between these tests, including what each tells them and when each might be used. The remaining parts #4 to #6 build toward creating all the pieces the students would need to provide a discussion of the results of the analysis, save an effect size, which was not learned at this point in the course.

The conceptual lessons in this worksheet begin to become apparent as the students complete questions #2. Some have only written down $e^{18.29}$, and others have a sentence that "The odds of survival are 87,969,437 times higher for the group receiving the drug, controlling for a patient's white blood cell count." Some will check their work, but typically many will go on to question #3, as no errors were indicated in the output. Calculating the likelihood ratio test for the effect of the drug, the students find a significant effect of the drug ($\chi^2(1) = 11.86, p < 0.001$). The AICs for the two models are 80.33 and 70.46 for the models without and with drug, respectively. The WALD statistic, however, returns a nonsignificant result ($z = 0.010, p = 0.99$).

The reactions to the results range from understanding why this has occurred to confusion or even indifference—all teachable moments. Depending on the students, several lessons can be emphasized as the instructor meets with each group. The most straightforward lesson might start with what happens when predictors perfectly distinguish between those who survive and do not survive, with a related discussion of small-sample inferences or types of substantive data that are likely to produce similar results. A secondary lesson can be related to relying not just on convergence but on the need to critically evaluate one's results. There is also the opportunity to talk about differences in the estimation of the different p-values, their different underlying approaches, and which is likely to be more accurate in this scenario. There is also the potential with increasing expertise to relate the differences in the observed p-values to details about maximum likelihood estimation. While one or more of these can be treated as a common core required of all students, some elements can be tailored to individual groups.

12.2.6   Details: Instructor and Graduate Teaching Assistant Roles

The instructor and GTA are critical to the success of the problem-solving sessions. During the problem-solving session, the instructor, and GTA if resources allow, circulate the classroom. They address questions that help students understand the conceptual points from the videos, connect those conceptual points to the analyses they are doing, address questions that relate the material to specific areas of study or other quantitative coursework, and help students move efficiently past roadblocks (e.g., what is the function for recoding a variable). My experience in two classes of this format and classes featuring interspersed days with a similar format is that a single instructor is sufficient with classes up to about 15 students. With 15 or more students, having a teaching assistant who is knowledgeable about the course material becomes invaluable. I have not, to date, tried expanding this design for larger classes.

With regards to division of responsibilities in the classroom, I usually let the GTA address any questions with which they felt comfortable. Not surprisingly, it is valuable to have a GTA who has previously taken the course, has more statistical experience, and has prior teaching experience that required interacting with students. The availability of GTAs meeting these criteria is usually very limited. Consequently, it is worth highlighting that one of the primary roadblocks for students was statistical programming, as the course was taught using R. I often would delegate more time-consuming programming roadblocks so that I could spend more time on conceptual issues. Familiarity with the course software would likely be valuable to prioritize when GTA availability is limited. As I also had my GTA review the write-ups provided by the students, the ability to interpret the output of an analysis was also a key skill, and consequently, a GTA who had done well in a prior rendition of the course was preferable.

12.3   Outcomes

The reverse classroom structure described was implemented for two iterations of the class (2013 and 2014) with 31 students and two different GTAs. In preparing a presentation on this course in 2017 (Deboeck, 2017), I decided to try to contact the students and GTAs and ask them for their impressions 2.5 and 3.5 years later. It is well known that many factors influence student course evaluations, and no doubt GTAs working towards their PhD might also feel pressures to respond in particular ways immediately following a class. As many of the students had graduated when I contacted them, and I had changed universities, there was little or no incentive to respond in a particular way about the course. The following two sections represent (1) the feedback received from the students and (2) the input received from the graduate teaching instructors.

12.3.1   Outcomes: Students

Of 31 students taking the redesigned class, contact information was located for 26 students, of which 20 responded to my inquiry for feedback. I expressed that their comments would be shared with other instructors of quantitative methods and that their honest feedback would be appreciated and could be influential; as I stated, "the best way to improve quantitative training would be to know the positives and negatives when something like reverse classrooms are tried." I provided five prompts: (1) How does learning in a reverse classroom compare to a lecture classroom? (2) Using a reverse classroom, what advantages are there for individual learning? (3) Using a reverse classroom, what disadvantages are there for individual learning? (4) What do you believe would be the consequences if more quantitative training occurred as reverse classrooms? and (5) Other comments/thoughts?

The 20 students who responded provided me a generous 6,700+ words of thoughts. To try to represent the students' voices fairly, I have read the 6,700+ words line by line and grouped them into related themes and recorded the frequency of each idea to try to summarize the information. I will offer this section with little additional commentary, save selecting a few students to quote, to try to minimize my voice in what the students provided. Generally grouping the responses into advantages and disadvantages, this is what the students shared with me (different ideas separated by semicolons):

The Advantages of the Redesigned Course Were

(6x each) ability to learn on one's own time or at one's own pace; hands-on experience/ application of statistical methods

(5x) ability to review/rewind lecture, watch multiple times

(4x each) less time spent on mundane coding issues; efficient immediate help when learning a (new) program from instructors

(3x each) help from peers; beneficial group work pushes students; more intensive practice

(2x each) helpful to practice explaining concepts to other students; more personalized guidance

(1x each) less boring; less stressful because surrounded by help; practice time without additional lab; positive view of being able to come to class prepared with questions from video; helpful for shy students; good for classes with students with diverse backgrounds

The Disadvantages of the Redesigned Course Were

(4x) unequal participation of group members/unprepared students

(2x each) can't ask videos real-time questions, which negatively impacts learning; takes some getting used to; requires quite a bit of time outside of class to get maximum value; if other members of the group understand the material much better, you can get left behind; can be annoying to have to work with other students

(1x each) video lectures are less engaging; no follow-up assignment, so no additional practice outside of class; leaves unmotivated students behind; having to work in groups lends itself to a lack of individualization; requires students to be highly motivated and self-disciplined; limits to possible class size, otherwise not enough time to approach every student

Quotes From a Few of the Student Responses

"I found the video lectures to be less engaging than an in-class lecture, and the biggest con was that I could not ask questions mid-lecture."

"I could see that if you had a problem with domineering personalities, conflict, lack of communication, social loafing, groupthink—all of these would come into play with a group, and they would decrease your individual learning."

"Being able to work through these difficulties [implementing statistical analyses] in class was extremely useful, rather than sitting at home banging my head on the table or throwing my computer out the window :)"

"even a few years out, I feel more competent in using and understanding categorical data analysis than I do other methods in which I completed coursework."

12.3.2   Outcomes: Graduate Teaching Assistants

In addition to the students, I was able to reach my two GTAs, one of whom had been a teaching assistant for the earlier lecture-only rendition of the class. As with the student responses, I will minimize my commentary in this section and try to reflect what the GTAs shared. Among the points that were highlighted, the GTAs expressed (1) that there were lots of teachable moments,

(2) students who would not typically ask questions felt more comfortable doing so, (3) "as a GTA in a reverse classroom, I never got to sit down," and (4) "in lecture classes it is easier to catch up if missing classes or when unable to prepare for class, as [in the new format] the interactions with instructors are not replaceable." The teaching assistant who served in both the lecture-only and reversed classroom designs reflected: "I believe that we saw some of our most ambitious and creative end-of-semester projects in the reverse-classroom environment. For the lecture classroom, the end-of-semester project served as a demonstration that the students could apply the material. With the reverse classroom, students had already demonstrated their application of the material every time we met, so it necessitated them to strive for something more to show in their projects.¹"

12.4   Conclusion

This chapter presented an approach to quantitative education that aimed at increasing the hands-on experience of students with statistical analyses, increase individual-level interaction with the instructor, and better match the course to the backgrounds of a diverse set of students. As could be seen in the prior outcomes section, there are mixed responses with regards to this classroom design, although my evaluation is that the reactions lean toward the positive. There are challenges for the instructor in preparing such a class, however, as this class design required far more preparation than lecturing from a book.

In preparing courses at a new university, I do not feel that I presently have a course developed enough that I can use this redesigned format. That has not precluded taking lessons from this format and incorporating elements into primarily lecture-based courses. Integrated into some of my recent classes, for example, are a few "practice days" where a general task is outlined, and the students work with each other to practice their skills to implement and to interpret an analysis. All the while I circulate, jumping on any chance to answer questions that might help a student take the next step in their learning. A mid-semester survey in one course seemed to indicate a desire for more of these practice days, but I have yet to explore interspersed practice days more systematically. But there seems to be the potential of getting some benefit, even from a more limited approximation of the course described in this chapter.

There is also the challenge that classes are much more mentally fatiguing for the students and the instructor. Group-based student questions seem to span a wider range than students will ask in front of an entire class, and this places a challenge on the instructor to address new questions or even to address common questions in a context suited to individual students. I held back two quotes, however, which I see as reasons elements of this redesign may be helpful for teaching quantitative methods in the 21*st* century. One student wrote:

> I found the reverse classroom course put A LOT of responsibility on the student. If you don't spend the effort to make sense of the video lecture, then going to class would be a waste of time. This is not a bad system at all, and in fact I found it to be preferable to a lecture-based course. *I had this feeling that I had much much more obligation to learn on my own, and in the end I think that made me learn a lot more.*
>
> [emphasis added]

And another wrote:

> I found myself challenged in new ways because I was faced with questions from my peers that you don't run into in a lecture class, because there's no real hands-on opportunity to encounter them, e.g.,—*does this make sense? Does this have validity? Is this model working or not? How do we know?*
>
> [emphasis added]

I cannot convey the depth of appreciation I have had for students in my redesigned courses. Most of the students were deeply engaged in the challenging assignments and left after hours of problem-solving mentally fatigued and in need of a break. I don't believe any of my lectures have ever been so mentally demanding of my students. The thought that the redesign might have also, even a little, encouraged a student to take ownership of their learning is profoundly moving. It is even more moving to think that years later, as in the second student's quote, the class might have conveyed to some to think carefully about their analysis—asking questions that not only apply to categorical methods but fundamentally will make her a better researcher.

It is not possible, due to many factors, for instructors of quantitative methods to offer every one of our students individualized education that ensures every student advances their understanding of conceptual and practical aspects of analyzing data. But we could take the step of first focusing on defining our goals and standards for quantitative training, independent of the content that should be conveyed. By doing so, there is the potential for reconceptualizing our approaches to teaching quantitative methods and putting better learning tools at the disposal of our students so that our courses come closer to our ideals for quantitative training.

Note

1. As was the case with the primarily lecture-based class, the students were required to apply the skills learned in class to their research for an end-of-semester paper.

References

Deboeck, P. R. (2017). *Generating hands-on experience in the classroom: A reverse classroom retrospective*. Presentation for Teaching Statistics and Quantitative Methods into the 21st Century, APA Division 5 Mid-Year Conference, Nashville, TN.

Deslauriers, L., Schelew, E., & Wieman, C. (2011). Improved learning in a large-enrollment physics class. *Science, 332*, 862–864.

Freedman, D. H. (2011, December). Impatient futurist: Science finds a better way to teach science. *Discovery, 32*, 28–30.

Freeman, S., Eddy, A. L., McDonough, M., Smith, M. K., Okoroafor, N., Jordt, H., & Wenderoth, M. P. (2014). Active learning increases student performance in science, engineering, and mathematics. *Proceedings of the National Academy of Sciences, 111*, 8410–8415. https://doi.org/10.1073/pnas.1319030111

Gibbs, G. (1982). *Twenty terrible reasons for lecturing*. Standing Conference on Educational Development Services in Polytechnics.

Wiggins, G., & McTighe, J. (2005). *Understanding by design*. Association for Supervision and Curriculum Development. Alexandria, VA.

## Chapter 13

Who Benefits From the Flipped Classroom?

Quasi-Experimental Findings on Student Learning, Engagement, Course Perceptions, and Interest in Statistics

Viji Sathy and Quinn Moore

"We want to make sure that we are exciting young people around math and science and technology and computer science. We don't want our kids just to be consumers of the amazing things that science generates; we want them to be producers as well. And we want to make sure that those who historically have not participated in the sciences as robustly—girls, members of minority groups here in this country—that they are encouraged as well. We've got to make sure that we're training great calculus and biology teachers, and encouraging students to keep up with their physics and chemistry classes."

President Barack Obama
National Academy of Sciences
April 2013

In recent years, there has been rising concern about producing more graduates with expertise in science, technology, engineering, and math (STEM) fields to advance economically and be globally competitive. The growth in STEM jobs from 2000 to 2010 was three times greater than that of non-STEM jobs (President's Council of Advisors on Science and Technology, 2012).

Despite the growing demand for STEM jobs, the pipeline of students interested in STEM fields diminishes from middle school through postsecondary education. In fact, at the undergraduate level, about half of the students who declare or intend to major in STEM fields ultimately leave STEM programs and do not earn STEM degrees (National Center for Education Statistics, 2013). Research suggests that students' decisions to leave STEM fields are likely to arise from a multitude of factors. Attrition rates are higher among women, underrepresented minorities, first-generation students, and students with lower income backgrounds as well as students with weaker academic preparation, lower motivation, confidence, and self-efficacy in one's capacity to learn STEM subjects (NCES, 2013).

Course-related factors may explain why students lose their interest in pursuing STEM subjects, including poor performance in STEM courses, especially relative to performance in non-STEM courses and negative experiences in introductory or gatekeeper math and science courses. Prior research indicates that students often feel apprehensive about quantitative courses (Dauphinee, Schau, & Stevens, 1997; Dunn, 2000). Studies have also shown that grades in STEM courses are markedly lower than grades in non-STEM courses (NCES, 2013).

An important strategy for engaging students in STEM courses and preparing them for success may be use of active learning techniques, yet not all implementations result in positive outcomes compared to lecturing (Freeman et al., 2014). When active learning is combined with high structure—preparation prior to class, active engagement during class through frequent formative feedback, and practice incorporated after class—there appears to be improved learning and retention of the material (Eddy & Hogan, 2014). Not all flipped classrooms incorporate high structure (i.e., the preclass work is considered optional, and students do not have incentive to attend or participate in class). In this instance, the flipped format was adopted with high-structure active learning where first exposure to the course material occurs prior to class either through readings or videos, and class time is used to engage in active learning and application of the material with the guidance of their instructional team and peers (for more information about this course and redesign, please see this post: https://www.apadivisions.org/division-5/publications/score/2018/04/active-learning).

The existing literature on flipped classrooms does not tell us whether it works for subgroups that have traditionally had lower levels of participation in quantitative courses, nor does it provide information on its effect on interest in quantitative education. This study presents findings from a quasi-experimental evaluation of flipped classroom techniques implemented in a large introductory statistics course offered at a large public university. Students in the flipped course were required to watch recorded course lectures before class and then attend class, where a greater emphasis was placed on application of knowledge and higher-order skills. Effects of the approach are assessed by comparing key student achievement, course engagement, and student perception outcomes for a group of students receiving traditional instruction to those receiving instruction in a flipped format. All analysis includes careful controls for initial student achievement and other baseline characteristics. The large study sample allows for analysis of effects for key subgroups, such as gender, minority status, initial skill, and initial quantitative anxiety. Further, the study examines whether effects of the flipped approach vary at different points of the student achievement distribution. Thus, findings from this study provide a rigorous assessment of whether the flipped approach incorporating high-structure active learning improves student performance in a large quantitative gateway course and whether this improvement is consistent across different groups of students, as well as how the flipped approach affects student attitudes toward the course and topic. More broadly, these findings provide important insight into the extent to which active learning techniques may facilitate student engagement in STEM fields.

Background and Related Literature

The difficulty in engaging students in quantitative courses has been well documented. In a large-scale study of introductory statistics students, Schau and Emmioğlu (2012) found that students believed that they had no gain in knowledge or skills from when they enrolled in the course, and their ratings of the value and their interest in statistics actually declined at the end of the course. Other studies corroborate that on average, students in quantitative courses don't change their negative attitudes about the topic, or in some cases they become more negative (Evans, 2007; Sizemore & Lewandowski, 2009).

Engaging teaching methods have been shown to help decrease learning anxiety (Tobias, 1994), increase feelings of empowerment (Townsend, Moore, Tuck, & Wilton, 1998), and improve attitudes about quantitatively focused courses (Carlson & Winquist, 2011; Posner, 2011; Harlow, Burkholder, & Morrow, 2002). Thus, these methods could encourage greater regard for and participation in quantitative science and research (Harlow et al., 2002).

Developments in active learning pedagogy, coupled with advancements in instructional technology, have prompted some educators to implement an educational model called the flipped classroom. In a flipped classroom (also known as the inverse classroom), what is normally done in class and what is normally done outside of class are reversed. For example, instead of students listening to a lecture on descriptive statistics in class and working on problems outside of class, students might view to a video or complete a reading on the topic prior to coming to class and work on more complex problems in class. The guiding principle in a flipped classroom is that class time is best used to practice higher levels of learning (analyzing, evaluating, and creating in Bloom's Taxonomy of Learning) through problem-solving and project work conducted under the guidance of the instructor and teaching assistants. Lower levels of learning (remembering, understanding, and sometimes applying in Bloom's Taxonomy of Learning), including but not limited to introduction to the material, is best done at home prior to class (Herreid & Schiller, 2013).

Proponents of the flipped approach argue that the weakness of a "traditional" approach relying heavily on lecture is that not all students come to class prepared to learn (Bergmann & Sams, 2012). This effect might be exacerbated in a quantitatively focused course, where the readings could be perceived as challenging or dry. Moreover, the traditional approach is less able to take advantage of the instructor's advanced expertise in the course topic because more class time is devoted to introducing topics and less is devoted to more complex problem-solving or discussion. Other cited advantages to a flipped classroom include: (1) students move at their own pace; (2) doing "homework" in class gives instructors better insight into student difficulties; (3) classroom time can be used more effectively and creatively; (4) learning theory supports the new approaches; and (5) the use of technology is flexible for individualized learning (Fulton, 2012).

Using preexposure to material to allow for class-time discussion has long been used in courses with smaller class sizes, but recent expansion of inexpensive video and internet capabilities has facilitated use of this format in courses that are larger or involve technical topics, as is often the case in introductory STEM courses. Specifically, lecture-capture software that enables instructors to record and broadcast their lectures to students over the internet has made preexposure through recorded lecture (in addition to or in lieu of reading) possible in a way that was not available even as little as a decade ago. With recorded lectures, students have active control over their learning. They can listen to entire recordings or segments, listen to recordings more than once, and pause, rewind, or fast-forward when necessary. Further, research suggests that it increases students' satisfaction and enjoyment with a course, reduces anxiety and stress about taking notes at their own pace, and aids students' understanding of complex information (Owston, Lupshenyuk, & Wideman, 2011).

As the technological infrastructure becomes increasingly efficient at providing course materials, it is critical to determine if the incorporation of these approaches has the potential to increase student learning, engagement, and interest in large STEM courses. Because the flipped classroom is a relatively new modality, research on its effectiveness is limited (for a thorough review of the literature, see Borman, 2014). Peer-reviewed literature includes research at the undergraduate and graduate or professional school levels with an emphasis on evaluating the impact of the flipped classroom over "traditional" classrooms in classes of fewer than 100 students (Borman, 2014). Initial results on the effect of flipped classrooms on student perceptions indicate that students expressed preferences for the flipped environment (Strayer, 2009, and Morin, Kecskemety, Harper, & Clingan, 2014; McLaughlin et al., 2014). Gundlach, Richards, Nelson, and Levesque-Bristol (2015) found that there were few differences in attitudes by course structure but that there was a general decline among all students' interest in learning about statistics and its relevance to them at the end of the semester.

Qualitative research suggest that an effective flipped environment cultivates critical-thinking skills by pushing lower levels of Bloom's Taxonomy outside class time and allowing for more higher-order thinking during class (Enfield, 2013; Rowe, Frantz, & Bozalek, 2013; Tune, Sturek, & Basile, 2013 in Borman, 2014; Murphree, 2014). Qualitative studies of student engagement suggest an increase in students' perceived engagement mainly due to redesign of class time in the flipped environment (Borman, 2014). Watching lectures outside of the classroom generated the most mixed criticism (Strayer, 2009; Davies, Dean, & Ball, 2013; Murphree, 2014). Students in these studies also reported student completion rates of outside activities ranging in the 70th percentile, but again, these are for courses that involved smaller class sizes. It is unclear whether students in a larger course would comply at the same rates. One study suggests that concerns that students would stop attending classes and only view recorded lectures is largely unfounded, with only modest reductions in attendance (Owston et al., 2011).

There is much less quantitative research on student achievement in the flipped environment. Although methodologies vary across studies, many use a summative assessment involving either identical or similar assessments across teaching modalities, although few of these studies control for initial achievement levels or other baseline characteristics. Unlike student perceptions, which tended to be favorable, student achievement results are mixed, with some finding no significant differences (Findlay-Thompson & Mombourquette, 2014; Morin, Kecskemety, Harper, & Clingan, 2013; Davies et al., 2013) and some finding improved achievement (Davies et al., 2013; Mason, Shuman, & Cook, 2013; Murphree, 2014; Talley & Scherer, 2013; McLaughlin et al., 2014; Strayer, 2009; Tune et al., 2013; Wilson, 2013; and McLaughlin et al., 2014). Studies that have found improvement in undergraduate courses demonstrate gains of approximately 5 percentage points (Davies et al., 2013; Wilson, 2013; Eddy & Hogan, 2014). Winquist and Carlson (2014) found that the flipped classroom format yielded better long-term performance of statistics knowledge as much as a year after the flipped course.

Studies of the impact of flipped classrooms on student achievement have focused on mean impacts and have not examined impacts at different points in the distribution. Thus we do not know if observed positive impacts are driven by improvements among higher-scoring students (as might be the case if out-of-classroom learning is most effective for students with already strong study habits) or lower-scoring students (as might be the case if videos are most useful for students that need more time to master lower levels of Bloom's taxonomy).

Existing studies were typically in classes with 100 or fewer students, for which implementation is arguably easier. Further, few studies to date have demonstrated whether achievement in the flipped classroom can be differentiated across student subgroups, such as groups based on achievement, gender, or underrepresented minority status. Additionally, the existing literature has not examined the effect of flipped classrooms on interest in statistics.

This study contributes to the existing literature on the effectiveness of flipped classrooms in several ways. It presents findings from a quasi-experimental evaluation of implementing the flipped classroom in a large introductory statistics course that serves as a major requirement and a prerequisite to other courses. The data cover multiple semesters and allow impact estimates to carefully control for initial achievement and other baseline characteristics. The study is the first to examine the effects of flipped classrooms at different points of the distribution of student achievement and to investigate effects for subgroups based on gender, achievement, quantitative anxiety, and underrepresented minority status.

Method

Study Design

This study uses a quasi-experimental research design based on data from students who took an introductory statistics course taught in a psychology and neuroscience department at the University of North Carolina at Chapel Hill. Impact estimates are based on comparisons between students who took a traditional-format version of the course in fall 2012 (comparison group) and students who took a flipped version of the course in spring and fall 2013 (treatment group).

Table 13.1 presents key characteristics of the traditional and flipped course formats. The validity of this design requires baseline equivalence of the groups being compared; this allows for differences in the outcomes of the groups to be attributed to the format of the course rather than to differences in baseline characteristics. During the time of the study, there were no systematic changes in the student body or in the population of students to whom the course was offered. Consequently, there are few differences in the baseline characteristics of the two treatment and comparison groups.

As shown in Table 13.2, only 2 of the 22 baseline characteristics evaluated show statistically significant differences between the groups, with students in the flipped course indicating that they

Table 13.1 Course Format Comparison

Format	Semester	Weekly PSYC 210 Structure (by hours)					
		Primary In-class Method	Assessments	Other Course Work (weekly assignments, online quizzes, exam study guides, etc.)	Number of Online Videos	Readings or Video Viewing Required	Number of Class Polls
Traditional	Fall 2012	Lecture	Same (3)	Same	0	No	74
Flipped	Spring 2013	Problem-solving	Same (3)	Same	80	Yes	160
Flipped	Fall 2013	Problem-solving	Same (3)	Same	80	Yes	184

Table 13.2 Student Characteristics at Baseline by Teaching Method (percentages of students unless otherwise indicated)

	Traditional Course	Flipped Course	p-value
Academic Characteristics			
Mean statistics pretest score	43.5	43.1	.79
Pre-test score missing	4.0	5.6	.46
Mean GPA	3.15	3.14	.83
Took at least one college-level statistics course	21.8	21.9	.98
Took AP statistics in HS	38.5	36.1	.60
Number of math classes taken in college[a]			
No math classes	35.1	32.7	.60
1 math class	40.1	37.9	.63
2 or more math classes	27.0	27.2	.97
Demographic Characteristics			
Underrepresented minority (URM)[a]			
Hispanic[b]	7.5	9.6	.43
Non-Hispanic URM[c]	19.5	14.5	.15
Non-URM[d]	74.7	76.5	.65
English as a first language	90.2	91.4	.68
Attitudes About Statistics			
Survey of Attitudes Towards Statistics (SATS)[e] *(1–7 Scale)*			
Mean SATS affect	4.58	4.49	.35
Mean SATS competence	4.97	4.92	.61
Mean SATS value	5.35	5.32	.73
Mean SATS difficulty	3.58	3.62	.51
Mean SATS interest	4.71	4.76	.64
Mean SATS effort	6.66	6.53	.01
Quantitative factors of student learning *(1–5 Scale)*			
Mean quantitative anxiety	2.38	2.41	.73
Mean quantitative self-confidence	3.20	3.19	.91
Mean quantitative hindrances	2.65	2.78	.11
Mean quantitative success factors	3.95	4.10	.01
Sample Size (Full Sample)	**174**	**324**	

a Differences between group distributions were tested using a chi-squared test.

b Student identified as either Hispanic or Latino exclusive of racial classification.

c Includes African American, Native American, Hawaiian Native, or non-Hispanic biracial or multiracial classifications.

d Includes Caucasian/White or Asian American.

e Prior to the first day of classes, students completed the Survey of Attitudes Towards Statistics (SATS), a 36-item scale providing scores for six attitude components on a 1 (strongly disagree) to 7 (strongly agree) scale: 1. Affect (students' feelings concerning statistics), 2. Cognitive competence (students' attitudes about their intellectual knowledge and skills when applied to statistics), 3. Value (students' attitudes about the usefulness, relevance, and worth of statistics in personal and professional life), 4. Difficulty (students' attitudes about the difficulty of statistics as a subject), 5. Interest (students' level of individual interest in statistics), and 6. Effort (amount of work the student plans to expend to learn statistics). Additionally, measures of quantitative anxiety, quantitative self-confidence, quantitative hindrances, and quantitative successes that were assessed prior to the first day of classes (Harlow et al., 2002). All measures have reasonably good internal consistency (alpha ranges from .64 to .91).

were slightly less likely to put effort into the course (SATS effort) and reporting slightly higher quantitative success factors (such as "Good study habits will help me do well in the course"). Critically, the groups had very similar mean scores on a statistics pretest completed on the first day of class. As discussed in more detail in what follows, the impact analysis controls for all measured baseline characteristics; thus it adjusts for any differences between the groups in these observed characteristics.

Implementation

Students in both the traditional and flipped courses were provided with identical skeletal notes on each topic, assignments, optional practice problems, exam reviews, and exams. Both courses met two times a week for a larger class meeting for 75 minutes and a 50-minute once-weekly recitation meeting led by a TA, generally used for review and working on practice problems. Course grade construction was identical for both courses, with 75% of the grade based on exam performance, 20% based on data analysis assignments and online quizzes, and 5% based on attendance. For the semesters included in the study time frame, the course was held in the same location and on the same days and times each term.

In the traditional course, the instructor used class time for lectures and practice problems that were incorporated through a web- and text-message-based classroom response system (Polleverywhere.com). In the flipped course, these lectures were broken out into mini-lectures, recorded through screencasting software (Camtasia), and offered to the students through a web-based portal. In all, 80 short videos were produced, and students were asked to watch five to seven videos weekly in the flipped course. Several of the videos also contained embedded recall questions before and after the video to encourage engagement and motivation to complete the front-loading required in the flipped format. Students in the flipped course were asked to watch the videos prior to the class meetings and quizzed at the start of class on the topic before proceeding to more challenging problem-solving activities. To offset the students' time spent outside of class in the flipped course preparing for class, a portion of time in class was earmarked to work on data analysis assignments (i.e., what was previously deemed "homework" was incorporated into class time) and complete practice problems through an online classroom response system.

For example, in a unit on variability, students watch a short (3-minute video) about standard deviation that includes a basic definition and formulas that describe the calculation of standard deviation. The video prompts them to answer the sample question that follows. In this case, the question appears before the video begins; students who have either read the text book or recall the material from a previous course can bypass the videos if they answer correctly. A similar question appears at the end for students to check their understanding of a concept:

What value is obtained if you add all the deviation from the mean scores for a population, then divide the sum by N?

a.   *The population variance*
b.   *The population standard deviation*

    c.   *You will always get zero*

    d.   *None of the other choices are correct*

At the start of class, students will respond via Polleverywhere.com to a short quiz (five questions or fewer). Students are allowed to consult their notes but must work independently to check their individual understanding of a concept reviewed in the module prior to class. A sample question from the quiz in this unit includes:

> *Suppose a researcher selects a sample of 16 participants and computes SS = 60. In this example, the standard deviation is 4.*

    a.   *True; Very certain of my answer*

    b.   *True; Somewhat certain of my answer*

    c.   *False; Somewhat certain of my answer*

    d.   *False; Very certain of my answer*

A common misstep for students is to forget to take the square root of the variance to obtain the standard deviation. The answer choices c and d are keyed correct for the purposes of this quiz. Quiz questions are scored more for participation than for accuracy. Debriefing regarding the quiz questions is interspersed throughout the class session alongside activities to explore concepts further collaboratively. An example question in this unit includes transformations to a set of data and the impact it has on measures of spread:

> *Suppose the average score on a national test is 500 with a standard deviation of 100. If each score is increased by 25, what are the new mean and standard deviation?*

    a.   *500, 100*

    b.   *500, 125*

    c.   *525, 100*

    d.   *525, 105*

    e.   *525, 125*

Students are encouraged to work in pairs or small groups to discuss their rationale for selecting the answer they chose and engage in peer instruction. During this time, the instructor, graduate student teaching assistants, and undergraduate learning assistants are circulating in the room to listen to responses and offer nudges when needed. For example, they might say, "What are the ways we could solve this? Could you construct a small data set to test the impact of adding a constant?" Students are expected to continue practicing concepts through a quiz on the unit through the learning management system as well as an assignment (typically focused on data analysis and interpretation).

Sample

The study sample includes 498 undergraduates who completed the traditional course in the fall 2012 term ($n = 174$) or the flipped course in the spring 2013 term ($n = 161$) or the fall 2013 term ($n = 163$). The majority of students (92%) were in their second or third year, and 7% were seniors. About two-thirds of the sample had taken at least one math class in college. The course is a required course for psychology majors and a prerequisite for upper-level psychology courses. While the group resembles the ethnic composition of the campus as a whole (66% Caucasian, 10% Asian American, 9% African American, 9% Hispanic, < 1% Native American, 5% Other), it was disproportionately female (58% on campus, 79% in this course).

Data Sources

The data sources for the study's analysis include a pretest of statistical knowledge on the first day of class, scores from the final exam, and responses to surveys administered at three points during the semester. Students completed a 15-item multiple-choice pretest on the first day of class to measure baseline knowledge of statistics. At the end of the semester, students completed a 50-item multiple-choice cumulative final exam. Students were asked to complete a background survey at the start of the semester, as well as midterm and end-of-course surveys of student perceptions. All surveys were administered using online polling software (Qualtrics). Completion rates were 98.8% for the precourse online survey and 88.3% for the postcourse online survey.

The precourse survey included the Survey of Attitudes Towards Statistics (SATS), an inventory of 36 items developed by Schau, Stevens, Dauphinee, and Del Vecchio (1995) with response options ranging from 1 (strongly disagree) to 7 (strongly agree). These responses to these items provide scale scores for six attitude components: 1. Affect (students' feelings concerning statistics), 2. Cognitive competence (students' attitudes about their intellectual knowledge and skills when applied to statistics), 3. Value (students' attitudes about the usefulness, relevance, and worth of statistics in personal and professional life), 4. Difficulty (students' attitudes about the difficulty of statistics as a subject), 5. Interest (students' level of individual interest in statistics), and 6. Effort (amount of work the student plans to expend to learn statistics). The survey also includes measures of quantitative anxiety, quantitative self-confidence, quantitative hindrances, and quantitative successes, which were assessed prior to the first day of classes, developed by Harlow et al., 2002). All measures have reasonably good internal consistency (Cronbach's alpha ranges from .64 to .91).

The end-of-course survey was distributed in the last week of classes to be completed prior to the course's final examination. The survey asked students to report about the utility of course resources offered, how often they came to class prepared, and their interest in the topic, as well as three global questions evaluating the instructor and course (1. Overall, this course was an effective course, 2. Overall, this instructor was an effective teacher, and 3. Overall, I learned a great deal in this course.). To provide context to quantitative findings, the discussion references qualitative feedback from end-of-course evaluations and findings from postcourse focus groups conducted with students from the flipped classroom group.

Outcome Measures

The evaluation of the effectiveness of the flipped format is based on impact estimates for outcomes in the four domains that the format was intended to influence: student achievement, course engagement, course perceptions, and student interest in statistics. Outcomes examined within each of these domains were selected at the outset of the evaluation before beginning analysis.

- Student Achievement. The primary measure of student achievement is the final exam score. The analysis examines differences in mean scores between the groups, as well as differences in the distribution of scores.
- Student Engagement. There are two primary measures of student engagement in the course: attendance and class preparedness. The percentage of class sessions attended is assessed based on the number of class sessions for which each student responded to an in-class poll. Whether the student came to class unprepared is based on self-report responses to the end-of-course survey, specifically whether the student indicated having come to class prepared.
- Course Perceptions. The student course perceptions measures include three items drawn from the end-of-course survey: (1) overall course evaluation; (2) overall instructor evaluation; and (3) assessment of learning from the course. Each of these scales ranges from 1 to 5, with higher values corresponding to a more favorable perception.
- Student Interest in Statistics. The measure of student interest in statistics is based on the task value component subscale of the Motivated Strategies for Learning Questionnaire (Pintrich, Smith, Garcia, & McKeachie, 1991). The subscale refers to students' perceptions of the course material in terms of interest, importance, and utility and includes the following items: I am very interested in the content of this course; I like the subject matter of this course; Understanding the subject matter of this course is very important to me; I think I will be able to use what I learn in this course in other courses; It is important for me to learn the course material in this class; I think the course material in this class is useful to me to learn.

Analytic Methods

Based on the similarity of the treatment and comparison groups, a simple comparison of means of the two groups would provide a valid estimate of program impacts. However, regression models can improve the statistical precision of these estimates. They can also adjust for small initial differences between treatment and comparison groups. Therefore, all impact estimates reported in this study adjust for baseline characteristics.

Mean impact estimates presented in this chapter are generated using ordinary least squares regression models. The regression models can be represented by the following equation:

$$Y_i = \alpha + \gamma Flip_i + \beta X_i + \varepsilon_i$$

where Y_i is an outcome variable for student i, $Flip_i$ is an indicator that equals 1 if the student was in the flipped course research group, X_i is a vector of baseline characteristics, and ε_i is a random disturbance term that is assumed to have a mean of zero conditional on $Flip_i$ and X_i. The impact estimate is the regression coefficient associated with the research group indicator, represented by γ in the equation. The covariates include variables that correspond to students' pretest scores, baseline academic and demographic characteristics, and baseline attitudes about statistics; these variables include all of those listed in Table 13.2.

The assessment of the impact of the flipped approach throughout the achievement distribution is based on quantile regression, a method for estimating functional relations between variables for all portions of a probability distribution (Koenker & Bassett, 1978). Whereas linear regression can answer the question "Does the intervention work on average?" it cannot answer the important question "Does the intervention work differently for low-performing students than for high-performing students?" Thus, quantile regression provides a more comprehensive picture of the effect of the course redesign that has not yet been addressed in the literature. The quantile regression analysis controls for the same factors described for the linear regression analysis. Not only does using a quantile regression allow for a more complete picture of impact across the distribution by focusing on more than the mean, it can overcome some of the problems presented in OLS. Because the focus is on the mean as a measure of location, information about upper and lower ends of the score distribution are lost. Furthermore, OLS is sensitive to extreme outliers, which can often occur in student exam performance data.

Lastly, the evaluation examined whether the flipped format is more effective for certain subgroups of students. These subgroups were selected before data analysis began and were based on the following characteristics: initial statistical skill, quantitative anxiety, gender, and underrepresented minority (URM) status. Regression adjusted impacts were estimated for each subgroup.

Results

Impacts on Student Achievement

The flipped format improved student achievement on average and throughout the achievement distribution. Table 13.3 provides impact estimates of the course redesign on student achievement, controlling for baseline characteristics. These findings indicate that, on average, students in the flipped course earned five more points on the cumulative exam than those in the traditional course ($M_{Flipped} = 75.8$ vs. $M_{Traditional} = 70.8$). This difference was statistically significant and with a medium effect size ($p < .001$, ES = 0.436).

OLS-regression-adjusted means for the percentage of students in each exam grade score band (< 60, 60–69, 70–79, etc.) are also presented in Table 13.3. These findings indicate that students were significantly less likely to earn very low achievement scores (corresponding to a failing grade) and significantly more likely to earn high achievement scores (corresponding to an A or B grade). Students were 2.5 times less likely to obtain scores less than 60 (or failing) in the flipped course than in the traditional course ($M_{Flipped} = 22.0$, $M_{Traditional} = 8.8$, $p < .01$, ES = 0.649) holding all other baseline characteristics constant. Students were at least two times more likely to earn scores between 80 and 89 ($M_{Flipped} = 30.6$, $M_{Traditional} = 13.7$, $p < .01$, ES = 0.620) and between 90 and 100 ($M_{Flipped} = 14.8$, $M_{Traditional} = 7.6$, $p = .035$, ES = 0.453).

Figure 13.1 presents impact estimates at different points in the student achievement distribution based on quantile regression, providing the adjusted difference between treatment and

Table 13.3 Impacts of Course Redesign on Student Achievement, Course Engagement, Course Perceptions, and Interest in Statistics

Outcome	Traditional Course	Flipped Course	Estimated Impact	p-Value	Effect Size
Student Achievement					
Mean final exam score (range: 0 to 100)	70.8	75.8	5.0***	<0.01	0.436
Final exam score was (percentage):					
Less than 60	22.0	8.8	−13.2***	<0.01	−0.649
At least 60, less than 70	24.3	20.5	−3.7	0.391	−0.130
At least 70, less than 80	32.3	25.2	−7.1	0.155	−0.212
At least 80, less than 90	13.7	30.6	16.9***	<0.01	0.620
At least 90	7.6	14.8	7.2**	0.035	0.453
Course Engagement					
Attendance (percentage of class sessions)	81.5	87.1	5.6***	<0.01	0.272
Come to class unprepared (percentage)	23.5	4.1	−19.4***	<0.01	1.196
Course Perceptions					
Overall course evaluation (range: 1 to 5)	3.33	4.04	0.70***	<0.01	0.667
Overall instructor evaluation (range: 1 to 5)	4.02	4.57	0.55***	<0.01	0.581
Assessment of learning from course (range: 1 to 5)	3.58	4.21	0.62***	<0.01	0.648
Interest in Statistics					
Task Value on MSLQ (range: 1 to 5)	3.37	3.74	0.37***	<0.01	0.461
Sample Size	**174**	**324**			

Notes: Means are regression adjusted. Effect sizes for continuous variables are calculated using Hedge's g, while those for binary variables are calculated with an adjusted logged odds ratio.

***/**/* Impact estimates are statistically significant at the .001/.01/.05 level, two-tailed test.

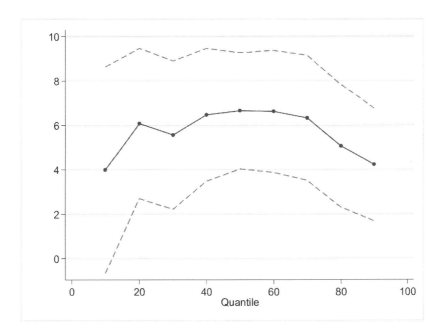

Figure 13.1 Impacts of course redesign on deciles of student achievement.

Note: Impacts are shown with solid lines. Upper and lower bounds for 95% confidence intervals are shown with dashed lines.

comparison groups at each decile. This figure also presents 95% confidence interval bands around these point estimates. These findings indicate that the course redesign produced roughly similar, positive results across the distribution. The impact was at least 4 points at each decile and was about 6 points for the 20th through the 70th deciles. Thus, impacts throughout the distribution are similar to the mean impact estimates presented in Table 13.3.

Impacts on Student Engagement in the Course

The flipped format improved student engagement in the course relative to the traditional format. Students in the flipped class were more likely to attend class than students in the traditional class ($M_{Flipped} = 87.1\%$, $M_{Traditional} = 81.5\%$, $p < .01$, ES = 0.272). In addition, students in the flipped class were less likely to report coming to class unprepared than students in the traditional class ($M_{Flipped} = 4.1\%$, $M_{Traditional} = 23.1\%$, $p < .01$, ES = 1.196).

Impacts on Student Perceptions of the Course

Students' overall ratings of the course were substantially higher in the flipped format relative to the traditional format. Students in the treatment group had more favorable responses than students in the control group to the questions "Overall this course was an effective course," "Overall, this instructor was an effective teacher," and "Overall, I learned a great deal from this course." These differences are all statistically significant and moderate, with effect sizes ranging from 0.581 to 0.667.

Impacts on Student Interest in Statistics

The flipped format improved student interest in statistics relative to the traditional format. Average scores on the task value component of the MSLQ were higher for students in the flipped class than for students in the traditional class ($M_{Flipped} = 3.74$, $M_{Traditional} = 3.33$, $p < .01$, ES = 0.461).

Impacts for Subgroups

Table 13.4 presents results from the subgroup analysis. For most subgroups that have traditionally had lower levels of participation in quantitative courses, we find favorable, statistically significant

Table 13.4 Impacts of Course Redesign on Different Subgroup Populations

Subgroup	Achievement	Course Engagement		Course Perception			Interest in Statistics
	Final Exam	Attendance	Come Unprepared	Overall Course Evaluation	Overall Instructor Evaluation	Assessment of Learning From Course	Task Value of MSLQ
Gender							
Women	5.01***	5.98**	−0.18***	0.69***	0.53***	0.60***	0.37***
Men	5.46*	3.79	−0.22**	0.78**	0.66**	0.69**	0.33**
Initial Statistics Knowledge							
Low (Below 50th percentile)	4.34**	5.49*	−0.23***	0.67***	0.58***	0.49***	0.41***
High (Above 50th percentile)	5.71***	5.76*	−0.16***	0.73***	0.52***	0.75***	0.33***
Quantitative Anxiety							
Low (Below 50th percentile)	6.27***	6.32**	−0.16***	0.64***	0.49***	0.60***	0.31***
High (Above 50th percentile)	3.81**	4.95*	−0.22***	0.75***	0.61***	0.65***	0.42***
Minority Status							
Underrepresented Minority (URM)	4.16*	6.17*	−0.23***	0.56**	0.49**	0.61	0.44***
Non-URM	5.33***	5.34**	−0.18***	0.74***	0.57***	0.62	0.35***

Notes: Coefficients are regression adjusted interaction terms. Test for impact differences compared with a Wald test.

***/**/* Impact estimates are statistically significant at the .001/.01/.05 level, two-tailed test.

impacts on all primary measures of program effectiveness (women, high quantitative anxiety, low initial statistics knowledge). For URM students, we find favorable, statistically significant impacts on all primary measures of program effectiveness except the assessment of learning from the course.

Discussion

The redesign of a large introductory statistics course from a traditional to a flipped format significantly improved student achievement controlling for baseline student characteristics, both at the mean and throughout the achievement distribution. Moreover, the flipped format increased student engagement in the course and perceptions of the course overall. Impacts were consistently positive for subgroups defined based on gender, initial statistical knowledge, quantitative anxiety, and underrepresented minority status.

The finding that mean student performance on the cumulative final exam was on average 5 points higher in the flipped format is consistent with much of the existing literature on the relationship between the flipped format and student achievement. However, the existing literature has not examined whether this effect is consistent for different groups or students at different points of the grade distribution. Quantile regression resulted in impacts of about 6 points throughout most of the distribution, with somewhat lower impacts for the 10th and 90th percentiles. At first glance, this finding would appear to contradict the findings presented in Table 13.2 for students at each score band, suggesting that students in the lowest category (< 60) benefit the most. However, the score band findings result from students at or near the cusp of the next category, where a 5-point gain would push a student into the next category, thereby moving them from failing the final to passing. Thus improved performance related to the flipped classroom is not concentrated among high or low performers; rather, improvements are made uniformly throughout the distribution.

The notion that the flipped format is beneficial to a broad set of students is further supported by the subgroup analyses. We found that the performance gains associated with the flipped format are consistently favorable and statistically significant irrespective of a student's gender, minority status, background knowledge of statistics, and quantitative anxiety. Thus the flipped format appears to be effective in improving performance, course engagement, course assessment, and interest in statistics for groups of students who have traditionally had lower levels of participation in quantitative courses.

Student engagement findings may suggest a few reasons for the positive impacts on student achievement. Students in the flipped research group were more likely than their traditional-group counterparts to attend class meetings and less likely to come to class unprepared. Increased attendance and class preparation could be linked to increased achievement, particularly given the class-time emphasis in the flipped format on practicing with the material, posing questions, and assessing understanding of the information. Student comments on the end-of-course focus group are consistent with this interpretation of the quantitative findings:

> I liked how [the instructor] had the poll everywhere quizzes at the beginning of class because it really
> forced me to actually do the work before I came to class instead of trying to learn it in class because it

was the kind of material that you probably couldn't pick up on just from class if you didn't do anything beforehand.

Focus group participant #2

Preparation was so crucial for this class. [The instructor] made it very easy to prepare by having all of these resources right there and all it was, was watching the video and taking notes. So it was something that I could easily motivate myself to do before class.

Focus group participant #6

A limitation of the quantitative findings on student engagement is that the preparation data are self-reported, and students may not accurately report their level of preparedness. Informal, periodic polls of students in the flipped classroom suggest that compliance with course preparation was quite high for the flipped group, ranging from 70% to 90% for most class meetings. Quiz performance further corroborated this self-report.

Learning gains could also be a result of having students be introduced to the material (videos or readings if they opted to) in a manner and rate that was appropriate for them. In quantitative feedback on the postcourse survey, students reported the videos to be very helpful in their preparation (97.2% rated the videos as either "helpful" or "very helpful") and that they watched certain videos more than once (94.7% reported going back to watch a previously assigned video, and 69.9% reported watching a video more than once). Performance gains could also be a result of students having access to easily navigable lecture videos.

I also really liked the videos that were made because I believe that you've got to go over something three-ish times before something solidifies. So doing the videos before, going over it in class, and then looking over it again it kind of creates a schedule to follow to I guess really get the information down if you need it.

Focus group participant #1

Being able to rewind and watch parts over again was so helpful because a lot of times, especially later in the semesters, I'd watch something, not be totally sure, and I could just watch it again and keep watching it until I understood, that was good, it's awesome.

Focus group participant #5

Especially since it's a math class, and having a video where somebody talks through a math problem and works through it and you can watch that process is a lot better for me learning than looking in a text book and seeing line by line how somebody worked it out [all focus group members in agreement] because having other math textbooks like that are much harder to follow and just watching the video, she's talking you through it so it was really helpful just for the subject matter for this course.

Focus group participant #5

Video use data indicated that students accessed videos multiple times during the semester, and particularly in the days prior to exams. The ability to pause, rewatch, and view videos at the time and setting the student prefers is often not available in a traditional lecture format and is often praised as one of the merits of lecture capture (Owston, Lupshenyuk, & Wideman, 2011). This self-pacing of content in combination with active learning exercises cements many practices that are effective to learning (retrieval practice, active engagement, etc.), thereby making good study practices "baked into" the course design. This is inherently inclusive, as not all students know how to approach studying, and when a course is taught in this way, it provides a roadmap for proper preparation and greater chances for success in the course.

Some may wonder if time can serve as a confound in the study, i.e., the instructor may have improved as a result of increased teaching experience. While possible, it is unlikely, as the instructor had already taught several semesters prior to the redesign. In this instance, the change between the traditional and redesigned format represents the seventh and eighth time through the course for this instructor, and vast improvement in teaching is unlikely to be observed. In fact, if anything, we would expect to see a dip in effectiveness as new methods are adapted and the instructor acclimates to these methods after several terms using a different modality.

Flipping a course requires a significant shift in the mindset of the student in terms of preparation and expectations about what occurs in class. However, in this study, course satisfaction ratings improved substantially. This finding is not consistent with prior studies of flipped classrooms, which typically find a decline in student perceptions of the course. Unfortunately, it is unclear why ratings improved in this study. One possibility is that, despite the perceived increase in out-of-class responsibilities, students may feel that in a flipped classroom, the quality of interactions they have with the instructor and peers in class is improved. Furthermore, preparing and granting access to lecture videos may suggest to students that the instructor is committed to fostering learning.

> *There were some class periods where we had worksheets that [the instructor] made up that we could do with whoever we were sitting near. I really liked that too because you know some people learn best by teaching others and so I really like that idea of listening to our peers, whoever were around us because they offer another way to do something or a different view or understanding so I also appreciated that opportunity to talk to other students in class.*
>
> Focus group participant #1

The emphasis on higher-order skills in the flipped classroom can translate to students gaining a deeper appreciation for the more nuanced aspects of the subject matter. Because the flipped classroom stresses a learner-centered approach to education, students may take ownership over their learning in a different way from a traditional classroom that is more passive.

> *I felt that this course was different from the math skills I learned in calculus in high school because success in statistics isn't about being able to work through a math problem because a lot of the calculations were simple algebra. It was more about reading a problem, what type of test you use, very analytical, so I think that was probably the biggest thing, that was one of the biggest skills that I learned. It was very different than solving a hard integral or something. It was about being able to use a situation and apply your knowledge to that.*
>
> Focus group participant #5

I came to class with the intention of them teaching me something, not elaborating on stuff that I was supposed to already have known. I just kinda went with that Freshman year and then taking this class I saw how useful it was to have the background knowledge and then having the professor just explain it further in class. And I've been keeping up with that this semester in other classes.

Focus group participant #1

By moving lecture outside the class, the class time can be less scripted and require the instructor to be more nimble in addressing the students' needs. Furthermore, careful selection of formative assessment questions and class exercises that are sufficiently challenging but not overwhelming are essential to a successful transition to a flipped classroom, but few instructors have formal training in these techniques. It is possible that the mixed review of flipped classrooms in the literature is a result of limited instructor training in these techniques, improper preparation of students for a flipped classroom, weak implementation, or combinations of all above. In all, there are many ways in which a flipped classroom can fail in the eyes of students, but in this case it did not. More research is warranted to evaluate the course, implementation, and instructor characteristics that lead to successful course redesigns. It is possible that the novelty of the course format engaged students differently, and such novelty may wear off if more courses adopt similar approaches.

While the literature on flipped classrooms using high-structure active learning is still in its infancy, this study demonstrates that it is possible to see improvement in achievement, engagement, and perceptions in large quantitative courses when they are flipped and that these impacts can translate into increased interest in the statistics field. These improvements are present across a broad range of students, including groups that traditionally have had lower levels of STEM participation. The consistency of these findings for different types of students may have important implications for maintaining student engagement in STEM courses. In particular, relatively poor performance in STEM courses and negative attitudes toward these courses are two likely barriers to students remaining engaged in STEM fields. Findings from this study indicate that flipped classrooms partially address these two barriers. Thus, effectively implemented flipped classrooms may represent an important strategy to keep STEM students motivated and engaged. When applied appropriately, high-structure active learning through a flipped classroom format has the possibility of not only keeping students interested in STEM fields but increasing the pipeline of students who feel a sense of ownership over their learning and are better able to increase skill and critical thinking abilities.

Acknowledgments: The author acknowledges and thanks the University of North Carolina at Chapel Hill's Center for Faculty Excellence for support.

References

Bergmann, J., & Sams, A. (2012). *Flip your classroom: Reach every student in every class every day*. Washington, DC: International Society for Technology in Education.

Bormann, J. (2014). *Affordances of flipped learning and its effects on student engagement and Achievement*. Master's thesis. Retrieved from www.flippedlearning.org/cms/lib07/VA01923112/Centricity/Domain/41/bormann_lit_review.pdf

Carlson, K. A., & Winquist, J. R. (2011). Evaluating an active learning approach to teaching introductory statistics: A classroom workbook approach. *Journal of Statistics Education* [Online], *19*(1). Retrieved from www.amstat.org/publications/jse/v19n1/carlson.pdf.

Dauphinee, T. L., Schau, C., & Stevens, J. J. (1997). Survey of Attitudes Toward Statistics: Factor structure and factorial invariance for females and males. *Structural Equation Modeling*, *4*(2), 129–141.

Davies, R. S., Dean, D. L., & Ball, N. (2013). Flipping the classroom and instructional technology integration in a college-level information systems spreadsheet course. *Educational Technology Research and Development*, *61*(4), 563–580.

Dunn, D. S. (2000). Letter exchanges on statistics and research methods: Writing, responding, and learning. *Teaching of Psychology*, *27*, 128–130.

Eddy, S. L., & Hogan, K. A. (2014). Getting under the hood: How and for whom does increasing course structure work? *CBE Life Sciences Education*, *13*(3), 453–468. https://doi.org/10.1187/cbe.14-03-0050

Enfield, J. (2013). Looking at the impact of the flipped classroom model of instruction on undergraduate multimedia students at CSUN. *Techtrends: Linking Research & Practice to Improve Learning*, *57*(6), 14–27. https://doi.org/10.1007/s11528-013-0698-1

Evans, B. (2007). Student attitudes, conceptions, and achievement in introductory undergraduate college statistics. *The Mathematics Educator*, *17*(2), 24–30. Retrieved from http://math.coe.uga.edu/tme/issues/v17n2/v17n2.pdf

Findlay-Thompson, S., & Mombourquette, P. (2014). Evaluation of a flipped classroom in an undergraduate business course. *Business Education & Accreditation*, *6*(1), 63–71. Retrieved from http://search.proquest.com/docview/1446438718?accountid=14691

Freeman, S., Eddy, S. L., McDonough, M., Smith, M. K., Okoroafor, N., Jordt, H., & Wenderoth, M. K. (2014). Active learning increases student performance in science, engineering, and mathematics. *PNAS*, *23*, 8410–8415

Fulton, K. (2012). Upside down and inside out: Flip your classroom to improve student learning. *Learning & Leading with Technology*, *39*(8), 12–17.

Gundlach, E., Richards, K. A. R., Nelson, D., & Levesque-Bristol, C. (2015). A comparison of student attitudes, statistical reasoning, performance, and perceptions for web-augmented traditional, fully online, and flipped sections of a statistical literacy class. *Journal of Statistics Education* [Online], *19*(1). Retrieved from www.amstat.org/publications/jse/v23n1/gundlach.pdf.

Harlow, L., Burkholder, G. J., & Morrow, J. A. (2002). Evaluating attitudes, skill, and performance in a learning-enhanced quantitative methods course: A structural modeling approach. *Structural Equation Modeling: A Multidisciplinary Journal*, *9*(3).

Herreid, C. F., & Schiller, N. A. (2013). Case studies in the flipped classroom. *Journal of College Science Teachers*, *42*(5), 62–66.

Koenker, R., & Bassett, Jr., G. (1978). Regression quantiles. *Econometrica*, *6*(1) 33–50.

Mason, G., Shuman, R. T., & Cook, K. E. (2013). Comparing the effectiveness of an inverted classroom to a traditional classroom in an upper-division engineering course. *Education, IEEE Transactions*, *56*, 430-435. https://doi.org/10.1109/TE.2013.2249066

McLaughlin, J. E., Roth, M. T., Glatt, D. M., Gharkholonarehe, N., Davidson, C. A., Griffin, L. M., . . . Mumper, R. J. (2014). The flipped classroom: A course redesign to foster learning and engagement in a health professions school. *Academic Medicine*, *89*(2), 236–243. https://doi.org/10.1097/ACM.0000000000000086

Morin, B., Kecskemety, K. M., Harper, K. A., & Clingan, P. A. (2013, June 23–26). *The inverted classroom in a first-year engineering course*. Paper presented at 120th ASEE Annual Conference & Exposition: Frankly We Do Give a D*mn.

Murphree, D. S. (2014). "Writing wasn't really stressed, accurate historical analysis was stressed": Student perceptions of in-class writing in the inverted, general education, university history survey course. *History Teacher*, *47*(2), 209–219.

Owston, R., Lupshenyuk, D., & Wideman, H. (2011). Lecture capture in large undergraduate classes: Student perceptions and academic performance. *The Internet and Higher Education*, *14*(4), 262–268. https://doi.org/10.1016/j.iheduc.2011.05.006

Pintrich, P. R., Smith, D. A. F., Garcia, T., & McKeachie, W. J. (1991). *A manual for the use of Motivated Strategies for Learning Questionnaire (MSLQ)*. Ann Arbor, MI: University of Michigan.

Posner, M. A. (2011). The impact of a proficiency-based assessment and reassessment of learning objectives system on student achievement and attitudes. *Statistics Education Research Journal*, *10*(1), 3–14.

President's Council of Advisors on Science and Technology. (2012, May). Federal Science, Technology, Engineering, and Mathematics (STEM) Education 5-Year Strategic Plan. https://obamawhitehouse.archives.gov/sites/default/files/microsites/ostp/stem_stratplan_2013.pdf

Rowe, M., Frantz, J., & Bozalek, V. (2013). Beyond knowledge and skills: The use of a Delphi study to develop a technology-mediated teaching strategy. *BMC Medical Education*, *13*(1), 51.

Schau, C., & Emmioğlu, E. (2012). Do introductory statistics courses in the United States improve students' attitudes? *Statistics Education Research Journal*, *11*(2), 86–94. Retrieved from www.stat.auckland.ac.nz/serj.

Schau, C., Stevens, J., Dauphinee, T. L., & Del Vecchio, A. (1995). The development and validation of the Survey of Attitudes Toward Statistics. *Educational and Psychological Measurement*, *55*, 868–875.

Sizemore, O. J., & Lewandowski, G. (2009). Learning might not equal liking: Research methods course changes knowledge but not attitudes. *Teaching of Psychology*, *36*(2), 90–95.

Strayer, J. F. (2009). *Inverting the classroom: A study of the learning environment when an intelligent tutoring system is used to help students learn*. Saarbrücken: VDM Verlag.

Talley, C., & Scherer, S. (2013). The enhanced flipped classroom: Increasing academic performance with student-recorded lectures and practice testing in a "flipped" stem course. *Journal of Negro Education*, *82*(3), 339–347.

Tobias, S. (1994). Interest, prior knowledge, and learning. *Review of Educational Research*, *64*(1), 37–54.

Townsend, M. A. R., Moore, D. W., Tuck, B. F., & Wilton, K. M. (1998). Self-concept and anxiety in university students studying social science statistics within a cooperative learning structure. *Educational Psychology: An International Journal of Experimental Educational Psychology*, *18*(1) 41–54.

Tune, J. D., Sturek, M., & Basile, D. P. (2013, December). Flipped classroom model improves graduate student performance in cardiovascular, respiratory, and renal physiology. *Advances in Physiology Education*, *37*(4), 316–320. https://doi.org/10.1152/advan.00091.2013

U.S. Department of Education, National Center for Education Statistics. (2013). *Digest of education statistics, 2012* (NCES 2014–015), Chapter 3. https://nces.ed.gov/programs/digest/d12/ch_3.asp

Wilson, S. G. (2013, July). The flipped class: A method to address the challenges of an undergraduate statistics course. *Teaching of Psychology*, *40*, 193–199. https://doi.org/10.1177/0098628313487461

Winquist, J. R., & Carlson, K. A. (2014). Flipped statistics class results: Better performance than lecture over one year later. *Journal of Statistics Education* [Online], *22*(3). Retrieved from www.amstat.org/publications/jse/v22n3/winquist.pdf

## Chapter 14

Teaching Research Methods Using Simulation

William Revelle

For those of us who teach research methods, the process of learning how to do research is the keystone of our psychological curriculum. Understanding how to do psychological research allows students to integrate the content of their substantive courses with the methods behind the findings discussed in those courses. Research methods considers the essence of experimental and correlational design and scientific inference. It is not a course to turn students into psychological researchers; rather it is a course to make our students intelligent consumers of science, whether it be psychological, physical, or biological. For teaching students the process of doing science in a particular field helps them appreciate the challenges and joys of science more broadly.

In this chapter, I outline a web-based simulation I have been using for a number of years that gives the students the experience of designing and analyzing their own experiment but with certain constraints. In addition, by using a simulation, I am able to know the "true" effects and can then discuss issues of power and inference.

At Northwestern, research methods (Psychology 205) is the fundamental course in our psychology curriculum. It is the second in a three-part sequence of research training, following a general introduction to statistics (201), and preceding the third course (3xx) which uses research methodology in a substantive field (e.g., personality research, research in social psychology, research in memory, etc.). Research methods is the gateway course to the major and is prerequisite for almost all of our advanced courses.

The students are typically sophomore or junior psychology majors or minors, although a few take it as part of requirements in other departments. The research methods course is taught in multiple sections every quarter, with a typical class size of 25 students. Because it is critical for upper-level courses, the faculty members of the psychology department agreed years ago on certain requirements for the course. These instructional guidelines include the need to cover correlational and experimental techniques, application of statistical reasoning, the ethics of human and animal research, and a writing requirement. The guidelines include doing three separate studies, either correlational or experimental, each of which is then written up in a standard scientific style (e.g., APA, but other styles are introduced). Because of the writing requirement, the emphasis upon statistical analysis, formal methods, and the need to actually do research, research methods at Northwestern is, like most such courses around the country, the "organic chemistry" course of the psych major. That is, it is the hardest course in the major but also the most important. Students typically dread taking the course but finish it with a degree of enthusiam for research that they did not think possible when they started.

A challenge in teaching the course is coming up with example studies for the students to conduct and report. Over the years, I have developed three types of studies for the students. The first is an actual experiment conducted in class on the first day. It is a replication and extension of the Roediger and McDermott (1995) study of false memories, which I use because it introduces substantively interesting results and demonstrates within- and between-person analyses. To help them understand the results, I do all the analyses for the students and show them how to integrate the findings into a 10–12 page paper. The third study is a research project designed and executed by each student individually. Each student writes a brief research proposal which I review before they undertake the final project. The statistical tools they learn in the second study are used for analysis of this third study. The second study is a computer-simulated experiment in which each student designs and executes their own study to test hypotheses discussed in class and in the readings for the assignment. The simulation uses a web-based interface to a simple model that includes three Subject Variables (SVs), two Independent Experimental Variables (IVs), and three outcome measures (DVs). The names of the variables can be specified by the instructor, as may the underlying relationships between the SVs, IVs, and DVs. In parallel with real research, the overall simulation is too complicated for one massive study, and students are expected to choose a particular subset of variables from the broader set.

The simulation code is written in PHP[1] as a general mixed model of SVs and IVs with multiple DVs. The parameters of the model can be modified for any particular implementation. For my class, I have instantiated the simulation with variables similar to those examined over many years at the Personality, Motivation, and Cognition (PMC) lab at Northwestern and reported in a number of article and book chapters. The code, however, is written in a general manner that allows it to be modified easily for other specific examples.

The Simulation

The basic simulation is a set of three interlinked PHP webpages that (a) give an overview of the study and ask for the number of subjects to run, (b) a data generation web page that prompts for specific values of the SVs and IVs and creates the values for three DVs; and (c) a page that displays the results for each subject suitable for copying into R (R Core Team, 2018) for further analysis. From the students' perspective, they just need to go to the experiment at https://personality-project.org/courses/205/ simulation/simulation.experiment. php and follow the instructions. From the instructors point of view, it is necessary to prepare a brief discussion of how the simulation works, what the variables are, etc. An example of such instructions is found at https://personality-project.org/courses/205/simulation/

simulating-experiments.pdf. The PHP code for these pages is included in the appendix to this chapter.

What the Students Are Told Before Doing the Study

Psychological theories are ways of organizing observable phenomena in terms of a limited number of unobservable constructs. In addition to describing known phenomena, theories allow for prediction of as-yet-unobserved phenomena. Theories may be stated as informal descriptions or may be stated in formal propositional logic or in mathematical equations. Complex theories that involve many variables may be stated as dynamic processes that change over time and that can best be captured in computer simulations.

This experiment simulates the complexity of a real research program by simulating the complex relationships between a set of observed characteristics of individuals, how they react to situations in terms of their motivational state, and how motivational state, in turn, affects cognitive performance. Prior work in the Personality, Motivation, and Cognition Laboratory at Northwestern has allowed us to formulate a complex model of human cognition in response to stress (Anderson & Revelle, 1982, 1994; Revelle & Loftus, 1992; Revelle & Oehlberg, 2008; Revelle & Anderson, 1992; Revelle, Amaral, & Turriff, 1976; Revelle, Humphreys, Simon, & Gilliland, 1980; Wilt, Oehlberg, & Revelle, 2011). This simulation is based upon that work. In a sense, the simulation is a theory of the relationship between these four sets of variables (person characteristics, situational characteristics, intervening motivational states, and cognitive performance). The parameters of the model have been set to reflect empirical estimates of the strength of various relationships. Several nuisance variables have been added to more properly simulate the problems of experimental design.

This simulation of the theory may be used as a test of the theory as well as a tool for understanding the complexity of research. That is, although one may want to study the full model, because of the limitations of one's time and energy, one may study only a limited aspect of the model. Your objective is twofold: to better understand a limited aspect of a particular psychological theory, and to try to understand what are the relationships that have been specified in the model.

Although the code is generic, the instantiation of the variables is shown in Table 14.1, and the particular model that is simulated is shown in Figure 14.1. Students are not shown this table nor the figure until after they have completed their papers.

The Students Are Further Told That

The simulation is a web-based program that allows you to "collect" the data on the web and then save the resulting output file to your computer to do subsequent analyses. The biggest question is what you should study. To answer this, you need to consider the variables available. The underlying model is a function of the IVs and SVs. Your job is to try to estimate the underlying model. The model is psychologically plausible and is based upon prior results.

Table 14.1 The Generic Variables in the Simulation With the Specific Values Given to Be Compatible With the Background Literature. Students are not shown the generic values, just the specific implementation. The program uses the generic equations but reports the results in terms of the specific implementation. The instructor can change the generic equations as well as the variable names by modifying the PHP code. The students' task is to hypothesize and test for various IV, SV, DV relationships. Although the underlying relationships are generally monotonic but nonlinear, with one nonmonotonic effect, the students are encourage to fit the data with linear approximations.

Generic Variable	Specific Implementation	Possible Values
ntrials	Subject Number	1 ... max
SV0	Sex	1–2
SV1	Anxiety	0–10
SV2	Impulsivity	0–10
IV1	Caffeine	Placebo, Caffeine
IV2	Time of Day	8–22
DV1	Energetic Arousal	0–100
DV2	Tense Arousal	0–100
DV3	Cognitive Performance	0–100

Weights	Specific values
wt1	.3
wt2	.2
errorwt	.3

Generic Equation	Specific Implementation
$DV1 = IV1 - \cos((IV2 - SV2)/4) + 1$	Arousal = f(Drug + Impulsivity x Time)
$DV2 = \dfrac{100}{(1 + \exp(3 - IV1 - wt1 * SV1 + wt2 * rnorm))}$	Tension = f(Drug + Anxiety)
$DV3 = \dfrac{100}{(1 + \exp(-DV1 + errorwt * rnorm))}$	Performance = f(Arousal)

They Are Then Given a Description of the Simulations

Independent variables that are under control of the experimenter may be categorized as experimental variables and subject variables. *Experimental variables or IVs* may be manipulated by the experimenter. *Subject variables or SVs* are characteristics of the subjects that may be measured but not manipulated.

In this experiment, the Independent Experimental Variables include Drug condition (placebo or caffeine), and Time of Day. Given the realities of volunteer subjects, Time of Day is assumed to vary only between 8 a.m. and 10 p.m. (22.00 hours). The Subject Variables that are "assessed" in this study include Sex, Trait Anxiety, and Trait Impulsivity, and when the subject appears during the quarter (Subject Number). Subject Number increases for every subject run in a particular experiment. This is modeled in the simulation as one subject per day, so later subjects are run later in the quarter.

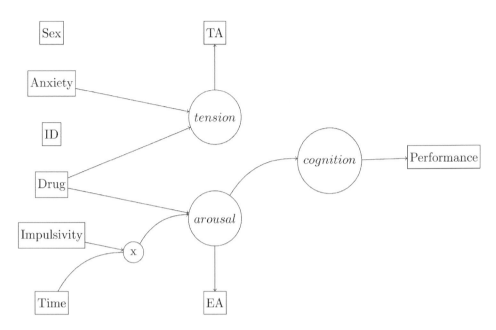

Figure 14.1 The simulation model as implemented. Boxes represent observed variables, circles latent variables. Straight arrows show linear effects, curved arrows are monotonic (arousal to cognition), or non-monotonic (time to arousal which is moderated by impulsivity). Some variables (i.e., Sex) have no effect, others (e.g., ID) have an effect if subjects are not assigned to condition. The specific values are calculated according to the formulae in Table 14.1.

The Dependent Variables are measures of motivational state (Energetic and Tense Arousal) as well as accuracy of Performance on a simple cognitive task (letter scanning). Energetic Arousal may be seen as reflecting how active and alert rather than sleepy and drowsy a subject reports being. Tense Arousal reflects how Tense and Frustrated rather than Calm and Relaxed a person reports being (Rafaeli & Revelle, 2006; Thayer, 1989). Both of these scales are reported in units ranging from 0 to 100. An additional variable is the Cost of running the experiment. This is a function of the scarcity of the subjects.

The values of the Independent and Subject variables may be specified by the experimenter for each subject or may be allowed to vary randomly. If allowed to vary randomly, the experimental variables will be assigned values in a uniform random distribution. The subject variables may either be specified (this simulates choosing particular subjects based upon a pretest) or be allowed to vary randomly. If varying, they will be assigned values based upon samples from a normal distribution. If subjects are selected for particular values on a personality dimension, this is the same as rejecting many potential subjects and thus the Cost of running grows more rapidly than the simple number of subjects who participate.

1. Drug has two levels (0 = Placebo or 1 = Caffeine). Caffeine is known to act as a central nervous system stimulant although it has some side effects such as tremor (Revelle et al., 1976, 2012, 1980).

2. Time of Day has 15 levels (8 a.m. . . . 10 p.m. or 8 . . . 22). Although most cognitive psychologists do not examine the effects of time of day on cognitive performance, there is a fairly extensive literature suggesting that performance does vary systematically across the day (Revelle et al., 1980; Revelle, 1993).

3. Sex of subject sometimes interacts with characteristics of the experiment (sex of experimenter, stress of experiment, type of task) and has sometimes been associated with levels of anxiety. In this study, Sex varies randomly taking on the values of 1 or 2. (Using the mnemonic of the number of X chromosomes, that is 1 = M and 2 = F).

4. Trait anxiety is a stable personality trait associated with feelings of tension, worry, and somatic distress. Trait anxious individuals are more sensitive to cues for punishment and nonreward and are also more likely to experience negative affect than are less trait anxious individuals (Gray, 1991; Wilt, Oehlberg et al., 2011). In this simulation, anxiety can take on values from 0 to 0.

5. Impulsivity is a stable personality trait associated with making up one's mind rapidly and doing and saying things without stopping to think. It has been shown in prior work to relate to an inability to sustain performance, particularly in the morning (Anderson and Revelle, 1982, 1983). Theories of impulsivity have also suggested that impulsivity is related to a general sensitivity to cues for reward and to a greater propensity toward positive affect (Gray, 1991; Revelle, 1997; Wilt & Revelle, 2009; Zinbarg & Revelle, 1989). In this simulation, impulsivity can take on values from 0 to 10.

Dependent Variables

1. Energetic arousal reflects self-reports of feelings of energy, activity, and alertness. EA has been shown to increase with exercise and to decrease with sleep deprivation (Thayer, Takahashi, & Pauli, 1988; Thayer, 1989). EA is also associated with feelings of positive affect (Rafaeli & Revelle, 2006; Watson & Tellegen, 1985; Wilt, Funkhouser, & Revelle, 2011).

2. Tense arousal reflects feelings of tension, frustration, and fear (Thayer, 1989) and is moderately associated with feelings of negative affect (Rafaeli & Revelle, 2006; Watson & Tellegen, 1985).

3. Performance in this simulation reflects accuracy on a simple decision task. A perfect score is 100, and performance deteriorates from that as a function of condition and motivational state. Abstractly, this may be thought of as accuracy on a vigilance task, or the ability to make accurate judgments on some sustained processing task (e.g., Anderson & Revelle, 1982, 1983, 1994; Humphreys & Revelle, 1984).

4. The cost of any experiment is a function of the number of subjects (it increases by 1 for every subject) and also of the scarcity of the subjects. Thus, if you choose to run just very high (10) and very low (1) anxiety subjects, this will require more prescreening to identify such subjects, and

thus the cost will be higher than if you just chose average levels of anxiety or if you just allowed anxiety to randomly vary. It is important to report the cost of the study you carry out.

Finally, They Are Told That

A reasonable approach is to have some theoretical reason to believe that a certain relationship exists and then perhaps conduct a series of "pilot" studies to determine the sensitivity of certain parameter values.

The goal of this project is to try to determine at least some of the relationships that have been built into the model. You will be evaluated on principles of experimental design, not on the significance of the results.

They are instructed to form some specific hypothesis (or hypotheses) and then test this by running the simulation.

Literature Review and Methodology

The students are given some background literature but are encouraged to use various search engines (e.g., Google Scholar, Web of Science) to find more recent references and potential hypotheses. When reporting their methods, they are required to report how they administered the caffeine and in what amounts (if they give caffeine), how they measured impulsivity or anxiety, and what were the measures of arousal and tension. The values they discuss in their paper need to be plausible. Thus, saying that they gave 0 or 1 milligram or 0 or 1 gram of caffeine suggests they have not read the literature enough to realize that 1 gram would be an overdose or that 1 milligram would have no effect. The choice of a performance task is important, for the simulated one actually has a monotonic relationship with arousal rather than some of the more complex relationships discussed in the personality × performance literature (e.g., Revelle et al., 1980). Thus, if students say they used a complex reasoning task but then failed to find a drug x personality interaction, this is not surprising given that the underlying model does not have such an interaction.

Data Analysis

An important part of research methods is learning how to apply modern statistical procedures to analyze research. To do this, the research methods students are introduced to the R statistical system (R Core Team, 2018). R is an open-source interactive statistical system that allows students to do basic and advanced statistics. One of the particular powers of R is the ability to use the output of any function as the input of any other function. This allows for rapid development of new functions, which add functionality to existing functions. Because of its open-source nature and the existence of a central repository for shared code (the comprehensive R archive network or CRAN), the R system encourages the development of additional packages for specific applications. In addition, because R is used in some of our advanced and graduate courses and in many graduate training programs and occupations, students are encouraged to learn R in Psychology 205. Class readings and web pages devoted to the use of R in general and the *psych* package (Revelle, 2018)

Table 14.2 The Observed Correlations From 100 Simulated Subjects

Variable	Sex	Drug	Time	Anxiety	Impulsivity	Arousal	Tension	Performance
Sex	1.00							
Drug	−0.07	1.00						
Time	−0.14	0.13	1.00					
Anxiety	−0.10	0.04	−0.06	1.00				
Impulsivity	−0.04	0.00	0.14	−0.17	1.00			
Arousal	−0.10	0.68	0.50	0.00	−0.07	1.00		
Tension	−0.12	0.60	0.01	0.76	−0.10	0.37	1.00	
Performance	−0.09	0.51	0.38	−0.03	0.03	0.68	0.23	1.00

in particular are given as additional handouts. In the following pages, R functions are shown in boldfaced fixed-pitch font.

Descriptive Statistics

The last page of the simulation generates a web page with the data arranged by "subjects," and the columns represent the IVs, SVs and DVs. The student may select everything on the page and then copy to R using the read.clipboard function. They are then ready for basic descriptive statistics, both quantitative (e.g., describe and describeBy) as well as graphic (e.g., pairs.panels, error.bars and error.bars.by). The importance of screening data for errors at entry or outliers is discussed.

Although encouraged to test specific hypotheses, students are also shown how to examine the overall correlational structure of the data (Table 14.2). The more adventurous students will run 100 subjects as a pilot study, examine the correlational structure, and systematically vary or control for specific variables in a subsequent study. The emphasis upon showing the correlations is for descriptive purposes, and the use of "magic asterisks" denoting statistical "significance" is discouraged.

Inferential Statistics

One of the many powers of R for teaching research methods is the emphasis upon the general linear model. Thus students are given the formulae for a single IV (1), two additive IVs (2), and then two IVs with interactions (3), and finally two IVs with an interaction and a covariate (4):

$$DY = Constant + IV1 \tag{1}$$
$$DY = Constant + IV1 + IV2 \tag{2}$$
$$DY = Constant + IV1 + IV2 + IV1*IV2 \tag{3}$$
$$DY = Constant + IV1 + IV2 + IV1*IV2 + Z \tag{4}$$

and told how if there is just one dichotomous IV, then this is just the *t-test* they were taught in introductory statistics. If *IV*1 is continuous, then this is regression. If *IV*1 and *IV*2 are both categorical, then this is just the Analysis of Variance they learned in their introductory statistics course . . .

If *IV*1 or *IV*2 are continuous, then this is multiple regression with or without moderation (Cohen, Cohen, West, & Aiken, 2003). The use of R and the general linear model approach is introduced.

Thus, equation 1 is implemented as a *t*-test and may be displayed using the error.bars.by function. This allows a discussion of confidence intervals of the group means and three different ways of displaying them (error bars representing one standard deviation around the mean, error bars representing 95% confidence versus "cat's eyes" showing 95% confidence).

```
my.data <- read.clipboard() #get the data from the web page
t.test(performance ~ drug, data = my.data) #perform the t.test
temp<-error.bars.by(performance~drug,data=my.data,sd=TRUE,eyes=FALSE)
#1 sd error bars
error.bars.by(performance ~ drug, data = my.data,eyes=FALSE) #conven-
tional error bars
error.bars.by(performance ~ drug, data = my.data) #cats eyes
```

Analysis of variance of categorical IVs with (equation 3) or without interactions (equation 2) is done by the aov function, and the error.bars.by function may be used to show the means by group.

```
summary(aov(performance~ sex+ drug,data=my.data)) #no interaction
summary(aov(performance~ sex* drug,data=my.data)) #with interaction
error.bars.by(performance~ sex* drug,data=my.data) #means plus cats eyes
```

The generalization to continuous IVs is discussed (Cohen et al., 2003). The concept of mean centering is introduced, and examples of mean centering versus not mean centering are shown, as are various ways of graphically presenting the effects. They are then given the R equivalent of equation 3 after zero centering and how to find the basic inferential statistics.

```
cen.data <- data.frame(scale(my.data,scale=FALSE)) # convert to a means
centered data frame mod1 <- lm(performance ~ drug * time* impulsivity,
data=cen.data) #test for 3 main effects, summary(mod1) #show the summary
statistics
```

There are, of course, multiple ways to display the results of the linear model. If using one categorical variable (e.g., drug or sex) and one continuous variable (e.g., impulsivity), a convenient way is plot all of the data, and then draw regression lines for each group.

```
# plot the data
with(my.data, plot(performance ~ impulsivity, pch = 21 - drug, data =
    my.data, main="Performance varies by impulsivity and drug"))
with(my.data, by(my.data,drug,function(x) abline(lm(performance ~
    impulsivity,data=x) ))) #add the lines for placebo and caffeine
text(9,56,"placebo") #add a label at the x, y coordinates
text(9,73,"caffeine") #add another label
#draw it using setCor
setCor(performance ~ drug * impulsivity, data = my.data,
    main="Impulsivity x Caffeine effects", std=FALSE)
```

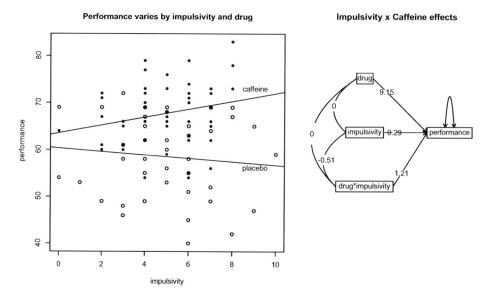

Figure 14.2 Two ways to show the results of a linear model. The left-hand panel shows the regression lines for performance as a function of impulsivity for both placebo and caffeine. The right-hand panel shows this as a path diagram with the interaction as a product term. By default, the setCor function standardizes the coefficients and means centers the data, but they may show as unstandardized by setting an option.

An alternative way to do and display linear model data is to use the setCor function, which shows the results as path coefficients. A comparison of these two approaches is shown if Figure 14.2.

Power, Type I and Type II Errors

The advantage of using a simulated experiment is that the instructor knows "truth." That is, the underlying model used to generate the data (see Figure 14.1) is known to the instructor but not to the students. Some of the variables (e.g., sex) have no effect on the outcome, some relationships are confounded (e.g., tension correlates with arousal because both are increased by caffeine), some effects are small (e.g., the interaction of impulsivity and time of day), and some effects are actually mediated through intermediate variables (the effect of caffeine on performance is mediated by the effect of caffeine on arousal, which in turn improves performance). Furthermore, the ease of doing two- and three-way ANOVAs and regressions and the resulting increase in various comparisons increases the likelihood that variables that have no real effect will show "significant" effects.

Because each student is designing his or her own study, but because they are limited to the number of possible variables to study, at the end of the second experiment, after all the results have been analyzed by the students and they have submitted their research papers, I conduct an informal meta-analysis of the results. That is, in class, it is easy to do a box-score count of how many people examined a certain variable or pair of variables and how many obtained "significant" effects. It seems as if the most motivated students are the ones most likely to get Type I errors, because they have done the most complex designs. On the other hand, those students who do not expend very much effort in doing the simulations are much more likely to commit Type II errors because of a lack of power. Having written a paper with a discussion of a result that turns out to be a Type I error is a particularly memorable experience for the best students. Although we are all susceptible to Type I errors, doing a simulation with a known model is the only time that we can be sure that what we found was indeed an error.

Confounding Variables

The simulation is meant to simulate what happens if data are collected from real subjects. An unfortunate characteristic of many undergraduate subject pools is that the more anxious subjects volunteer earlier in the quarter than do the less anxious subjects, and the more impulsive subjects tend to put things off to the end of the quarter. This is simulated by inducing a slight negative correlation between anxiety and subject number and a slight positive correlation between impulsivity and subject number. This is not a problem if subjects are randomly assigned to condition but does lead to a confound if all of one condition (e.g., placebo or caffeine, morning versus evening) is done before the other condition.

The problem of how to create random numbers is addressed (even coin flips are not truly random), and computers generate pseudo-random numbers. A problem of complete randomness is the tendency for cell sizes to be unbalanced. This is particularly a problem with small samples. Randomization with filling out of cell sizes at the end of the study introduces systematic biases due to end-of-quarter effects. Students are shown examples of such confounding and encouraged to make use of the block.random function to help them assign subjects to control for this confound. The correlation of subject number with any of the experimental or subject variables should be near zero if the conditions are assigned by block randomization.

Mediation and Moderation

Although far beyond the scope of the normal research methods course, an occasional student will notice that caffeine and time of day affect arousal as well as performance. They then discover that the relationship between caffeine and performance is much weaker when they introduce arousal into their model. That is, they have discovered that arousal mediates the effect of caffeine and time of day on performance. This does not happen often, but they (and I) are very excited when they find this. I can then show them how to test mediation models using the mediate function, which tests the mediation effect through bootstrap resampling (Figure 14.3).

Mediation

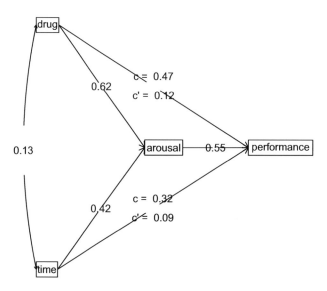

Figure 14.3 An analysis of the mediating role of arousal on performance. Both drug and time of day affect performance, but this effect is mediated through their effect on arousal. The direct effects of caffeine or of time are shown to vanish when controlling for the effect of arousal.

Conclusion

Learning how to do research is best done by doing it. Designing their own studies, running their own (simulated) subjects, and analyzing their own data helps students appreciate the complexity of research. How to read the appropriate literature to generate hypotheses, how to operationalize these hypotheses in an experimental or correlational study, and then how to analyze and report their results are important parts of doing science. In addition, in the process of analyzing and displaying their results, the students are also learning how to use modern statistical techniques and developing confidence in their ability to do real research.

Author Note

contact: William Revelle revelle@northwestern.edu Draft version of March 22, 2019

Note

1. PHP is an open-source language that was originally written to allow for Personal Home Pages but in the Unix tradition has come to have a self-recursive definition: PHP: Hypertext Preprocessor. It is a "server-side" aid to allow dynamic features in HTML (Hyper Text Markup Language) and access to databases such as MySQL and

resides on a remote computer running a webserver such as Apache. From the end user's point of view, webpages appear as if they were written in normal HTML but with dynamic features not available in HTML. As is true of much of the open-source community, there are extensive help pages available on the web for programming assistance.

References

Anderson, K. J., & Revelle, W. (1982). Impulsivity, caffeine, and proofreading: A test of the Easterbrook hypothesis. *Journal of Experimental Psychology: Human Perception and Performance*, *8*(4), 614–624. https://doi. org/10.1037/0096-1523.8.4.614

Anderson, K. J., & Revelle, W. (1983). The interactive effects of caffeine, impulsivity and task demands on a visual search task. *Personality and Individual Differences*, *4*(2), 127–134. https://doi.org/10.1016/0191-8869(83)90011-9

Anderson, K. J., & Revelle, W. (1994). Impulsivity and time of day: Is rate of change in arousal a function of impulsivity? *Journal of Personality and Social Psychology*, *67*(2), 334–344. https://doi.org/10.1037/0022-3514.67.2.334

Cohen, J., Cohen, P., West, S. G., & Aiken, L. S. (2003). *Applied multiple regression/correlation analysis for the behavioral sciences* (3rd ed.). Mahwah, NJ: L. Erlbaum Associates.

Gray, J. A. (1991). The neuropsychology of temperament. In J. Strelau & A. Angleitner (Eds.), *Explorations in temperament: International perspectives on theory and measurement* (pp. 105–128). New York: Plenum Press.

Humphreys, M. S., & Revelle, W. (1984). Personality, motivation, and performance: A theory of the relationship between individual differences and information processing. *Psychological Review*, *91*(2), 153–184. https://doi. org/10.1037/0033-295X.91.2.153

Rafaeli, E., & Revelle, W. (2006). A premature consensus: Are happiness and sadness truly opposite affects? *Motivation and Emotion*, *30*(1), 1–12. https://doi.org/10.1007/s11031-006-9004-2

R Core Team. (2018). *R: A language and environment for statistical computing* [Computer software manual]. Vienna, Austria. Retrieved from https://www.R-project.org/

Revelle, W. (1993). Individual differences in personality and motivation: 'Non-cognitive' determinants of cognitive performance. In A. Baddeley & L. Weiskrantz (Eds.), *Attention: Selection, awareness, and control: A tribute to Donald Broadbent* (pp. 346–373). New York: Clarendon Press/Oxford University Press.

Revelle, W. (1997). Extraversion and impulsivity: The lost dimension? In H. Nyborg (Ed.), *The scientific study of human nature: Tribute to Hans J. Eysenck at eighty* (pp. 189–212). Amsterdam, Netherlands: Pergamon/Elsevier Science Inc.

Revelle, W. (2018, December). *psych: Procedures for personality and psychological research* [Computer software manual]. Retrieved from https://CRAN.r-project.org/package=psych. (R package version 1.8.12)

Revelle, W., Amaral, P., & Turriff, S. (1976). Introversion-extraversion, time stress, and caffeine: Effect on verbal performance. *Science*, *192*, 149–150. https://doi.org/10.1126/science.1257762

Revelle, W., & Anderson, K. J. (1992). Models for the testing of theory. In A. Gale & M. Eysenck (Eds.), *Handbook of individual differences: Biological perspectives* (pp. 81–113). Chichester, England: John Wiley and Sons.

Revelle, W., Condon, D., & Wilt, J. (2012). Caffeine. In V. S. Ramachandran (Ed.), *Encyclopedia of human behavior* (2nd ed., pp. 423–429). Oxford: Elsevier. https://doi.org/10.1016/B978-0-12-375000-6.00078-1

Revelle, W., Humphreys, M. S., Simon, L., & Gilliland, K. (1980). Interactive effect of personality, time of day, and caffeine: A test of the arousal model. *Journal of Experimental Psychology General*, *109*(1), 1–31. https://doi. org/10.1037/0096-3445.109.1.1

Revelle, W., & Loftus, D. A. (1992). The implications of arousal effects for the study of affect and memory. In S.-A. Christianson (Ed.), *The handbook of emotion and memory: Research and theory* (pp. 113–149). Hillsdale, NJ: Lawrence Erlbaum Associates, Inc.

Revelle, W., & Oehlberg, K. (2008). Integrating experimental and observational personality research: The contributions of Hans Eysenck. *Journal of Personality*, *76*(6), 1387–1414. https://doi.org/10.1111/j.1467-6494.2008.00526.x

Roediger, H. L., & McDermott, K. B. (1995). Creating false memories: Remembering words not presented in lists. *Journal of Experimental Psychology: Learning, Memory, and Cognition*, *21*(4), 803–814.

Thayer, R. E. (1989). *The biopsychology of mood and arousal* (xi, 234 p.). New York: Oxford University Press.

Thayer, R. E., Takahashi, P. J., & Pauli, J. A. (1988). Multidimensional arousal states, diurnal rhythms, cognitive and social processes, and extraversion. *Personality and Individual Differences*, 9(1), 15–24. https://doi.org/10.1016/0191-8869(88)90026-8

Watson, D., & Tellegen, A. (1985). Toward a consensual structure of mood. *Psychological Bulletin*, 98(2), 219–235. https://doi.org/10.1037/0033-2909.98.2.219

Wilt, J., Funkhouser, K., & Revelle, W. (2011). The dynamic relationships of affective synchrony to perceptions of situations. *Journal of Research in Personality*, 45, 309–321. https://doi.org/10.1016/j.jrp.2011.03.005

Wilt, J., Oehlberg, K., & Revelle, W. (2011). Anxiety in personality. *Personality and Individual Differences*, 50(7), 987–993. https://doi.org/10.1016/j.paid.2010.11.014

Wilt, J., & Revelle, W. (2009). Extraversion. In M. R. Leary & R. H. Hoyle (Eds.), *Handbook of individual differences in social behavior* (pp. 27–45). New York: Guilford Press.

Zinbarg, R., & Revelle, W. (1989). Personality and conditioning: A test of four models. *Journal of Personality and Social Psychology*, 57(2), 301–314. https://doi.org/10.1037/0022-3514.57.2.301

Appendix to Chapter 14

Web-Based Tutorials for the Simulation and the Data Analysis

Following instructions at https://personality-project.org/courses/205/ simulation/simulating-experiments.pdf, the simulation is run by going to https:// personality-project.org/courses/205/ simulation/simulation.experiment.php.

Simplified instructions for analyzing the data are at http://personality-project.org/revelle/ syllabi/205/analysing-data.pdf (a handout written by a former undergraduate). A slightly longer tutorial is at http://personality-project.org/r/r.205.tutorial.html, as well as a much longer tutorial on the of R in general http://personality-project.org/r/.

The PHP Code for the Simulation

The following three pages need to be installed on a remote web server that has initiated PHP.

Page 1 The basic description of the simulation and the names of the variables. The instructor can change these names to match the simulation.

```
<!DOCTYPE html PUBLIC "-//W3C//DTD XHTML 1.0 Strict//EN"
    "http://www.w3.org/TR/xhtml1/DTD/xhtml1-strict.dtd">
<html xmlns="http://www.w3.org/1999/xhtml">
<head>
    <title>Simulating a Psychology Experiment - Preface</title>
    <meta name="generator" content="BBEdit 8.7" />
</head>
<body>
<?php
echo '
<head>
    <title>Simulating a
    Psychology Experiment - Preface</title>
    <meta name="generator" content="BBEdit 8.7" />
</head>
<p>
The simulation is a web based program that allows you to "collect" the
data on the web and then save the resulting output file to your computer
```

to do subsequent analyses. The biggest question is what should you study. To answer this, you need to consider the variables available. Make sure to read the <a href="https://personality-project.org/courses/205/simulation/simulating-experiments.pdf">handout<a/> discussing this experiment before starting.

<h2 align="left">What are the variables you can specify in this simulation?</h2>

<B> Independent variables</B> that are under control of the experimenter may be categorized as <U>experimental</U> variables and <U>subject</U> variables. Experimental variables may be manipulated by the experimenter. Subject variables are characteristics of the subjects that may be measured but not manipulated. </P>

<P>In this experiment the Experimental Variables include
<ol>
<li> Drug condition (placebo or caffeine),
<li>Time of Day</B>. Given the realities of volunteer subjects, Time of Day is assumed to only vary between 8 am and 10 PM (22.00 hours).

</ol>

<p> The <B>Subject Variables</B> are that are "assessed" are:
<ol>
<li> Sex (Male=1, Female=2)
<li> Trait Anxiety (0-10)
<li> Trait Impulsivity (0-10)
<li> Subject Number reflects when the subject appears in the quarter.
</ol>

<p> The <B>Dependent Variables</B> are measures of motivational state and cognitive performance
<ol>
<li> Energetic Arousal
<li>Tense Arousal)
<li> Performance (accuracy on some attention task)
</ol>

<P>The values of the IVs and DVs may be specified by the experimenter for each subject, or may be allowed to vary randomly. If allowed to vary randomly, the experimental variables will be assigned values in a uniform random distribution. The subject variables may either be specified (this simulates choosing particular subjects based upon a pretest) or may be allowed to vary randomly. If varying, they will be assigned values based upon samples from a normal distribution. If subjects are selected for particular personality types, this is the same as rejecting many potential subjects and thus the Cost of running grows more rapidly than the simple number of subjects who participate.</P>

It is a good idea to think carefully about your design before you run it.

<U><P>Subject Number</U> increases for every subject run in a particular experiment. Currently, it can not exceed 1000, but most runs will use

less than 100. You will be asked to specify the number of subject that you want to run.

```
<h2 align="left">Run the experiment</h2>

<p> How many subjects do you want to run?

<form action="simulation.specification.php" method="post">
<input name="ntrials" type="text" size="4" maxlength="4" />
<input type="submit" name="enter the data"></button>
</form>
';
?>
</body>
</html>


Page 2
<!DOCTYPE html PUBLIC "-//W3C//DTD XHTML 1.0 Strict//EN"
   "http://www.w3.org/TR/xhtml1/DTD/xhtml1-strict.dtd">
<html xmlns="http://www.w3.org/1999/xhtml">
<head>
   <title>Specify the Experimental and Subject Conditions</title>
   <meta name="generator" content="BBEdit 8.7" />
</head>
<body>
<?php
#simulation of personality by drug study
#converted from Pascal to php November 1, 2007
#Annotated July, 2018

#this file collects the data from the user

#the generic model can be made specific by specifying the names
#Here we specify particular ranges (and names) for the IVs
#Change the names and ranges of the variables to fit the model
#The current names of variables are
#Sex (SV1) 1 or 2
#Drug (IV1) Placebo or Caffeine
#Time of day (IV2) 8 - 22
# Anxiety (SV2) 0 - 10
# Impulsivity (SV3) 0 - 10
#The current names of variables and their ranges match prior work in the
PMC lab
#And the 2018 chapter

#Fix these to match the particular study

function show_the_selection($num) {
for ($snum=1; $snum < $num+1 ; $snum++ ) {
echo '<p>
Enter the conditions for the subject ',$snum, '
<form action="simulating.personality.results.php" method="post">
 <br> Sex Random <input type = "radio", name= "sr',$snum,'", value = -1
checked="yes"> or
```

```
Male <input type="radio" name="sr',$snum,'" value = 1 />
Female <input type="radio" name="sr',$snum,'" value =2 />
<br> Drug Random <input type = "radio", name= "dr',$snum,'", value = -1
checked="yes"> or
Placebo <input type="radio" name="dr',$snum,'" value=0 />
Caffeine <input type="radio" name="dr',$snum,'" value=1 />
<br> Time of Day Random <input type = "radio", name= "tr',$snum,'",
value = -1 checked="yes"> or Fixed
8 <input type="radio" name="tr',$snum,'" value =8 />
9 <input type="radio" name="tr',$snum,'" value =9 />
10 <input type="radio" name="tr',$snum,'" value =10 />
11 <input type="radio" name="tr',$snum,'" value =11 />
12 <input type="radio" name="tr',$snum,'" value =12 />
13 <input type="radio" name="tr',$snum,'" value =13 />
14<input type="radio" name="tr',$snum,'" value =14 />
15 <input type="radio" name="tr',$snum,'" value =15 />
16 <input type="radio" name="tr',$snum,'" value =16 />
17 <input type="radio" name="tr',$snum,'" value =17 />
18 <input type="radio" name="tr',$snum,'" value =18 />
19 <input type="radio" name="tr',$snum,'" value =19 />
20 <input type="radio" name="tr',$snum,'" value =20 />
21 <input type="radio" name="tr',$snum,'" value =21 />
22<input type="radio" name="tr',$snum,'" value =22 />
<br> Anxiety Random <input type = "radio", name= "ar',$snum,'", value =
-1 checked="yes"> or Fixed
0 <input type="radio" name="ar',$snum,'" value=0 />
1 <input type="radio" name="ar',$snum,'" value=1 />
2 <input type="radio" name="ar',$snum,'" value=2 />
3 <input type="radio" name="ar',$snum,'" value=3 />
4 <input type="radio" name="ar',$snum,'" value=4 />
5 <input type="radio" name="ar',$snum,'" value=5 />
6 <input type="radio" name="ar',$snum,'" value=6 />
7 <input type="radio" name="ar',$snum,'" value=7 />
8 <input type="radio" name="ar',$snum,'" value=8 />
9 <input type="radio" name="ar',$snum,'" value=9 />
10 <input type="radio" name="ar',$snum,'" value=10 />
         </br>
<br> Impulsivity Random <input type = "radio", name= "ir',$snum,'",
value = -1 checked="yes"> or Fixed
0 <input type="radio" name="ir',$snum,'" value=0 />
1 <input type="radio" name="ir',$snum,'" value=1 />
2 <input type="radio" name="ir',$snum,'" value=2 />
3 <input type="radio" name="ir',$snum,'" value=3 />
4 <input type="radio" name="ir',$snum,'" value=4 />
5 <input type="radio" name="ir',$snum,'" value=5 />
6 <input type="radio" name="ir',$snum,'" value=6 />
7 <input type="radio" name="ir',$snum,'" value=7 />
8 <input type="radio" name="ir',$snum,'" value=8 />
9 <input type="radio" name="ir',$snum,'" value=9 />
10 <input type="radio" name="ir',$snum,'" value=10 />
```

```
                    <br> <br>
};
echo '
<input name="ntrials" type="hidden" value =',$snum,' />
<br> Ok, I am finished, show me the data <input type="submit" value="submit"
" /></p>
</form> ';
}; #end of get the selection

#these are global parameters
#this first part is the basic model with no interactive input
#first lets get some basic parameters
#then we set some weights
#
#not clear if these actually do anything
$IV2wt = 1;
$SV2wt=.3;
$errorwt=.3;
$tensewt = .2;
$n =10;
$dynamic = FALSE;
$total_cost =0;
$snum = 1;
$max_trials = 10;

$ntrials = $_POST['ntrials'];
#echo 'ntrials = ' ,$ntrials;

echo 'This form will allow you to run up to the ',$ntrials,' subjects
that you specified.
For each simulated participant you need to specify the experimental
conditions.
When you are finished with specifying all the subjects, you can enter
submit (at the end of the page).
 If you specify less than ',$ntrials,' participants, the last N will be
filled with random participants.
 You can edit these out later in the statistical analysis if you choose.'
;

show_the_selection($ntrials);

?>
</body>
</html>

Page 3 This page actually does the simulation and reports the results.
<!DOCTYPE html PUBLIC "-//W3C//DTD XHTML 1.0 Strict//EN"
   "http://www.w3.org/TR/xhtml1/DTD/xhtml1-strict.dtd">
<html xmlns="http://www.w3.org/1999/xhtml">
<head>
   <title>Simulating Personality - the Results (copy to R for analysis)
</title>
```

```
   <meta name="generator" content="BBEdit 8.7" />
</head>
<body>

<?php

#first we create a function to produce N(0,1) numbers
#Based upon the central limit theorem that the distribution of means
tends towards normal
 function rnorm() { $x = 0;
 for ($i=1; $i < 17; $i++ ) { $x = $x + mt_rand();}
 $x = ($x )/16; #find the mean of the 16 replications
 $x = $x/32768; #convert to sd 1
 $x = ($x -32768)/ 32768;
 return $x/.144;
 };

#alternatively
# function rnorm() {return stats_rand_gen_normal ( 0,1 )}

#this next function gets the data from the posting and stores as an array
function post_the_data($snum) {
$sr = $_POST['sr'.$snum];
$dr = $_POST['dr'.$snum];
$tr = $_POST['tr'.$snum];
$ar = $_POST['ar'.$snum];
$ir = $_POST['ir'.$snum];
$values = array($snum,$sr,$dr,$tr,$ar,$ir);
return($values);
}; #end of the post_the_data function

#these are global parameters
#this first part is the basic model with no interactive input
#first lets get some basic parameters
#then we set some weights
#
$IV2wt = 1;
$SV1wt = .3;
$SV2wt=.3;
$errorwt=.3;
$tensewt = .2;
$n =10;
$dynamic = FALSE;
$total_cost =0;
#now process the data

$ntrials = $_POST['ntrials'];
#echo 'ntrials = ' ,$ntrials;
$trials = $ntrials-1;
#first echo out titles
#change if using different IVs, SVs, and DVs
#These are the variable labels
```

```
# Change the following to match your experiment

# echo 'Trial SV1 IV1 IV2 SV2 SV3 DV1 DV2 DV3 DV4';
#e.g.,
echo 'snum sex drug time anxiety impulsivity arousal tension performance
cost';

#$trials =100;
#begin Trials loop
for ($i=1; $i < $trials + 1; $i++ ) {
$result[$i]= post_the_data($i);

$resarray = array_values($result[$i]);
$trialnum = $resarray[0];
$sr = $resarray[1];
$dr = $resarray[2];
$tr = $resarray[3];
$ar = $resarray[4];
$ir = $resarray[5];

# convert the input into our IV and SV values
#cost increases if we select subjects
$cost =1;
if ($sr < 0) {$sex = mt_rand(1,2) ;} else {$sex = $sr; $cost=$cost+1;}
if ($dr < 0){ $IV1 = mt_rand(0,1);} else {$IV1 = $dr; $cost=$cost+1;};
if ( $tr < 0) {$IV2 = mt_rand(8,22);
} else {$IV2 = $tr; $cost=$cost+1;}

if ($ar < 0 ) {$SV1 = intval(2* rnorm() +5 -$i/$ntrials);} else {$SV1 =
$ar; $cost=$cost+1;}
if ($ir < 0 ) {$SV2 = intval(2* rnorm() + 5 + $i/$ntrials);} else {$SV2
= $ir; $cost=$cost+1;}
#Echo the condition and then the results

echo '<br>',$trialnum, ' ',$sex,' ', $IV1,' ',$IV2,' ',$SV1,' ',$SV2,' ';

#Find the DVs as functions of the IVs
#this section can be modified by the instructor to specify the particular
model
$DV1 = $IV1 - $IV2wt * cos(($IV2 - $SV2)/4)+1; #curvilinear function
$DV1 = $DV1/3;
$DV2 = 100/(1+exp(3 -$IV1 - $SV1wt* $SV1 + $tensewt * rnorm())); #mono-
tonic function
$DV3 = intval(100/(1+ exp(-$DV1+ $errorwt* rnorm())))); #monotonic of DV2

#show the results
echo intval($DV1*100),' ' ,intval($DV2),' ',$DV3,' ',$cost ,' ';

}
#end of trials loop

?>
</body>
</html>
```

Chapter 15

Teaching Statistics With a BYOD (Bring Your Own Device) Student Response System

R. Shane Hutton and Derek Bruff

Introduction

Classroom response systems are instructional technologies that allow instructors to rapidly collect and analyze student responses to questions posed during class. Wired versions of these systems have been used since the 1960s, but it was the advent of wireless systems using radio frequency communications that led to rapid adoption of classroom response systems in college and university classrooms in the early 2000s (Abrahamson, 2006). These systems consisted of three parts: software running on the instructor's computer, a receiver unit attached to the instructor's computer, and handheld response devices, often called "clickers." The instructor would pose a multiple-choice question projected on a screen at the front of the classroom, and students would respond with A, B, C, or D using their clickers. The response system software would then display a bar chart summarizing the student responses for the instructor and students to see.

One typical use of classroom response systems is an instructional technique known as peer instruction. As popularized by Mazur (1999), peer instruction involves posing a question to students, having students answer the question individually using their response devices, then, assuming there isn't general agreement on the right answer, asking students to discuss the question in pairs. Students submit potentially different answers using their clickers, and the instructor uses the resulting bar graph to guide a classwide discussion toward the correct answer and the correct reasoning for the answer. This sequence provides students with a chance to practice what they're learning and receive feedback on that practice, a critical component of learning (Ambrose, Bridges, DiPietro, Lovett, & Norman, 2010). It also provides instructors with insight into student learning they can use to be more responsive to student learning needs, what some call "agile teaching" (Bruff, 2009).

When used to support active learning pedagogies such as peer instruction, classroom response systems provide a number of benefits, including increased student participation and engagement during class; useful feedback on student learning to both students and instructors; and, in some cases, greater learning outcomes and student success (Yourstone, Kraye, & Albaum, 2008; Kay & LeSage, 2009; Smith et al., 2009). When students consider classroom response systems, they appreciate the ability to see other students' answers (and, thus, compare their own answers to their peers'); the ways in-class polling engages them in learning during class; the immediate feedback on learning that polling activities provide; and the opportunity to test their knowledge and skills during class through polling activities (Graham, Tripp, Seawright, & Joeckel, 2007; Hoekstra, 2008; Nagy-Shadman & Desrochers, 2008).

More recently, as smart phone ownership among students has increased, "bring your own device" (BYOD) options have become available for classroom response systems. BYOD systems leverage students' personal mobile devices (phones, tablets, laptops), allowing students to respond to questions via web browsers, text messaging, or dedicated mobile apps. BYOD classroom response systems offer some logistical advantages over clicker-based systems. By making use of existing student devices and campus Wi-Fi networks, BYOD systems avoid some of the costs and administrative overhead of managing student-purchased clickers and classroom-installed receivers. Also, students who might forget to bring a clicker to class aren't likely to forget to bring their phone.

One common concern expressed about BYOD systems is the potential for distraction that mobile devices pose in the classroom. However, instructors who use BYOD systems report that giving students something engaging and on-topic to do with their mobile devices during class leads to less use of phones and tablets for off-topic pursuits such as looking at Facebook or ESPN (Imazeki, 2014; Savary & Gifford, 2017). Other concerns about BYOD systems are logistical in nature—What about students who don't own a phone or laptop or tablet? Will dozens or hundreds of students going online concurrently overwhelm classroom Wi-Fi access points? Colleges and universities are finding ways to address these questions as more institutions move toward adoption of BYOD systems (Roll, 2017).

One reason is that the pedagogical advantages of BYOD response systems are potentially significant. Clickers were largely limited to multiple-choice questions, but given the input capabilities of mobile devices like phones and tablets, BYOD systems offer robust support for free-response questions. For instance, questions can ask students to respond with text then display the aggregate responses as a word cloud. Or students might be shown an image of some kind and asked to click on a location within the image, with the collected student responses showing up on the image like pins on a map. Some BYOD systems allow students to respond to questions with drawings (perhaps using a tablet and stylus) or with photos taken on the spot. These free-response questions open up a range of pedagogical applications for classroom response systems, as we will explore in this paper.

Teaching Statistics With a BYOD Response System

One of the authors (Hutton) has used a BYOD response system, Top Hat. In his undergraduate introduction to statistics class, he made use of three main tools provided by Top Hat: polling questions, discussion forums, and lecture note annotation. Although the specific tools provided by individual BYOD systems vary, most systems provide some version of these three tools. What follows is a description of Hutton's use of the system and the benefits he sees in the system, using the first person for clarity.

Polling Questions

Incorporating polling questions into my lectures has been the single most effective teaching strategy I have utilized. Many BYOD systems on the market today support various types of polling questions. They are not limited to multiple-choice questions; however, I find well-formulated multiple-choice questions particularly useful for my class. I typically ask polling questions at the beginning of class over material that was covered in the previous lecture, but I also ask polling questions during the lecture to gauge students' understanding of the material as I am teaching. Overall, I tend to group the polling questions into five categories: (1) terminology, (2) notation, (3) conceptual, (4) problem-solving, and (5) graphical.

Terminology

One of the major challenges in learning statistics is understanding terminology. I find students sometimes struggle with understanding the meaning of statistical terms or the slight differences in terminology, e.g., the difference between a sample distribution and a sampling distribution. Being able to ask questions about terminology and obtaining real-time feedback helps me adjust my teaching to the needs of the class. It gives me an opportunity to address misunderstood terminology during class based on the responses of my students. I find questions about terminology are best asked in multiple-choice format, but other appropriate formats can be used.

For example, I ask a question about the term "between-subjects" during a review from a previous lecture where I introduced the independent-samples t-test. This allows me to determine if students understood the independent nature of the groups. Even though I highlight this as I am introducing the material in lecture, I find students sometimes get lost in the complexity of the material. By asking a polling question about this, I help students to avoid any confusion prior to discussing further topics such as the "within-subjects" design.

Sample Polling Question: The term "between-subjects" refers to observing:
  a. groups of the same participants
  b. groups of different participants

"Significance" is another term with which students tend to struggle initially. In the lecture after introducing hypothesis testing, I ask students a question about finding a significant result. I typically find that a majority of students struggle with understanding that a significant result corresponds with rejecting the null hypothesis. This could be because many students are still trying to understand the concept of hypothesis testing, and the differences in terminology may seem secondary at that point. But having the ability to highlight terminology and ask students during lecture about that terminology is invaluable.

Sample Polling Question: When making the decision to reject the null hypothesis, the effect is said to be _____.
  a. Significant
  b. Nonsignificant

Note that when asking polling questions with only two answer choices, some interpretation of the results is required, since it's likely some students will answer correctly by guessing. If, for instance, 75% of students answer correctly, that would be an overestimation of the proportion of students who understand the term. However, the results are still useful for guiding review of terminology during class. Some instructors will include "I don't know" or "I'm not sure" as a third answer choice, mitigating this issue.

Notation

Another major challenge in statistics is understanding notation. I typically ask questions about notation at the start of class to review material from the previous class, to clarify student misunderstandings about notation, and to prepare them for new material that utilizes the notation. Questions about notation are usually short, which allows me to review every question even if the majority of the class selected the correct answer. Even for students who answer correctly, this review provides useful retrieval practice (Brame & Biel, 2015) that helps cement their understanding.

One of the primary reasons for asking questions about notation is to determine if students clearly understand what each symbol represents. However, it can also be used to bring attention to the differences in notation. For instance, when asking a question about population standard deviation, I am able to determine if students understand that σ is the notation for population standard deviation. In addition, asking this question in multiple-choice format also allows me the chance to point out the difference in notation between population and sample standard deviation as well as the difference in notation between standard deviation and variance.

Sample Polling Question: What notation is used for the population standard deviation?
   a. s
   b. s^2
   c. σ
   d. σ^2

Additionally, questions about notation can be used to tell if students have knowledge of a broader concept. For example, in order to ensure students have an understanding of ANOVA and the conventional notation, I ask them to compute degrees of freedom. I do not tell them what k and N represent in the problem, because I want them to recall that notion. However, to successfully compute the correct degrees of freedom, students must not only know the notation but also how to compute the correct degrees of freedom. I ask this as a multiple-choice question because I want students to see other possible degrees of freedom in the response options, i.e., within-groups degrees of freedom and total degrees of freedom, so I can address them while reviewing responses. Selecting wrong answer choices that represent common student misunderstandings is a key element in designing effective multiple-choice questions for in-class polling.

Sample Polling Question: Suppose $k = 4$ and $N = 75$. What are the between-groups degrees of freedom for a one-way ANOVA?

a.   3
b.   70
c.   71
d.   74

Conceptual

My introductory statistics course emphasizes understanding statistics at a conceptual level. I have found that sometimes students get anxious about conceptual questions. Having a low-stakes environment in which students can think through the question and get immediate feedback is beneficial for both the student and the instructor. When writing conceptual questions, I typically use multiple-choice or true/false questions. I try to make questions that are both fairly straightforward and challenging.

For example, during the lecture on confidence intervals, I spend a good amount of time discussing the alpha level and how that is related to the confidence level. I also introduce the confidence interval in terms of an interval estimate for the population parameter. After doing this, I poll students about what happens to the precision of the estimate after increasing the confidence level from 90% to 95%. Even students who can successfully compute the width of a particular confidence interval can struggle with this question, indicating that their computational skills are not founded on sound conceptual understanding, making this kind of question important.

Sample Polling Question: Suppose the confidence level is increased from 90% to 95%. The interval estimate will _____.
a.   Increase in precision
b.   Decrease in precision
c.   Not change

It is also important to ensure students understand the conceptual nature of the statistical tests being utilized in the course. For example, after teaching students about two-way ANOVA, I will ask them a question about the number of factors in a 2×3 design. Many students will select 6 for this question because they recall multiplying the number of levels of each factor together to obtain the number of cells. However, there is a fundamental conceptual misunderstanding of two-way ANOVA if a student responds with anything other than 2.

Sample Polling Question: How many factors are in a 2×3 ANOVA design?
a.   2
b.   3
c.   5
d.   6

If most students respond with the correct answer, that's an indication that their understanding of this concept is high. I can fairly quickly move on during class to other topics on which students need more help. More often, however, a number of students answer incorrectly. Since the BYOD response system reports results on the fly, I can address those wrong answers immediately. The response system allows me to practice a form of agile teaching (Bruff, 2009) in which I can be more responsive to student learning needs during class, before they attempt problem sets and other assignments.

Problem-Solving

Problem-solving questions are a vital part of any statistics course. It is typically more straightforward for students to watch a problem being solved but more challenging when they are asked to do it on their own. I have always had active problem-solving exercises during lecture, but using a BYOD response system provides an excellent platform to ask these same types of questions with immediate feedback. I typically use open-ended questions for problem-solving exercises because I do not want students to see possible response options. This also mimics the short-answer-type questions I ask on exams. However, there may be some situations in which multiple choice is a better option.

After teaching about finding probabilities under the normal curve, I have students compute the probability of being within one standard deviation of the mean. I ask this as an open-ended question so that students can type in the probability they obtain. I use this to introduce the empirical rule, but being able to view polling responses helps me to know if students are comfortable computing the probability and allows students to develop the empirical rule on their own.

Sample Polling Question: Find $P(-1 < z < 1)$. Express answer as percentage and round answer to 2 decimal places.

The free-response format of the question means there's not a bar chart that quickly summarizes results. Instead, I have a list that summarizes every response, with the most frequently occurring responses listed first. I can quickly scan the answers to see how accurately the students are responding, and I can point out and discuss wrong answers as we debrief the question. One advantage of asking a free-response question is that I will occasionally be surprised by student responses that I wouldn't have predicted. This provides useful insight into the misunderstandings students have in their statistical thinking.

During the lecture on binomial distributions, I ask students to use the binomial distribution to compute a binomial probability. I have found that students sometimes have trouble with these calculations, and this is a great opportunity for students to practice what they have just learned. I normally ask this question as an open-ended response because I want to see if students can arrive at the correct probability without seeing an answer that is close to correct. Having students do this exercise while I am teaching the material allows me to diagnose any common mistakes in calculations.

Sample Polling Question: Use the binomial distribution to compute the probability of obtaining three heads in five coin tosses. Round to 2 decimal places.

Graphical

Understanding graphs is an important skill to master in statistics. Many BYOD response systems will allow for including graphics in polling questions. These questions can be asked in a variety of formats including multiple choice or short answer. One unique feature of some BYOD response systems is the ability for students to respond by clicking on parts of an image. For example, when I am introducing scatter plots to my students, I give them a few data points to plot then have them plot those points on a set of coordinate axes I have saved as an image and loaded into the BYOD response system. Students see the axes on their mobile devices and click to indicate where they would plot the given coordinates. The results are displayed in a heat map (see Figure 15.1) that aggregates students' responses. As seen here, most students plot the given points correctly, but the heat map allows me to see student errors in plotting, such as switching the X and Y axis.

Another way I ask students about graphical questions is to ask questions about a particular graph or plot. Most BYOD response systems have the ability to embed graphics or tables within the question. For example, after introducing terminology to describe the shape of a distribution, I will ask students to describe shapes of particular distributions. I ask these in multiple-choice format and allow more than one response to be selected so that the distribution can be described using more than one term if needed. Figure 15.2 shows a leptokurtic, positively skewed distribution, so students would select both B and C.

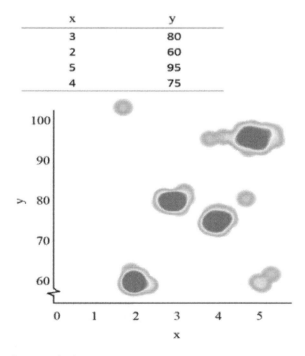

Figure 15.1 Example of scatter plot heat map.

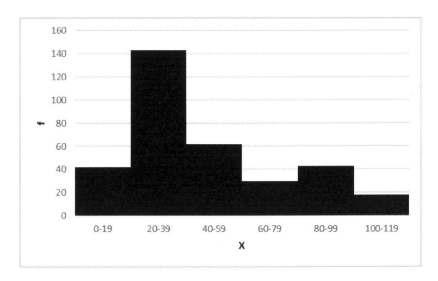

Describe the shape of the distribution. Select all that apply.

a.   Platykurtic
b.   Leptokurtic
c.   Positively skewed
d.   Negatively skewed
e.   Normal

Figure 15.2 **Example of graphical question.**

Lecture Note Annotation and Discussion Forum

In addition to polling questions, I use both the annotation feature and discussion forums during class. I find both to be extremely useful in teaching statistics, and it helps to keep a dynamic and engaging atmosphere in the classroom. I will discuss how I use both of these features in class, but there are certainly other ways they can be utilized.

Lecture Note Annotation

Many BYOD systems have the ability to upload lecture notes so that students can access them through the BYOD platform. There are benefits to uploading slides, because many BYOD response systems allow embedding of polling questions into the lecture slides, which creates a seamless transition between polling questions and lecture material. However, annotation is the primary reason I upload lecture slides. I am able to annotate on the slides during lecture, and students can

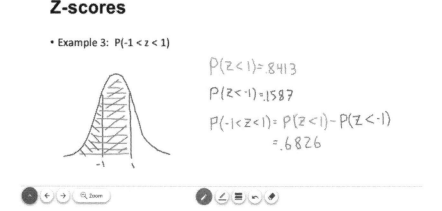

Figure 15.3 Example of lecture note annotation for normal probabilities.

view these annotations in real time on their electronic devices. The annotations are saved so that students can access the material at any time.

Lecture note annotation is helpful to be able to draw graphs. For example, when I teach finding probabilities under the normal curve, I always utilize lecture note annotation (see Figure 15.3). In this instance, it is more helpful for students to watch me find the probability step by step. I can also change the colors for each probability so that students can clearly see the components of calculating the final probability. Additionally, I use annotation to underline or circle important text in the lecture slides. This helps draw students' attention to key terminology or concepts.

Discussion Forum

There are several uses of a discussion forum in teaching statistics. Discussion forums could be used for students to discuss a particular problem or allow students the ability to debate statistical questions posed by the instructor. However, I use the discussion forum as a tool to enhance engagement during lecture, as a kind of backchannel for student questions (Baron, Bestbier, Case, & Collier-Reed, 2016). For each lecture, I create a discussion forum in which students can type questions they have about the material. Students are sometimes reluctant to ask questions, especially in a large lecture setting, so the discussion forum gives those students the ability to ask questions through the BYOD response system.

I usually pause about halfway through the lecture to check the discussion forum for any questions and then again at the end of class. Figure 15.4 shows an example of questions asked during a lecture. I do my best to answer the questions during class but I also provide written answers to the questions after class. Students seem to find this very useful, because they can scroll through

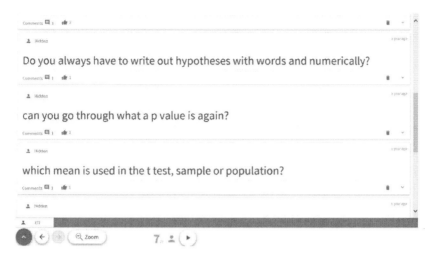

Do you always have to write out hypotheses with words and numerically?

can you go through what a p value is again?

which mean is used in the t test, sample or population?

Figure 15.4 Example of a discussion forum during lecture.

the questions and responses at any time. Allowing students to ask questions in this manner allows me the ability to diagnose any problems students are having from lecture. Students even have the ability to "like" other students' questions or to ask follow-up questions to my response, which gives me a sense of how common certain questions are among the students.

I have also used discussion forums for exam reviews, homework questions, and class feedback. It is important to organize discussion forums carefully so that students do not get confused with question content. For instance, if I use a discussion forum for students to ask questions about an upcoming assignment, I want that to be clearly different than the lecture forums. Finally, I find that having a discussion forum active during the entire course where students can provide anonymous feedback is important. This allows students to raise any concerns they have about the course. This helps to create an atmosphere of open communication with my students.

Conclusion

Classroom response systems have been a useful tool for college and university educators for more than a decade. Bring-your-own-device systems provide certain advantages over traditional clicker-based systems, both logistical and pedagogical. We have outlined a number of uses of these systems in an introductory statistics course taught by the first author. BYOD systems support a variety of in-class interactions, from multiple-choice and free-response polling questions to backchannel discussion forums. Such interactions support active learning instruction, known to be more effective for student learning and student success than traditional lecture (Freeman et al., 2014). Developing useful polling questions and practicing agile teaching takes a degree of intentionality and effort, but the benefits for student engagement and learning are worth it. As the capabilities of mobile devices continue to expand (i.e., better network capabilities, access to portable electronic devices for all students), creative educators will have even more tools in their teaching toolboxes to promote student learning during class.

References

Abrahamson, L. (2006). A brief history of network classrooms: Effects, cases, pedagogy, and implications. In D. A. Banks (Ed.), *Audience response systems in higher education: Applications and cases*. Hershey, PA: Information Science Publishing.

Ambrose, S., Bridges, M., DiPietro, M., Lovett, M., & Norman, M. (2010). *How learning works: 7 research-based principles for smart teaching*. San Francisco, CA: Jossey-Bass.

Baron, D., Bestbier, A., Case, J., & Collier-Reed, B. (2016). Investigating the effects of a backchannel on university classroom interactions: A mixed-method case study. *Computers & Education*, *94*, 61–76.

Brame, C., & Biel, R. (2015). Test-enhanced learning: The potential for testing to promote greater learning in undergraduate science courses. *CBE—Life Sciences Education*, *14*(2).

Bruff, D. (2009). *Teaching with classroom response system: Creating active learning environments*. San Francisco, CA: Jossey-Bass.

Freeman, S., Eddy, S., McDonough, M., Smith, M., Okoroafor, N., Jordt, H., & Wenderoth, M. (2014). Active learning increases student performance in science, engineering, and mathematics. *Proceedings of the National Academy of Science*, *111*(23), 8410–8415.

Graham, C. R., Tripp, T. R., Seawright, L., & Joeckel, G. L. (2007). Empowering or compelling reluctant participators using audience response systems. *Active Learning in Higher Education*, *8*(3), 233–258.

Hoekstra, A. (2008). Vibrant student voices: Exploring effects of the use of clickers in large college courses. *Learning, Media, & Technology*, *33*(4), 329–341.

Imazeki, J. (2014). Bring-your-own-device: Turning cell phones into forces for good. *Journal of Economic Education*, *45*(3), 240–250.

Kay, R., & LeSage, A. (2009). Examining the benefits and challenges of using audience response systems: A review of the literature. *Computers & Education*, *53*, 819–827.

Mazur, E. (1999). *Peer instruction: A user's manual*. Upper Saddle River, NJ: Prentice Hall.

Nagy-Shadman, E., & Desrochers, C. (2008). Student response technology: Empirically grounded or just a gimmick? *International Journal of Science Education*, *30*(15), 2023–2066.

Roll, N. (2017, August 2). Communications crossroads. *Inside Higher Ed*. Retrieved from www.insidehighered.com/digital-learning/article/2017/08/02/mobile-apps-gaining-ground-handheld-clickers.

Savary, M., & Gifford, K. (2017). The benefits of a real-time, web-based response system for enhancing engaged learning in classrooms and public science events. *Journal of Undergraduate Science Education*, *15*(2), E13–E16.

Smith, M. K., Wood, W. B., Adams, W. K., Wieman, C., Knight, J. K., Gulid, N., & Su, T. T. (2009). Why peer discussion improves student performance on in-class concept questions. *Science*, *323*(5910), 122–124.

Yourstone, S. A., Kraye, H. S., & Albaum, G. (2008). Classroom questioning with immediate electronic response: Do clickers improve learning? *Decision Sciences Journal of Innovative Education*, *6*(1), 75–88.

## Chapter 16

Personally Relevant Project-Based Learning in Graduate Statistics Curriculum in Psychology

Rachel T. Fouladi

Aiken, West, Sechrest, and Reno (1990) and Aiken, West, and Millsap (2008) provided surveys of quantitative training in doctoral programs of psychology in the U.S. and Canada. A primary purpose of the authors, particularly in their 2008 paper, was to assess the extent to which statistical innovation had infused graduate quantitative curriculum in psychology. Based on the surveys, the authors indicated that statistical innovations were scarce in standard graduate curriculum in psychology—with core coursework constituting coverage of one-way and factorial ANOVA and multivariate statistics with an emphasis on multiple regression through the equivalent of two courses (~77/78% of a year). Based on the percentages of departments reporting regular coverage of these topics (c.f., Aiken et al., 1990, 2008), it is not unreasonable to state that these topics constitute the mainstay of required graduate statistics curriculum in psychology.

Although the Aiken et al. (1990, 2008) articles did not speak to pedagogical approaches directly, in the same way that course content of required statistics graduate courses has not seen much innovation, the methods of teaching used for these courses are also likely to be largely unchanged. There are a variety of ways we can innovate our teaching, one of which is through the use of project-based learning. Statistics courses are well-suited for project-based or problem-based learning (e.g., Smith, 1998; Siswono, Hartono, & Kohar, 2018). In the current chapter, I address the use of personally relevant project-based learning in our teaching. I begin the chapter with an overview of key concepts and terminology used in descriptions of teaching "innovations" regarding authentic, project-based, and problem-based learning. This is followed by an example framework for authentic statistics assignment design that considers instructor/student experiences and workload. I follow this with an outline of one strategy to develop a course with project-based learning using a sequence of authentic assignments (e.g., article critique, proposal, report) with guidelines for how these specific assignment types can be personalized. I highlight instructor/student processes and include implementation examples illustrated with reference to student work and reflections. Closing comments emphasize the value of project-based learning and ease of incorporating flexibly structured personally relevant projects in our teaching.

Authentic, Project-Based, and Problem-Based Learning: Concepts and Terminology

A variety of terms arise in readings regarding pedagogical "innovations" in higher education. The following focuses on concepts and terminology in discussions of problem-based learning and project-based learning and the use of authentic assessments that promote active learning.

Hulsizer and Woolf (2009), in their book *A Guide to Teaching Statistics: Innovations and Best Practices*, provide an overview of standard and innovative strategies for teaching introductory statistics to undergraduate students. As psychologists dedicated to examining teaching methods, they draw on a wide body of research (317 references) to support their arguments. Included in their book is reference to the value of authentic assessments and active learning (see Sathy et al., Chapter 13 in current volume for further discussion on active learning). Regarding authentic assessments, Hulszier and Woolf write:

> Authentic assessments have the benefit of active learning, student ownership of the material, . . . increased sense of responsibility, and the development of higher order thinking skills. . . . Authentic assessments also have the benefit of increasing student motivation, particularly if . . . [the students] see the connection to real-world usefulness.
>
> (p. 75)

The recent release of the American Statistical Association–endorsed *Guidelines for Assessment and Instruction of Introductory Statistics in College* (GAISE College Report ASA Revision Committee, 2016) provides six recommendations for consideration in teaching introductory statistics; these include (a) teach statistical thinking, (b) focus on conceptual understanding, (c) integrate real data with a context and a purpose, (d) foster active learning, (e) use technology to explore concepts and analyze data, and (f) use assessments to improve and evaluate student learning. Importantly, even though written in the context of teaching undergraduate students, these comments and recommendations also have relevance to teaching statistics to graduate students.

Projects are one way in which to integrate authentic learning and assessment into a course. Although not widely implemented in many disciplines, learning through projects is a centuries-old approach to formal education (c.f., Knoll, 2014). Knoll (2014) recognizes "the project method, also discussed under headings like project work, project approach, and project-based learning, is one of the standard teaching methods" (p. 665). Although there are many variations, according to Pecore (2015), one of the early approaches put forward in North America was Kilpatrick's approach (Kilpatrick, 1918), referred to in the education literature as the Project Method, wherein Kilpatrick "advocated for student-initiated projects that utilize the laws of learning to intrinsically motivate the student to emerge with a high degree of skill and knowledge, [and] view school activity with joy and confidence" (Pecore, 2015, p. 158).

The student-centered project is fundamental to early conceptualizations of what has been termed in recent decades "problem-based learning" (Barrows & Tamblyn, 1980; Wilkerson & Gijselaers, 1996; Boud & Feletti, 1997)—which some have described as "perhaps the most innovative instructional method conceived and implemented in education" (Hung, 2009, p. 118). Although some authors have strict interpretations of the term, in their paper "Introducing Problem Based Learning in Higher Education", the editors of the recently launched *Journal of Problem Based Learning in Higher Education (JPBLinHE)*, acknowledge that "problem based learning covers an amazing diversity of educational practices" (Ryberg & Nørgaard, 2013, p. V). Quoting from Barrows's paper "A Taxonomy of Problem Based Learning" (1986) and Kalmos and Graaff's paper "Characteristics of Problem-based Learning" (2003), the editors of the journal set the stage for a broader perspective on problem-based learning than appears in many writings (e.g., Hung, 2009; www.edutopia.org/project-based-learning):

> The term problem-based learning must be considered a genus for which there are many species and subspecies. Each addresses different objectives to varying degrees. All description and evaluation of any PBL method must be analysed in terms of the type of problem used, the teaching learning sequences, the responsibility given to students for learning and the student assessment method used.
>
> (Barrows, 1986, p. 485)

> As even superficial inspection of a few of the available sources can reveal, the label "PBL" is used to cover an amazing diversity of educational practices, ranging from problem-oriented lectures to completely open experiential learning environments aimed at improving interpersonal relations.
>
> (Kolmos & Graaff, 2003, p. 657)

In my recent readings of pedagogical practice, I have noticed the alternating use of the terms for problem-based learning and project-based learning (e.g., www.edutopia.org/project-based-learning). In these writings, some authors use the term project-based learning to refer to the strictest interpretation wherein all course content is learned through completion of the focal problem/project; in other instances, project-based learning is used simply to refer to the inclusion of authentic projects through which students engage in active learning but which do not necessarily provide the fundamental structure from which all learning takes place. I am not alone in this recognition of alternating use of terminology (c.f., Campbell, 2014; Knoll, 2014). According to Knoll (2014),

> Frequently, the phrase project-based learning is interchangeably used with problem-based learning, but—in accordance with Dewey—one should clearly distinguish between both concepts. Whereas problem-based learning is inquiry-centered and restricted to abstract problem solving, project-based learning is production-centered and requires the use of theoretical as well as practical problem solving strategies.
>
> (Knoll, 2014, p. 668)

That said, according to Campbell (2014), "it is probably the importance of conducting active learning with students that is worthy and not the actual name of the task. Both problem-based and project-based learning have their place in today's classroom and can promote 21st Century learning".

In recognition of the heterogeneity in usage and understandings of "problem-based learning" and "project-based learning", the editors of the *JPBLinHE*, seek to have "authors explicate their theoretical understanding of PBL, as well as their actual course design or methods" (2013, p. V). It is in this spirit that I clarify that for the purpose of the current chapter, unless citing the work of an author who describes their work as being on "problem-based learning", I prefer the terminology of "project-based learning" and that I use the term "project-based learning" to refer to any course in which projects serve both as learning and assessment tools, without excluding that learning may also be taking place through traditionally structured and organized lecturing. For this definition, I focus on the first characteristic of project-based learning indicated on the University of Lethbridge Teaching Centre web-page (www.uleth.ca/teachingcentre/project-based-learning), on which they describe project-based learning as:

> an approach to teaching in which students are engaged by having them tackle authentic problems. The facts and knowledge needed to solve problems are often segregated from the application skills needed to apply the information in a critical way. Project based learning is a way to bridge this gap and produce learning that integrates facts, knowledge, skills and the application of those to a real problem.

The University of Lethbridge resource provides several guidelines to keep in mind for the development of "assessments and assignments using this method, one of which is:

> Projects should try to be based around an authentic problem. At the very least the project should emulate a real world problem. The problem should be challenging and push the students to utilize higher order thinking skills such as analysis, evaluation, synthesis and creation. In no way should the project be thought of as optional or extra. This will take away from the student's motivation to complete the assignment.

A Framework for Authentic Statistics Assignment Design to Personalize Project-Based Learning

Jennifer D. Timmer and Carolyn J. Anderson (Chapter 17 in current volume) address the use of projects in undergraduate and graduate statistics courses. Karpiak (2011) considered the use of "problem-based learning" in statistics courses with psychology undergraduate students. Studies of student experiences in College of Education Educational Psychology offerings of required graduate-level statistics courses provide examples of the use of "application-oriented teaching methods" (Pan & Tang, 2004) and "problem-based learning" teaching strategies (Mercier & Frederiksen, 2007) with graduate students in these programs.

Although I have not conducted a formal survey, based on 25+ years of teaching and interacting with other instructors of graduate-level quantitative courses in psychology departments and informal review of available course syllabi, the standard curriculum for required graduate statistics courses in psychology focuses on the introduction of data analytic strategies with assignments involving short prespecified research scenarios and sample datasets that are provided to the students for analysis. This highly structured approach to assignments to promote and assess learning dominates required courses (e.g., ANOVA). It is less common for more advanced special-topics courses (e.g., structural equation modeling, multilevel modeling, test theory) to be completely based on fully prespecified research scenarios and datasets (e.g., McGrath, Ferns, Greiner, Wanamaker, & Brown, 2015). Importantly, however, flexible authentic assignments including project-based learning can be implemented in required graduate statistics curriculum in psychology, with generally positive student outcomes (c.f., Pan & Tang, 2004; Mercier & Frederiksen, 2007).

The use of authentic projects naturally permits the contextualization of specific content, knowledge, and skills that the student learns and develops while tackling the focal project; content learning and skill development unfold as the student works through the project by engaging in active reasoning, inquiry, and critical and creative thinking. However, a primary issue that we need to address when we are developing curriculum that involves authentic learning/assessments and personalization to student interests to differing degrees is the management of workload for the instructor (Chiang, Wu, & Baba, 2009) and the increased load/stress that may result for students due to large-scale assignments (Ruiz-Gallardo, Castano, Gomez-Alday, & Valdes, 2011). Considering the implementation of "problem-based learning" in undergraduate information technology courses, Chiang et al. (2009) provide an overview of workload issues to the educator and student, as well as to other teaching staff. Although personalization of assignments comes at cost in terms of increased workload for instructors in terms of grading and increased stress for students, there are reported student benefits in terms of increased interest, motivation, and appreciation of the relevance of their learning to their current and future work.

Table 16.1 provides an overview of an example framework for how authentic statistics assignments might be tailored to differing degrees as a function of specification of the source of the research scenario and dataset, and for thinking about how authentic statistics assignment design can have differential consequences to the instructor and student. The table illustrates how carefully designed personalized project-based statistics assignments can provide opportunities for greater student interest while managing student stress and instructor workload. Importantly, assignments can be tailored to student interests/needs in a variety of ways. This includes but is not limited to offering choices on whether to personalize variables and which research questions to address. Providing flexibility in formats of how to communicate the completed assignment (e.g., oral/written; report/poster) is another way by means of which authentic and project-based learning can be assessed and personalized to the student.

Table 16.1 Authentic Learning/Assessment Design as a Function of Flexibility in Scenario and Dataset Specification

Scenario	Dataset		
	Instructor-specified dataset	Instructor-specified dataset; Student-personalized variable names	Student-specified dataset (variable names, score structure, etc.)
Scenario(s)* completely specified by instructor	Low workload for instructor (Single answer key)	Low+ workload for instructor—must keep track of variable names/ groups (Single answer key template)	High workload for instructor—challenge of certainty with respect to accuracy of student work across multiple criteria; results & follow-ups vary as a function of data
	Low interest for student Low stress for student	Medium interest for student Low+ stress for student	High interest for student Medium stress for student
			Problem for both instructor and student with respect to appropriateness of dataset
Scenario(s) partially specified by instructor* (Provides student choice of select research questions, analyses, etc.)	Medium workload for instructor—select analyses/follow-ups student determined (Multiple answer keys)	Medium+ workload for instructor—must keep track of variable names/ groups; analyses/follow-ups are student determined (Multiple answer key templates)	High+ workload for instructor—challenge of certainty with respect to accuracy of student work across multiple criteria; analyses student determined; results and follow-ups vary as a function of data
	Low/Medium interest for student	Medium+ interest for student	High interest for student Medium/high stress for student
	Low+ stress for student	Medium stress for student	Problem for both instructor and student with respect to appropriateness of dataset
Scenario specified by student	Medium/high workload for instructor (analyses and follow-ups student determined)	Medium/high+ workload for instructor—must keep track of variable names/ groups; analyses and follow-ups are student determined	High++ workload for instructor—challenge of certainty with respect to accuracy of student work across multiple criteria (analyses student determined; follow-ups vary as a function of data)
	Medium interest for student	Medium/high interest for student Medium+ stress for student	High interest for student High stress for student
			Problem for both instructor and student with respect to appropriateness of dataset, research questions.

Note: Variations to further increase personalization to students: * students may be provided with choice from a set of prespecified scenarios (rows 1 and 2); ** students may be provided with choice of dissemination format (e.g., report vs. poster)—any of above cells.

Incorporating Personally Relevant Project-Based Learning in Courses and Assignment Categories

Although highly touted, according to Hung (2009), the literature on "problem-based learning" is mixed—which Hung attributes in part to the lack of systemization with which focal problems are developed and implemented. Although I do not consider my course offerings to adhere to the principles of a "full-on" problem-based learning course, my structured pedagogical approach does overlap in some areas with the processes described in Hung (2009)—necessarily beginning with a "front-end analysis of the [course goals/objectives], course content and context area" (p. 124) for the development of the authentic assignments through which key student learning takes place.

In this section, I discuss a general pedagogical approach, with emphasis on specific assignment categories that I have used to varying degrees in my teaching of required graduate statistics courses over the past 25+ years—first in a department of educational psychology, now in a department of psychology. The approach that I have used in most iterations of these courses includes projects of personal relevance to the students, with the requirement of rigor in proposal and report writing/results communication. Throughout the courses, students learn the importance of research planning and varied diagnostic and alternative data analytic/modelling strategies that are not in many old-school courses on ANOVA and multiple regression (see Aiken, West, & Millsap, 2008, p. 43), including modelling considerations under challenging data conditions.

A brief overview of key components in my development of required graduate statistics courses utilizing authentic project-based learning/assessment is detailed in this list.

- Context: Students are in their first or second term of their graduate program in psychology and are taking their first or second required course in a required statistics course sequence. A small number of upper-division undergraduate students may also be enrolled. Class size is 15 to 25 students.
- Learning goals include (a) learning statistical theory and practice, (b) learning skills that include the development of writing skills for preparation of proposals as well as research reports, (c) the development of critical and creative thinking, analysis, and research capabilities, and (d) increased appreciation of the importance of methodological thinking and skills.
- Primary course elements include (a) a review of exemplar literature, (b) consideration of motivating examples and research questions (RQs), (c) review of relevant statistical theory, and (d) a discussion of research planning and practice in the disciplines.
- Activities and assignments are specified as a mechanism by means of which students can (a) develop their knowledge and skills and (b) demonstrate learning—that is, they are learning tools as well as assessment tools.

In my course delivery, I provide core material (e.g., motivating examples, statistical theory) in lecture format, which provides the foundation on which students scaffold their project-based learning. The primary assignment categories I use are article critique, proposals, and reports.

Exemplar literature/article critique, proposals, and reports are valuable vehicles on which to structure a required graduate statistics course in psychology using authentic project-based learning. In the following, I review a design strategy for assignments in each of these categories, which adhere to principles of authentic learning/project-based learning and to which increasing levels of student tailoring/personalization can be ascribed in order for the learning to be increasingly personally relevant to the student. Key strategies used include but are not limited to the provision for student choice and personalization of research scenarios (see Table 16.1 for example framework for assignment design). For each assignment type (e.g., "article review/critique"), I consider student and instructor experiences and provide implementation examples.

Article Review/Critique

The development of skills of article critique with regard to methodology and analyses is an important component of a statistics course with a focus on authentic learning/assessment. These skills can be developed in a variety of ways. The instructor:

a.   can assign an article that all students must review (AC),
b.   can have students select/choose and review an article from a prespecified set (AC-choice), or
c.   can ask students to identify their own article (from their own area of study/interest) to review, with very limited constraints on the choice of the article except that RQs/analyses described in the article must be of types covered in the current course (AC-student specified).

With these three formulations of the article review/critique assignment, we see three increasing levels by means of which personalization of assignments can take place—from no personal relevance (AC) to complete personal relevance (AC-student specified) with regard to the article (AC → AC-choice → AC-student specified). In the different variations of the assignment, it is reasonable to expect that the student is generally more interested in the article if they have chosen it. With AC and AC-choice, the workload for the instructor is reasonable, particularly if the number of candidate articles in AC-choice is small; however, student interest/motivation can be low or varied depending on the match of student interests to the topics of the articles. The highest level of personal relevance of the assignment to the student (AC-student specified), however, comes at a cost to the instructor in terms of workload due to the necessity of the instructor having to familiarize themselves with the content of every article selected by the students in order to verify the accuracy and appropriateness of each student's summary and critique of the article. Although there is the cost of additional workload with the student-identified articles, there is a benefit to the instructor. By having students select and review articles that are of interest to them, the instructor benefits by becoming more familiar with the specific interests of the students, which can be useful in the generation of in-class examples/scenarios and discussion of relevant exemplar literature. These articles can also be a valuable source for the prototype exemplar scenarios for later assignments (e.g., research proposals).

Implementation Example

One version of the fully personalized article review/critique assignment that I have utilized in some of my iterations of required graduate statistics courses is one in which students are asked to conduct a literature search to find an example article in their own area of study that makes use of the data-analytic strategy being considered in the course (e.g., ANOVA, multiple regression). Whether set up as a low- or medium-stakes assignment, it is useful to provide an explicit structure by which to prepare an article review/critique, which includes full discussion, using APA format, of primary relevant article critique components (purpose, methods, results, summary, other analyses that could have been conducted). With regard to the description/critique of the methods section, students are asked to address the fullness with which (a) study participants were described, (b) measures (scoring, reliability, validity, item level missing data) were detailed, and (c) analyses (score level missing, descriptive, assumption checking/remedial analyses, research question–focused analyses, and follow-up analyses including error rate control strategies) were described.

With this assignment, students can see current practices in their own area, develop skills of critique, and consider strategies by means of which a paper can be improved. Additionally, students can develop ideas of how they might approach these types of data in a secondary analysis in a future replication study or follow-up research. As mentioned previously, the article critique exercise, when conducted early in the term can provide excellent resources for generating examples and scenarios that are of specific student relevance—which can be well received; one student wrote, "I . . . appreciated your . . . effort to incorporate relevant topics from our different research areas".

Research Proposal

The development of skills of writing a research proposal is important in graduate psychology curriculum. Over the course of one's academic career, one must write thesis/dissertation proposals as well as grant proposals. Although some graduate programs have courses in which students write their thesis/dissertation proposals, when available, these course offerings are not generally taught by the faculty members who are teaching the statistics courses in the department.

Power and sample size considerations are of fundamental relevance to the topics in most required statistics courses (e.g., ANOVA, multiple regression). Although consideration of power, power calculations, or calculations regarding sample size requirements is a valuable component of graduate statistics curriculum (c.f., Aiken et al., 2008), only one-third of reporting programs in Aiken et al.'s (2008) survey provided "in-depth training in power analysis" (p. 36). Assignments, such as a simulated grant application, in which these topics are included can simultaneously facilitate the development of the skills of proposal writing, including but not limited to clear communication of research questions and corresponding data analytic plans.

There are a number of ways to frame research proposal assignments. The instructor:

a. can assign a scenario for which all students must write a proposal (RP),
b. can have students select/choose from a set of candidate scenarios regarding which to write a proposal (RP-choice), or

c. can ask students to write a proposal for a project completely of their own choosing, using their own RQs/variables, etc., in the context of their own research area, with very limited constraints except that RQs/analyses must include those types covered in the current course (RP-student specified).

With these three formulations of the research proposal assignment, we see three increasing levels by means of which personalization of assignments can take place—from no personal relevance to complete personal relevance (RP → RP-choice → RP-student specified). As in the article review/critique assignments, it is reasonable to expect that a student is generally more interested in a proposal topic if they have chosen or specified it themselves. However, the highest level of personal relevance with RP-student specified can be accompanied by increased student stress, because the student has to take greater responsibility for the direction of the proposal and the correctness of the match of the research questions, design, variables, and analysis to each other. This highest level of personal relevance to the student comes at a cost to the instructor in terms of workload in order to verify the appropriateness and accuracy of each student's proposal; however, the instructor gains by becoming more familiar with the specific interests of the students, which can be useful in the generation of in-class examples/scenarios.

Although student interest might be lower with RP and RP-choice than with RP-student specified, student stress and instructor workload should be lower, because the instructor has carefully structured/standardized the research questions and, consequently, the answer key/template. If the instructor has based the scenario(s) for RP and RP-choice on topics of student relevance established from earlier classroom discussions in the course or from AC-student specified, student interest can be increased while maintaining a reasonable workload for the instructor.

Importantly, however, there are other variations of RP and RP-choice by means of which to maintain most of the ease of grading that comes through having standardized research questions for which proposals can be written but which make the assignments more personally relevant and compelling for the students. Students can be invited (or even required) to reframe the research questions using variable names from their own areas of interest. To accomplish this type of personalization through transformation of RP and RP-choice assignments, the instructor:

a. describes a single scenario (RP); students use the exemplar scenario as a basis from which to generate/write up a proposal in the context of their own research area (e.g., change sample description, variable names) (RP-personalized), or
b. describes a set of candidate scenarios (RP-choice); students choose one of the exemplar scenarios as a basis from which to generate/write up a proposal in the context of their own research area (e.g., change sample description, variable names) (RP-choice/personalized).

With RP-personalized and RP-choice/personalized, students scaffold their personalized proposals on the exemplar scenarios provided by the instructor. The value of the personalization of RP and RP-choice, through the RP-personalized and RP-choice/personalized variants, is that students begin to imagine the application of the methodologies to their own area; at the same time, this allows the instructor to have a clear grading template and to gain additional insights into the interests of the students for use in continued generation of in-class examples and scenarios.

Implementation Examples

The primary focus of the research proposal assignment that I commonly assign in my teaching of required graduate statistics courses includes some variation whereby students are tasked with writing a five- to seven-page project proposal. This assignment includes expectations for clear specification of their research questions in an introduction, measures and analysis (main and follow-up analyses including full specification of diagnostics, treatment of missing data, error control, etc.) in their methods section, power analysis and target sample size including budget justification if I have framed the research proposal assignment as a grant application. For example, instructions might include:

> For this assignment, pretend you are the researcher applying for grant/scholarship funding. Develop a brief but appropriately detailed proposal. Your main purpose with this proposal is to convince the funding agency that you have the scientific/statistical competence for this project—keeping in mind the usual issues, e.g., scoring, reliability/validity, missing data/dropouts, full descriptives, outliers/diagnostics, assumptions/assumption checking, omnibus tests, follow-up tests, Type I error control, power, effect sizes, confidence intervals, alternative procedures in case of assumption violations, etc. . . . Your proposal must follow APA guidelines. Include an introduction section.

For many years, I opted for "fully" student-specified research proposals and research reports (e.g., RP-student specified and RR-student specified, the bottom right cell of the authentic assignment design framework in Table 16.1) as the sole basis of assessment in my courses (particularly my offering of Correlation/Regression). Along with the provision of the information on the expected organization of the proposal (introduction, etc.), the instruction set for the RP-student specified assignment can be very simple. For example:

> Summarize a data analytic problem on which you are/will be working or in which you are interested, which can be analyzed using any of the techniques described in this course. The data analytic problem may involve real data to which you already have access or will be collecting; you might like to use some previously published data; or you can use artificial data that you make up.

Although RP-student specified is highly personalized and interesting to many students, it can be stressful for students, particularly if this is in their first required statistics graduate course, in which case they are in their first month of graduate school and typically have not yet decided what their research focus might be. This format of research proposal assignment involves many one-on-one student–instructor meetings as the instructor supports the students in the development of appropriate research questions and analytic plans for the kinds of data they might imagine collecting. Although there is a heavy workload in helping students prepare their assignments, for an experienced instructor, the workload associated with grading fully student specified research proposals is not excessive.

More recently, as I have tried to figure out a way of reorganizing my workload at the same time as maintaining interest for students and reducing some of their stress of working through fully student-specified projects, I have been trying a variation of project-based learning, shifting more to structured authentic learning in which students are provided with a general scenario they are encouraged to personalize (c.f. Table 16.1). The following is an adapted excerpt from the instructions that accompanied a research proposal assignment (RP-personalized) for a recent iteration of a required graduate statistics course. In contrast with the simplicity of the RP-student specified instructions, along with the provision of the information on the expected organization of the proposal (e.g., introduction, etc.), this RP-personalized assignment began with a variant of the following instructions:

> Develop a brief proposal for a project in which the researcher has the purpose of studying the effect of two different factors (i.e., 2 IVs: Factor A and Factor B) . . . [detailed description of number of levels and whether/which factors are between/within]. You can write a proposal for the project in the Example Scenario described below. Alternatively, you can generate a proposal inspired from your own context, e.g., by renaming the variables. . . . Keep in mind that you must address the assigned research questions and keep the number of factors, levels, and type of design the same.

This was followed by a detailed, roughly one-single-spaced-page description of the example scenario and corresponding research questions.

Notably, when provided with the option of personalizing an assignment, not all students choose to personalize the assignment with imagined personally relevant data collection scenarios or their own variable names. Nonetheless, their appreciation of the authentic assessment and its personal relevance when they are asked to reflect on what they learned from the assignment comes through. Students particularly appreciated the value of the power/sample size/budget calculations. Example quotes include:

> Q: Inventing the study procedures were fun, and I found it to be a helpful reminder of what to include in research proposals . . . this was especially relevant in my own life.
>
> Q: . . . the required sample size (and surprising associated budget) was quite revealing . . . calculating power before beginning any data collection is a strategy that I will employ in the future.

Research Reports (and Other Dissemination Strategies)

Writing a detailed empirical research report that conforms to APA guidelines is a valuable skill. Although the writing of manuscripts in graduate school is often done under the tutelage of one's primary supervisor, required graduate statistics courses are a context in which the practice of complete and clear writing of analyses and results can be developed. This is sometimes a skill that is developed and practiced in advanced topics statistics/methodology courses; however, it is not a common part of standard required graduate statistics curriculum in psychology.

In a research report assignment, students are typically tasked with writing a research report, including a brief introduction with specification of research questions, methods, results, and discussion section. If the students have already largely been graded on their skills of writing of research questions and data analysis plans in a previous assignment (e.g., a research proposal assignment), the grading can focus on the novel type of writing in which the student is engaging (e.g., results).

Research report assignments are strong examples of assessments that promote authentic learning. Variations can be structured in a similar way to the research proposal assignments described in the previous section. Specifically, variations of research assignments include ones in which the instructor:

a. assigns a scenario and corresponding data for which all students must write a research report (RR),
b. has students select/choose from a set of candidate scenarios/datasets regarding which to write a report (RR-choice), or
c. asks students to write a report for a project completely of their own choosing, using their own RQs/variables, etc., in the context of their own research area, with very limited constraints except that RQs/analyses must include those types covered in the current course (RR-student specified).

Personalized variants of RR and RR-choice include assignments in which the instructor:

a. describes a single data scenario (RR); students use the exemplar data scenario as a basis from which to generate/write up a report in the context of their own research area (e.g., change sample description, variable names) (RR-personalized), or
b. describes a set of candidate data scenarios (RR-choice); students choose one of the exemplar scenario/datasets as a basis from which to generate/write up a report in the context of their own research area (e.g., change sample description, variable names) (RR-choice/personalized).

Importantly, research reports are not the only mechanism by which to disseminate findings. When I have already established that students have achieved a general acceptable level of mastery of writing/preparing research reports, I provide options for other methods of communication of research findings. Given that the research poster is a commonly used vehicle to share research, providing this format as an option for their assignment "product" allows students to develop and practice their skills with written and visual communication in posters. Oral presentations can also be used, but special consideration is needed by the instructor in terms of effective use of class time, particularly for assignments where all the students are using the same dataset and assigned scenario. The issues around student interest/stress and instructor workload in the different variants of the research report assignment are much the same as with the research proposal assignment, with the complexities of any variant that includes student specification of research scenario, research questions, and/or dataset.

Implementation Examples

As is common in most standard graduate statistics classes, students must complete an analysis and provide a description of their findings. In my course offerings, I often ask students to simulate preparing a brief report to their supervisor or that the research report is a brief report to be submitted to a journal. In my offerings, depending on the specifics of the report, I have assigned anywhere from an 8- to 10-page or 12- to 15-page report. In all contexts, I ask the students to provide full and complete reporting of their methods, including analysis, and results sections such that anyone reading their report will be able to repeat and verify their analyses and findings and will know that they have considered issues of missing data, diagnostics including possible assumption violations, and error rate control. Specifically, students are tasked with providing complete communication of methods, analysis, and results in such a way that demonstrates their statistical competence to conduct and communicate relevant analyses, including consideration of missing data, diagnostics, and error rate control. But beyond asking the students to demonstrate excellence in meeting, if not exceeding, research reporting standards (c.f., APA Publications and Communications Board Working Group on Journal Article Reporting Standards, 2008; APA, 2009), I have either had fully student-specified project research reports (RR-student specified) or invited students to personalize their reports in order to maximize their interest and the possibility that they will make use of these procedures in the future in their own research (e.g., RR-personalized, RR-choice/personalized).

Course offerings, in which I utilized both RP-student specified and RR-student specified assignments, produced a variety of course projects—work that formed a component of later conference presentations, master's thesis projects, or journal articles (e.g., Smit, Gukova, Weisgeber, & Mistlberger, 2012; Craig & Moretti, 2012; Shaffer et al., 2014). In these iterations, beyond specifying expectations for report structure/content (e.g., introduction, etc.), instruction sets for RR-student specified assignments were short. Instructions for RR-student specified assignments can be similar to those for RP-student specified assignments and as simple as:

> Summarize your analysis of a dataset using data analytic strategies described in this course. Demonstrate that you have learned the appropriate use of data analytic techniques involving principles of [topics in the current course]. . . . You may use real data to which you have access; you might like to use some previously published data; or you can use artificial data that you make up.

However, as with RP-student specified assignments, instructor workload with the RR-student specified format was high. In RR-student specified format, there are multiple one-on-one meetings with most students and the major grading challenge of fully following through on each student's work.

More recently, in order to reduce the instructor workload associated with research reports that I had with RR-student specified assignments, at the same time as trying to optimize student interest and reduce some of their stress of working through fully student-specified projects, I have opted for more structured formats of assignments. Most recently, when providing the research report assignment to the students, I provide a detailed description (approximately 1 page single-spaced) of a research scenario, including participant, measures, and data collection description, along with relevant research questions. Included with the scenario description is the specification for the expectations and format for the research report. Depending on the timing of the assignment in the semester and my learning objectives for the specific assignment (I may assign one to three unique or scaffolded research report assignments depending on the course), I offer fewer or more choices of research question/design to the students; in all, I include the option to personalize the scenario description and variable names.

For the last assignment (RR-choice/personalized with dissemination option) in an offering of a course on experimental design, students were provided a general scenario, data and variable names, and research questions. I provided three levels of choice to the students: (a) variable/scenario personalization, (b) research design, and (c) final product format. Students were invited to personalize their description of the data scenario and variables using the described scenario as a template; regarding this option, one student wrote, "I really appreciated how we could choose our own variables of interest when writing . . . it definitely made it more fun for me". Additionally, students were given a choice of conducting the analysis and writing up a report with the scenario/data framed as though it were from a between-between, between-within, or within-within design; the provision of a choice for scenario (e.g., research design) to students is a valuable mechanism by means of which personalization of assignments can be structured, as it allows students to consider and recognize that the "same" data could have been collected in different ways. Although all the students ended up choosing the between-between design for their final writeup for this specific assignment, students acknowledged having explored the data analysis options. One student wrote, "I . . . liked . . . we had several design options to choose from (i.e., between-between, between-within, and within-within, . . . it allowed us to further personalize our assignments, and to practice playing around with different data". As this was the final assignment for the term and I was pleased with the level of writing the students had achieved in previous reports, I also provided students with the option of producing a poster. Whether students selected the standard paper report or poster option, they all demonstrated creativity as they explored different approaches to communicating their formulated quantitative research findings. Sample titles include:

- The Effect of Testing Location and Gender-Based Stereotyping Threat on Female Test Anxiety (poster, variable names not personalized)
- The Effects of Self-Expansion on Relationship Satisfaction in Non-Relational and Relational Contexts (report, fully personalized)
- Have Yourself a Merry Little Christmas: The Effects of Snow and Music on Christmas Spirit (poster, fully personalized)

Conclusion: Closing Comments

Many of us use project-based learning in our advanced graduate statistics courses. I argue that there is little reason for us not to use project-based learning in our offerings of required graduate statistics courses in psychology as well. Projects permit students to develop critical thinking and problem-solving skills as well as communication skills in authentic contexts.

There are many ways to talk about and to implement project-based learning. Problems/projects can be the primary method of student assessment and serve alongside lectures as a vehicle for authentic student learning and skill development. Use of an organizing framework when designing authentic assignments can help organize assignment-specific learning objectives and activities with consideration of student/instructor experiences. Instructor-specified authentic assignments that students can personalize in terms of variable names and choices for analyses depending on their research priorities and how they have conceptualized the variables enhances the opportunity for appreciation of the personal relevance of the material and enhances their confidence that they will be able to apply these concepts in meaningful and personally relevant ways in the future. Building a statistics course using carefully designed assignments of article review/critique, research proposals, and research reports is one strategy to incorporate project-based learning.

Use of project-based learning in required graduate statistics courses may be one way to bring teaching of statistics and quantitative methods in psychology into the 21st century. Importantly, project-based learning does not have to be onerous for the instructor or for the student; with careful structuring of authentic assignments, grading workload can be eased, and stress to the student from a large-scale assignment can be mitigated. Providing

- choices to students for articles, research questions, analyses and dissemination, and
- invitations for students to reframe provided scenarios and variables to their own area

are two easy ways structured project-based learning can be personalized and made personally relevant to the student.

References

Aiken, L. S., West, S. G., & Millsap, R. E. (2008). Doctoral training in statistics, measurement, and methodology in psychology: Replication and extension of Aiken, West, Sechrest, and Reno's (1990) survey of PhD programs in North America. *American Psychologist, 63*, 32–50. https://doi.org/10.1037/0003-066X.63.1.32

Aiken, L. S., West, S. G., Sechrest, L. B., & Reno, R. R. (1990). Graduate training in statistics, methodology, and measurement in psychology: An international survey. *American Psychologist, 45*, 721–734.

American Psychological Association. (2009). *Publication manual of the American Psychological Association* (6th ed.). Washington, DC: American Psychological Association.

APA Publications and Communications Board Working Group on Journal Article Reporting Standards. (2008). Reporting standards for research in psychology: Why do we need them? What might they be? *American Psychologist, 63*, 839–851. https://doi.org/10.1037/0003-066X.63.9.839

Barrows, H. S. (1986). A taxonomy of problem-based learning methods. *Medical Education, 20*, 481–486. https://doi.org/10.1111/j.1365-2923.1986.tb01386.x

Barrows, H. S., & Tamblyn, R. (1980). *Problem-based learning*. New York: Springer.

Boud, D., & Feletti, G. (Eds.). (1997). *The challenge of problem-based learning* (2nd ed.). London, UK: Kogan Page.

Campbell, C. (2014, September 16). Problem-based and project-based learning. *Teacher Magazine*. Retrieved from www.teachermagazine.com.au/articles/problem-based-learning-and-project-based-learning

Chiang, A., Wu, P. H., & Baba, M. S. (2009, March). A study of educator workload in problem-based learning. In *Proceedings of the IASTED International Conference Web-based Education* (WBE 2009), March 16–18, 2009, Phuket, Thailand. Retrieved from www.researchgate.net/publication/228602104_A_study_of_educator_workload_in_problem-based_learning

Craig, S. G., & Moretti, M. (2012). *The impact of depression on conduct disordered adolescent girls versus boys: Gender matters.* Oral paper presentation presented at the 13th Biennial Conference of the European Association for Research on Adolescence, Spetses, Greece.

GAISE College Report ASA Revision Committee. (2016). *Guidelines for assessment and instruction in statistics education college report.* Retrieved from www.amstat.org/education/gaise

Hulsizer, M. R., & Woolf, L. M. (2009). *A Guide to teaching statistics: Innovations and best practices.* West Sussex, UK: Wiley-Blackwell. https://doi.org/10.1002/9781444305234.

Hung, W. (2009). The 9-step problem design process for problem-based learning: Application of the 3C3R model. *Educational Research Review, 4*, 118–141.

Karpiak, C. P. (2011). Assessment of problem-based learning in the undergraduate statistics course. *Teaching of Psychology, 38*, 251–254.

Kilpatrick, W. H. (1918). The project method. *Teachers College Record, 19*, 319–335.

Knoll, M. (2014). Project method. In C. D. Phillips (Ed.), *Encyclopedia of educational theory and philosophy* (pp. 665–669). Thousand Oaks, CA: Sage.

Kolmos, A., & Graaff, E. D. (2003). Characteristics of problem-based learning. *International Journal of Engineering Education, 19*, 657–662.

McGrath, A. L., Ferns, A., Greiner, L., Wanamaker, K., & Brown, S. (2015). Reducing anxiety and increasing self-efficacy within an advanced graduate psychology statistics course. *Canadian Journal for the Scholarship of Teaching and Learning, 6*. http://doi.org/10.5206/cjsotl-rcacea.2015.1.5

Mercier, J., & Frederiksen, C. H. (2007). Individual differences in graduate students' help-seeking process in using a computer coach in problem-based learning. *Learning and Instruction, 17*, 184–203.

Pan, W., & Tang, M. (2004). Examining the effectiveness of innovative instructional methods on reducing statistics anxiety for graduate students in the social sciences. *Journal of Instructional Psychology, 31*, 149–159.

Pecore, J. L. (2015). From Kilpatrick's project method to project-based learning (Chapter 7). In *International handbook of progressive education* (pp. 155–171). Retrieved from https://ir.uwf.edu/islandora/object/uwf%3A22741/datastream/PDF/view

Ruiz-Gallardo, J. R., Castano, S., Gomez-Alday, J. J., & Valdes, A. (2011). Assessing student workload in Problem Based Learning: Relationships among teaching method, student workload and achievement. A case study in Natural Sciences. *Teaching and Teacher Education, 27*, 619–627.

Ryberg, T., & Nørgaard, B. (2013). Introducing problem-based learning in higher education. *Journal of Problem Based Learning, 1*, I–VI.

Shaffer, C. S., Gray, A. L., Viljoen, J. L., Douglas, K. S., Tweed, R. G., & Bhatt, G. (2014, March). *The predictive validity of the Antisocial Process Screening Device in male and female adolescents.* Poster presented at the Annual Meeting of the American Psychology-Law Society, New Orleans, LA.

Siswono, T. Y. E., Hartono, S., & Kohar, A. W. (2018). Effectiveness of project-based learning in statistics for lower secondary schools. *Eurasian Journal of Educational Research, 75*, 198–212.

Smit, A. N., Gukova, K., Weisgeber, D., & Mistlberger, R. E. (2012, May). *Associations among chronotype, sleep duration and academic performance.* Poster presentation at SRBR International Conference, Sandestin, FL.

Smith, G. (1998). Learning statistics by doing statistics. *Journal of Statistics Education, 6*(3). Retrieved from https://amstat.tandfonline.com/doi/pdf/10.1080/10691898.1998.11910623

Wilkerson, L., & Gijselaers, M. H. (Eds.). (1996). Bringing problem-based learning to higher education: Theory and practice. In *New directions for teaching, no 68.* San Francisco, CA: Jossey-Bass Inc., Publishers.

Chapter 17

Using Projects to Teach Statistics in Social Sciences

Jennifer D. Timmer and Carolyn J. Anderson

Engaging students in statistical thinking is critically important given the current availability of data and interest in data-informed decision-making. Applied statistics courses at all levels, covering a variety of methods, should involve learning not only the mathematical foundations inherent in statistical methods and quantitative research more generally but also how data are turned into evidence to answer research questions. Students can learn the mechanics and critical decision-making essential to data analysis in a practical, applied manner through the integration of projects into a course. To ameliorate the difficulty that some students have with the abstract nature of statistical concepts, course projects provide students the opportunity to engage with statistical concepts in a concrete way. Additionally, student projects enhance engagement, aid in learning, increase interactions with the instructor, and lead to benefits beyond the course. For example, course projects may lay the foundation for honors projects, master's theses, dissertations, conference presentations, publications, and other outlets important for professional development; further, the skills honed through projects can benefit students in their future careers. Projects can also help instructors engage with students and assess student learning.

In this chapter, we will review some of the challenges of teaching statistics, discuss how student projects can be used to address these challenges, and provide suggestions for incorporating student projects in a variety of statistics courses. This chapter is structured as follows. In the first section, we consider how course projects can aid student learning by making statistics less abstract and encouraging data literacy and critical thinking. In the subsequent section, we discuss practical steps to incorporate projects into a statistics course. These multiple steps include students submitting proposals outlining their research questions and proposed methods and final papers in which they interpret and communicate their findings. In the final section of this chapter, we discuss several instructional considerations, including course organization, grading, time demands, and diverse student needs.

Why Use Projects?

A unique challenge in teaching and learning statistics is the balance between focusing on the mathematical foundations and the application of the methods. As De Veaux and Velleman (2008) describe, "The challenge for the student (and teacher) of introductory statistics is that, like literature and art, navigating through and making sense of it requires not just rules and axioms, but life experience and 'common sense'" (p. 2). Students must learn the methodological foundations, but experience applying the concepts in a meaningful context is critical to greater comprehension and appreciation of the complexities of the quantitative research process. Course projects may be used to advance a number of educational goals; here we focus on two in particular: (1) making statistics less abstract and (2) increasing data literacy through elucidating the critical thinking and decision-making inherent in quantitative analysis.

Statistics as Abstraction

Statistics uses mathematical formulas to express statistical concepts (e.g., variance, sampling distributions, standard errors, measures, models, etc.); in other words, statistics uses an abstract language to represent abstract concepts. These abstractions make the methods difficult to learn and to fully understand. Additionally, students often conflate statistics with mathematics, the latter being a subject many students dislike, and as a result, they come into their statistics courses with a sense of intimidation (Ben-Zvi & Garfield, 2004; Gal & Garfield, 1997). Thus, although math is often the dreaded but required course that a student must take, statistics is mathematics' even more confusing cousin. Course projects add a practical and concrete element to students' learning process (Blumenfeld et al., 1991; Carver et al., 2016). Relevant statistical examples can help connect students' lives and interests to course material, and projects can push these connections even further by encouraging students to explore the statistical nature inherent in their own interests. Students often ask how course concepts can be applied to their own data, especially graduate students in more advanced courses who have selected the course specifically because the methods are needed for their research. Projects encourage students' learning through engagement with a goal-driven data analysis applying statistical concepts, procedures, and techniques to their own data. By analyzing data, students can see how the abstract concepts relate and provide solutions to data analysis problems.

Of course, this abstract-to-real connection is why we use examples in lectures to which we think/hope students will connect more generally. For example, when considering measures of central tendency (i.e., mean, median, and mode), we may use examples in which one measure would provide meaningfully different conclusions about the data. As an example, suppose a town of 100 residents has 99 who work in a factory making $50,000 per year and the factory owner makes $1,000,000 per year. The mean income is $59,500, whereas the median and mode incomes are $50,000. If the goal of determining an average has policy implications for services provided in a community, obtaining an estimate that overstates 99% of the sample by about 20% could be misleading in a manner that even novice statistical learners can appreciate. Although not a real data set, this hypothetical example demonstrates how assigning numbers to an understood context can make the abstract more concrete, which helps students make connections between statistical concepts and their world and interests and better understand the decision-making process inherent in statistical work.

The type of example given still may not actually be helpful in illustrating the concepts for all students, particularly because it is a contrived situation. Although students can understand the concept somewhat more clearly given the example and may understand the implications of the choice of a statistic in the policy context, examples using real data can be even more compelling. Using census data to illustrate the prior example to show an actual community in which those differences might lead to different policy decisions highlights the current ways that statistics operates in society. Other real, nonsimulated or nonhypothetical examples provided in the courses we have taught used real data that students tend to find interesting (and generate discussion). Examples include who survived the sinking of the *Titanic*, who survived the travels and trials of the Donner Party, the admission of students to various universities under different policies, math and reading scores from students on large standardized tests, multiculturism and peer-group formation within classrooms of children, the performance of various university athletic teams, and many more. For the adult learners found in college and university undergraduate and graduate programs, these real-world connections can lead to increased engagement and learning (Chan, 2010; Knowles, 1984; Ozuah, 2016).

While meaningful connections between course concepts and real-world applications can be created through thoughtful examples in lectures, assigned readings, and homework problems, they can be strengthened further through experience engaging in the research process via a goal-driven project of individual interest. Student-led projects can provide students the opportunity to see how these concepts apply to real data of interest by exploring the complexities of analysis and interpretation.

Data Literacy and Critical Thinking

Data literacy and critical thinking are related but distinct concepts. Both are necessary to data analysis and are required in a research project. Projects can demystify statistical thinking and show the mathematical building blocks in action. The critical thinking and judgment inherent in statistical work helps students understand that numbers are only part of the story. As De Veaux and Velleman (2008) note, "We can help students by giving them a structure for problem solving that incorporates the requirement that they exercise their judgment" (p. 3). Projects require critical thinking as well as the many (nonstatistical) judgments and complex decision-making that goes into analyzing data and communicating findings.

For example, one of the first decisions that students must make in creating projects is determining what data are required to answer their questions about a subject or topic. A student must choose a data source and ensure that the data set has all relevant variables and information that will be needed, including the sampling design—how the data were collected and under what conditions. Students must also recognize the nature of their data, whether it is numerical, qualitative, or a combination. The nature of the data and the sampling design, combined with the research questions, have implications for the statistical methods and procedures needed, as well as the inferences that can validly be made from the analysis. Recognizing the statistical design and nature of the data are critical elements that require statistical and substantive knowledge; that is, students must recognize that data are not just numbers in a file.

Students may think data will provide one "true" answer or that there is only one way to approach an analysis. Projects are much less structured than homework problems where the correct analysis is relatively obvious and there is one correct answer. We have found that students are often able to follow along in lecture and even successfully complete homework problems, but when faced with a project that challenges their knowledge and understanding, they are not sure what to do or where to start. A student must engage in critical thinking to decide what analyses could and should be done given their selected data and their stated reasons for conducting the analyses. Further, projects provide instructors the opportunity to assist students in thinking through the many decisions involved in the quantitative research process. As instructors, we often guide students by asking more questions in response to student questions rather than attempting to provide a "correct" answer, thus prompting more critical thinking.

Course projects facilitate students' development of data literacy skills, encourage a better understanding of how data are used to inform arguments, and lead to better critical thinking when faced with data-based arguments found in their daily lives (e.g., news, politics, other coursework)—in short, teaching what constitutes data and how data are turned into evidence. By going through the process of making decisions at each step of the research process, students can gain a better grasp of the judgments based on their chosen research goals as well as data limitations and the scope of any inferences given the sample. The development of these analytic tools and skills will aid students in evaluating other research, policy arguments, and any research-based arguments in general.

To summarize, using student projects in statistics courses enhances learning as students gain experience in the process of research and connecting abstract concepts to concrete research questions and data sets. Undergoing this process also encourages critical thinking, as students work through the decisions and judgments (many nonstatistical) involved in the analysis of data. Homework assignments can help to some extent with the mechanics of applying abstract concepts to data, but they are too often contrived and artificial. Instructors need to be able to grade all submissions efficiently, and one-off assignments may not allow for the in-depth and detailed analyses a project can provide. Analyzing data requires making many decisions, including what data are needed to answer research questions, what variables should be examined or included in a model, what model should be used, and how data should be summarized. Projects are ideal for providing students with experience making these decisions, from selecting research questions and appropriate data and methodological approaches to determining how best to present their data and communicate findings and implications. By going through the process of making decisions and applying what they are learning, students develop skills in identifying what is needed throughout the research process and implementing it in their analysis.

Designing Projects

We provide suggestions for designing and incorporating projects in statistics courses based on our experiences teaching both undergraduate and graduate students from a variety of disciplines in the social sciences in both introductory and more advanced statistics courses, including categorical data analysis, multilevel modeling, and Bayesian statistics and modeling. We discuss multiple possible components of student projects, which will be applicable to varying degrees given specific course organization and expectations. Specifically, we discuss: (1) helping students create a research proposal that includes selecting feasible research question(s), stating their hypotheses both verbally and statistically, and finding relevant data; (2) guiding students as they work to apply methods and engage in data analysis and interpretation; and (3) some of the opportunities and challenges inherent in implementing course projects in statistics, including considering and planning for diverse student needs, particularly regarding novice as compared to more advanced students.

Initial Considerations

We acknowledge that student projects are not suitable for all courses. For example, an unsuitable course could be a very large course in which an instructor cannot feasibly give individual attention to students or grade all projects. Another problematic context are courses that cover many different topics such that demonstrating competence in even a sub-set of methods might require multiple data sets. Still, we believe they can be a useful component in many courses that emphasize applied statistics or modeling. In introductory courses, students may need more suggestions regarding possible data sets, and the goals of the project may be fairly simple, perhaps involving only basic descriptive statistics; in these situations, students may benefit from starting to work with their data early in the semester and applying various course concepts to their chosen data set as the semester progresses. In more advanced courses, students may already have research questions in mind and access to relevant data but may need guidance regarding more complex methodological challenges; in many cases, these students will have a fuzzy idea of what they need to do and will work to connect course material to their data throughout the semester, which can lead to more nuanced and developed research and deeper understanding of the methods. In both introductory and more advanced courses, projects provide students the opportunity to deal with a data set, statistical software, and coding in the context of a research project in a low-stakes environment.

When selecting a topic, ideally the project will be of *high value* to the student and applicable to their own interests, particularly for graduate students. Undergraduate and more novice students may not have defined research agendas, but they should still seek to choose a project they find interesting. In these situations, it may be useful to provide students with several options from which they can choose; a few possible data sets with accompanying research questions can make the task less daunting for students without a clearly defined project in mind. In our experience, students tend to struggle most if they are just trying to find data to meet course requirements without considering what interests them; providing multiple options with data can help avoid that pitfall. Furthermore, providing options ensures that students with ill-defined ideas will still gain the experience of performing goal-driven data analysis.

To help students select a topic, individual meetings with the course instructor are ideal; whether or not this is possible, we recommend having students complete a project proposal both to help organize their ideas and to provide an opportunity for the instructor to redirect students whose ideas may not be feasible or appropriate for the course. Written proposals can also be particularly useful for students who might be somewhat intimidated by the notion of meeting with an instructor or asking for help in person. In what follows, we describe considerations for project proposals and some of the possible components.

The Proposal

The proposal starts with student interests and can best be thought of as the beginning of a conversation with students about their research. Motivation, especially in introductory courses, can be a problem; however, projects encourage greater engagement in learning and applying statistics as students become more active in their own learning process. If a student has well-defined interests and their own data, which is true for many honors, graduate, and professional students, then research questions may have already been determined in conjunction with their academic adviser or other collaborators. In such cases, the project may also be a part of a larger research project. In situations when students have access to a particular data set that drives their choice of topic, care should be taken by the student and instructor to ensure the data are appropriate for the course. For many novice and introductory students, the instructor will need to encourage students to articulate their interests and think about questions they may have on a topic; places to start are within a student's major, possible career paths that they envision, or even hobbies. Ideally, research starts with a theory that leads to questions that in turn lead to designing a study or seeking data that can be used to answer our questions and finally confirm aspects of the theory (or not). However, the process can be a bit different for a course project; that is, searching through available data sets may spur research questions about topics for which data are available. A data-driven project is more exploratory in nature; however, students must have some inkling regarding what they might want to learn from the data. A data-driven project without focus is not ideal because there is no guidance regarding what analyses should be performed. Regardless of how students decide on a topic and questions, the decision should be made by the student and approved by the instructor.

The instructor's role is to ensure that the project is well defined and feasible for completion within the term of the course and to provide feedback on planned analyses and uses of methods covered in the course. In graduate courses, proposed research may require methods that go beyond what is covered, but it is the student's responsibility to learn the material and the instructor's responsibility to guide the student to relevant literature if needed. For example, if a student proposes a project for a course on categorical data analysis but the data are nested or clustered (a topic not covered), the student can either simplify their analysis, ignoring the clustered structure of the data, or do outside work to learn about multilevel versions of models for categorical data. Students who choose simplification can then expand their project in subsequent semesters either in other (project-based) statistics courses or for their thesis or publication.

Most research done solely for use within the course does not need to go through review by campus Institutional Review Board (IRB) offices. Graduate students already involved with research generally come to a course already having their project approved by the IRB; however, some students may want to pursue projects that are not exempt. If a project does not fall into an exempt or expedited case, IRB review might not be attainable in the desired time frame. In other words, depending on typical approval timing on a particular campus, these projects may not be feasible within the course timeline and should be avoided. However, in cases where students are doing secondary data analyses, IRB approval could be a matter of days at some institutions. Students should realize this a required component of ethical research, and, as appropriate, students should submit evidence of IRB approval to the instructor. Students may also wish to seek IRB approval independently after the course is over. In any case, instructors should confirm any IRB requirements with appropriate campus authorities.

The written proposal provides the instructor an opportunity to assess whether the project meets the requirements of the course as well as provide feedback and suggestions on the proposed work. If a plan does not include enough detail, the instructor may ask for more details, or better yet, meet with a student to talk through their ideas and plan. The decision on students' proposals should be prompt.

When designing requirements for the project proposal, appropriate expectations given students' research and statistical experience is critical. For advanced students, we recommend project proposals around two to three pages, including the topic of interest with a brief indication of the motivation, specific research questions or goals of the proposed analysis, a description of the data and its source, and planned analyses. A substantial literature review is typically not the focus of the course; therefore, it is not a required part of the proposal. The written proposal is an opportunity for students to think through their project and articulate it in a manner that gives the instructor the best opportunity to provide useful feedback and guidance. For more novice students or students without data, the instructor can still use projects by providing a selection of data sets with accompanying research questions from which a student may choose. In such cases, a proposal still provides students the chance to think through the research process in depth and plan how they will tackle the project. This is an excellent opportunity for instructors to identify and address any major issues in students' understanding of the methods and the process as a whole. We here further discuss several components of the proposal in more depth.

Data

Within their proposal, students should describe their chosen data set, including how the data were collected (the source) and how they will be used to answer the research question(s). Importantly, instructors can then assess the feasibility and appropriateness of the project given student experience and expertise as well as course constraints. Some data sets may simply be too complex for a class project, and instructors should steer students toward a more practical data set, a simpler analysis, or just one part of a larger project. Attention to the sampling design is important because it in part determines what conclusions may be validly drawn from an analysis. For example, if participants are randomly assigned to one of two treatment groups and observe the results on behavior, then a case could be made for causation. If data on the same individuals are collected over time, then conclusions can be made about change.

There are many ways to help students find data. Depending on course structure and learning objectives, in some cases, students may collect data independently, in small groups, or as a class. Many students, particularly more advanced students, will have data from their own research labs. Additionally, both novice and advanced students may be employed in jobs in which they have access to data; for example, school administrators may have specific data sets they are interested in analyzing. In these cases, it is important to make sure students handle data appropriately to ensure confidentiality and abide by all applicable legal and ethical standards. Again, IRB approval may need to be obtained, especially for nonsecondary analysis.

If a student does not already have data, obtaining data matching their interests can be a very challenging task, particularly given the large and ever-rising number of publicly available data sets. For example, at the time of this writing, the U.S. government site www.data.gov had more than 300,000 data sets. To avoid students feeling overwhelmed or getting bogged down in their search for data, the instructor should provide a list of possible sites to obtain data, or perhaps a smaller list of specific recommended data sets, especially in undergraduate courses. When compiling such a list, the instructor should become familiar with the site and test the ease of using and accessing data housed on it. The instructor may want to illustrate in class how to access sites, obtain information about a study, and download data.

Many online resources exist that house data, including the General Social Survey (http:// gss.norc.org), World Bank Open (https://data.worldbank.org), Data World (https://data. world/datasets/open-data), and National Longitudinal Surveys (www.bls.gov/nls). Preferred sites are those organized by topic, which narrows a search considerably and provides students a more streamlined process. Other aspects to consider are sites with documentation on how data were collected, data citation information, and a codebook providing the meaning of variable names. Another consideration is the ease of downloading the data and using it—most students will be best served by a clean, ready-to-analyze data set. Useful sites will provide data in a variety of formats for use in various statistical software programs, including Excel, SAS, SPSS, R, and/or Stata, which are commonly used in statistics courses. If data come in one format but need to be converted to another format, the instructor should be ready to instruct students on how to handle such problems. For example, SAS can import data from many different formats, the foreign package in R can import data in a variety of formats, and Excel can be used to convert an .xls file to a .txt or .csv format, which can be easily imported into most statistical software programs.

Other data sources that we have found useful are online media, magazines, journals, and newspapers. Often in online articles, there are links to references, especially in science- and health-related papers. With the move toward more open science and concerns regarding reproducibility, data from research papers published in journals are also becoming more prevalent, and data collected under federal grants are required to be accessible in stable online sites. Many journals strongly encourage or require that software and data be provided as online supplemental material (e.g., journals published by the American Psychological Association, Psychometric Society, Association for Psychological Science, Society of Research in Child Development, and others). Some creative students may also pull data from multiple websites focused on topics such as sports or weather. Again, the data should be appropriate for addressing the students' research questions and should align with student interest.

Methods

Projects provide students the opportunity to apply the methods and procedures taught in the course to the chosen data set. The proposal is the students' first effort to explain statistical methods and demonstrate conceptual understanding. Depending on the timing of covering topics in a course, relevant methods are likely learned both before and after a proposal is submitted. Therefore, it is important to scaffold learning through a comprehensive course overview and thoughtful examples, so students can start the proposal even not having learned everything necessary to complete their analyses.

In the proposal, students should describe the methods to be used in the project and why those methods are appropriate for answering the proposed research question(s). Ideally, students will do this using both statistical and nontechnical language, demonstrating their understanding of the concepts. Depending on the nature of the course, the methods may involve only basic descriptive statistics or may entail complex modeling. In any case, students can define relevant variables and their anticipated models, which helps them get a sense of the many decisions involved in the research process. For example, should they use mean or median to measure central tendency, should an ordinal predictor variable be treated as nominal or numeric, should explanatory variables be standardized, or is a logistic or log-linear formulation of a model for discrete data more advantageous given the context of the analysis? These are only a small sample of the decisions students might encounter. Additionally, students can present hypotheses regarding possible findings and what those results would mean. Students can also outline their model-building approaches, as well as their plans for examining assumptions. Particularly at this stage of the project/research process, if a method is not fully understood, thinking through the application of the methods to the concrete problem of an actual data analysis can lead to building understanding, knowledge, and skills.

Data Analysis

After designing their projects and obtaining instructor approval, students can embark on using a statistical software package to compute statistics, design models, and interpret output, which for introductory students may be their first experience using statistical software. As appropriate given course expectations, it is often useful for instructors to provide examples of necessary code as well as instructions on how to access software help manuals and online resources. Students, especially novice students, may be intimidated by coding and the precision required, as well as by the technical output and the process of extracting results; providing resources and examples can help alleviate their concerns and preemptively address common questions, issues, and mistakes. Students may also benefit from online forums in which they and their peers can pose and answer questions, thereby learning from each other.

Students may be unfamiliar performing common steps using statistical software, such as accessing data, importing data into the software program, cleaning data, and examining whether assumptions of a procedure are tenable. Simply getting the data into the program is often a significant challenge and should not be overlooked, particularly as struggling with this first step of data analysis can discourage students from the beginning if not handled well. Once data are imported, it is often preferred to use data that is already "clean," especially for novice students. For more advanced students, problems such as missing values will need to be addressed. Once data are ready to analyze, students will often still need to manipulate their data to suit their research questions. Examining data closely both numerically and graphically can help students better understand their data and its relevant distributions. The instructor should cover and the student implement various methods of "looking" at data to determine whether the planned statistical analysis is an appropriate approach.

Particularly for novice students, focusing on understanding the structure of the coding scheme can demystify the process as well as provide scaffolding for further analyses they may perform in the future. Having students explain code in both statistical and nonstatistical language can help them think through the logic of the code and how it applies to their research questions. For example, a basic line of Stata code analyzing the relationship between participation in an academic program and a test score might read: *reg score program*. While this may seem abstract, if students can explain that the code indicates the program should run a regression model (command *reg*) with *score* as the dependent variable and *program* as the independent variable, this can help them better understand how to apply the same code structure to a new command and/or model. Further, if students can also explain that this is a linear regression examining the relationship between *program* participation and *score* and that the model will show if participation in the *program* can be used to predict *score*, they have an even better chance of internalizing the structure and process in a way that demonstrates real learning and paves the way for more complicated analyses. Of course, more advanced students who already have experience working with these programs may not need this type of intermediate check on their understanding.

The instructor should be mindful of the fact that some students may never run a statistical analysis again. For such students, it is probably appropriate to provide necessary code they can apply to their own data sets, spending instructional time talking about how the code was made and describing what the code is doing; the main goal is basic exposure. For more advanced students who will use statistical methods beyond the course, learning how to use the statistical software is very important. For these students, we recommend that they thoroughly annotate and include comments in the code created throughout the course, which allows them to go back to their coursework to see how they implemented an analysis. The instructor should use such practices in all material presented or made available to students. Lastly, for the more advanced students, learning how to make sense of cryptic error messages is an important skill. One strategy an instructor can employ is to purposively make mistakes and have students detect a problem and determine how to fix it.

For more advanced students, analyses are more complex, and more focus is placed on process, decisions, and implementation of methods. The specific decisions of utmost importance are what exploratory analyses were done (and what was learned from them), what type(s) of model(s) were used, their modeling strategy, how they arrived at their final models, test statistics used, and consideration of assumptions. By the end of their projects, students should have developed a toolkit that they can use and expand beyond the course. Even when a project is one provided by the instructor, it has been our experience that such students subsequently use the knowledge, tools, and skills developed later in their own work.

Communicating Results

To complete their projects, students must be able to interpret their results accurately and then communicate the answers to their research questions effectively. This is yet again a good opportunity for students to explain their results in both statistical and common language—What do the findings mean? What did we learn? Depending on the goals of the course, the amount of detail presented and the emphasis on the results themselves or the process of reaching them may vary. Generally, in a final paper writing up their projects, students can expand/revise the methods they explained in the proposal and then present their results, demonstrating how they have interpreted the statistical output using careful and precise language. At this point, they can provide a discussion of their results and explain the implications (and limitations) of their findings.

Instructors should be clear about expectations for final reports in their instructions. Students may not know what information they should present nor how to report it. While much of the work students undertake during the semester involves the *process* of statistical analysis, the final paper will likely focus on the *results* and subsequent *conclusions*. We suggest having students write what would be appropriate for a published paper in their field, in particular details on the data, methods, and findings—the information necessary for someone with the exact data to reproduce their results. The report should end with a paragraph or two summarizing their findings for a non-technical audience. This approach emphasizes that while there is a lot of work involved in statistical analyses, only a small portion of that work is typically reported.

We suggest that instructors not focus on specific grammar or formatting issues, because the goal of the course is for students to learn and apply statistics and communicate results. More emphasis should be placed on the logic and clarity of presentation. The writing of results especially helps nonnative English speakers/writers practice communicating their work in English. Students can be encouraged to write their results in a format customary in their field, with proper citations as appropriate, and standard table/figure labeling. One pitfall we have observed in writing by students is inappropriate causal language, as students often imply causation in their language despite not using data/methods allowing for causal claims.

Additional Considerations

We have described the overall structure of student projects, and in this section, we briefly discuss several additional considerations for implementing projects in statistics courses. Specifically, we discuss the organization of the project components throughout the semester, grading, demands on the instructor, and some considerations for addressing diverse student needs.

Organization

We recommend discussing the project and various components at the beginning of the course to give students time to start thinking about their research interests and how they might want to approach the task. This also allows for the proposal to be submitted fairly early in the semester, at least by the halfway point, which provides the instructor time to meet with students prior to proposal submission as well as time to provide adequate feedback. Importantly, this also allows time for students to encounter problems, as they inevitably will. Depending on course structure, instructors may choose to have small groups of students complete projects together, or some components could even be completed as a class if appropriate given the desired course learning outcomes. (For example, if data collection is a component of the course, the class may want to work together to collect data and create a data set, or small groups may work together to analyze code they will use independently.)

Students often request sample projects. Although these may be beneficial in some circumstances, it is important to be cautious in providing anything students may be tempted to inappropriately use as a template. Additionally, before a former student's work can be given to current students, the instructor should ask the former student for permission and remove all identifying information. Instead of distributing sample projects, there are two possible strategies we have found useful. One course of action is pointing students to research journals in their field for those seeking this type of guidance. Another strategy is giving students detailed instructions regarding what most projects should include. This is particularly useful because a clear statement of the instructor's expectations can be used as a guide by the students, and grading can be based on a rubric detailing the quality of each element or component in the statement. The specificity of the statement should apply to all projects within a course and can be adjusted to meet the student's selected data analysis procedure and instructor's learning goals. In particular, if a student does a nonstandard project (e.g., uses procedures not covered in the course, writes computer code), students should provide more detailed explanations of their procedures.

In some courses, especially more introductory classes, it may be useful to have students submit portions of the larger project at various points throughout the semester. This timing can prompt students to tackle analyses one piece at a time rather than waiting to attempt the full project at the end of the semester, and it also provides opportunities for the instructor to assess understanding along the way. In more advanced courses, the presentation of lecture material and homework can also be timed so that students are exposed to examples of the various methods and procedures they should be undertaking in their projects. While these students may not need the intermediate step of submitting individual components throughout the semester, this scaffolding still provides students guidance as to how to complete their projects.

Grading

By their very nature, student projects will be unique, as students create individualized products based on their interests and chosen research questions and methods. Clear guidelines regarding what information should be included in the final write-up can help instructors in determining how to grade projects, and in many cases, a rubric outlining the various required components may be useful. Students thus must meet all reporting requirements regarding a thorough and complete description of the data, methods, results, and implications/discussion. If various components are assessed throughout the semester, the final product should include appropriate revisions. Overall, projects may differ by field and course structure, but students should demonstrate an understanding of the methods and include appropriate implementation and accurate conclusions. While findings will differ across students and course content, student projects should demonstrate critical thinking, data literacy, and a concrete application of the statistical concepts involved.

Time Demands

Projects can be time consuming for instructors, an important consideration when deciding whether to include a project in a given course. Over the course of the semester, students will benefit from discussing their research design, chosen data set, code, results, and interpretation, and we encourage student-instructor meetings throughout the process to provide one-on-one guidance. Additionally, some students may request additional feedback or advice even after the semester is over. While these time demands on already-busy schedules may seem discouraging, we believe the benefits to student learning and their research literacy outweigh these concerns. Instead, we look at the process as an opportunity to build strong researchers, not just get students to complete the course.

We have frequently used course projects in classes of 50 to 60 students as sole instructors/ graders. Without support from a teaching assistant, it may not be feasible to devote enough time to each student throughout the semester in a larger course. However, we have also found that regular communication with students about their projects can actually lead to more efficient use of instructor time, as minor questions and mistakes can be resolved before they become major analytical and statistical errors. Instructors should both be cognizant of the increased demands of a larger course and also consider how careful planning and communication with students can alleviate some of these demands.

Diverse Student Needs

As we have pointed out throughout this chapter, well-designed projects will take into account differing levels of student experience with research and students' future research goals. Student immersion in their chosen topics may differ, as may access to appropriate data for their research questions. Projects for undergraduates and novice researchers provide them with valuable experience that may better prepare them for being able to reason in a quantitative way, which is good preparation for being an informed citizen and consumer of quantitative information, graduate school, and various careers. Instructors should be ready to provide these students more specific instructions and additional guidance on the basics of the research process. Alternatively, more advanced students tend to experience many of the same benefits, but their focus may be aimed more specifically at complex research problems encountered due to more complicated research questions and/or thorny data situations. In many ways, these more advanced students may need even more one-on-one guidance than more novice researchers, though again, this is time well spent in training thoughtful, creative, and knowledgeable scholars. In both cases, if students are doing original independent work, they will need multiple opportunities for guidance to afford best practices.

In considering diverse student needs based on student interest and experience, instructors might also allow students to pursue alternative projects dealing with code, macros, or programming. This may especially be useful for more advanced students and those in fields in which they anticipate writing extensive code. For example, a student in a multilevel modeling course taught by one of the authors did not think he would ever use hierarchical linear models after the semester was over but wanted to learn SAS macro programing, so he and the instructor devised a project for which he wrote a macro that computed a statistic not included by the software. The student published the macro, and it is now used in that same course as a benefit to current/future students. Additionally, as course sequences allow, many students may choose to start a project for one class (e.g., multilevel models) and then expand it in a subsequent course (e.g., categorical data analysis). In our experience, these projects have been expanded into conference presentations, dissertations, and publications—even winning research awards!

To conclude, we believe incorporating student projects in statistics courses in the social sciences provides students with the opportunity to engage with course concepts more deeply, enhances learning and enthusiasm for research, and ultimately helps to build a stronger research community. Students (and many others) have a tendency to think of statistics as formulaic rather than creative and full of interpretation. Projects can expose that misconception and show the many complex decisions involved in statistical thinking and the research process. While projects can be demanding for instructors, they provide students with the full experience of completing a research project, including designing a proposal that defines the research project, working with data in a manner that demystifies the experience, making the many decisions inherent in the research process, interpreting statistical output to answer research questions of interest, and communicating results in both technical and plain language. In our experience, students genuinely appreciate the opportunity to engage in such a project and find it useful for developing their research skill set. Projects make the work relevant to students' real-world experience, give them hands-on experience, and allow them to see how statistical analyses can be used to answer real-life questions. Helping students understand how to use data to answer their research questions and the critical thinking involved in doing so leads to benefits that can be found far beyond the end of the semester—students develop skills that can help them secure jobs or compete for grants, for example. Not only does this provide important training for future researchers, it also gives students a better appreciation for statistics more generally and enhances research and data literacy, skills they may not learn elsewhere.

References

Ben-Zvi, D., & Garfield, J. (2004). Statistical literacy, reasoning, and thinking: Goals, definitions, and challenges. In *The challenge of developing statistical literacy, reasoning and thinking* (pp. 3–15). Dordrecht: Springer.

Blumenfeld, P. C., Soloway, E., Marx, R. W., Krajcik, J. S., Guzdial, M., & Palincsar, A. (1991). Motivating project-based learning: Sustaining the doing, supporting the learning. *Educational Psychologist*, *26*(3–4), 369–398.

Carver, R., Everson, M., Gabrosek, J., Horton, N., Lock, R., Mocko, M., . . . Wood, B. (2016). *Guidelines for assessment and instruction in statistics education*. (GAISE) College Report 2016.

Chan, S. (2010). Applications of andragogy in multi-disciplined teaching and learning. *Journal of Adult Education*, *39*(2), 25–35.

De Veaux, R. D., & Velleman, P. F. (2008). Math is music; Statistics is literature (or, why are there no six-year-old novelists?). *Amstat News*, *375*, 54–58.

Gal, I., & Garfield, J. B. (1997). Curricular goals and assessment challenges in statistics education. In *The assessment challenge in statistics education* (pp. 1–13). IOS Press (on behalf of the ISI).

Knowles, M. S. (1984). *Andragogy in action: Applying principles of adult learning*. San Francisco, CA: Jossey-Bass.

Ozuah, P. O. (2016). First, there was pedagogy and then came andragogy. *Einstein Journal of Biology and Medicine*, *21*(2), 83–87.

## Chapter 18

Teaching Statistical Concepts Through a Scale Development Project

Kevin J. Grimm and Jonathan L. Helm

Most undergraduate statistics courses in the social and behavioral sciences contain a computer-based lab section, wherein students learn to perform statistical analysis via statistical software (e.g., SAS and R). The lab section represents an essential ingredient of the course because most statistical analyses are too labor intensive to be performed by hand. However, lab sections typically contain one-third to one-quarter of the total class time; necessitating efficient and purposeful use of this time. To that end, we developed a student-led, scale development project that highlights the research process and facilitates the teaching of statistical programming. This chapter describes the project and the students' responses to it.

Course Background

We implemented the lab-based project in an undergraduate elective course, in a Department of Psychology, recommended for students with aspirations of attending graduate school (as an aside, enrollment required completion of an introductory statistics course from the Department of Statistics). Most enrollees were sophomores and juniors, and tended to be above the 50th percentile on academic achievement for the university. The total enrollment ranged from 60 to 70 students, which was (approximately) equally divided across two lab sections. The course spanned a 10-week quarter (as opposed to a semester), with 3 hours and 40 minutes of lecture time per week and 1 hour and 50 minutes of total lab-section time per week.

The course provided an introduction to statistics commonly applied in the social sciences. Course topics included measures of central tendency, variability, central limit theorem, hypothesis testing, *t*-tests (one-sample, dependent samples, and independent samples), and analysis of variance (one-way between-subjects and factorial between-subjects). Students learned to perform statistical analysis using the programs SAS and R.

Project

The project began with students' development of a psychological scale, continued with students' analysis of data collected from the scale, and concluded with students' writing of an American Psychological Association (APA) formatted manuscript that summarized the results from the statistical analysis. The project contained a sequential set of goals, with some (Goals 1 through 3) completed in groups and others (Goals 4+) completed individually. The tasks were embedded in each week's lab section and directly corresponded to one of the sequential goals, which provided structure and direction for the lab. In the remainder of this section, we describe these goals to provide a detailed overview of the project.

Goal 1: Design a Psychological Scale

The first goal of the project is to design a scale (i.e., survey, questionnaire) to measure a psychological construct. Scale construction was completed as a group activity (groups usually comprised three or four students). Students were initially introduced to resources on developing psychological scales, including www.scalesandmeasures.net/search.php and Schwarz (1999), which highlighted issues in the design of psychological scales. Using those resources, the members of each group brainstormed potential psychological constructs and then collectively agreed upon a single psychological construct to measure. Importantly, groups were required to obtain the course instructor's approval for their proposed construct, which ensured that items designed to measure the construct were unlikely to cause psychological discomfort to the respondents.

At this time in the class, we discussed ethical issues when conducting research. We reviewed several studies that were not ethically conducted as well as controversial studies to help students think deeply about these issues. We also reviewed the Belmont Report and discussed the importance and responsibilities of Institutional Review Boards and the review processes that studies undergo to ensure they are conducted responsibly.

The group members designed the scale after obtaining the course instructor's approval. Design included (1) creating a title, (2) writing instructions, (3) determining a response format, (4) writing items to measure the psychological construct of interest, and (5) generating grouping variables that can be used to predict the psychological construct (i.e., levels of a factor from ANOVA).

Students were asked to write 15 to 20 items that would measure their psychological construct. The lab instructor discussed features of good items such as clear, concise, and direct language (i.e., items should contain as few words as possible without the loss of meaning; items should be understandable to persons with an 8th grade reading level), asking one question (i.e., avoid multipart questions, which may be confusing), and using positive language (e.g., avoid negative terms, which may be confusing). Students began to craft items with these instructions in mind, and the lab instructor consulted each of the groups during the item construction to provide detailed guidance as needed. As noted, the students had to consider the response format. Likert-type scales were most common, but other formats were sometimes chosen. If a Likert-type response format was used, the students had to make important decisions regarding the number of scale points and the labels for each scale point. Students typically chose a 4-, 5-, or 7-point scale (using values of $\{-2, -1, 0, 1, 2\}$ or $\{-3, -2, -1, 0, 1, 2, 3\}$), with labels that varied between 'Strongly Disagree' to 'Strongly Agree' (e.g., $\{-2 = $ 'Strongly Disagree', $-1 = $ 'Disagree', $0 = $ 'Neither Disagree nor Agree', $1 = $ 'Agree', $2 = $ 'Strongly Agree'$\}$).

The students then developed three to five additional questions that could be used to predict the psychological construct. The response scale for these additional questions were categorical to ensure that students could use them as predictors in a *t*-test or ANOVA, and therefore had two to three response options. These additional questions could collect demographic information or measure a separate construct. As an example of the former, students asked for the respondents' biological sex (with responses {'Male', 'Female'}), and year in school ({'2nd', '3rd', '4th', '5th'}). As an example of the latter, the question 'Do you consider yourself to be an introvert or an extravert?', which could be measured with responses {'Yes', 'No'} or {'Very Much', 'Somewhat', 'Not at all'}. We encouraged students to attempt the latter because students tended to be more motivated to test hypotheses regarding the relation between constructs rather than the relation between one construct and demographic information.

As an important final check, the scales were reviewed by the course instructor. Similar to the initial approval by the lab instructor, the second approval (after construction of the scale) provided a second opportunity to ensure the scales did not contain offensive or inappropriate material.

The majority of scales that students created were focused on introversion/extraversion, alcohol consumption, or stress. One example scale, called the **Lifestyle** survey, measured how often the respondent participated in healthy lifestyle activities (see the Appendix). This survey contains 18 statements rated on a 4-point scale with the following scale points: Strongly Disagree, Disagree, Agree, and Strongly Agree. The statements describe activities or behaviors that were associated with living a healthy lifestyle. Example questions include "I make an effort to walk or bike to school" and "I take a multivitamin daily." The authors also included negatively valenced items, such as "I watch TV in my spare time" and "I eat fast food more than once a week." The additional questions that could be used to predict the scores on this scale included biological sex, year in college, age, number of siblings, and birth order.

Goal 2: Collect the Data

Once scales were approved by the instructor, the students collected data on their scales during the following lab section. There were (typically) between 18 and 23 scales designed for a class of 60 to 70 students, and a full lab session (~2 hours) was required for the students to complete all of the questionnaires. Successful data collection required specific preparation before the lab section and a well-orchestrated lab section. The following paragraphs outline these two components.

First, the lab instructor (usually a teaching assistant) prepared for data collection. The lab instructor needed a large box, several manila envelopes, time for creating photocopies, and a dolly. Using these resources, the lab instructor would (1) make 60 to 70 photocopies of each group's questionnaire, (2) insert the 60 to 70 photocopies into a single manila envelope, and (3) place each manila envelope into the large box. The manila envelopes ensured that each set of photocopies remained separate, the large box allowed for easy containment of the manila envelopes (i.e., it is easier to transport a box than a stack of manila envelopes), and the dolly enabled transportation of the large box from the photocopier to the lab section (the box was quite heavy, especially for walks across campus to a classroom). As an aside, the large box also protected against inclement conditions while transporting the photocopies to and from the lab.

Second, the lab instructor orchestrated data collection during lab section. The lab instructor would begin with specific instructions for students and continued with a specific procedure for the students to complete the questionnaires. The lab instructor directed students to (1) anonymously complete each of the questionnaires (i.e., to *exclude* identifying information from each questionnaire, such as name or student identification number), (2) not feel obligated to respond to questionnaires or items, and (3) carefully and appropriately respond to each questionnaire. Anonymity was emphasized to ensure that each student's responses could not be traced to their originator. Lack of obligation enabled students to avoid or ignore questions that were perceived as offensive or inappropriate (although we did not expect this to occur given our careful review of each questionnaire and recognized that people may find discomfort in questions despite our review).

The lab instructor continued with a specific approach to facilitate data collection with the lab section. The lab instructor (1) opened a single manila envelope, (2) dispensed fresh copies of each questionnaire to each student, (3) instructed students to complete the questionnaire with care, (4) prompted students to look at the front of the classroom when finished with the questionnaire (usually 3 to 5 minutes), (5) collected the completed questionnaires, (6) placed the completed questionnaires back into the manila envelope, and (7) repeated steps 1 through 6 with a new questionnaire. This seven-step approach helped ensure that students took appropriate time to complete the questionnaires (i.e., students could not rush to complete all questionnaires in order to leave lab section early) and maintained the original organization of the questionnaires (i.e., the lab instructor left with each group's set of questionnaires in separate manila envelopes).

As a final note, online computer software (e.g., Qualtrics or Survey Monkey) may be used in place of paper questionnaires. Online computer software provides the benefits of (1) not needing to use a large amount of paper to create the questionnaires, (2) not requiring the time of the lab instructor to copy and organize the paper questionnaires, (3) not needing to transport the questionnaires with a hand truck, and (4) not requiring time for students to input data into an Excel file. However, online computer software requires (1) the instructors to be highly familiar with the software and (2) extra time to teach the students to use the software. Readers should weigh the benefits and drawbacks and then choose the delivery method (i.e., online versus paper questionnaires) they deem to be the most appropriate for their class.

Goal 3: Code the Data

The third goal requires each group of students to translate the students' responses to their psychological scales into an analyzable format (e.g., an Excel table). Similar to data collection, coding the data was facilitated by a specific set of instructions delivered by the lab instructor. We begin with a cautionary note regarding the required time for coding the data and then describe the specific set of instructions that helped make coding the data a smooth process.

Coding the data may require more time than expected by an instructor new to implementing this course project. During our initial implementation, we expected coding the data to be quick, straightforward, and simple. In the initial implementation of this project, the class size was much smaller (~12 students), and each group of students had to code approximately 20 questionnaires (far fewer than the 60 to 70 questionnaires that needed to be coded in this class), and we naively allotted 30 minutes for this activity. To our surprise, this activity took more than an hour. Thus, we now set aside an entire lab session (~2 hours) for students to code their data.

The lab instructor followed a specific procedure for directing students to code the data. This included (1) creating an ID number for each questionnaire, (2) creating an Excel file with a user-friendly structure for inputting data, (3) using a 'buddy system' for inputting the data, and (4) triple-checking the responses. First, students were prompted to give each questionnaire an ID number by writing a *large*, *unique*, *sequential*, and *clearly written* number (e.g., 1, 2, 3, 4, . . .) at the top of each questionnaire. This ID number allowed students to link each row of the Excel spreadsheet to a specific questionnaire and therefore enable double- and triple-checking of the inputted responses.

Next, students created a user-friendly structure for inputting the data. In particular, the lab instructor displayed a blank Excel file to the lab section, labeled the first column 'ID' and the next five columns {'Q1', 'Q2', 'Q3', 'Q4', 'Q5'}, and filled in the rows below 'ID' with values {1, 2, 3, 4, 5, 6, 7, 8, 9, 10}. The lab instructor explained that each row would correspond to one respondent's questionnaire and that the columns would contain the responses to the items. Finally, the lab instructor prompted students to create their own user-friendly structure, with the appropriate labels for each of the responses in their group's questionnaire (i.e., student typically included labels 'Q1' through 'Q20' to represent responses to items that measured the construct of interest and different labels for the additional questions, such as 'Sex', 'YrInSchool', and 'Extraversion').

Next, students were prompted to input the data using a buddy system. In particular, one student was designated as the 'typer' (i.e., the person that types the response into the Excel file), another was designated as the 'reader' (i.e., the person that reads the response for a given item), and the remaining members were 'overseers' (i.e., one or two individuals would watch both the typer and reader to check that responses were inputted correctly). To demonstrate the importance of the buddy system, the lab instructor told students to try and input one participant's responses (i.e., one individual) without the buddy system (i.e., performing the input independently). Students quickly learned that the buddy system was more efficient and accurate and continued to use this approach until all data were inputted into the Excel file.

Finally, students were instructed to triple-check the responses from each of the questionnaires. Students reused the buddy system but exchanged roles (the 'typer' became the 'reader', the 'reader' became the 'overseer', and the 'overseer' became the 'typer'). Naturally, the 'typer', did not actually type when checking responses; rather, that role was simply to view the Excel file to make certain that the response matched the reader's dictation. Importantly, students learned that the only way to double- or triple-check responses to the questionnaires was to have a unique ID associated with each questionnaire. Furthermore, students usually identified a few coding errors when double- or triple-checking and learned the importance of accounting for human error while inputting psychological data into an analyzable format.

Coding the data was the last activity completed as a group. Students independently completed the remainder of the project, and therefore projects from individuals within the same group began to diversify.

Goals 4 and 5: Analyze the Data and Write an APA-Formatted Paper

Finally, the students could begin analyzing their data as part of the class and for their final project; excited by the opportunity to test a few simple hypotheses regarding their construct of interest. Here we describe goals 4 and 5 simultaneously because those goals were approached concurrently.

Initially, students created reverse scores for any of the relevant items (e.g., negatively worded items). Students learned that ordinal response items centered around 0 (e.g., scores from $\{-2, -1, 0, 1, 2\}$, as given earlier) could be reverse scored by multiplying responses by -1. For example, if the variable 'Q1' was score using values $\{-2, -1, 0, 1, 2\}$, then the reverse scores for Q1 may be computed by performing Q1 $\times$ (-1).

Next, students examined the psychometric properties of the scale. At this point in the academic term, students learned about reliability and validity during lecture, along with the conceptual underpinnings of Cronbach's Alpha. The lab section complemented lecture by prompting students to calculate Cronbach's Alpha for the sum score calculated by adding up the item responses. Students determined which items to retain using the information from calculating Cronbach's Alpha. Stated differently, students may exclude items based on their impact on Cronbach's Alpha. Therefore, students received an opportunity to refine their measure using Cronbach's Alpha. As an aside, it may be beneficial to include alternative forms of validity (e.g., predictive validity) to help students gain a deeper breadth for measurement of psychological constructs.

Subsequently, students applied the statistical approaches learned during lecture to their data. As the weeks progressed, students moved from calculating descriptive statistics to performing independent samples t-tests to one-way analysis of variance and between-subjects factorial analysis of variance. The lab assignments involved using a statistical program (SAS and R in our case) to perform the statistical technique to their data and write a brief results section, which followed APA formatting for statistical notation (e.g., $F(2,67) = 5.21$, $p < .05$). Consequently, students made weekly progress on their projects because the brief results are a subset of the project, and during the final weeks, the students stitched the brief results together into a single, coherent paper.

Summary of Project

The preceding five goals provided a solid foundation from which students built their course projects. These enabled students to follow a coherent structure throughout the semester and also generated analytic tasks that existed well within students' zone of proximal development (i.e., learning R and SAS for the first time).

Student Experience

From our perspective, students both enjoyed and benefited from the course project. The benefits included an opportunity to generate and analyze their own data set, but also generate and test hypotheses, and experience the process of planning an executing a research project.

From our experience, students learn statistical concepts more deeply when they are applied to an interesting and familiar data set. The course project empowered students to learn in this manner because students created their own measure and conducted data collection, coding, and analysis throughout the academic term. Students often echoed this sentiment by showing heightened enthusiasm during the lab section. For example, students relished the opportunity to measure their own construct of interest and were delighted to test whether their hypotheses regarding that construct were supported by the data. This came as a contrast to having a single data set that all students received and analyzed, which tended to only create enthusiasm from the small subset of students that happened to be interested in the chosen data set.

Students also showed excitement based on the opportunity to analyze 'real' data. In other courses, students received a data set that was simulated to have certain pedagogical properties. However, students sometimes showed a lack of interest when analyzing those data because fabricated data do not warrant conclusions to be drawn. Given that students were psychology majors, one of their main interests encompassed the understanding and testing of real psychological phenomena. Therefore, students completing this project showed more enthusiasm based on the potential to draw conclusions regarding their constructs of interest. And many students shared this enthusiasm during lab section and via evaluations.

Students benefited from completing all stages of the research project. Other approaches may provide students with a canned data set wherein all students complete the same analysis. Here, students had the opportunity to obtain more insight into the true scientific process from start to finish. Many students noted that they gained much insight into the scientific process that underlies psychological measurement and research and that they were grateful to not simply receive and analyze a data set.

Another interesting benefit surrounded students' desire for further knowledge. Students often realized that they wanted to test their constructs in more nuanced ways than those offered by a *t*-test or an analysis of variance. Students often spent time during the lab section or office hours asking for new statistical approaches that could be applied to data. We were delighted by these requests but also felt the need to harness students' interests to remain within the confines of the class topics. Nevertheless, we believe these motivations remained in students and propelled them to enroll in higher level courses to gain further insights into more complex statistical analyses.

Students appreciated the opportunity to build their projects throughout the semester. Many showed anxiety regarding the course project because they had not engaged in writing a full research project prior to this course. The structure embedded in the project (i.e., completing subsets of the project week by week) alleviated most of this anxiety. Students completed reasonable strides each week and often found joy in tying the final series of assignments into a single narrative.

One drawback that we encountered arose from poorly designed questionnaires. Although these did not occur often, it is natural to expect that some questionnaires may have very low reliability (i.e., as estimated using Cronbach's Alpha) despite the ability to select a subset of items. When these low reliabilities did occur, they were often not foreseeable from the group's, lab instructor's, or course instructor's perspective. Instead, this was the unfortunate consequence of the scientific process: questionnaires need to be refined to improve measurement properties. Nevertheless, the students were committed to using these responses (i.e., the course did not have enough time to redevelop the questionnaire). Therefore, students had to analyze a construct with relatively low reliability and sometimes lost motivation to perform the subsequent analyses knowing that the results showed little potential for drawing conclusions.

A second drawback was the amount of grading time for the lab instructors. In our class, there were two 20-hour teaching assistants who shared the responsibility of leading the lab sections and guiding the scale development project. For a class of this size, having two teaching assistants was necessary. In addition to leading the scale development project and grading weekly assignments, the teaching assistants were responsible for grading the papers. Grading 60 to 70 papers that typically ran 10 to 15 pages was very time consuming. To help ensure consistency in the grading across teaching assistants, the teaching assistants and the instructor graded a few papers following a very specific rubric. Once those were graded, the teaching assistants and instructor met to discuss the papers and compare their evaluations. Discussions of the grades took place, and modifications to the grading rubric were made when necessary.

Evaluation

Overall, we believe that this project truly provided a great learning opportunity for students' knowledge of applied statistics in the social sciences. Importantly, the project required extra work from the lab and course instructors (e.g., making several photocopies, reviewing all of the questionnaires). Nevertheless, we believe this cost to be well worth the students' increased motivation for learning the course topics. At times, the students gave comments in the course evaluations about the project that indicated they were nervous about the project at the beginning of the semester, but the enjoyed the project and appreciated how the project took place in phases. Given the feedback and our experience with the project, we think this project has achieved the goals we set out, and we happily report that this project has been adopted by colleagues who work in psychology and human development departments across the United States.

Extension

There are ways to extend the project for more advanced courses in psychology and human development. For example, in a multivariate statistics course or psychometrics course, factor analysis and item response models can be fit to data collected as part of a scale development project. Additionally, there are alternate options for the written paper including presenting a poster or giving a lecture presentation.

Reference

Schwarz, N. (1999). Self-reports: How the questions shape the answers. *American Psychologist*, *54*, 93–105.

Appendix to Chapter 16
Lifestyle Survey

Please use the following scale to answer questions 1–18.

Strongly Disagree   **Disagree**   **Agree**   **Strongly Agree**
       1   2   3   4

_____1.   I care about my fiber intake.
_____2.   I take a multivitamin daily.
_____3.   I drink soda often.
_____4.   Exercise is a high priority in my life.
_____5.   I watch TV in my spare time.
_____6.   I exercise for at least 30 minutes every day.
_____7.   I make an effort walk or bike to school.
_____8.   I am a health-conscious person.
_____9.   I eat at least 5 servings of fruit and vegetables daily.
_____10. I choose whole grain when I can.
_____11. I stay educated by reading health articles.
_____12. I get 8 hours of sleep every night.
_____13. I drink heavily on the weekends.
_____14. I use tobacco products regularly.
_____15. I admire others who live a healthy lifestyle.
_____16. I make healthy choices in part because of my family and/or friends.
_____17. I eat fast food more than once a week.
_____18. I enjoy physical activity.

Please answer the following questions based on the options given to the right.

_____   Gender: (M/F)
_____   Year in college: (1, 2, 3, 4, 5+)
_____   Age: (in years)
_____   Number of siblings: (0, 1, 2, etc.)
_____   Birth order: (First, Second, etc.)

Index

Note: Page numbers in *italics* indicate figures and in **bold** indicate tables on the corresponding pages. Underlined page numbers indicate chapter authorship.

alpha = .05 97–98
AAU STEM redesign grant 37–38
abnormal psychology 144–145
abstraction, statistics as 267–268
academic design for STEM education **33**, 33–39
Achinstein, P. 23
Ackerman, L. 106–108
Adkins, D. 48
Against Method 24
agile teaching 238
Aiken, L. S. <u>55–69</u>, 79, 80, 126, 249, 257
American National Election Study (ANES) 148
American Psychological Association (APA) 30
American Psychologist 105
American Statistical Association (ASA): on authentic assessments 250; on curricular reform 65–67
anarchism, epistemological 24
Anderson, C. J. <u>266–279</u>, 252
ANOVA *F*-tests using model-comparison formula 130–132
antirealism 20–22
Arnau, J. 104–105
Association for Psychological Science (APS) 30, 58, 80
assumption violations 103–104; as informative 106–108
astrology, tests of 148–149, **150**
authentic assessments 250
Avant, L. 171

Barer, M. L. 162
Baron, R. M. 77
Barrows, H. S. 251
Barry, A. E. 75
Basic and Applied Social Psychology 96
Bathke, A. 106
Bayesianism 22–23

Bayesian thinking and inference *165*, 165–166
Bem, D. J. 70
Benbow, C. P. <u>xvi–xvii</u>
Bendayan, R. 104
Best, J. 91–92, 93
between-group heteroscedasticity 105
Blanca, M. J. 104–105
Bloom's Taxonomy of Learning 199
Bono, R. 104–105
Borkenau, P. 116
Bornstein, M. H. 106
Bruff, D. <u>238–248</u>
Bruner, J. S. 171
Bryk, A. 107, 108, 115
But What If We're Wrong? 25
BYOD (bring your own device) student response system: conclusions on 247–248; introduction to 238–239; lecture note annotation and discussion forum 245–247, *246–247*; polling questions and 240–245, *244–245*; teaching statistics with 239–247

Cain, M. K. 105, 110
Campbell, C. 251
Cardiff, K. 162
Carlson, K. A. 200
Carnegie Foundation for the Advancement of Teaching 56
Carroll, A. 161, 162
Cartwright, N. 23–24
Center for Epidemiologic Studies-Depression Symptoms Scale (CES-D) 111–114, *111–114*, **113**
Center for Integration of Research, Teaching and Learning (CIRTL) 47
Chalmers, A. F. 14–15, 17, 19, 23
classroom response systems (CRS) 46; *see also* BYOD (bring your own device) student response system

climate change and regression *163–164*, 163–165
clinical psychology 144–145
Clinton, H. 158
Cobb, G. 55, 66, 67
Cohen, J. 95–96, 98, 99, 126
Cohen, P. 126
Cokely, E. T. 156
Cole, D. A. 77
Collaborative Psychiatric Epidemiology Surveys 145
confounding variables 227
constructivism 21–22
construct validation practices, scale use and 72–74
correlation: "correlation does not equal causation" axiom 99; development of concept of 175–178, *176–177*
covariance structures 105–106
Cover, J. A. 14–15
Cowles, M. 97–98
Cozby, P. C. 96
critical thinking and data literacy 268–269
Cronbach, L. J. 72
cross-cultural psychology 148
Curd, M. 14–15, 23
curricular reform 68–69; ASA on 65–67

Damn Lies and Statistics 91
data analysis: in clinical psychology and abnormal psychology 144–145; conclusions on 151–152; in courses in social psychology 142–144; in cross-cultural psychology 148; and dashboards for understanding students being taught 38; in developmental psychology 145–146; in gender studies 146, 148; in human sexuality 146, *147*; in personality theory 145; in psychology of religion 148; relevant to other psychology courses 144–148, *147*; in substance use 145; Survey Documentation and Analysis (SDA) interface 137–142; in tests of astrology 148–149, **150**
data literacy 268–269
data visualization 153–154; descriptive statistics and survival curves 161, *162*; inference and Bayesian thinking *165*, 165–166; interactive experiences in, for students 166–167; many goals of 154–156; measurement and the MPG illusion 158–159, *159*; meta-analysis of food-cancer association 159–161, *160*; pie charts and health care use 162, *163*; regression and climate change *163–164*, 163–165; sampling and the 2016 presidential election *157*, 157–158; types of graphs used in 156–166
Data World 273
Dauphinee, T. L. 205
Davidson, I. J. 70–83
Davis, C. 97–98
Deboeck, P. R. 182–196, 66, 67
deduction 16–17

degrees of freedom 128–129
Delaney, H. D. 126
Del Vecchio, A. 205
Demon-HauntedWorld, The 95
descriptive, concept of 19
descriptive statistics 161, *162*, 224
De Veaux, R. D. 267–268
developmental psychology 145–146
dialectics 123–124; of implementation of new innovations in teaching statistics 132–134; of past due new curricula, approaches, and textbook TOC organizational structures 127–128; of whether introductory statistics teaching should have changed in the past and whether it should change in the future 125–127
Dierker, L. 66
distributional nonnormality 104–105
Dunning-Kruger effect 153

Early Head Start Research and Evaluation Study 145–146
ecological fallacy 164, *164*
Edwards, M. C. 13–28
Emmioğlu, E. 198
empiricism, logical 16
epistemological anarchism 24
Erceg-Hurn, D. M. 105
Evans, R. G. 162
explanation versus prediction 23
exploratory data analysis (EDA) 125

facticity and laws 23–24
faculty: curricular reform and tiny numbers of quantitative 65; with focus including undergraduate statistics and research methods 61–63, **62**; observations on 67–68; with quantitative expertise across departments of psychology 63–65, **64**; for teaching undergraduate statistics and research 58–61, **59, 60**
faculty learning communities (FLCs) 44–46
Faig, J. 161
falsifiability 17–18
Farebrother, R. W. 181
F-distributions 130
Feyerabend, P. 24
finish line project (FLP) 45
Fisher, R. A. 97, 98, 130, 131
Flake, J. K. 70–83
flipped classrooms 197–198; analytic methods on 206–207; background and related literature on 198–201; data sources on 205; discussion of 211–214; outcome measures of 205–206; sampling of 204–205; student achievement impacts of 207–209, **208**, *209*; student engagement impacts of 209; student interest in

statistics impact of 210; student perceptions of courses impact of 209–210; study design for **201–202**, 201–203; study implementation for 203–204; study results on 207–211, **208**, *209*, **210**; subgroups impacts of **210**, 210–211
food-cancer association 159–161, *160*
Fouladi, R. T. <u>102–120</u>, <u>249–264</u>
Freedman, D. H. 183
Fritz, M. S. <u>87–101</u>
Fundamentals of Modern Statistical Methods Substantially Improving Power and Accuracy 108
Fundamental Statistics in Psychology and Education 55–56

gambler's fallacy 95
Garcia-Retamero, R. 156
Gelfand, L. A. 77, 78
Gelman, A. 154
gender studies 146, 148
General Social Survey (GSS) 137–141, **139**, *140–141*, 273; in clinical psychology and abnormal psychology 144–145; in courses in social psychology 142–144; in human sexuality studies 146, *147*; in psychology of religion 148; in tests of astrology 149
generic word processor (GWP) 170–171
Godfrey-Smith, P. 14–15, 24
Gomez-Benito, J. 104–105
Google 166
Gould, S. J. 161
Graaff, E. D. 251
graph literacy 155–156; *see also* data visualization
Gravetter, F. J. 88
Gray-Little, B. 49
Grimm, K. J. <u>281–289</u>
Grissom, R. 107, 108, 115
Guidelines for Assessment and Instruction in Statistics Education (GAISE College Report) 133, 153–154
Guide to Teaching Statistics: Innovations and Best Practices, A 250
Guilford, J. P. 55
Gundlach, E. 200

hands-on experience: class time and classroom for 189–190; conclusions on 195–196; how to use 184–193; instructor and graduate teaching assistant roles in 192–193; meeting goals of students 184–187, *186*; outcomes of 193–195; reasons for 182–184; videos and 187–189, *188*; worksheets for 190–192
health care use and pie charts 162, *163*
Helm, J. L. <u>281–289</u>
high-structure active learning (HSAL) 41–45, **43**
Hoffrage, U. 156
Hogan, K. A. <u>30–51</u>
Howson, C. 23
How the Laws of Physics Lie 23

Hulsizer, M. R. 250
human sexuality 146, *147*
Hung, W. 255
Hutton, R. S. <u>238–248</u>

Improving How Universities Teach Science: Lessons From the Science Education Initiative 32
induction 16–17
inference and Bayesian thinking *165*, 165–166
inferential statistics 224–226, *226*
informative assumption violations 106–108
InfoVis 154
innovation, classroom 109; considering distributional form of scores on questionnaire in 111–114, *111–114*, **113**; "full" distribution in 110–111; implementation of new 132–134; research questions beyond the mean and **115**, 115–119, *117–119*; *see also* flipped classrooms; hands-on experience
innumeracy 92
Institutional Review Board (IRB) 271–272
Inter-university Consortium for Political and Social Research (ICPSR) 142
Introduction to Robust Estimation and Hypothesis Testing 108–109
introductory statistics courses: additional readings for 89–100, **91**; additional suggestions for 99–100; for applied researchers in the 21st century 123–134; dialectics on 123–128; fueling the pedagogical revolution in 128–132; memorization in 87–88; Peer Review of Teaching Project on learning objectives in 88–89, **89**; stasis in teaching 124–125; teaching ANOVA *F*-tests using model-comparison formula in 130–132; teaching degrees of freedom in 128–129; teaching sampling distributions through resampling theory in 130
Ioannidis, J. P. 161, 165
I Wear the Black Hat 25

Jaccard, J. 106–108
Jones, L. V. 48
Journal of Consulting and Clinical Psychology 108
Journal of Experimental Psychology: General, and *Psychological Science* 71
Journal of Personality and Social Psychology 71
Journal of Problem Based Learning in Higher Education 251, 252
Judd, C. M. 126, 133
just-in-time teaching (JiTT) 42

Kahneman, D. 95, 97
Karpiak, C. P. 252
Katz, S. J. 162
Kazdin, A. 90
Kenny, D. A. 77

Keselman, H. J. 105
Kilpatrick, W. H. 250
Kirk, R. 36
Klosterman, C. 25
Knoll, M. 250, 251
Kogan, L. R. 74
Kolmos, A. 251
Kosara, R. 154
Kosslyn, S. M. 156
Kuhn, T. 19–20, 24

Lady Tasting Tea, The 98
Lakatos, I. 20
Lambert, B. 180
Larrick, R. P. 158
Laudan, L. 20
Law of Large Numbers 95–96
Law of Small Numbers 95–96
laws and facticity 23–24
lecture note annotation and discussion forum, BYOD
    response system for 245–247, 246–247
Levesque-Bristol, C. 200
Loevinger, J. 73
logical empiricism 16
logical positivism 16
Longitudinal Study of Generations 146
López-Montiel, D. 104
low- and medium-tech teaching: cognitive background
    for 171–172; development of concept of correlation
    175–178, 176–177; generic word processor (GWP)
    170–171; representation of multilevel models 178–180,
    178–180; shortcomings of 180–181; simplified theory
    of regression 172–175, 173–175
Luck, S. J. 104, 106

MacCallum, R. C. xviii–xix
Madden, L. V. 106
Maldonado, A. 156
Marital Instability Over the Life Course/Work and
    Family Life Study 146
Maxwell, S. E. 77, 126
Mayo, D. 23
Mazur, E. 238
McClelland, G. H. 126, 133
McCrae, R. R. 116
McDermott, K. B. 218
McTighe, J. 183
measurement and the MPG illusion 158–159, 159
mediation practices: literature review on 77–79; research
    design and 75–77, 76; simulation models and 227, 228
Meehl, P. E. 72
mesothelioma survival curves 161, 162
meta-analysis of food-cancer association 159–161, 160

methodological research training: construct validation
    practices in 72–75; crisis in 79–80; introduction
    to reform efforts for 70–72; mediation practices
    and research design and 75–77, 76; pervasive poor
    practices in 72–79; suggestions for improving 80–83
Methodology 105
Micceri, T. 104
Midlife in the United States Survey 146
Miller, G. A. 171
Millsap, R. E. 63, 249
Mirosevich, V. M. 105
Modern Statistics for the Social and Behavioral Sciences: A
    Practical Introduction 108–109
Moore, Q. 197–214
More Damned Lies and Statistics 93
Motivated Strategies for Learning Questionnaire 206
MPG illusion 158–159, 159
Mueller, P. A. 180
multilevel models, representation of 178–180, 178–180
multiple-regression models 99

National Center for Early Development and Learning
    Multistate Study of Pre-Kindergarten 146
National Comorbidity Survey (NCS) Series 144–145
National Couples Survey 146
National Longitudinal Surveys 273
National Survey on Drug Use and Health 145
Nelson, D. 200
New Statistical Procedures of the Social Sciences: Modern
    Solutions for Basic Problems 108
Norcross, J. C. 56
normative, concept of 19
null hypothesis 97
null hypothesis significance testing (NHST) 17–18, 124,
    127–128, 131–132
Nunnally, J. C. 103–104

Obama, B. 197
Okan, Y. 156
Okasha, S. 14–15, 19
Oppenheimer, D. M. 180
overgeneralization 96

Panter, A. T. 30–51
paradigms 19–20
Pascali, M. 162
Pearson's Learning Catalytics 46
Pecore, J. L. 250
Peer Review of Teaching Project (PRTP) 88
Peer Visits Program 47–48
Pek, J. 70–83
Permutation Test 130
personality theory 145

philosophy of science 13–14; Bayesianism in 22–23; deduction and induction in 16–17; definitions in 15; descriptive or normative in 19; falsifiability in 17–18; grand narrative of 14; included in statistics courses 24–25, 27; laws and facticity in 23–24; logical positivism and logical empiricism in 16; paradigms in 19–20; prediction versus explanation in 23; realism, antirealism, and scientific realism in 20–22; statistical programs and 25–26; and what is science? 15–16

Philosophy of Science: A Very Short Introduction 14

Philosophy of Science: The Central Issues 14

pie charts and health care use 162, *163*

Pincock, C. 14–15

polling questions and BYOD response system 240–245, *244–245*

Popper, K. 17, 20, 24

positivism, logical 16

power=80 97–98

power in simulation models 226–227

prediction versus explanation 23

presidential election predictions 157–158, *158*

President's Council of Advisors on Science and Technology 48

probability, making decisions based on 94–96

problem-based learning 250–251; article review/critique 256–257; research proposal on 257–260; research reports on 260–263

project-based learning 249; closing comments on 264; communicating results of 276; concepts and terminology of 250–252; data analysis in 274–275; data literacy and critical thinking with 268–269; designing projects for 269–279; diverse student needs in 278–279; framework for authentic statistics assignment design to personalize 252–253, **254**; grading in 277–278; incorporating personally relevant 255–263; organization of 276–277; proposal for 271–274; reasons for using 266–269; scale development project 281–288; selecting topics for 270–271; statistics as abstraction and 267–268; time demands in 278

pseudo-science 17

PsychMAP 80

Psychological Assessment 110

Psychological Bulletin 104

Psychological Science 71

psychology of religion 148

Psychometric Theory 103–104

Psychophysiology 105–106

Putnick, D. L. 106

p-values 96–97

Quantitative Pipeline Task Force 31, 36

quantitative methods 3–4, 31, 34–36, 55; bridging the gap between substantive and 82; curricular reform in teaching 68–69, 195–196; faculty teaching and mentoring responsibilities in 60, **62**, 63–67; in graduate programs 58; overcoming lack of training in psychology 94, 104, 120, 133; students with prior experience in 184–185; in undergraduate programs 56–57, **57**

quantitative psychology: academic design for 34–37; ASA curricular reform considerations for 65–67; faculty in (*See* faculty); statistics on undergraduate training in 56–57, **57**; Statistics Road Map for 93–94, *94*; as STEM field 30–31; teaching, feedback, and assessment of 43–44

R 26, 142; in simulation modeling 223–227, *224*, *226*, *228*

Raudenbush, S. W. 107, 108, 115

realism 20–22

regression: climate change and *163–164*, 163–165; simplified theory of 172–175, *173–175*

Reichardt, C. S. 137–152, 66

religion, psychology of 148

resampling theory 130

research design 75–77, *76*

Revelle, W. 217–237, 217–236, 66–67, 130–131

revolution 3, 14, 165; data science 154; information visualization 154; postmodeling 18; in statistical pedagogy 123, 128–132

Richards, K. A. R. 200

Rindskopf, D. 170–181

Roche, B. 105

Rodgers, J. L. 1–10, 123–134, 18, 55, 66

Roediger, H. L. 218

Rosenthal, R. 98

Rosnow, R. L. 98

Rosopa, P. 107

Ruscio, J. 105

Saari, I. A. 148

Salmon, W. C. 23

Salsburg, D. 98

sampling and the 2016 presidential election *157*, 157–158

sampling distributions 130

SAS 142

Sathy, V. 30–51, 197–214

scale development project: course background on 281; data analysis and writing APA-formatted paper goal in 286; data coding goal in 284–285; data collection goal in 283–284; designing a psychological scale goal in 282–283; evaluation of 288; extensions of 288; goals of 282–286; lifestyle survey 289; purpose of 281–282; student experience with 286–288

Schabenberger, O. 106

Schau, C. 198, 205
Scheffé, H. 98
Schoenfeld, J. D. 161
Schrodt, P. 170
Schumacher, E. F. 181
Schwarz, N. 282
science, defining 15–16
scientific method, statistics as one piece of 90
scientific realism 20–22
Sechrest, L. B. 249
significance testing 17, 55, 94, 96–97, 99, 124, 127
Silver, N. 157–158
simplified theory of regression 172–175, *173–175*
Simpson's paradox 164, *164*
simulation models 217–218; conclusions on 228;
    confounding variables in 227; data analysis using
    223–227, **224**, *226, 228*; descriptive statistics and
    224; inferential statistics and 224–226, *226*; mediation
    and moderation and 227, *228*; PHP code for
    229–236; power, Type I and Type II errors 226–227;
    setup and process of 218–223, **220**, *221*; web-based
    tutorials for 229
Slaney, K. 75
Small Is beautiful 181
Social Justice Sexuality Project 146
Society for Experimental Social Psychology 80
Society for Personality and Social Psychology 80
Soll, J. B. 158
Some Things You Learn Aren't So 99
SPSS 26, 142
Standards for Educational and Psychological Testing 73
Stapel, D. 71
STATA 142
statistical assumptions 102–103; classroom innovation
    and pedagogy reframed as way forward for 109–119,
    111–114, **113**, **115**, *117–119*; closing comments on
    119–120; considering distributional form of scores on
    questionnaire and 111–114, *111–114*, **113**; coverage
    of assumption violations and distributional conditions
    and 103–108; current textbooks and software as way
    forward in 108–109; "full" distribution in 110–111;
    research questions beyond the mean and **115**,
    115–119, *117–119*
statistical literacy 93
Statistical Principles in Experimental Design 56
statistical programs 25–26
statistical significance tests, misuse of 96–97
statistics: as abstraction 267–268; ANOVA *F*-tests using
    model-comparison formula in 130–132; burden of
    proof resting with the author of 92–93; correlation
    does not equal causation axiom in 99; created to
    answer real-world questions 98; degrees of freedom
    as measure in 128–129; descriptive 161, *162*, 224;

evaluating all 91–92; humans not good at making
    decision based on probability and 94–96; inferential
    224–226, *226*; as one piece of the scientific method
    90; psychologists required to take very few 93–94,
    94; resampling theory in 130; sources of bad 92
statistics and research teaching: adding philosophy of
    science to 24–25, 27; faculty positions with focus
    including undergraduate statistics and research
    methods and 61–63, **62**; faculty with quantitative
    expertise across departments of psychology and
    63–65, **64**; hiring of faculty for undergraduate
    58–61, **59**, **60**; introductory (*See* introductory
    statistics courses); Rodgers challenge on 1–2;
    teaching reform and 3–5; textbook content in 55–56;
    top 10 pieces of advice for 8–10
STEM (science, technology, engineering, and
    mathematics) education: AAU STEM redesign
    grant for 37–38; academic design for **33**, 33–39;
    APA guidelines for undergraduate psychology
    majors and 39; conclusions on 48–51; curriculum
    development using pedagogy of 38–39; data analytic
    tools and dashboards for 38; elements of 21st century
    32–48; flipped classrooms for 197–198; quantitative
    psychology included in 30–31; teaching, feedback,
    and assessment in 39–48, **40–41**, **43**, **45**
Stevens, J. 205
Stigler, S. M. 99
Student Evaluations of Teaching (SETs) 48
substance use 145
Summer Science Institute 47
Survey Documentation and Analysis (SDA) interfaces
    137; General Social Survey (GSS) 137–141, **139**,
    140–141; World Values Survey (WVS) 137, 141–142
Survey of Attitudes Towards Statistics (SATS) 205
survival curves 161, *162*

Tabarrok, A. 165
Task Force for Increasing the Number of Quantitative
    Psychologists 31
t-distributions 130
Terracciano, A. 116
Terry, R. <u>153–167</u>, 63, 66, 67
textbooks, statistics 3, 102–104, 183; demand for 4, 67;
    stability of topics in 36, 55; software and future of
    108–109, 119–120; suggestions for 123, 124–129,
    132–134
*Theory and Reality: An Introduction to the Philosophy of
    Science* 14
Thinking About the Present as if It Were the Past 25
Thode, H. C., Jr. 109
Thompson, B. 74, 96–97
Timmer, J. D. <u>266–279</u>, 252
Tobias, R. D. 106

Top Hat *see* BYOD (bring your own device) student response system
Transparency and Openness Promotion (TOP) guidelines 71
Treatment Episode Data Set 145
Trump, D. 157–158
t-test 98
Tufte, E. R. 180, 181
Tukey, J. 125, 167
Tversky, A. 95, 97
Type I errors 98, 226–227
Type II errors 98, 226–227

Understanding and Applying Basic Statistical Methods Using 109
"undesired" covariance structures 105–106
Unwin, A. 154
Urbach, P. 23

Vacha-Haase, T. 74
validity 28n1
van Fraassen, B. C. 21
variance ratio (VR) 105
Velleman, P. F. 267–268

videos 187–189, *188*
visualization *see* data visualization

Wallnau, L. B. 88
West, S. G. 63, 126, 249
What Is This Thing Called Science? 14
Wieman, C. 32, 34, 36, 39, 43, 183
Wiggins, G. 183
Wilcox, R. R. 108–109, 115
Winer, B. J. 56
Winquist, J. R. 200
Woolf, L. M. 250
worksheets for hands-on experience 190–192
World Bank Open 273
World Values Survey (WVS) 137, 141–142; in courses in social psychology 142–144; in cross-cultural psychology 148

Ybarra, V. 153–167
YouTube 166, 180
Yuan, K. H. 105

Zhang, Z. 105